OCR
A LEVEL

CW01501570

SOCIOLOGY

Sue Brisbane
Kath Roberts
Paul Taylor
Laura Pountney

HODDER
EDUCATION
AN HACHETTE UK COMPANY

Author acknowledgements

Sue Brisbane: All my love and thanks to Martin for going beyond the bounds of reason to help me – Evans-Pritchard strikes again! Love and thanks also to Keir and Finlay for your encouragement and joie de vivre. **Kath Roberts:** I would like to thank Martin, as ever, for his continued support, belief and love, I couldn't do it without you xx. **Paul Taylor:** I would like to acknowledge Jo for supporting me with love and cups of tea through writing the book and all my students past and present who have helped to inspire my love of teaching sociology. **Laura Pountney:** Thanks to all of my family for supporting me, as always, with love.

The Publishers would like to thank the following for permission to reproduce copyright material.

Photo credits

p.1 *tl* © iStockphoto.com/sweetym, *tr* © bloomua – Fotolia.com, *b* © Eray – Fotolia; **p.2** © JUSTIN SUTCLIFFE/REX Shutterstock; **p.11** © The Guardian via Getty Images; **p.17** © Gill Harle/Alamy Stock Photo; **p.19** *t* © Carsten Reisinger – Fotolia.com; *c* © Alex Segre/Alamy Stock Photo; *b* © Melinda Fawver – 123RF; **p.26** © RubberBall/Alamy Stock Photo; **p.30** © GIANLUIGI GUERCIA/AFP/Getty Images; **p.35** *tl* © paulcraven – Thinkstock/Getty Images, *tr* © ehabeljean – Fotolia, *bl* © Manuel Faba Ortega – Thinkstock, *br* © epa european presspphoto agency b.v./Alamy Stock Photo; **p.45** *tl* © loganban – 123RF, *tr* © Luis Louro – 123RF, *b* © Charlotte Nation via Getty Images; **p.47** *t* © tomas – Fotolia, *c* © Carmen Taylor/WireImage via Getty Images, *b* © serezniy – 123RF; **p.51** *l* © sdecoret – Fotolia, *r* © Dan Istitene/Getty Images; **p.52** © Paul Thompson/FPG/Hulton Archive/Getty Images; **p.54** © JOEL SAGET/AFP/Getty Images; **p.55** *tl* © Photographee.eu – Fotolia, *tr* © Ingram Publishing Company/Ultimate Business 06, *cl* © Photographee.eu – Fotolia, *cr* © Chris Ratcliffe/Getty Images, *b* © JackF – Fotolia.com; **p.66** *l* © Universal Images Group via Getty Images, *c* © Paul France/REX Shutterstock, *r* © PYMCA/UIG via Getty Images; **p.70** © Guy Corbishley/Alamy Stock Photo; **p.72** *l* © cmspic – 123rf, *r* © don jon red/Alamy Stock Photo; **p.77** © Chip Somodevilla/Getty Images; **p.84** © Mark Bourdillon/Alamy Stock Photo; **p.90** © PicturesofLondon/Alamy Stock Photo; **p.98** *tl* © Monkey Business – Fotolia, *bl* © Purestock – Thinkstock/Getty Images, *r* © Wavebreak Media Ltd – 123RF; **p.100** *l* © David Leahy/Digital Vision/Getty Images – UK_Education_DV1183, *r* © Fredrik Kippe/Alamy Stock Photo; **p.104** © Carl Court/Getty Images; **p.108** © Tommy (Louth)/Alamy Stock Photo; **p.115** © Travel21 Impact/Heritage Images/topfoto; **p.118** *l* © Janine Wiedel Photolibrary/Alamy Stock Photo, *r* © Ilike – Fotolia.com; **p.120** © Christian Schwier – Fotolia; **p.126** © John Kershaw/Alamy Stock Photo; **p.136** © Janine Wiedel/REX Shutterstock; **p.139** © Design Pics Inc/Alamy Stock Photo; **p.145** *l* © ANessiR – iStock via Thinkstock/Getty Images, *r* © Cathy Yeulet – 123RF; **p.149** © Shehzad Noorani/Majority World/UIG via Getty Images; **p.157** © M. McNeill/Fox Photos/Hulton Archive/Getty Images; **p.166** Background picture © eugenesergeev – Fotolia; **p.168** *cl* © Mario Tama/Gettty Images, *bl* © Paul Thompson Images/Alamy Stock Photo, *tr* © Hodder Education, *cr* © GARETH FULLER/epa/Corbis; **p.170** © TC/Alamy Stock Photo; **p.171** © Sygma/Corbis; **p.177** © VINCENZO PINTO/AFP/Getty Images; **p.179** © Clichesdumonde – Fotolia; **p.180** © Rodrigo Varela/WireImage; **p.183** © Leif Skoogfors/CORBIS; **p.187** © PRISMA ARCHIVO/Alamy Stock Photo; **p.189** © Dunca Daniel –123RF; **p.190** *t* © Kevin Mazur/WireImage/Getty Images, *b* © robertharding/Alamy Stock Photo; **p.191** © The Guardian/Alamy Stock Photo; **p.193** *tl* © PhotoStock – Israel/Alamy Stock Photo, *tr* © fotogiunta – Fotolia, *b* © Louise Batalla Duran/Alamy Stock Photo; **p.194** © Thomas Cockrem/Alamy Stock Photo; **p.202** © Phil Banko via Getty Images; **p.205** © Pascal Deloche/Godong/Corbis; **p.209** © Robert Hoetink – Fotolia; **p.210** © Photofusion/REX Shutterstock; **p.216** PA Graphics/Press Association Images; **p.218** © Borislav Marinic –123RF; **p.221** Reproduced with the kind permission of Sea of Faith; **p.225** © Michael Fair – 123RF; **p.228** Reproduced with permission from freshexpressions.org.uk/about/whatis, copyright © 2015 Fresh Expressions freshexpressions.org.uk.

Acknowledgements

p.48 From The globalisation of organised crime, by UNODC – UN Office on Drugs and Crime, © 2010 United Nations. Reprinted with the permission of the United Nations; **p.116** Item B Source: Sippitt, A. (2014) 'Measuring social mobility: How does the UK perform?' https://fullfact.org/education/social_mobility_what_is_it_how_measure-31277/ Copyright © Full Fact or fullfact.org. Used by permission; **p.140** Source: Centre for Education and Employment Research (CEER), University of Buckingham; **p.141** *Item A* Source: Joint Council figures on grades. © JCQ; **p.142** *Item B* Source: Provisional GCE Results Data Summer 2014 for the UK, *bottom* Source: *Social Trends*, 2007, 2011 and HESA https://www.hesa.ac.uk/stats Copyright © HESA. Used by permission; **p.150** Source: EFA Global Monitoring Report. Copyright © UNESCO; **p.196** Credit: Linda Woodhead and the AHRC/ESRC Religion and Society Programme; **pp.209–10** Credit: Linda Woodhead and the AHRC/ESRC Religion and Society Programme.

Every effort has been made to trace all copyright holders, but if any have been inadvertently overlooked, the Publishers will be pleased to make the necessary arrangements at the first opportunity.

Although every effort has been made to ensure that website addresses are correct at time of going to press, Hodder Education cannot be held responsible for the content of any website mentioned in this book. It is sometimes possible to find a relocated web page by typing in the address of the home page for a website in the URL window of your browser.

Hachette UK's policy is to use papers that are natural, renewable and recyclable products and made from wood grown in sustainable forests. The logging and manufacturing processes are expected to conform to the environmental regulations of the country of origin.

Orders: please contact Bookpoint Ltd, 130 Park Drive, Milton Park, Abingdon, Oxon OX14 4SE. Telephone: +44(0)1235 827720. Fax: +44(0)1235 400454. Email education@bookpoint.co.uk Lines are open from 9 a.m. to 5 p.m., Monday to Saturday, with a 24-hour message answering service. You can also order through our website: www.hoddereducation.co.uk

ISBN: 9781471839450

© Katherine Roberts, Sue Brisbane, Paul Taylor and Laura Pountney 2016

First published in 2016 by

Hodder Education,

An Hachette UK Company

Carmelite House

50 Victoria Embankment

London EC4Y 0DZ

www.hoddereducation.co.uk

Impression number   10 9 8 7 6 5 4 3

Year   2012 2019

Cover photo © istockphoto/scanrail

Illustrations by Integra Software Services and Peter Lubach

Typeset in 10.75/13.5 pt Bliss Light by Integra Software Services Pvt. Ltd., Pondicherry, India

Printed in India

A catalogue record for this title is available from the British Library.

Contents

How to use this book

This book has been written and designed specifically for the new OCR A Level Sociology specification introduced for first teaching in September 2015.

OCR Sociology for A Level 2 covers the content required for:

- Component 03 Debates in contemporary society of OCR A Level Sociology (H580).

Components 01 and 02 are covered in **OCR Sociology for A Level 1**.

To view the full specifications, and examples of assessment material, for OCR AS or OCR A Level Sociology, please visit OCR's website: www.ocr.org.uk.

The content of this book, as well as **OCR Sociology for A Level 1**, covers all topic options in the new specification. Each chapter has a range of features which have been designed to present the course content in a clear and accessible way, to give you confidence and to support you in your revision and assessment preparation. It is important to remember that the linear A Level is more demanding than the AS, and to plan your studies accordingly.

Getting you thinking

Each section starts with an activity that has been designed to get you thinking about the topic.

Activity

Activities appear throughout the book and have been designed to help you develop your understanding and sociological skills.

Study

Sociological studies are summarised in these boxes. The studies included are not required by OCR but have been added to help develop understanding and support further discussion.

Quick question

Quick questions are exactly that – questions to answer quickly that will help you think about, and understand, different topics in the book.

Check your understanding

These questions have been designed specifically to help to check that you have understood different topics.

Section summary

These boxes contain summaries of what you have learned in each section but we have left some blanks for you to fill in!

Practice questions

These have been designed to offer study practice.

Glossary

Key terms in **bold** in the text are defined in the glossary at the end of the book.

Chapter 1

Globalisation and the digital social world

Component 3 Section A
Globalisation and the digital social world

Content

1 **What is the relationship between globalisation and digital forms of communication?** Definitions of globalisation, developments in digital forms of communication in a global society, applying sociological theories including Marxism, feminism and postmodernism.

2 **What is the impact of digital forms of communication in a global context?** The impact of digital forms of communication on people's identity, social inequalities, relationships and the impact of digital forms of communication on culture.

1.1 What is the relationship between globalisation and digital forms of communication?

Getting you thinking ...

What is globalisation?

Look at the images above. Describe some of the effects of these changes. Think about: communication, shopping, travel.

What is globalisation?

Globalisation is a much used term which has been interpreted in a number of different ways by different groups. This section explores some of the challenges of defining globalisation and offers some different definitions for discussion.

Globalisation is a word which is used to describe a process which has been going on for a very long time. In fact, it started when early humans began moving out of Africa around 1.8 million years ago to spread all over the world. As communication and transportation developed with greater efficiency, more and more groups of people became connected. The internet, which was created in 1983 led to some of the most significant advances in communication technology; it is easier for people to communicate with others instantly without being physically close to them.

As a result of globalisation, people who were previously uncontacted became part of a wider global society resulting in a whole array of consequences. For example, national boundaries become less significant, businesses are able to operate internationally and the economy now has a global dimension. It is important to acknowledge that globalisation is not an even process. While globalisation has occurred in many parts of the world there are other areas where people remain marginalised and excluded from the process, often suffering great inequality as a result.

Why the recent sociological interest in globalisation?

As you will probably have begun to understand, social change has always occurred to some degree, at varying speeds. However, Giddens, Duneier and Appelbaum

---

Activity

Uncontacted tribes

At risk of extinction from disease and land loss, in the depths of the Amazon rainforest in Brazil live tribes such as the Awa, who for long periods of time have had no contact with the outside world. However this part of the world is rich in resources and the land is highly sought after by businesses. Globalisation has led to increasing demand for land, often due to the spread of **transnational corporations (TNCs)**. For example, the high demand for timber products have led to legal and illegal logging, which caused the destruction of some habitats in the rainforest.

Brazil's Amazon rainforest is home to more uncontacted tribes than anywhere in the world. There are thought to be at least 77 isolated groups

in this particular area of the rainforest, according to the government. The Tribes' decision not to maintain contact with other tribes and outsiders is almost certainly a result of previous disastrous encounters and the ongoing invasion and destruction of their forest home. For example, the uncontacted groups living in the state of Acre are probably survivors of the rubber boom (which occurred from 1879 to 1912), who managed to avoid having their way of life permanently changed.

Today these societies are fighting for their right to live in the area as western developers want to clear the forest for farming as well as extracting natural resources from the land. Interestingly, many uncontacted tribes may be forced to fight for their rights through new forms of communication to ensure that they can maintain their culture and lifestyle. For example, campaigns led by internet based organisations such as Survival International provide public, legal and practical support to these tribes. Often, this involves helping these groups win the right to lands which they have lived on for thousands of years, without any formal legal evidence of ownership.

Source: Adapted from www.survivalinternational.org

1 What effects has globalisation had on tribes such as the Awa?
2 How might digital communication be used to protect the rights of these groups?

(2005) suggest that if human history (about half a million years) were equivalent to a twenty-four-hour day, not much would have happened for the first 23 hours. Agriculture would appear at 11:56:30 pm. The great civilizations would appear at 11:57pm. We would see modern societies emerge at 11:59:30 pm. More change has taken place in the remaining 30 seconds than in the entire time that preceded this. They conclude that the trend is unmistakable: not only are societies changing, but the pace of change is accelerating beyond any pace previously recognisable.

In the past few decades, sociologists have become increasingly aware of the need to understand the globalisation process and ensure that their explanations of the world need to encompass the causes and effects of the process. There has also been a growing interest because of the rapid advances in technology which have meant that the rate of globalisation has accelerated rapidly over recent years. However, Wiseman (1998) warns us that the term 'globalisation' can be misused and misunderstood and therefore needs careful consideration when it is being used and defined in sociology.

What are the problems with trying to define globalisation?

So far it is clear that globalisation is a complex process that involves a variety of social, economic and political factors, which may or may not be occurring in a uniform way everywhere. As well as this, there are those who suggest the effects of globalisation are generally positive whereas there are others who claim that the effects are generally negative for particular groups. For example, leading to the further reinforcement of inequalities in society. Other sociologists argue that the effects of globalisation are both negative and positive in different ways. Therefore it should be no surprise that attempts to define the process in a simple way is very difficult without revealing some assumptions about the view the person has of the process.

Below are some different definitions of globalisation:

The first definition can be seen to be problematic since it suggests that globalisation is occurring at the same rate everywhere at the same time. The second definition appears to suffer from the same problem, but does acknowledge the different aspects of globalisation which is perhaps more accurate. Neither of the first or the second definitions accurately defines the complexity of the process, and the way that is connected to technological advances. The third definition relates to one specific aspect of globalisation which underpins many of the other features of globalisation, namely increasing interconnectivity.

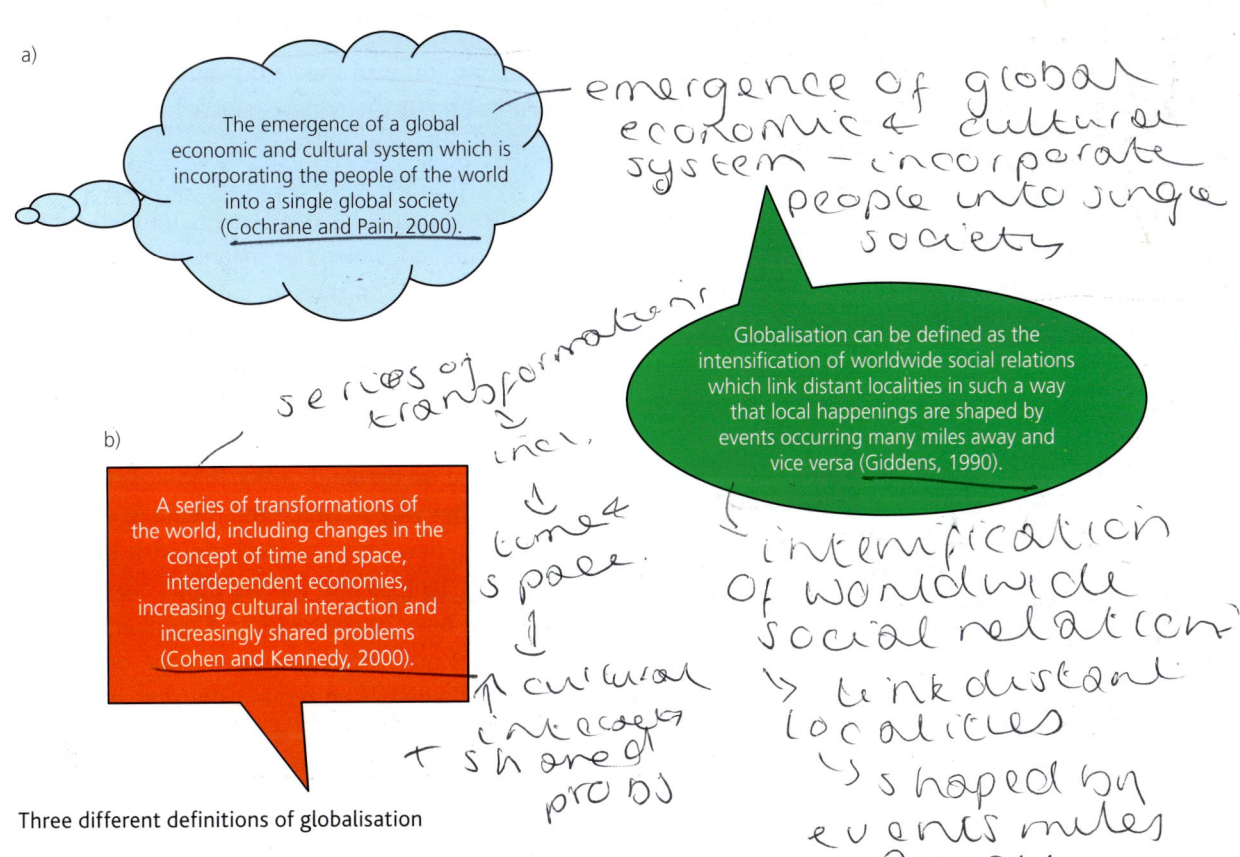

a) The emergence of a global economic and cultural system which is incorporating the people of the world into a single global society (Cochrane and Pain, 2000).

b) A series of transformations of the world, including changes in the concept of time and space, interdependent economies, increasing cultural interaction and increasingly shared problems (Cohen and Kennedy, 2000).

Globalisation can be defined as the intensification of worldwide social relations which link distant localities in such a way that local happenings are shaped by events occurring many miles away and vice versa (Giddens, 1990).

Three different definitions of globalisation

1. The definition may assume that globalisation is a positive process	For some, globalisation results in marginalisation and exclusion. For example those without access to the internet. For example, those in poverty or those unable to access the internet due to state restrictions.
2. The definition may assume that globalisation occurs everywhere at an even pace	One thing is clear and that is that globalisation occurs at different rates in different places. So in less developed countries for example, digital communication may be less well used.
3. The definition may assume that globalisation results in cultural homogenisation	In fact globalisation has brought people spread out all over the world with similar or unique cultural characteristics together to protect their rights and culture. For example tribal people.
4. The definition may assume that globalisation is only an economic or political or cultural process	In fact, globalisation affects with all of these different areas of social life, in different ways.
5. The definition assumes that globalisation all results in social change towards postmodern characteristics such as individualism and choice	Globalisation can result in people wishing to react to defend themselves against change, as a form of cultural resistance. For example, some people see the spread of western liberal ideas as threatening and seek to protect their own alternative culture. For example, religious fundamentalists.

Table 1.1 A summary of some of the problems with defining globalisation

---

Activity

Defining globalisation
1 Explain two problems with trying to define globalisation.
2 Which of the three parts of globalisation (cultural, economic and political) do you think is most significant, and why?
3 Write your own definition of globalisation. Did you find it difficult to do so and if so, why?

Developments in digital forms of communication in a global society

The digital revolution

The digital revolution refers to the massive and rapid advances in technology which have transformed people's lives over the past few decades. Society has moved from being based on analogue, mechanical and electronic technology to being based on digital technology and communication. The growth of digital technology over the past two decades has had huge impact on the way information is stored and communicated. This means that all new forms of communication are created by computer technology using internationally recognised programming systems meaning that it is possible that information can be shared everywhere around the world.

This section explores some of the features of advances in digital forms of communication in a global society. The speed of technological advances has been so rapid that sociologists are only just beginning to understand some of the effects of these changes. As well as thinking about these key developments it is also important to consider those who are not able to access digital forms of communication (we will discuss this further in the second part of the chapter).

These new forms of digital communication are sometimes known as new media. These fall into two categories.

1 Initially there is the extension and development of existing forms of media on various new platforms. For example, many newspapers have now got significant readership online as well as on paper. Another important way in which traditional forms of media have evolved is through satellite transmission, which has meant that people can now access television through cable or satellite. This form of transmission allows a much larger amount of information to be shown, meaning a whole range of television and radio stations transmitting simultaneously. For example, television can now be watched on demand rather than at set times.

2 The other way in which the media is 'new' is through new forms of platform, such as mobile phones, laptops and tablets which are used in various new ways and allow a number of different types of programmes, such as 'apps' or applications that help people communicate more easily and in much more novel and dynamic ways. These new forms of media are also used to help people manage

their lives, relationships, shopping, diet, health and so on. These are often highly individualised, so that the person using them can adapt them to their own specific needs.

Activity

Forms of media

- TV on demand
- podcast
- facebook messenger
- newspaper apps
- apps like flappy birds, snapchat and instagram
1 Which forms of media listed above are new and which are an extension of traditional forms of media?

The global village

Marshall McLuhan 1964

Digital communication has led to an increasing volume of communication which does not involve face to face contact. This has led to the idea that as time and distance shrink, the world is becoming a much smaller place. This idea is sometimes known as the global village, which increases people's ability to create and maintain social relationships both with people they already know or people who live far away, who they might only ever interact with online. The ease with which people can make contact with others who share similar interests from across the world means that it is much easier for people to maintain these interests. For example, people can search for particular online communities and interact with others who share similar interests and concerns. Indeed the relationships which people have on line with people may in fact be as significant as relationships that they enjoy offline.

Virtual communities

A virtual community is a social network of individuals who create an online community which may or may not reflect their offline lives. This community crosses geographical, political and social lines. These virtual communities are becoming increasingly complex and in some cases, very realistic. These allow people to share interests and create and transform their identities. There are many forms of virtual communities:

- message boards
- online chat rooms
- virtual worlds
- social networks
- specific services communities (where people who share a specific type of knowledge or skills can share ideas)

Study

Virtual communities: Cybercity, Carter (2005)

The social anthropologist Carter (2005) explores the ways that digital forms of communication are used in creating and maintaining relationships in an increasingly globalised context. Carter conducted research in one particular virtual community which the author names Cybercity. Cybercity is a virtual community with over 1, 062, 072 registered users in June 2004. It has all the characteristics of a city. Carter spent three and a half years in her fieldwork from September 1999 to April 2001. She visited the community at least once every day and used a predominantly Western sample. Carter carried out participant observation and questionnaires as well as offline semi-structured interviews. Carter's research illustrates how, for many people, cyberspace is just another place to meet people with similar interests.

She suggests that people in Cybercity are investing as much effort in maintaining relationships in cyberspace as in other social spaces. She asked three questions: What kinds of relationships are formed online? Do relationships formed online migrate to other social settings? How are real life and virtual life interwoven in terms of lived experiences? She was looking at friendship and how the trustworthiness and authenticity of these affect social relations. Carter found out that people who meet a person online do in fact often then continue these online friendships in their offline lives, by meeting them in person. Carter also argues that cyberspace is becoming increasingly embedded in people's everyday lives.

Activity

Global village

1 How does Carter's study support the idea that we now live in a global village?
2 Using a simple world map, note where all of your friends live. How important is digital forms of communication in maintaining these friendships?

What are social networks and how do these shape communication?

Until recently, many forms of social networks have existed in a face-to-face form. For example, people have different groups of friends who they might meet up with periodically, face-to-face. However the recent rapid increase in digital technology has led to a range of different forms of social networks which go beyond face-to-face to form virtual networks. In fact many people now form all types of different relationships online. Think about the types of social networks people have:
- friendship groups
- work networks
- family networks
- networks linked to hobbies, interests or religion

How does digital communication affect the way that people create and maintain social networks in employment?

As globalisation has accelerated, the way the economy and employment have changed is significant. People rely on the internet for creating and maintaining work based relationships, as well as finding and applying for jobs. This is so significant now that it could be argued that unless a person has access to digital forms of communication they are at a real disadvantage.

Networked global society refers to the idea that in the post-industrial society, the focus is on information as a result of new forms of communication. Those with the access to information create social networks, often which result in greater employability and hierarchical status. In other words, having relationships or connections with people and groups at a global level leads to material rewards, known as social capital.

One good example of this is the website LinkedIn. LinkedIn, founded in 2002 is a social network created for people to develop employment based connections. It is designed specifically to allow people to find a job. It now has more than 20 million users world wide.

Quick question

Think of some ways in which employment based networks help people find a greater range of job opportunities.

Study

Network Society, Castells (2000)

Castells (2000) offers an interesting interpretation of the impact of digital communication drawing upon Marxist ideas. He claims that we are moving from the industrial age into an age defined by information. This significant change has occurred as a result of the evolution of new information technologies, particularly those for communication. Castells argues that although society remains capitalist, the focus has shifted from a focus on energy such as oil, gas and electricity, to a focus on information. This information is of central importance in determining economic productivity. Communications technologies allow for the removal of the issue of space and distance and for globalisation; the potential for rapid, multiple forms of communication also changes the relationship that people have with time: communication is instantaneous. Furthermore, while Castells explains that networks are not a new form of social organization, they have become a central characteristic of society. This is because communication technologies, such as the internet, allow for decentralisation of control, increasing the effectiveness of networks and hierarchical structures.

According to Castells, power now rests in networks. Some networks, such as that of financial capital, are global in scale. Networks also exist within and between businesses and can also be temporary, project-by-project. Resources, by which Castells means employees, consultants, and other businesses are brought together to work on a particular project, then dispersed and reallocated when the task is complete. The people at the bottom are those who, with nothing to offer the network, are excluded. These people include labourers and factory workers who are low paid and less able to invest in the development of their skills. They are likely to be poorly educated and have very little chance of social mobility.

Activity

Networks

1 What is necessary today to create a social network?
2 What is the relationship between global networks and power?

What is media convergence?

Media convergence refers to the way that a whole range of different kinds of information can be combined and delivered in one format. For example, videos, text and images can all be stored and accessed on one website. Media convergence also refers to the ways in which social media platforms are able to communicate with each other to share contacts, for example. So, someone is able to access information about their Facebook friends on Instagram, for example. This has also led to the convergence of various cultural ideas as well as economic markets becoming increasingly global rather than just national. Because digital forms of communication have developed most rapidly in the west, western capitalist ideas have become dominant across all forms of media. So, it follows that these ideas support and perpetuate capitalist ideas such as the pursuit of profit, private ownership and material objects being seen as important.

Imagine, for example, advertising when it is possible to advertise on a whole range of platforms and gain maximum engagement from your potential customer. The result is a much more effective advertising strategy and increased sales. The various combinations of different ideas has also led to the creation of new ideas and products which themselves have become successful as a result of media convergence. Boyle (2005) explains how the process of digitalisation allows media convergence. Boyle explains that these once separate forms of media can now be accessed through one device. For example, having a phone on which you can watch television programmes, films and also listen to the radio (as well as make phone calls). New digital media are also often highly interactive meaning that people can shape new forms of convergent media in individualistic ways.

What is Big Data? Understanding the data that is produced by digital forms of communication.

In the past, data, or information was stored on paper and available only to those few who had access to such information. This relied upon people being literate and being physically close enough to the information. Encyclopedias for example, were used by children to find out about different parts of the world whereas today, search engines such as Google can be accessed by many millions of children all over the world at the touch of a button.

Today, the way information is being collected and used has changed massively. Because of the internet and the increase in the volume of data being recoded and collected, there are now huge amounts of information about almost every area of social life.

Big data refers to extremely large data sets that may be analysed digitally and non-digitally to reveal patterns, trends and links, especially relating to human behaviour and interactions. This data is collected usually through commercial companies and other bodies.

There are several features of Big Data, which make it different to other forms of data that exist:

- **Volume** – Many factors contribute to the increase in data volume. Information is now stored about online communications, purchases and transactions which produces a large amount of data which is stored for a possibly infinite amount of time. Unstructured data streaming from social media also forms another source of data and increasing amounts of information is being collected. In the past, excessive data volume was a storage issue, however as information has become possible to store digitally, there has been a decrease in the cost of storing it. As a result other issues have emerged, including how to decide what data is relevant and what can be discarded.
- **Velocity** – Data is streaming at unprecedented speed and must be dealt with promptly.
- **Variety** – Data today comes in all types of formats. Structured, numeric data in traditional databases as well as unstructured text documents, email, video, audio, stock market data and financial transactions.

- **Variability** – In addition to the increasing velocities and varieties of data, data flows can be highly inconsistent. For example, where an event or idea is trending in social media it suddenly becomes widely popular and briefly high profile. Daily, seasonal and event-triggered peak data loads can be challenging to manage. This is even more so with unstructured data.
- **Complexity** – Today's data comes from multiple sources. And it is still an undertaking to link, match, sort and transform data across systems, as well as to connect and correlate relationships.

Big Data is 'big', not only in terms of the terabytes of storage space it can require, but in the number of people talking about it and the myriad of opportunities it presents. It's debatable whether market research data can be categorised as Big Data. Some research (such as the GP Patient Survey) involves several million interviews but even this is not big or complex enough for many to consider it Big Data. Big Data analytics tends to focus more on the data trails or impressions we generate as we all communicate, consume and conduct our day-to-day lives; the (often digital) breadcrumbs we leave behind after any interaction.

What is social media and how does it relate to globalisation?

Social media refers to any form of digitally based platform for making, confirming or developing social networks which have a global reach, such as Second Life which was discussed above in relation to virtual communities. The first mass usage of social media networks was probably Cyworld, launched in South Korea in 1999 (Miller 2012). However the best known example is probably Facebook, which was the result of an experiment carried out by students as a way of connecting and communicating with each other at Harvard University. Within six years the site had half a billion users. Social media has many of the qualities of postmodern society; it allows its users to personalise their page, reflecting increased individualism.

The use of new social media has exploded in popularity, which can be seen from these statistics:

- 15 million users of Twitter in the UK in 2014, 80 per cent of whom use Twitter via their smart phones.
- In 2014 there were 31 million users of Facebook in the UK, mainly used by 24–35 year olds. As Facebook has become more mainstream its growth has begun to slow down.

- In 2013 Linkedin passed the 20 million users mark globally. This is a site where people can share their professional skills and create work based social networks.
- In 2014, Pinterest and Instagram were the fastest growing forms of social media and they are more used by women than men.
- Snapchat, launched in 2011, is hugely popular too. In 2014 its average age users were aged between 13 and 20 and 70 per cent are female.
- According to Ofcom's annual News Consumption study (2014) 41 per cent of the population use the net to keep up-to-date with current affairs.

Source: Adapted from www.socialmediatoday.com and www.ofcom.org.uk

Activity

Trends in social media use

1 What do these statistics reveal about trends in the use of new social media today?
2 Discuss with a partner what the possible effects of people using new forms of social media more frequently are (more on this later in the chapter).

Applying sociological theories to digital forms of communication

Getting you thinking ...

What are the problems with trying to apply traditional theories to new forms of digital communication?

Due to the fact that digital forms of communication have only recently emerged there have been relatively few attempts to interpret them theoretically. However this is an interesting and growing area of sociology. In this section we explore three key theoretical interpretations; Marxist, feminist and postmodernist.

The Marxist perspective

This perspective argues that digital communication is not new, simply a different version of other forms of communication whose effects have been exaggerated by postmodernists and other sociologists. This critical view, led by Cornford and Rob there is a range of evidence to

Study

The continuation of power being the hands of a few, Cornford and

Cornford and Robins argue that digital communication is presented as a new for democratic, open communication which to greater equality in the creation and spread of new ideas and communication. In reality, however, they are doubtful of these claims and argue that the people who own and control the digital media are capitalists who not only want to make profit but also to ideologically control the masses. In the past, the ruling class owned the means of production, that is the factories and machinery which led to the production of goods to be sold for a profit. Today, power and money come from a variety of different sources, the media being one of these. The media includes the news and entertainment which are powerful in shaping the ideas of the population.

In many ways this reflects the changes recently seen in the general non-digital media where the media is owned by a smaller and smaller number of media moguls who influence the content and organisation of their media with their predominantly conservative values (Bagdikian, 2014).

As we have seen there has been an increasing number of ways to access the media through digital devices such as mobile phones, tablets and computers, sometimes known as media convergence. For the owners of media companies this creates greater opportunities for cross fertilisation of ideas and marketing strategies, meaning that they can sell their media in a number of different formats, creating vast opportunities to make profit. Marxists would argue that this also means that the media has an even greater platform for shaping people's ideas, encouraging people to accept capitalism and not question the inequalities that exist.

Therefore this approach argues that new forms of digital communication reinforce and maintain inequalities in society and ideologically control people in new and subtle ways.

The proposed merger of the media mogul Rupert Murdock's media companies would mean that he controls over a fifth of UK news consumption. The question should not be focused on whether you like Rupert Murdoch but simply whether the companies he owns, News Corp/Sky are too large. Those who have dealt with Ofcom, the communications regulator grappling with the merger of Murdock's major companies, say that the researchers are trying to understand the issue by producing some data that determines media power and dominance in the UK. As companies such as these are now available on a range of different hand-held devices, there is a growing sense that the media is playing a more and more powerful role in people's lives.

Source: Adapted from *The Guardian*, Dan Sabbagh, 30th December 2010

1 How does this article support the Marxist view that the ownership of the media reflects capitalist ideology?
2 Why do you think it is a problem for the media to be controlled by so few people?
3 What implications does this have for digital media?

De-regulation of the media and digital communication

One part of the critical argument has been the apparent lack of regulation in relation to digital communication. The fact that digital communication is mediated by private companies rather than the state means that there are few laws governing its moral responsibilities. There have been growing concerns about the lack of social control over what occurs as a result of digital communication, either in virtual reality or in people's offline lives (see the figure on page 11).

Marxists would also argue that the internet and digital forms of communication are yet another method of surveillance, a form of subtle observation as a way to control and regulate people, in the interests of the wealthy. It is possible to argue that as there is little economic incentive for protecting vulnerable groups such as children and women online, little is done to prevent their exploitation.

Critics of capitalism and digital communication also argue that adults may be spending excessive amounts of time online, to the extent that the balance between sleep and screen based activities has now tipped. The typical adult spends eight hours and 41 minutes each day communicating or consuming media, including books and newspapers, and just eight hours and 21 minutes asleep (Garside, 2014). Marxists would suggest that the internet and digital communication is a way of entertaining people which presents no real threat to the existing capitalist society.

Digital communication provides a new form of surveillance

There have been recent concerns over the monitoring of personal digital communication between individuals by the state, see below for information on The Snowden Report. Alternatively, private companies gather information on people's use of social media as well as their consumer habits and their 'breadcrumbs', which means their movements around the internet, often without the knowledge or consent of the person who is being monitored.

This has caused some to suggest that digital communication threatens individual liberty and freedom. Cornford and Robins argue that digital communication is simply a way of capitalism controlling people more subtly through their use of various social media under the guise of protecting people from extremism or criminal acts. This represents a huge challenge to people's individual privacy, and has caused considerable controversy. These forms of surveillance are little understood by the consumer. For example, it is often unclear if or how the company owning the software program such as Facebook are collecting information on individual's choices and decisions. It is even less clear what the rules are relating to personal information in digital communication since it is such a new issue. For example, what happens to the information we provide online? Are people fully aware of how it is used but the owners of the social media, or what their rules are on managing people's private data?

Formal social control through the law has not yet fully caught up with the changes and is often ill equipped to deal with such problems. The prevailing lack of clarity over how personal information is being used is considered highly problematic by many critical sociologists and others.

Activity

The Snowden Report

In 2013 the US National Security Agency (NSA) specialist Edward Snowden revealed widespread misuse of surveillance of digital forms of communication. He provided evidence that the US and British government had been accessing personal and private communications claiming that it was in the interests of 'national security'.

But the intelligence agencies dismiss such claims, arguing that their programmes are necessary and legal. Surveillance, they say, is essential to meet their overriding aim of protecting the public from terrorist attacks.

The debate has raged across time zones: from the US and Latin America to Europe and to Asia. Barack Obama cancelled a trip to Moscow in protest at Russian president Vladimir Putin's protection of Snowden. Brazilian president Dilma Rousseff cancelled a state visit to Washington in protest at the US spying on her. Bolivian president Evo Morales's plane was forced down in Vienna amid suspicion that Snowden was being smuggled out of Russia.

In Germany, a 'livid' Angela Merkel accused the US of spying on her, igniting a controversy that has seen the White House concede that new constraints on the NSA's activities may be necessary. Meanwhile, in Britain, Prime Minister David Cameron accused the Guardian of damaging national security by publishing the revelations, warning that if it did not 'demonstrate some social responsibility it would be very difficult for government to stand back and not to act'.

Source: Adapted from *The Guardian*, Ewen Macaskill and Gabriel Dance, 1st November 2013

1 What did Snowden's revelations about the NSA show had been happening?
2 What were the effects of the revelations?

Key points	Problems with Marxist views
Globalisation results in the spread of western, capitalist ideas	Globalisation has resulted in class becoming just one part of many that shapes our identity. Ethnicity for example, is very significant.
New forms of communication reflect the ideas of the owners of the media companies who represent the ruling class	Digital forms of communication allow people to challenge the ruling class through more interactive participation in public issues and the news for example.
Digital forms of communicaiton encourage passive acceptance of capitalism	There have been examples of where digital forms of communication have actually led to social protest, challenging inequality (more on this later in the chapter).

Table 1.2 A summary of Marxist views on global forms of digital communication

Evaluation of Marxist ideas about globalisation and digital forms of communication

Despite the fact that Marxist ideas were developed over a hundred year ago, it is clear that they still offer an interesting way of looking at the role of digital forms of communication in a global context. Marxists argue that globalisation has led to the spread of capitalist ideology and as a result, new opportunities to make profit. Marxists are pessimistic about the role of digital communication, arguing that it simply offers a new and more sophisticated way for the ruling class to ideologically control and watch the working class masses. According to Marxists the owners of the media and new media companies alike use their positions to manipulate people into accepting society as it is.

The feminist view

Feminist views on digital communication include theoretical interpretations as well as practical and socio-political movement. This section explores the way in which feminists interpret the existing patterns in digital communication as well as exploring what they are doing to challenge and change these patterns.

Statistics reveal the following facts about gender and digital communication:

- Women use social media slightly more than men, however, Pinterest and Instagram are overwhelmingly used by females – over 70 per cent are women.
- Only 13 per cent of the contributions to Wikipedia are by women (New York Times, 2011)
- The latest list of Britain's top 100 influential Twitter users in 2013 contained just 17 women (Peer Index and The Independent).
- This may reflect patterns in employment where women still represent under a fifth of IT managers, 21 per cent of computer analysts, and 14 per cent of software professionals (Cooper, 2013).
- Linkedin the social network site for creating stronger and further reaching work based contacts has considerably more male users than women.

Quick questions

1 What do these facts reveal about the use of digital communication and gender?
2 How might a feminist explain these patterns?

Feminist theory and the digital

Feminist studies of the digital world are a relatively recent development in the field of digital humanities as a whole. Feminist views have emerged partly due to recent criticism of the digital to further patriarchal or dominant (hegemonic) discourses. Some of the research into gender and the digital world focuses on the exclusion of women from the history of technology and the use of technology to develop feminist ideas. Feminists challenge the male-dominated nature of digital media, emphasising the role of women, feminists, and cyber-feminists, (feminists whose interests lie in researching cyberspace, the internet and technology) in developing digital communication. They seek to challenge and overturn ideas such as the suggestion that men are the innovators of the internet and digital communication.

One of the earliest feminist discussions of the role of technology was by Haraway (1985) who wrote a ground breaking article entitled 'A Cyborg Manifesto: Science, Technology, and Socialist-Feminism in the Late Twentieth Century' in the *Socialist Review*. Haraway felt strongly that women should be included in all forms of knowledge relating to technologically based information, which appeared to be produced mainly by men. She argued that feminists must not be excluded from the technological advances that were taking place and instead, be part of them and inform them. Haraway's manifesto argues that women cannot be essentialised, or, in other words, seen as sharing something essentially similar about what it means to be a woman. Rather, Haraway argues that what is considered to be female is highly politicised and socially constructed. She suggests that cyborgs, which are part-machine, part-human entities, might allow people to transcend or rise above gender-bound ideas of what it means to be a person. In other words, Haraway suggests that technological advances offer the possibility for women to create new forms of identity not bound by traditional ideas or dominant patriarchal discourses about gender.

In her later book Simians, Cyborgs and Women: The Reinvention of Nature (1991), Haraway uses the cyborg metaphor to explain how problems with feminism and capitalism might be overcome through greater understanding of identity through cyborg theory. Haraway is interesting therefore as she was among the first feminists to consider technology to be a way for women to become more empowered, offering possibilities beyond those which traditional social life can offer.

Activity

Social media use and gender

1 Using questionnaires or interviews, carry out some research in your class on the way girls and boys use different forms of social media and digital communication. Focus on:
   - How much time people spend using new forms of digital media
   - Which sites they use
   - Why they use social media
   - If girls or boys have different views on digital forms of communication
2 What did you find?
3 Does your evidence support the view that there is a gender divide in the way that girls and boys use digital communication differently?

Today, there are a number of ways in which feminists are exploring the links between feminist theory and the digital global world. For example, Nakamura (2011) notes that women from a range of ethnic minorities are gaining an increasing presence in digital communication and this enables their particular interests. For example, there are support networks for women who might have been unable to access support previously. These networks offer practical and emotional support for women who are experiencing discrimination for example, The Everyday Sexism Project founded by Laura Bates.

Globalisation and the exploitation of women

Globalisation has had many effects, including new opportunities for criminals to exploit already vulnerable groups. As a result, women and children who were already at increased risk of exploitation are now at further risk of, becoming commodities to be bought, sold and consumed. The criminals involved include, for example, tourists, organised crime rings, traffickers, pimps, and those seeking sexual entertainment.

Women and children throughout history have been in a vulnerable position due to the fact that those who hold the power in terms of government and law-making have not made passing legislation to protect women and children a priority. Most feminists would argue that this is because men largely control governments and legal systems worldwide. Protecting women and children from exploitation has not only not been prioritised, but is exceedingly difficult as those who operate human trafficking networks do so as covertly as possible. The internet has made it easier for such activities to be organised in an unregulated digital world.

The global sexual exploitation of women and children that is accompanying globalisation is a human rights disaster. As national boundaries have become less significant, the illegal movement of people has become much easier to coordinate and as a result, people trafficking has risen. Arlaccki (1997), who led the United Nations efforts to fight organised crime, states that exploitation has been one of the most undesirable consequences of globalisation. Regrettably, he stated that this is not currently considered a priority by any country.

How is exploitation of women and children furthered through new forms of digital communication?

There are increasing concerns about the exploitation of children through various forms of digital communication. For example, the Child Exploitation and Online Protection Centre (CEOP) play a leading role in protecting children, and in the year 2012–13 reported that:

- 790 children were subject to safeguarding or protection as a result of CEOP activity.
- There were 18,887 reports relating to child sexual exploitation.
- 2,866 intelligence reports were sent to UK and overseas law enforcement agencies relating to individuals suspected of being involved in child sexual abuse.
- 192 people suspected of online child exploitation were arrested.

Some of the many negative impacts of exploitation of women include:

- Physical, sexual, emotional abuse with both short and long term effects and implications.
- The further commodification of women (women becoming something to be bought and sold).
- The ability to share the eroticising of men's violence towards women.

Establishing Britain as a world leader in the fight against modern slavery, The Centre for Social Justice (2013)

This study reflects the result of research carried out by a range of academics on the nature and extent of slavery in the UK. The study takes evidence from over 180 individuals and organisations across all sectors involved. They conclude that slaves include UK nationals and those from abroad – who are exploited in the sex industry, through forced labour, domestic servitude in the home, and forced criminal activity. This exploitation takes place in factories, fields, construction sites, brothels and houses. Their research shows that a large proportion of cases are never recognised or reported, and do not appear in any statistics or measures of the size of the problem.

This is not just a problem for women: the study reveals that in 2011, of the 2077 potential victims of modern slavery identified by the UK Human Trafficking Centre, 40 per cent of the individuals were male. This problem can no longer be viewed only as a manifestation of violence against women, and must be recognised as a significant issue for vulnerable men as well. Despite this, the majority of sexual exploitation continues to affect women; in 2011, 94 per cent of those identified as trafficked into sexual exploitation were women.

1 How might globalisation have lead to greater opportunities for the exploitation of women and children?

2 Explain why exploitation is difficult to research.

- Objectification – women become increasingly regarded as objects without feelings, dignity or rights due to increased access to images depicting them in this way being easily accessed on the internet.
- Sexualised violent imagery becomes seen as less serious as it is prevalent.
- Viewing violence against women, such as exposing pictures of their ex partners naked, provides a new form of social control over women, which reflects the continuation of patriarchy which goes largely unchallenged. Few men are ever detected, found responsible or prosecuted. The lack of regulation in the digital world makes it even less likely for perpetrators to be found.

Feminists acknowledge that men are also included in this exploitation, however they point out that that online forms of abuse reflect the rate and societal patterns already exsisting in society where overwhelmingly it is women who experience violence at the hands of men.

Therefore it appears that new forms of digital communication in fact not only allow for the reproduction of patriarchy but also offer new ways in which women, children and other vulnerable marginalised groups can be exploited. At present, despite attempts to punish these behaviours, much exploitation goes undetected and un-policed. This presents a real challenge to policy makers and law enforcement both locally and globally.

Apart from slavery, feminists also point out the ways in which digital forms of communication can offer new ways in which patriarchal ideology can exert further control over women. The types of sexual exploitation on the internet include: bride trafficking, sex tourism (where people visit parts of the world where sex can be bought with little risk of punishment) exchange of information on where to buy prostitutes and live sex shows through videoconferencing (Hughes 1999).

Because there is little regulation of the internet, the traffickers and promoters of sexual exploitation have rapidly utilised the internet for their purposes.

Practical responses by feminists

There have been practical responses to the perceived and real lack of women in digital communication. For example, through the work of FemTechNet, a network of scholars, artists, and students who work on technology, science and feminism in a variety of fields. Feminist academics write blogs about the structures in place that have kept women from engaging in digital humanities.

The fourth wave of feminism

Interestingly, there has been a revitalisation of feminist discourse through what is known as the fourth wave of feminism, which arguably emerged between

Digital communication reproduces patriarchy	Digital communication allows women to challenge and potentially overcome patriarchy
Digital communication simply provides new ways to exploitation of women and children	Women are able to utilise digital communication to mobilise support for activities which challenge patriarchal practices and ideology.
Patriarchal ideology is perpetuated through imagery and representation of women	Cyborgs and other online identities can be created which transcend gender.
Digital communication companies are perceived to be masculine and women often play a secondary role in the development and maintenance of them, for example, new social media companies are largely designed and run by men.	Women who might have previously been 'muted' have a voice through new forms of digital communication and are able to contact others all over the world.

Table 1.3 A summary of feminist views on global forms of digital communication

2000–2010, is defined by the importance placed on technology as a method for communicating and sharing ideas and plans. This has had a significant effect on many women who might previously have been unheard. Women in many parts of the world are not allowed to be educated or to express their views, making their thoughts part of a muted group.

New forms of digital global communication are being used as tools that are allowing women to build a strong, popular, reactive movement online. This is evidenced at all ages, for example, The Girl Guides organisation introduced a campaigning and activism badge this year and a survey of Mumsnet users found 59 per cent consider themselves feminists, double those who do not (Cochrane, 2013). Other examples of their activities include:

- Ikamara Larasi, 24, started a campaign to address racist and sexist stereotypes in music videos, just as students began banning the hit Blurred Lines on many UK campuses, in response to its sexist lyrics.
- Jinan Younis, 18, co-founded a feminist society at school, experienced online abuse from some boys in her peer group. She wrote an article about it that went viral. She is now helping out with a campaign to encourage feminist societies in schools countrywide.
- Thousands more feminists raised their voices online. Bates and Chemaly were among those who set up a campaign against misogynist (sexist) pages on Facebook, convincing the owners of social media to change their moderation policies.

Source: Adapted from *The Guardian*, Kira Cochrane, 10th December 2013

This discussion alone illustrates the range of exciting new ways that feminism is responding to the rise of global digital communication. The fact that globalisation leads to the proliferation of a variety of different gendered identities means that digital communication can reduce the problem of women being essentialised (seen as sharing the same experience of being a woman). So, there are positive and negative effects of the internet on women – on the one hand it provides new ways for women to gather force in overcoming oppression, on the other hand, it leads to greater opportunities for the exploitation of women.

Evaluation of feminist views

Feminists are critical of the new opportunities that globalisation and digital forms of communication create to exploit women. They argue that some forms of new digital communication are simply an extension of the older forms of traditional methods which reflect patriarchal ideology. However, other feminists are optimistic and claim that these new forms of communication give rise to new ways of women being able to express themselves without falling into traditional assumptions about men and women, gender politics.

Postmodernism and digital global communication

Postmodernists explore the ways in which digital global forms of communication are emerging as a part of postmodern society. Postmodern society is very much linked to globalisation and the rapid technological progress that accompanies it. Rather than taking a position arguing that digital communication in a global context is positive or negative, postmodernists explore what is possible with new forms of technology and how it is being used. In essence, these new forms of communication reflect a shift towards greater individual choice. With the huge amounts of information sharing that is possible as a result of the internet, people have a greater scope for developing different parts of their identity as well as building a range of different social networks.

Activity

Postmodernity

Think about the characteristics of postmodernism and consider ways in which they are linked to postmodern society. The first one has been done for you.

Characteristic	Link to digital forms of communication	Example
Diversity	The internet means that contact with a wider range of different cultural groups or practices is possible.	The rights and interests of smaller ethnic groups can be protected for example, through social networks.
Fluidity		
Fragmentation of identity		
Choice		

Identity and digital forms of communication

In the past, the 'self' (the way we see ourselves) has been understood through interpretivist sociologists such as Mead and Goffman and then through the poststructuralist Foucault. More recently, postmodernism has attempted to make sense of how identity is created, negotiated and confirmed, including through technological advances. Global digital forms of communication offer a whole range of different ways in which identity can be created. The ways in which people use Facebook, for example, reveals much about how individuals create their own identity, how they see themselves and how others see them. Postmodernists, such as Collins (2005), suggest that to understand society, the chains of interaction between people must be understood. He suggests that by looking closely at how individuals construct their identity through social network sites such as Facebook, using a 'micro' sociological approach, it may be possible to learn about how people see the world around them. It is also interesting to consider the difference in people's on- and offline lives. For

example, *Catfish* a TV series was developed which follows the journey of couples who have formed an online relationship but have never met in person. Each programme tells the stories of people hoping to meet romantic partners online, and each hourlong episode is filled with mystery, surprises, and sometimes even shocking revelations as one partner discovers the difference between peoples on and offline lives.

Activity

Online identity

1 Think about different platforms for global communication such as Twitter, Instagram and Facebook. How can these be used to create identity online?
2 Why might people create different identities online to their real identities?

Facebook as a new form of autobiography?

Bjorklund (1998) explains that until recently, individuals have used autobiographies to describe their lives as they near the end of their life. However in a postmodern world, she suggests that people take a different view of defining the self. Digital forms of communication offer an ongoing autobiography which can be continually manipulated and updated. Facebook, she suggests, is like an autobiography in that it keeps a record of how people see their lives. Similarly, according to Hart (2011) individuals today are writing and rewriting their autobiographies on a daily basis, which reflect their own values and the values of their particular society. Identity, therefore is now created both online and offline, in multiple ways. For example, by posting a picture on Facebook the construction of the self occurs and from this, social networks are developed by finding similar like-minded friends. The effects of this use of social media are to some extent less known, and will need researching over the coming years before any definitive conclusions can be drawn. Case (2007) suggests that this can present a challenge especially to adolescents who in effect have two adolescences; one online and one offline. She claims that the nature of new social media makes it harder to remove mistakes as every interaction is visible, like an audit trail. For example, many people do not realise that much of what they say is stored by social media companies and is hard to remove or edit. This can cause tension and conflict between individuals, for example, resulting in disputes due to the disclosure of private information.

Some sociologists such as Elliot (2001) are pessimistic about the fragmented nature of identity as a result of sites such as Facebook, whilst others prefer to see new ways of seeing the self as only problematic when considered using 'modern' theories. Hart (2011) suggests for example that there is a tendency of traditional interpretations of the self to regard postings on Facebook as trivial or superficial. However if one is to take a postmodern approach, events on Facebook such as status updates can be understood as culturally significant as they reflect people's feelings and actions in a particular social context. Therefore digital communication is an important way of exploring and understanding the complex ways in which identity is created.

Quick question

According to some postmodernists, how is Facebook useful for understanding identity?

Digital media and surveillance

As we have seen, some Marxists argue that digital forms of communication provide new and more sophisticated ways for the state and commercial companies to control people. Postmodernists also explore the role of digital media in acting as a form of surveillance. For example, the post structuralist Foucault (1977) argues that in fact surveillance is likely to become the most effective means of regulating behaviour and reducing crime in contemporary society. According to Foucault, a person who knows that they are being watched is less likely to commit a crime as their chances of being caught are that much greater. In a different yet interesting new way, people are controlled through increasing amounts of information being collected, building a profile of their behaviour. Supermarkets, for example, collect information about the tastes, preferences and habits of their customers through customer loyalty cards, and online shopping.

Activity

Information gathering online

1 Think about a website that you have visited where you have brought something. What kinds of information might be gathered about you on the basis of your buy?
2 Were you recommended other similar products as a result?
3 What does this suggest about the kinds of information being collected about you?

Study

The Global Media Impact Study, Miller (2016)

The Global Social Media Impact Study, led by Miller, aims to study and report on the use and consequences of social media for peoples all around the world. Using the ethnographic method, Miller and his team of researchers explore peoples social lives both on and offline.

The aims of the study are:

- To carry out nine ethnographic studies, each of 15 months, in order to investigate how people actually use social media today.
- To explore the impact of social media on people's relationships, especially the family, gender roles, intimate relationships and friendships.
- To examine how social media has impacted upon key issues such as politics and privacy.
- To explore the way social media has been used within institutions such as education, commerce, the state and religion.
- To provide insights on what an in-depth ethnographic study of social media might bring to social science more generally.
- To consider the current state of the 'digital divide' and how social media relates to the problems of low income populations and their welfare.
- To examine other possible welfare benefits, which in practice have ranged from the use of social media by the hospice movement in the UK to its impact on the restrictions traditionally experienced by women in certain societies.

Activity:

Miller's project

Find and visit the 'Why We Post' website and explore the project, including the online course available alongside the research, which explains the research and the main findings.

1 What are the strengths and weaknesses of the methodology of the project?
2 How does research into digital communication vary from traditional forms of research?
3 What is polymedia, and why is it important to include it in this research?

Digital communication reflects the greater fluidity of identity	Individuals can chose which parts of their identity are most relevant to them and explore and maintain these online
Digital communication is linked to globalisation	Technological advances represent the shift from modern society to post modern society
Digital communication represents new ways in which people can create their identity giving them greater agency	People create online biographies which do not always reflect their actual offline identities – this provides important and interesting information for sociologists about what people select to make visible
Digital communication has both positive and negative effects on social relationships.	Social life is complex and digital communication simply reflects those compexities

Table 1.4 A summary of postmodernist views on global forms of digital communication

Evaluation

Each theoretical perspective takes a very different interpretation of the role of digital communication. It is clear that the digital communication needs to be understood within the context of the globalisation process. Although Marxists regard the changes as favouring the powerful, both feminists and postmodernists explore the way in which digital communication has positive and negative effects simultaneously.

Check your understanding

1 Identify two problems with defining globalisation.
2 What does homogenisation mean?
3 What is meant by the following terms and give an example of each:
   a Global village
   b Social capital
   c Media convergence
4 Why have new forms of social media given rise to greater levels of exploitation?
5 What does the 'commodification of women' mean?
6 What are the two different views that feminists have about new forms of digital communication?
7 What is the Marxist view of digital communication?
8 How are postmodernist views on digital communication different to Marxist views?

Section summary

Make a copy of the following passage and fill the spaces using the words listed below.

_____, the process whereby space and distance have become compressed, is a complex concept which is difficult to define. This is partly because its effects are _____ and broad, including cultural, _____ and political changes. What is certain, however, is that the development of digital communication accelerated globalisation, so dramatically that it is now known as a digital revolution. This has been assisted through _____ where different forms of digital communication are increasingly combined on the same device, which has led to innovative and effective forms of communicating with people all over the world. One effect of this is that global social _____ are increasingly important in providing people with _____. Those without access to new forms of digital communication find themselves disadvantaged and possibly _____ as a result.

There have been attempts to interpret these changes through different theoretical perspectives. There are those who regard the relationship between globalisation and digital forms of communication as making some positive contributions to social life such as some _____ and_____. However there are others who disagree and argue that in fact, digital communication within globalisation has led to new ways of reproducing inequalities in society, such as _____.

marxists, feminists, globalisation, uneven, postmodernists, networks, marginalised, economic, media convergence, social capital

1.2 What is the impact of digital forms of communication in a global context?

Getting you thinking ...

1 What are the benefits of digital communication?
2 What are the negative effects of digital communication?
3 Make a list for each and compare them; do the strengths outweigh the benefits?
4 How might it be a challenge for sociologists to fully understand if there are more benefits or negative effects?
5 In terms of your own life, would you say that digital forms of communication are more beneficial or do they have more negative effects?

So far this chapter has explored the various characteristics of digital forms of communication within a global context. This section begins to explore the effects of global communication which are complex and as you will now know, occur at different rates in different places.

Despite being heralded as a more democratic way of sharing information and communicating, new social media appears to reflect some already exiting social inequalities in society as well. This section explores the ways in which different groups interact with digital communication and what effect this may have on their on and offline lives.

Identity

Technological advances have made it possible for there to be a much greater capacity of information passed to individuals in their own homes, workplaces and during their leisure time. This means that people have a greater range of choices and information on different lifestyles and cultures all over the world. This has without doubt given rise to a much wider range of resources through which to develop identity. For example, if a person wished, they could easily discover religious practices from other areas of the world and share these traditions with people all over the globe, without needing to find a group nearby.

Globalisation and the proliferation of technological advances, coupled with other wider changes in society such as increasing affluence in some parts of the developing world have also meant that traditional sources of identity such as social class in the UK have become less clear. The blurring of lines between different social classes by no means results in a more equal society: inequalities still exist. However ethnicity or gender may have become a more important factor in defining a persons' identity than social class, for example. Of course, many of the changes linked to identity are increased by the increase in migration or population movement that accompanies globalisation.

Identity as chosen and not given

The emergence of online identities or avatars as they are sometimes known provides people with the opportunity to decide which kinds of identity and appearance that they might like to choose, as opposed to certain characteristics such as gender and class, which are often (but not always) given. The kinds of identity that people want to take on and the ways that they represent themselves reveals important information about the individuals and attitudes in wider society. If you remember

We are all cyborgs now, Case (2007)

According to Amber Case (2007) because people's use of technology is so embedded in their daily lives, they are becoming cyborgs. By this she means that people are part human part machine. She argues that the way that people interact with technology defines their identity. In her study of the effects of mobile phone use, Case argues that people are now in a post modern era much more able to select and develop different aspects of their identity in a global rather than a local context. Case regards this as potentially beneficial, but warns about the dangers of digital communication which results in a trail of information about someone that can be difficult to remove. For example, the usual mistakes made in adolescence (such as saying the wrong thing, or acting inappropriately) are recorded through digital media, whereas in the past such errors were not as visible.

from the previous section, the feminist Haraway explained how cyborgs could offer women the chance to transcend their gender to avoid traditional assumptions about women and allow them to engage differently with others online.

In online settings such as social network sites, chat rooms, or discussion groups, identity processes are complicated because many identity cues (such as gender or age) are masked and can be selectively shared, withheld, or misrepresented. In these and other online contexts, identity is essentially constructed by the user. Individuals can adopt multiple online personalities, and online activities often leave visible traces which can be captured, tracked, packaged, and shared (Ellison, 2013).

People's online identities continue to overlap with their offline lives, sometimes with positive or negative effects. For example, the UK's first youth police and crime commissioner, Paris Brown, resigned from her post following criticism of messages she posted on Twitter. Police investigated Paris Brown following investigations into tweets she posted between the ages of 14 and 16 which could be considered racist and anti-gay.

Activity

Achieved and ascribed characteristics

1 Which parts of your identity are chosen (achieved) and which are given (ascribed)?
2 Why might people want to choose an alternative identity to their offline identity?
3 What are the benefits and problems with being able to choose your own identity?

Age and digital communication

Age has a considerable effect on the way is which digital communication is used.

The Ofcom Report (2014) revealed the following patterns.

- More UK adults, especially older adults, are now going online, using a range of devices.
- Privacy and security attitudes and behaviour continue to vary considerably by age group.
- Over eight in ten (83 per cent) of adults now go online. Nearly all 16–24s and 25–34s are now online (98 per cent), and there has been a nine percentage point increase in those aged 65+ ever going online (42 per cent vs. 33 per cent in 2012).
- The number of adults using tablets to go online has almost doubled; from 16 per cent in 2012 to 30 per cent in 2013. While almost all age groups are more likely than previously to use tablets, the use by those aged 35–64 has doubled, while use by 65–74s has trebled; from 5 per cent to 17 per cent. This undoubtedly means greater use of digital communication.
- Six in ten UK adults (62 per cent) now use a smartphone, an increase from 54 per cent in 2012.
- Gaming has grown in popularity, driven by older age-groups and mobile phones.
- Compared to 2012, those aged 45–54 are twice as likely to play games over the internet (18 per cent vs. 9 per cent).
- 65 per cent of men and 48 per cent of women age 18–34 use Wikipedia, compared with 40 per cent of men and 28 per cent of women age 35+.
- Two thirds (66 per cent) of online adults say they have a current social networking site profile.

Activity

Age and technology
Six-year-olds understand digital technology better than adults

The average six-year-old child understands more about digital technology than a 45-year-old adult, according to a new report. The introduction of broadband in the year 2000 has created a generation of digital natives, the communication watchdog Ofcom says in its annual study of British consumers. Born in the new millennium, these children have never known the dark ages of dial up internet, and the youngest are learning how to operate smartphones or tablets before they are able to talk.

The report suggests that as a result, younger generations are shaping digital communication. Children are developing fundamentally different communication habits from older generations. While half of all adults claimed to know a lot about smartphone and tablet apps, nearly half had never heard of Snapchat, the picture messaging service launched in 2011, which is overwhelmingly used by people under the age of 25.

The most remarkable change is in time spent talking by phone. Two decades ago, teenagers devoted their evenings to monopolising the home telephone line, dissecting love affairs and friendships in conversations that lasted for hours. For those aged 12 to 15, phone calls account for just 3 per cent of time spent communicating through any device. Today's children do the majority of their remote socialising by sending written messages or through shared photographs and videos. "The millennium generation is losing its voice," Ofcom claims.

Source: Adapted from *The Guardian*, Juliette Garside, 7th August 2014

1 What does this article suggest about the generational difference in the use of digital communication?
2 What effects might this have on young and older people's offline lives?
3 How would cultural pessimists such as Marxists interpret this article?

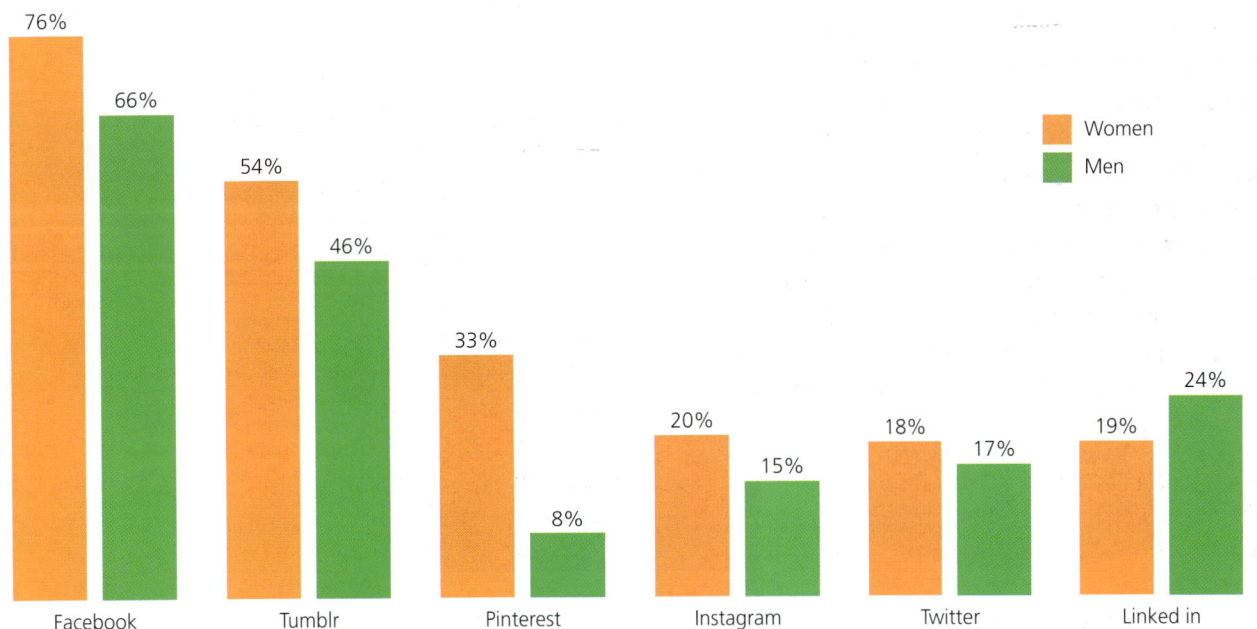

Percentage of US Online Adults Using the Top Social Media in 2013

	Women	Men
Facebook	76%	66%
Tumblr	54%	46%
Pinterest	33%	8%
Instagram	20%	15%
Twitter	18%	17%
Linked in	19%	24%

Source: Adapted from Zeendo.com

The sociologist Boyle (2007) argues that with each successive generation, the greater the reliance on and use of digital communication. So much so, that this has contributed to the idea that there is a 'digital generation divide' between the old, who are less likely to use digital communication and the young, who are very proficient and reliant on it.

Quick question

Why do you think young people are more likely to use digital forms of communication?

Boyle argues that the generational divide is not particular to digital communication, but can be seen within the media more generally, with younger generations taking an interest in different forms of music such as rock and pop while adults prefer alternative types of music and taste in art and so forth. Boyle also suggests that young people are more receptive to learning new skills demanded by new forms of technology and communication. It may also be because young people are perhaps more keen to explore and assert their emergent adult identities and digital communication can be the most effective way to do this. Young people are likely to place greater importance on their peer group and social networks, which are highly influential in their lives during their adolescence, which may be another reason why they are more likely to use digital forms of communication.

Another factor to consider is that some (but by no means all) is that parents are spending more money on their children. For example it now costs on average £230,000 to raise a child to the age of 21 (Centre of Economic and Business Research with London Victoria, 2015). Therefore, young people today have much greater access to expensive phones, tablets and laptops which enable them a wide range of ways in which to engage with digital forms of communication. In the past, not only did people have less money to spend on their children, but there were simply less technological devices available.

The other obvious reason why younger people are more likely to be users of digital communication; they have more free time on their hands as they generally have less responsibilities such as jobs, caring responsibilities and duties and therefore the immediacy of the communication means that it is possible for them to communicate with many different people in a highly effective way. It is also true that adults are spending increasing amounts of their free time on new forms of social media, but their free time amounts to proportionally less than that of young people and teenagers.

Activity

Impacts of digital communication on young people

1 Sort the following statements into negative and positive categories.

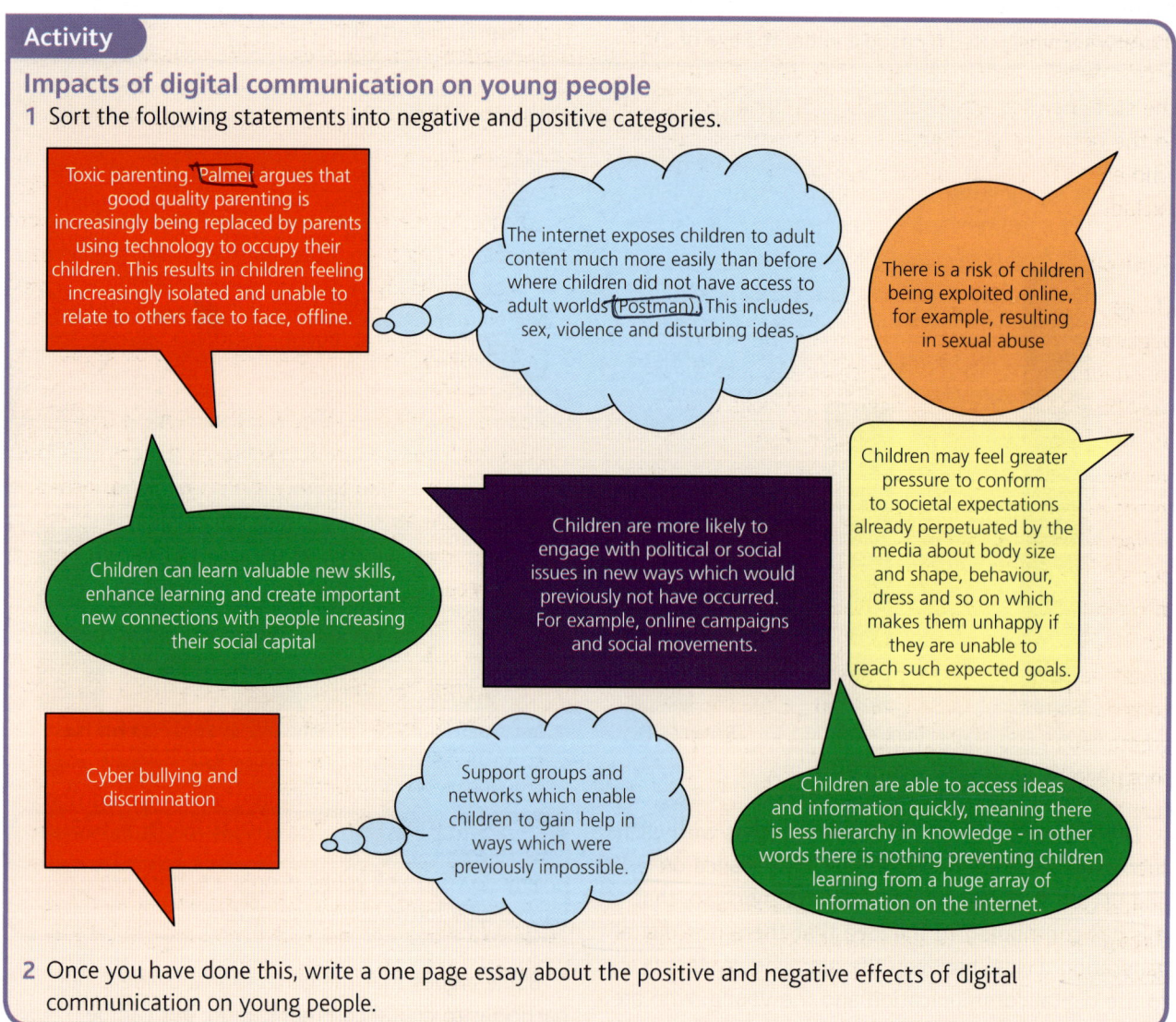

2 Once you have done this, write a one page essay about the positive and negative effects of digital communication on young people.

Older users of the internet, Berry (2011)

Berry carried out research on secondary data focusing on the way older people use the internet. His research findings reveal that among those who do not have access to the internet, most people cite non-material reasons such as lack of skills or lack of interest to explain why they are not online. Other research has highlighted the psychological barriers preventing older people from accessing the web. These reasons appear to be more significant than material factors such as cost or lack of physical infrastructure. Older people who do use the internet tend to do so less frequently than younger people. The ONS data shows of all internet users log on every day, while only 59 per cent of older users (above 65) do this.

Berry notes that there has been content designed specifically to encourage older people to use the internet, based on the use of accessible web design. For instance, the website Finerday is a social network designed to encourage older people to use it: it has a number of the functions of other networks such as Facebook, but with high contrast colours, large font and a simplified format.

1 How might the term 'digital divide' be applied to older people?
2 What are the main reasons for older people not using the internet?

Older users of digital communication

According to recent research findings, 79 per cent of households below the state pension age have internet access, while only 37 per cent of households above the state pension age do so. This difference gives rise to the notion of the digital divide, between those who enjoy access to the internet and those who are excluded (Berry, 2011).

Evaluation

Things are changing, and older generations are beginning to use digital forms of communication much more frequently. This may be because they may have taken longer to acquire the skills which are necessary to use them. It might also be because people are becoming aware of the need to use digital forms of communication for work, for example, as a way to create social networks. It might also be because of increased affluence, that some people can afford to buy various devices today which they may not have been able to previously. Another reason might be that the wide range of ways in which digital communication is being used means that there is greater appeal for older people, for example, online shopping, lifestyle applications and so forth, meaning that they have more practical appeal.

Social class and digital communication

Digital communication relies upon various devices through which the internet can be accessed. These devices are expensive, need maintaining and regular updating. For example, tablets can cost over five hundred pounds and monthly internet connection fees are on average £15, a month. Further there are areas of the country where access to high speed broadband connection is possible whereas in other parts of the country it is not available. There is considerable consumer choice and competition, for example, owning the latest phone or tablet has become seen as important by many. For those who cannot afford these items, known as the digital underclass, this results in even greater disadvantage and less social capital. This is because:

- Social networks are largely dependent on digital communication.
- Education for children now relies a lot on digital communication, thus disadvantaging many children who cannot afford to have smartphones or access to the internet.
- A knowledge gap is created between those who have access to the internet and can quickly access information, services and ideas and those who cannot.
- People may feel inferior or lacking because they are not sharing in digital forms of communication.
- Information shared through digital communication can shape cultural ideas and if excluded from this people may feel removed from what is happening in society.

There have been a number of studies around the world which have found evidence of a digital divide based along the lines of social class.

The digital divide, Mertens and D'Haenens (2010)

Mertens and D'Haenens (2010) found in their study of the digital divide in Brussels that lower social class was linked with lower internet use (81 per cent are users, compared to 94 per cent of middle class). Moreover, individuals with low social class tended to focus their technology use on entertainment rather than knowledge and information (79 per cent owned game consoles, compared to 65 per cent for higher social class). While they originally sought to measure digital inequality by ethnicity and gender, they found that social class is the most powerful social variable. In reality, this relationship between social class and use of the internet and digital media may be even greater than the research suggested because of embarrassment to admit low status, although the questionnaire was anonymous. Similar results are found in digital access divides in Latin America (Brazil and Uruguay), which showed that social class was more important than other factors such as age, gender and education level.

1 Describe the patterns in relation to social class and use of the internet
2 How do the working class use the internet differently compared with the middle class according to this study?

Activity

Access

1 In pairs think about who might be less likely to have access to the internet in the UK.
2 Make a list of all the different ways this might affect them negatively in terms of
   a) education
   b) health
   c) employment
   d) leisure
   e) maintaining relationships
3 Describe the barriers to people's use of the internet and how these might be overcome.

Gender and digital communication

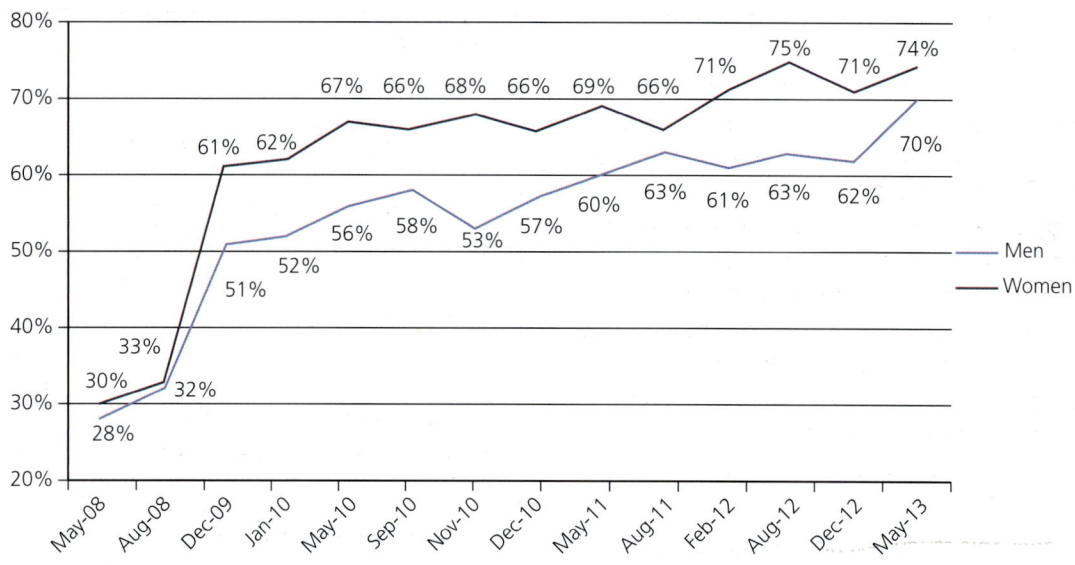

Source: Pew Research Centre's Internet and American Life Project Tracking Surveys, May 2008 – May 2013, from socialmedialondon.co.uk, adapted from socialmedialondon.co.uk

Gender differences reveal interesting patterns about the different ways in which men and women engage with digital communication. Earlier in the chapter we discussed some feminist theoretical interpretations of the gender divide in relation to digital communication (see page 12). Statistics

Activity

Gender and social media

1 Carry out some research in pairs on the ways in which the use of social media is affected by gender, using interviews or questionnaires.

2 In your research make sure that you investigate the different ways that boys and girls vary in their use of e-mails, social network sites and games to highlight any patterns.

3 Write a report on your findings, suggesting some reasons for the results using the following concepts:
   a) patriarchal ideology
   b) gendered socialisation
   c) gender stereotypes

Study

Attitudes towards the internet and computers, Li and Kirkup (2007)

Li and Kirkup (2007) investigate differences in use of, and attitudes toward the internet and computers generally for Chinese and British students, and gender differences in this cross-cultural context. Using a sample of 220 Chinese and 245 British students, they carried out a self-report survey questionnaire. They found significant differences in internet experience, attitudes, usage, and self-confidence between Chinese and British students. Most significant however, were the gender differences that were also found in both groups. Men in both countries were more likely than women to use email or chat rooms. Men played more computer games than women. Interestingly, men in both countries were more self-confident about their computer skills than women, and were more likely to express the opinion that using computers was a male activity and skill. Gender differences were higher in the British group than the Chinese group. The study illustrates the continued significance of gender in students attitudes towards, and use of computers, within different cultural contexts.

1 What does this study reveal about gender and the use of digital communication?

2 Name a potential problem with self-report questionnaires.

reveal the following about gender and digital communications in the USA:

- Younger women are much more likely to use digital forms of communication to maintain social relationships: 42 per cent of women use social media to stay in touch, compared with 34 per cent of women age 18–34.
- Younger users (particularly men) use social media for a wider variety of reasons other than maintaining relationships, particularly entertainment (28 per cent).
- Younger women spend the least amount of time using social media to find information (16 per cent).
- Women have an average number of 394 posts on Facebook and 69 per cent of Facebook gamers are women, again outnumbering the men.
- In each month in 2014, 40 million more women visited Twitter than men and among the top 50 brands followers on Instagram, 53 per cent were woman. Google+ was 64 per cent male user based and 25 per cent of men watched a video daily on YouTube.

Location and digital communication

Evidence about the use of the internet in different parts of the world reveals interesting patterns of access, which may partially help to explain the uneven distribution of globalisation. In general, more developed affluent countries have greater access to and consumption of the internet, which comes as no surprise.

Activity

Internet usage

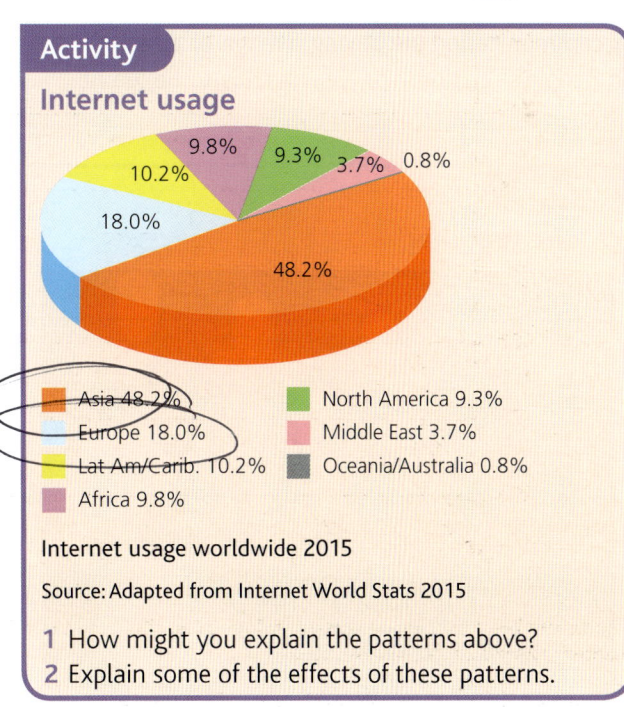

9.8% 9.3% 3.7% 0.8%
10.2%
18.0%
48.2%

- Asia 48.2%
- Europe 18.0%
- Lat Am/Carib. 10.2%
- Africa 9.8%
- North America 9.3%
- Middle East 3.7%
- Oceania/Australia 0.8%

Internet usage worldwide 2015

Source: Adapted from Internet World Stats 2015

1 How might you explain the patterns above?

2 Explain some of the effects of these patterns.

Social group	Patterns	Explanations
Age groups	Young people are more likely to use digital forms of communication, but this pattern is changing and there are increasing numbers of older people beginning to use them too.	Younger people: Have more time Are more affluent More able to learn new skills More keen to use new forms of digital communication to develop and express their emerging identities
Social class	Those with less money have higher rates of non-participation in digital forms of communication leading to a 'digital underclass'. The more affluent are able to increase their social capital through networks online, strengthening their position socially and economically in society.	There are considerable costs linked with digital forms of communication including set up and maintenance. This digital divide leads to increasing social inequalities in society.
Gender	Men and women use digital forms of communication very differently; the digital world is perceived to be overwhelmingly masculine, and women use social media much more than men. Thus, gender roles and identities are often reinforced and reproduced through digital forms of communication.	Women are more likely to engage with social media while men contribute more to the work-based networking sites.
Locality	Developing countries are increasing their use of digital communication but are still significantly behind compared with the usage of developed westernised countries.	Globalisation is not occurring evenly and many parts of the world lack the money or freedom to access western forms of digital media which require considerable start-up costs. This results in poorer people being further marginalised and disadvantaged.

Table 1.5 A summary of the way different groups interact with digital communication.

How has digital communication affected people's relationships?

As a recently emerging phenomenon, digital forms of communication are having a range of effects on people's relationships, yet much is to be learnt about what these effects are and if there are any general patterns emerging. There are two issues worth thinking about here: how do new forms of digital communication affect both the quality and also the quantity of relationships.

Activity

'Alone together'

Turkle (2011) expresses concerns about the ways in which our communication tools distance us from one another because we are 'alone together' – in the same room but using our devices to communicate with others or engage in other tasks.

1 What effects might being 'alone together' have on offline relationships?
2 Name some of the benefits of online relationships.

What kinds of relationships are created through digital forms of communication?

Relationships consist of social ties, which are the connections between individuals that link them together, which vary in strength. According to Granovetter (1973) the strength of ties between two individuals can be measured as follows:

1 The amount of time spent together.
2 The emotional intensity of the relationship.
3 The level of intimacy.
4 The degree of reciprocity (how much the other person responds in a similar way back).

Relationships with other people are typically broken into two major categories: weak ties, or individuals who are considered mere acquaintances, are differentiated from strong ties, such as close friends and family members.

Granovetter argues that weak ties are in many respects more important than strong ties. The strength of weak ties is that they create connections between members of the network. Weak ties connect an individual to people with whom he or she has little in common and would likely not be able to connect with through strong ties, such as a celebrity. Therefore the removal of an average weak tie would potentially do more 'damage' to the person's social network than the removal of an average strong tie.

This can be directly applied to the social networks created online where weak and strong ties may be equally as significant. With the rise of the internet and digital communication, much recent research has looked at the impact of online forms of communication on social ties.

Activities that connect individuals directly to one another (such as email, chat) tend to have positive correlations to social ties, meaning that they strengthen relationships, while those activities that are more solitary in nature, such as surfing the internet, tend to have more negative correlations to social ties

(Zhao, 2006). Research from the 1990s found negative correlations between internet use and social ties, but these findings were later disproven, especially as most individuals using the internet for social purposes also maintained their offline relationships (Kraut et al. 2002). In addition, Kraut argues that online social ties tend to be weaker than relationships formed and maintained offline.

Feld (1981) suggests that people use social networks to evaluate both themselves and others. In other words, an individual's identity is, in part, determined by the network of friends he or she maintains. Much of the research on friendship networks has focused on how people make friends or how many friends individuals have (Feld, 1981, 1991). One's social network is directly linked to the number of strong and weak ties a person can maintain.

We will now turn to some of the potential positive and negative effects of digital communication on relationships.

Positive effects	Negative effects
Another opportunity to meet people	A lack of privacy or differing ideas about privacy between people resulting in conflict
Immediacy: people can be contacted instantly	Hard to switch off
An opportunity to meet people who you would not normally come into contact with	Having to come into contact with people that the person may not want to
A way of people overcoming traditional barriers to meeting people such as disability, shyness, geographical distance	People's offline relationships suffer as a result of the time spent with online relationships

Table 1.6 A summary of some of the potential positive and negative effects of digital communication

Quick question

Can you think of any other positive or negative effects of digital communication on relationships?

Study

Tales from Facebook, Miller (2011)

Facebook was once seen as a media site for the young, however more recently the largest increase in usage is amongst the older sections of the population. Until recently, no major study of the impact of these **social networking sites** upon the lives of their users had been carried out. In his book, *Tales from Facebook,* Miller (2011) demonstrates that the impact can be profound. The tales in this book reveal how Facebook can become the means by which people find and cultivate relationships, but can also be instrumental in breaking up relationships and even marriage. Each chapter reveals how Facebook can bring back the lives of people isolated in their homes by illness or age, by shyness, but equally Facebook can challenge people's ideas about privacy and create social problems and scandal. For example,

exposing people being unfaithful in relationships. Miller found that some people believe that the truth of another person lies more in what you see online than face-to-face. Miller's research demonstrates how Facebook has become a vehicle for business, the church, sex and remembering people who have passed away.

Miller concludes that after a century in which we have assumed social networking and community to be in decline, Facebook has suddenly hugely expanded our social relationships in a global context.

1 What has happened to the average age of people who use Facebook in recent years? Suggest some reasons for this trend.

2 Identify two potential problems which Miller identifies with Facebook.

Activity

The Twitter effect: Why using social media too much can lead to divorce

Researchers have previously found the damaging influence that Facebook can have on relationships and now they've turned to Twitter, concluding that 'Twitter-related conflict' can lead to 'negative relationship outcomes, including emotional and physical cheating, breakup and divorce' according to new research by Russell Clayton, a doctoral student at the University of Missouri.

Clayton spoke to 581 Twitter users of all ages, asking various questions about their level of activity on the social network and if any conflict arose with partners or former partners as a result of Twitter use. Clayton found that the more active an individual was on Twitter, the more likely they were to report 'Twitter-

related' conflict with partners. This included people feeling frustrated at the amount of time their partner spent online, or conflict resulting from what was being said online. These then resulted in significantly negative effects on people's relationships, such as infidelity or even divorce.

However, the news that people who use social networks frequently are more likely to have arguments about those social networks doesn't seem too surprising – any hobby that consumes too much of an individual's time is likely to become a bone of contention.

Source: Adapted from *The Independent*, James Vincent, 29 April 2014

1 What is the relationship between Twitter use and conflict in relationships?

Study

The positive effects of the internet, Shaw and Gant (2002)

According to Shaw and Gant (2002) as more people connect to the internet, researchers are beginning to examine the effects of internet use on users' psychological health. Previous studies had concluded that internet use is positively correlated with depression, loneliness and stress, which led to public opinion about the internet has often been negative. In contrast, Shaw and Gant's study was designed to test the hypothesis that internet usage can affect users beneficially. Participants engaged in five chat sessions

with an anonymous partner. At three different intervals they were administered scales measuring depression, loneliness, self-esteem and social support. Changes in their scores were tracked over time. Internet use was found to decrease loneliness and depression significantly, while perceived social support and self-esteem increased significantly.

1 How does this study challenge the idea that the internet damages the individual and their relationships with others?

2 Suggest some ways in which digital forms of communication might improve relationships

This discussion alone reveals some of the ways in which relationships seem to be affected, often negatively through digital communication. It is important to remember that this can be a challenging area of life to carry research out on, and that the effects are relatively new and unresearched.

Conflict and change

This section explores the ways in which digital forms of communication have contributed to social conflict and change. There are some examples of ways in which digital communication has actually changed the course of history on a small and large scale and so these effects can be profound and widespread.

Religious fundamentalism

The recent concerns over the activity of religious fundamentalist groups such as Islamic fundamentalist group ISIS have been linked to the rise of digital communications. Fundamentalist religious groups often want to interpret their religious text literally, and in many respects want a return to a more 'traditional' way of life. Despite this, they often use modern day technologies to gain support, plan and share their activities.

Study

The role of digital communication in fundamentalist religious groups, Howard (2011)

According to Howard (2011) in 1999 it was already clear that the internet was playing a key role in Christian fundamentalist groups, he found in his study of online network of Christians, a virtual church built around those who embraced a common ideology.

Howard's study entitled 'Digital Jesus' shows how like-minded individuals created a large web of religious communication on the internet, in essence developing a new type of new religious movement—one without a central leader or institution. Based on over a decade of interaction with figures both large and small within this community, Howard offers the first sustained ethnographic account of the movement as well as a realistic view of how new communication technologies can both empower and disempower the individuals who use them.

Activity

The Taliban's internet strategy

The Taliban once banned photography, movies, and use of the internet on the grounds that they were all 'un-Islamic'. Now, however, the terrorist group's perspective has radically changed. Throughout the duration of their government (1996–2001), which was toppled after the 9/11 attacks, social media was much less developed. There was not even a mobile-phone service. Nonetheless, over the past decade, the Taliban has dramatically improved its public-relations skills.

It now possesses several internet domains, which host official content and have backup domains in case of an attack on the main website. Taliban members also use e-mail on a daily basis to communicate with journalists. Despite persistently launching attacks on officials and killing civilians, the Taliban has yet to have a decisive military success. However, it has been trying hard to compensate for its military losses with effective propaganda warfare. The militant group cannot deny the potential of such media as tools of propaganda and recruitment.

Now, films are distributed on Taliban websites, passed from mobile phone to mobile phone, and reach broader audiences through other outlets, such as Facebook, Twitter, and YouTube. It does not interact with its followers and is mainly used as one-way dissemination tool.

Source: Adapted from www.rferl.org

1 How have the Taliban used new forms of digital communication to further their interests?
2 Why might this be in conflict with their fundamentalist beliefs?

Social movements and new social media

The Facebook Effect (Kirkpatrick, 2010) starts with a story about how a Facebook site became a catalyst for a popular movement in Colombia, mobilising 10 million people in street demonstrations, which curbed the violence and kidnapping by the Revolutionary Armed Forces of Colombia. This is not an isolated case, indeed there is a growing awareness of the role that new social media plays in contributing to and shaping the course of major social movements. There are several reasons why new forms of digital communication are able to mobilise change including:

- Immediate communication with others which can warn them/prepare them of an occurrence;
- Information can reach a huge number of people simultaneously;
- Information about, for example, human rights abuses can be shared anonymously;
- Groups or individuals who are usually unable to speak out or act through conventional means are able to speak to a wide range of people through digital forms of communication. For example, women in countries where it is forbidden for them to speak out publically, such as in Syria;
- News presented about events that may be inaccurate or biased can be actively challenged and possibly changed;
- Where political activism is suppressed, digital communication offers a way for people to speak out against the regime.

Conflict and change in the Middle East

One interesting emergent areas of sociology is the exploration of the effects of social media on social protest in the Middle East. Before the recent revolutions in the Arab World, the use of social media could be described as limited and largely limited to the social elite, mainly due to the fact that access to the internet had been so restricted by the state. This was mainly because there were fears by the ruling groups that western ideas were damaging to traditional ideas. However the events across the Arab world in 2011 brought social media to the forefront, with many claiming that Facebook, weblogs, Twitter and YouTube, had an important role to play in the revolutions that have taken place there.

It is quite difficult to clearly understand or measure the ways in which social media have affected events, either through actual protest on the streets or through influencing mainstream forms of media. Sociologists and journalists are not clear why social media was particularly effective in mobilizing protest in some contexts and not others. These events present a real challenge to sociologists trying to research the relationship between events and the role of social media. The very nature of social media means that it is private and there are not necessarily ways to record interactions that take place online.

In the well documented case of Egypt, through the spread of information online, internet activists were able to establish networks of resistance within Egyptian political society. Despite the relative weakness of the ties between members of these networks, social media emerged as an effective tool to facilitate collective action. Through being permanently connected to each other, activists were able to access a huge number of networks of trust and multiply the impact of social protest through the creation of an uprising, protesting community. Internet activism made political action easier, faster and more universal in Egypt. Social media sites became a place where many could express their anxieties and vocalise their feelings. But it was not, of course, in any way a complete solution to the problems there.

It is important not to over emphasise the role of technology in the revolutions in Egypt or indeed anywhere else. Political activists use new forms of communication, especially digital and online social media, such as Twitter, Facebook, and YouTube as a means of highlighting the government abuses of their citizens, promoting citizen interaction and participation in reporting of events, shaping public opinion, and organising and mobilising people to protest against repression. Activists integrate these online activities with offline activities, such as staging demonstrations and protests and launching on-the-ground campaigns. The regimes in both Egypt and Syria also use communication tools to protect their interests and to counter the political activists' efforts, whether via traditional, state-owned media avenues or new media tools.

What evidence is there that new forms of digital communication lead to cultural homogenisation?

It is clear that the developed world has the greatest use of the internet and therefore digital communication. This is reflected in the fact that the majority of information written on the internet is written in English (see the graph below). This means that many ideas and the content is driven by an English speaking, western cultural perspective. Some argue that this means that a process of cultural homogenisation is occurring, whereby western culture threatens to dominate over other cultures, creating one culture that is characterised by the following world view:

- Capitalist ideology – a specific economic system whereby there is a distinct ruling class who extract profit from the workers, where people are driven by the need to make profit. This comes with a particular set of ideas about relationships, inheritance and ideas about education all of which are shaped to perpetuate the economic system.
- Patriarchal ideology – a set of ideas which support the view that men dominate over women in all areas of life.
- Consumerism being central – people's identities are increasingly shaped by the products they choose to buy, with an emphasis on buying expensive items as a signifier of status.
- Secular ideas – western society has significant rates of secularisation and an increasingly rational scientific world view. *moving away from religion*
- Increased individualism – increased emphasis on individual wishes and priorities over societal or communal expectations.

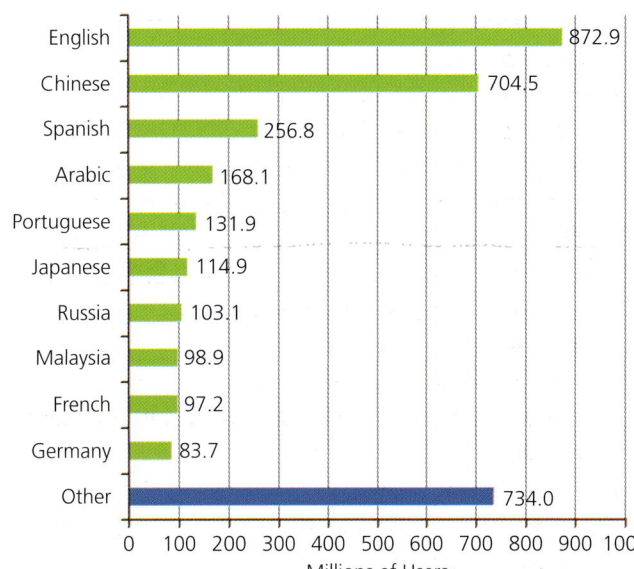

Top ten languages in the internet 2015

Source: Adapted from Internet World Stats 2015

How digital communication is leading to homogenisation of culture	Evidence
Computer software is not localised therefore programs such as Microsoft Word reflect westernised ways of thinking	Microsoft is geared to the US English speaking market, despite the fact that Spanish, Chinese Mandarin are also widely spoken. Assumptions are made about organising written work, dates, style and so on.
Advertising generated by the west is broadcast globally	Thus spreading ideas about what is desirable and acceptable e.g. particular sporting events or products get greater exposure from western companies who can afford bigger budgets for advertising, thus increasing their sales and becoming more powerful.
Antisocial behaviour on the internet is creating a universal global redefinition of harm against others which may reflect western ideas about morality and deviance.	These include unauthorised access to people's information online, launching of viruses, racism and harassment.
Digital communication does not have the same kind of rules about moral guidance and ethics that are usually entrenched within local cultures. The rise of digital communication is largely unregulated	Some countries in the middle east (such as Egypt) wanted to prevent access to western liberalist ideas which they saw as threatening their cultural practices and beliefs.

Table 1.7 Arguments and evidence for cultural homogenisation

Adapted from Fairweather and Rogerson: The Problems of Global Cultural Homogenisation (2003)

The fact that much of the internet is written in English has important cultural implications; language reflects cultural assumptions which are being spread around the globe. This is known as cultural homogenisation. In other words, western cultural practices begin to influence other non-western cultures. However, there is some evidence to suggest that in response to the threat of loss of local cultures through cultural homogenisation, a process of cultural defence has emerged, through which local cultures are being protected and promoted.

There have been challenges to the claims that cultural homogenisation is occurring. These are based on the idea that they ignore evidence against this view. For example, Sreberni Mohammadi (1996) points out that the simple image of western media and cultural domination over all of the rest of the world is exaggerated and ignores important complex interactions that occur between different cultures. Giddens (1991) points to a process of 'reverse colonisation' where it is not the western powers dominating over less powerful groups culturally but the other way round. For example, the recent 'Mexicanisation' of California. This has resulted in Mexican food, dress and music becoming increasingly part of Californian culture. This is interesting because Mexico is significantly poorer than America. This suggests that it is not simply the powerful who impose their culture on the less powerful. Clearly in this example, it is the poorer culture which has influenced the richer cultural group.

More generally it is argued that global digital media companies have been forced to take into account local practices and adapt their material accordingly, linking with local partners or people in order to make sure that their companies grow and succeed (Croteau and Hoynes, 1997). There has also been some evidence of resistance by American media and digital forms of communication. For example, people using the internet to promote their own language and cultural characteristics.

How digital communication is leading to cultural defence	Evidence
Local practices are defended through the internet and western non-governmental organisations	Greenpeace transmitted video footage of nuclear testing to whip up international protest to protect the local wildlife which is essential to the cultural practices of those living nearby.
Local conflicts get international recognition leading to the protection of people's rights locally	Zapatista rebels in Mexico used their support through the internet to win international sympathy for their cause (Park and Curran, 1997)

How digital communication is leading to cultural defence	Evidence
Glocalisation – global ideas have been adapted to local practices	Blogs focus on local interpretation of events, it is possible to adapt many forms of profile pages to reflect cultural differences. Facebook have recently added the facility to produce specially designed global pages which make it even easier for users from different parts of the world to share business ideas and practices which reflect local issues.
Indigenous (non westernised) peoples use the internet to protect their environment and way of life	Organisations such as survival international and Tribalnet empower indigenous people, raising awareness and fundraising through the internet to help them fight for the right to their land and way of life.
The role of the internet amongst religious groups especially fundamentalist groups	Extremist terrorist religious groups such as the Taliban, Islamic fundamentalists, for example, use the internet to gain support and protect their interests.

Table 1.8 Evidence and arguments for the ways in which new social media maintains cultural difference.

Quick question

Can you think of any other ways in which the internet supports or reflects local cultural practices?

Check your understanding

1 What is meant by the digital divide?
2 Identify some evidence which suggests that cultural homogenisation might be occurring.
3 How might new forms of digital communication affect relationships positively?
4 How might digital forms of communication reinforce class inequalities?
5 Identify a problem with much of the internet being written in English.
6 Give three examples of glocalisation through digital forms of communication.
7 What is cultural homogenisation?
8 How have digital forms of communication contributed to social change?

Section summary

Make a copy of the following passage and fill the gaps using the words in the list below.

Digital forms of communication have a number of complex effects on different groups. Until recently new forms of _____ were predominantly used by the _____, however, things are changing and more and more _____ are using these platforms. In terms of social class, digital communication reinforced inequalities, known as the _____. This is because social connections created through the internet are a very important source of _____ today, and so being unable to access the internet may really limit people and restrict their work opportunities. People use digital forms of communication to reflect their _____ for example, personalising their pages, describing their views and interests and changing their appearance through creating _____.

The impact of digital forms of communication also occurs on a larger scale, for example, through its use in _____ and _____. Often digital communication enables people who are otherwise _____ to speak to a large audience, which can result in the mobilisation of _____ such as in the middle east.

Finally there is a debate about the extent to which digital forms of communication leads to _____ where one global world culture becomes dominant. There is evidence for and against this view, with some suggesting the opposite is occurring, known as cultural _____.

social capital, identity, cyborgs, social media, adults, digital divide, conflict, social protest, cultural homogenisation, young, change, muted, defence

Practice questions

Source A

Globalisation is a concept which is used regularly; however its meaning is often unclear. Some people see globalisation as being linked to changes in the way the economy works, while others see globalisation as a process based on changes within cultural practices. By contrast, globalisation can refer to political changes. Therefore the concept can be difficult to define. However one thing is clear; the role of technology is central to the process.

Source B

There are various forms of digital communication such as Facebook, which offers each member the chance to personalise their page. There are also virtual online communities which offer people the opportunity to find people with similar interests to themselves much more easily. Interestingly, these programs are available on a whole range of devices such as phones, tablets and computers meaning that they can be accessed on the move as well as in the home.

1 With reference to the sources, explain some of the problems with defining globalisation   [9]

2 With reference to the sources, explain how digital forms of communication are linked
   to globalisation   [10]

3 Evaluate the view that globalisation and the development of digital forms of communication
   simply reinforces capitalism   [16]

Chapter 2

Crime and deviance

2.1 How are crime and deviance defined and measured?

Getting you thinking ...

1 Which of these activities are criminal?

2 Which are deviant?

3 What's the difference?

Defining crime and deviance

Consider these definitions:

- **Crime:** A legal wrong that can be followed by criminal proceedings, which may result in punishment; an action or omission which constitutes an offence and is punishable by law.
- **Deviance:** Behaviour which is disapproved of by most people in a society or group, which does not conform to shared norms and values.

> **Quick question**
>
> Give some examples of:
>
> - Crimes which are not deviant
> - Deviance which is not criminal

Crime and deviance are both 'socially constructed', that is, they are created and defined by society. Crime and deviance can also be said to be 'relative': they will vary according to time, society and circumstance. The same behaviour or actions may be deviant or criminal in some cases but not in others.

> **Activity**
>
> ### The relativity of deviance
>
> Copy the following table, adding your own examples to each category:
>
> | Relativity of: | Deviant/Criminal Act | Non-deviant Act |
> |---|---|---|
> | **Time** | Alcohol consumption in the US in the 1920s | Alcohol consumption in the US today (if over 21) |
> | **Culture** | Women exposing their legs in some Islamic societies | Women wearing shorts/ mini-skirts in Western societies |
> | **Circumstance** | Killing a person in cold blood (killing in an unemotional way) | A soldier killing an enemy in the course of battle |

Due to the cultural diversity of contemporary societies such as the UK, views on what constitutes deviance may often vary within societies. For example, what may seem deviant to the wider population may not be deviant within some subcultures.

> **Quick question**
>
> Can you think of examples of behaviour which is seen as deviant by some groups and not others within the UK? (Hint: consider differences based on age, ethnicity, religion, region, social class etc.)

A crime will often require certain circumstances to be fulfilled, in addition to the action itself. For example, the act of sexual intercourse is not illegal in itself, but could become so according to age and/or whether consent has been given by both participants. Another example is driving at 50 miles per hour. This will be deviant in a 30 mph zone, but not in a 50 mph zone.

The opposite of deviance is conformity: behaviour which does fit in with the norms and values of a society or group.

> **Quick questions**
>
> 1 In what ways are we taught or pressured to conform to shared norms and values?
> 2 Are some people more likely to conform than others?

- **Social order** – general conformity to the shared norms and values, so that society is peaceful and predictable. Sociologists do not always agree about how and why social order is achieved, and in whose interests it works.
- **Social control** – the processes by which people are persuaded to obey the rules and conform. The agencies of social control are institutions that serve to ensure conformity. Sociologists also disagree about whether social control is a good or bad thing, and whether it operates in a fair way. Social control can be formal or informal:
- **Formal social control** – carried out by the government, the armed forces and the Criminal Justice System, including the police, the courts and the prison service.
- **Informal Social Control** – carried out by agencies such as the education system, the family, the peer group, the media and religion. We may be less aware of informal social control, but it is arguably more important and more effective than formal social control.

> **Activity**
>
> ### Social control, crime and deviance
>
> 1 Which sociological theory would tend to support social order and social control arguing that it is in the best interests of society as a whole?
> 2 Which sociological theory would argue that social order is merely the enforcement of the norms and values of the ruling class, and that social control operates in their interests to maintain this order?
> 3 What is meant by the following terms:
> a) Crime
> b) Deviance
> c) The social construction of crime
> d) The relativity of deviance
> e) Formal and informal social control

Measuring crime

The Official Crime Statistics (OCS) include statistics produced from police, court and prison records, as well as data collected in the Crime Survey for England and Wales (CSEW), a victim survey which asks people about their experiences of crime. All of these are collated by the Home Office and published by the Office for National Statistics.

Police recorded crime figures

These statistics include all police recorded crime in England and Wales. Separate figures are published for Scotland and Northern Ireland. They are supplied by the 43 territorial police forces of England and Wales, plus the British Transport Police, via the Home Office to the Office for National Statistics. They are sometimes used as a definitive measure of the amount of crime which has taken place, but only include crime which the police become aware of and which the police then record.

Strengths of using the police recorded crime statistics include:
- They are easy to access and have already been compiled;
- They are up-to-date and standardised – the time lag between occurrence of crime and reporting results tends to be short, providing an indication of emerging trends;
- They cover the whole population and go back many years, so trends and patterns can be identified;
- The ethical problems of studying criminal behaviour in other ways are not an issue;
- They provides 'whole counts', rather than estimates that are subject to sampling variation – the whole country is included.

However, there are many limitations of the police recorded crime statistics:
- They do not include undetected or unreported crimes – many victims may not report crimes to the police, or the crime may go undiscovered.
- They do not include unrecorded crime – the police have a certain amount of discretion over whether to record a crime which has been reported, and how to record it. Collectively these unrecorded offences are known as 'The Dark Figure of Crime' – we will consider this further below.
- They do not provide a complete picture about each crime – some information is not collected, for example the employment status or family background of the offender.
- Accuracy may vary between areas, for example if one area has a particular focus or target to meet.
- Changes in public perception may influence them. For example, a certain crime may be noticed and reported more if it has recently been publicised.
- Definitions, laws and police counting rules change – so they are not strictly comparable over time.
- Changes in police practice and government policy may influence them, as policies about dealing with certain offences may change.
- Pressure on the police to meet crime reduction targets may lead to some crimes 'disappearing' from the figures, or being downgraded. The impact of police discretion is considered below.

The dark figure of crime

This is the term used for all unrecorded crime. It is hard to estimate how large this figure is, because it includes crimes which are not even known about. It is unlikely to be in proportion to the police recorded crime statistics, so we cannot just estimate, for example, 50 per cent more crime on top of the known figures. In addition, some types of crime are more likely to be in the dark figure than others.

Activity

The 'dark figure' of rape and sexual assault

Item A

A survey on rape and sexual assault carried out by Mumsnet in 2012 found that 83 per cent of those who had been raped or sexually assaulted did not report it to the police. About half said they would be too embarrassed or ashamed to report such an incident and two-thirds said they would hesitate because of low conviction rates. Nearly three-quarters (70 per cent) of respondents feel the media is unsympathetic to women who report rape.

Source: Mumsnet, (2012) – 1609 respondents

Item B

Kier Starmer, former Director of Public Prosecutions, said in 2012 that 9 out of 10 rapes and other sexual attacks are never reported to the police, arguing that it is partly because victims do not believe the criminal justice system will help them. In 2014, the Ministry of Justice revealed that the conviction rate for sexual offences was just 55 per cent, even lower than in 2013, when the rate was 61 per cent.

Item C

In 2002, rape victim Lindsay Armstrong, 17, was put through a second ordeal by the defence lawyer in the court case, which included being made to hold up the underwear she had been wearing at the time of the attack. The accused, who was 14 at the time of the attack, was found guilty, but the following morning Lindsay took an overdose and was found dead by her mother.

1 Using the items above and your own ideas, suggest reasons why rape and sexual assault may be highly likely to be part of the 'dark figure' of crime, and be underestimated by the police recorded figures.

Police discretion

One problem with police recorded crime figures is that they will be affected by the discretion and decisions made by the police. Some individual police officers may be corrupt or have their own reasons for misrecording individual crimes. However, recent evidence suggests that practices which compromise the accuracy of the statistics are widespread.

Activity

The manipulation of the police recorded crime statistics

Item A

Manipulation techniques:

Coughing: An offender might be encouraged to admit a number of offences in return for being charged for less serious offences which would result in a reduced sentence. This would greatly improve the 'clear-up rate' for the police force in question.

Cuffing: This refers to crimes, which have been reported and initially recorded, being removed from the statistics at a later date. The official term for this practice is 'no-criming'. This may be for various reasons, such as officers deciding they did not believe complainant or reassessing the offence following further investigation. However, it has been alleged that, to improve figures, officers may inappropriately take crimes off the books, even trying to persuade a victim to withdraw their allegation.

Skewing: This involves forces putting resources into those areas measured by performance indicators, to the detriment of other areas, thus 'skewing' the figures.

Item B

James Patrick – whistleblower

Allegations relating to the routine manipulation of police crime statistics were made in 2013 by a whistleblower called James Patrick, who gave evidence to a Parliamentary Committee about his concerns. He was disciplined by the police force and left his job as a result.

Patrick, a serving police officer at the time, spent 12 months analysing data from the Metropolitan Police and found that even serious sexual offences were routinely 'no-crimed', and that burglary was commonly downgraded to a lower type of offence. Patrick's allegations were supported by other senior police officers. In their report, 'Caught red-handed: why we can't count on police recorded crime statistics', the Public Administration Committee (2014) said 'the attitudes and behaviour which led to the misrecording of crime have become ingrained, including within senior leadership.'

1 Which particular crimes do you think are likely to be under-recorded because of the practices mentioned in Item A?

2 Write an analysis of the evidence regarding the manipulation of crime statistics from the following theoretical perspectives:
   a) Functionalist
   b) Marxist

The police could also be influenced by the stereotype of the 'typical criminal', leading to more stop and searches and more arrests for some types of people, creating misleading figures. This issue can be linked to concerns about institutional racism and chivalry, which will be discussed later in this chapter.

What do the sociologists think of the police recorded crime statistics?

Note: It may be helpful to reconsider this question once you have learned about the different sociological theories of crime and deviance in the next section. However, we will briefly discuss the response of these theories here.

The police recorded statistics give us a picture of the 'typical criminal'. While it is clear that there are flaws in the statistics, which even the police themselves acknowledged, some theories broadly accept the police statistics as accurate social facts, and go on to explain why people with the typical criminal's characteristics commit crime:

- Functionalists believe in the existence of social facts and measuring social behaviour scientifically. They would trust quantitative data produced in the statistics and see it as reliable and representative. Functionalists also believe there is a value consensus in society, so would see the police as representing all of us, and not question their motives. Thus most functionalist and subcultural explanations use the 'typical criminal' presented in police recorded figures as their starting point in explaining crime, focusing on young, working class males in particular.

- Similarly, the New Right and right realists accept the official picture of the typical criminal presented by the police recorded figures, since they too believe that laws are made for the benefit of society and applied equally, and that the police are representing the interests of the whole society. They focus on explaining criminality amongst the most deprived sections of society, referred to as the 'underclass', since statistics suggest that most crime is committed by such people.

- Left realists recognise the police figures are not perfect, but they should not be dismissed, because they are about real crimes. They suggest police recorded figures should be supplemented by other methods, such as victim surveys.

- Some feminists accept the official picture that females commit significantly less crime than males, and try to explain why. They look at the high levels of social control applied to females, for example.

On the other hand, several sociological theories have a problem with police statistics, for various reasons, and challenge the idea of the 'typical criminal':

- Marxists see the police recorded crime figures as a tool used to control the working class and justify their control and oppression. Police statistics are used to scare us and justify more policing.

- Interactionists agree to an extent with Marxists. They focus on the social construction of crime statistics, paying particular attention to police labelling and the consequences of interactions between certain powerless groups in society and the police and the courts.

- Radical criminologists combine aspects of Marxism and interactionism in their approach to understanding crime, thus they tend to focus on the power of the police to label for political reasons. Such ideas have also been used to challenge the over-representation of certain ethnic minority groups in the police recorded figures.

- Some sociologists, including feminists, focus on the way that female offenders are treated differently by the police and in the courts. Feminists also argue that, if anything, male crime against women is underrepresented in the police figures. So they do not challenge the idea of the typical criminal being male, but do challenge the accuracy of the statistics.

So there are both strengths and limitations of the police recorded crime figures. The two main alternative approaches to the measurement of crime are victim surveys and self-report studies.

Victim surveys

This is an alternative way of measuring crime which involves surveying people about which crimes they have been victims of in a given period. Victim surveys are likely to include some crimes which have not been reported to the police. A major contribution made by victim surveys to the measurement of crime is the doubt they cast on the accuracy of police recorded crime figures. The biggest example of a victim survey is the Crime Survey for England & Wales (CSEW) which is included as part of the official crime statistics by the Government.

The Crime Survey for England and Wales (CSEW)

The CSEW is one of the largest social surveys conducted in Britain. It is currently carried out by the British Market Research Bureau on behalf of the Home Office, and mainly involves face-to-face structured

Comparing the police recorded crime statistics and the CSEW

Consider the police recorded crime statistics and the CSEW:

1 Which is more valid?
2 Which is more representative?
3 Give some examples of crimes which may be in the CSEW, which may not be in the police recorded crime statistics.
4 Give some examples of crimes which may be in the police recorded crime statistics, but not in the CSEW.
5 Which do you think is the more useful measure of crime and why?
6 Are there any crimes which you think may not be recorded by either measure? Give examples.

interviews. It has been carried out since 1982, though it was called the British Crime Survey (BCS) until April 2012. Initially it was biennial, but since 2001 it has been carried out annually. Only those over 18 were originally included, and then those over 16, but since 2009, children aged 10–15 are also included, usually as part of their parents' survey.

The CSEW has a nationally representative sample of around 35,000 adults and 3,000 children per year. The response rates for the survey in 2013–14 were 75 per cent and 68 per cent respectively, which is relatively high. The survey is weighted to adjust for possible non-response bias and to ensure the sample reflects the profile of the general population.

Respondents are interviewed in their own homes by trained interviewers using a structured questionnaire that is administered on a laptop computer. Respondents are asked about property crimes (such as burglary) and personal crimes (such as theft from the person or violence) which they themselves have experienced. The reference period to which these questions relate is from the first of January in the calendar year preceding the survey, up to the date of interview.

The CSEW tends to show that crime is much higher than the police figures suggest, for some crimes up to 4 times higher. In order to classify incidents, the survey collects extensive information about the victims of crime, the circumstances in which incidents occur and the behaviour of offenders in committing crimes. The CSEW has been successful at developing special measures to estimate the extent of domestic violence, stalking and sexual victimization, which are probably the least-reported to the police but among the most serious of crimes in their impact on victims. The survey also includes questions on people's attitudes about crime-related topics such as anti-social behaviour and the effectiveness of the police.

Limitations of the CSEW

Though many commentators and politicians claim that the CSEW is a more accurate measure of crime in England and Wales than the police recorded statistics, it does have its limitations, including:

- Victimless crimes, or crimes where the 'victim' is a large corporation, such as fare evasion or shoplifting, will not appear;
- Only people over 16 have been asked in the past so crimes with child victims were not picked up, though this has now changed;
- The CSEW only surveys a sample, so overall trends are an estimate which may not be representative (especially for rare crimes);
- The response rate is around 75 per cent, missing potentially important data (see below for more on this issue).

However, most of these problems will be constant over time, and it is carried out every year, so trends may be identified. Hough and Mayhew (1985) who carried out the first British Crime Surveys commented that, 'the value of crime surveys should be assessed not against the yardstick of perfection, but against the existing alternatives: survey and police statistics combined enable the contours of crime to be mapped far better than police statistics alone.'

Other victim surveys

The Islington Crime Survey (Jones, Maclean and Young, 1986) was first conducted by the Centre for Criminology in inner city London. A second survey was carried out in 1990, and a similar survey was carried out in Merseyside (Kinsey, 1984). These surveys not only focused more on specific geographical areas than the CSEW, but also focused on the impact of crime on individual's lives and particularly on vulnerable groups.

The first Islington survey showed that a third of all households had been touched by serious crime in the last twelve months, and crime was rated as a major problem, second only to unemployment. Because there was a qualitative nature to the questions, the survey was also able to uncover the degree to which crime shaped people's lives. For example, a quarter of all people *always* avoided going out after dark, specifically because of fear of crime, and 28 per cent felt unsafe in their own homes. More than half of women stated that fear of crime meant that they did not often or ever go out after dark. Young argues that the Islington survey shows that fear of crime is real and rational, pointing out that it is understandable that 46 per cent of people admitted to worrying 'a lot' about mugging, given that over 40 per cent of the population actually knew someone who had been mugged in the previous twelve months.

Police recorded figures suggest that males are more likely to be victims of crime than females, but women's fear of crime is not just caused by a moral panic according to Young (1988). He claimed that by the use of carefully trained researchers who were able to sympathetically conduct interviews, the Islington Survey found a considerably higher rate of female victimisation, due to the non-reporting of sexual and domestic offences through official channels.

Victims have also been studied even more qualitatively, for example Dobash and Dobash's research into domestic violence (1979) which involved in-depth interviews with women at a refuge. Such qualitative research is not aiming to compete with police recorded figures, but rather to access a particular group of victims and to understand the impact of crime on their lives.

General limitations of victim surveys

Most victim surveys will be subject to similar limitations to the CSEW (see page 40), and do not have the benefit of such representativeness. However, those which take a more qualitative and less official approach may gain enhanced validity.

Young (1988) presented a comprehensive evaluation of victim surveys, despite having been prominently involved in the Islington Crime Survey himself. He argues that a 'dark figure' is also present in victim surveys, for various reasons. The accuracy of victim surveys relies on the memory and honesty of the victim. Some people may get the timescale wrong and people may not tell the truth for various reasons, including shame or guilt. Additionally, people's threshold of 'crime' may differ. For example, some may be unaware they have been a victim of a crime, whilst others may include things which are not technically crimes, such as trespass.

Another problem relates to response rates. If the response rate is low, this affects the representativeness of the final sample and the generalisability of the results. Those who do not respond may disproportionately include victims of particular offences such as sexual offences, people who are hostile to official surveys and people from particular social groups. Additionally, non-victims may not respond, not seeing the survey as relevant to them, which could result in an overestimation of crime.

Self-report studies

The other main method of measuring crime involves asking people which crimes they themselves have committed. This technique is known as a self-report study.

There are obvious logistical and ethical problems in carrying out self-report studies on large-scale samples of adults. They are often carried out on young people and tend to focus on certain types of crime and deviance, often quite minor, rather than gaining a comprehensive picture. However, this does not necessarily mean they lack value, since it is often these minor offences which are not picked up, in either the police recorded crime figures or the CSEW.

Self-report studies may be qualitative. For example, *The Jack-roller* (Shaw, 1966) involved a series of unstructured interviews to build-up a 'life history' of a criminal. Rather than measuring crime, this method gives an insight into criminality, so is favoured more by interpretivist sociologists.

However, most self-report studies are quantitative and usually involve a list of offences requiring the respondent to tick the ones they have committed. Their findings often provide a challenge to the picture of the 'typical criminal' which is presented by the police recorded crime statistics. For example, in her self-report study, conducted on young females and some young males, Campbell (1981) found that levels of crime and deviance admitted to by females and males were much closer than the police recorded figures tend to suggest. Similarly, some self-report studies suggest that statistics overemphasise working class male involvement in crime.

Self-report studies are often longitudinal in nature. This means they follow the same group of participants over a number of years to get an overview of their criminality. These usually measure several different variables, such as family background, peers, education, area, gender and ethnicity. A well known example of a longitudinal self-report study is the Cambridge study, carried out by Farrington et al over a number of years, which has generated much data (for example,

Farrington 1989, 2000a, 2001). The Cambridge Study followed the criminal careers of 411 South London boys, from the age of 8 to 32, and first started in 1961.

Another, more recent, example is the Edinburgh Study of Youth Transitions and Crime, a longitudinal self-report study of the offending careers of over 4000 young people. The Edinburgh Study focuses on gender differences, whereas the Cambridge Study was confined to males. The cohort consists of all the young people in the City of Edinburgh in the relevant age group and information is collected from multiple sources about all members of the cohort once a year. At each sweep, the period covered is the previous 12 months, so that the study provides a continuous account of events in the lives of the cohort, and not just an account of selected time segments.

Quick question

Which types of crimes from the 'dark figure' would self-report studies be more likely to uncover?

Issues affecting the usefulness of self-report studies

- **Validity** – How far do self-reports produce a true picture the number of offences committed?

Because of the subject matter, there are obvious concerns about the truthfulness and accuracy of the data gained. Participants may conceal offending or make false claims about what they have done. The validity of self-reports is usually assessed by comparing them against recorded arrests or convictions which, as we have seen, contain their own flaws. However, by comparing what participants say they have done with official records, their honesty can be evaluated to an extent.

For example, West and Farrington (1977) found that, at age 18, 94 per cent of convicted boys admitted that they had been convicted, whilst only 2 per cent of unconvicted boys claimed to have been convicted. Farrington (2001) found some evidence that while young males may readily admit their convictions, this may not be true for older males or for females. He suggests that this may be because older people and females are concerned to present a façade of respectability whereas young males, who offend more often, are more truthful.

Self-reports can also be compared with more direct measures of offending. For example, Farrington et al (1980) gave young people an opportunity to steal and compared actual stealing with self-reported stealing.

- **Attrition** – This refers to participation and drop-out rates in studies.

This is an important issue because participants who are most difficult to find and interview tend to commit the most offences according to evidence from Farrington et al (1990). This suggests that a survey with a high attrition rate is likely to miss out a number of frequent offenders and to under-estimate the true number of offences committed.

One issue identified in the Cambridge Study was co-operation. The most elusive and unco-operative men at age 32 tended to have had unco-operative parents at age 8 and were unco-operative themselves at age 18. However, in the Edinburgh study, the participation rate after four 'sweeps' continued to be extremely high, at 94.4 per cent of the final cohort.

- **Ethics** – Ethical issues are clearly important to consider in any research into criminality.

With self-report studies, key issues to consider relate to informed consent, confidentially and the right to withdraw. For example, the Edinburgh Study gained the informed consent of parents, through a letter from the researchers. Parents who wished to withdraw their children from the study were invited to return a tear-off slip. Children were fully informed about the purpose of the study and are free to refuse at any time. Children were also required to sign a consent form allowing access to their police files.

Other limitations of self-report studies include the problem of matching the offender's definitions of criminal behaviour with police categories. Additionally, self-report studies usually focus on relatively small groups of people, and on particular types of crime, so do not give us an overall picture, reducing representativeness.

Check your understanding

Briefly explain the following measures of crime:
- Police recorded crime figures
- The CSEW
- Victim surveys
- Self-report studies

2.2 What are the patterns and trends in crime?

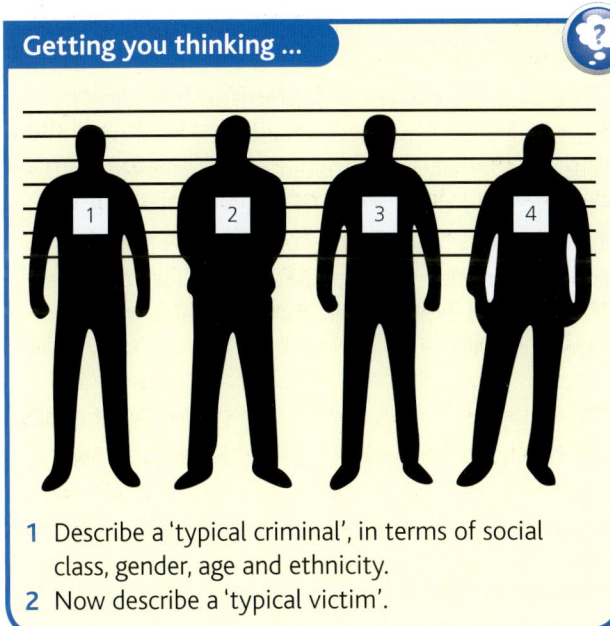

Getting you thinking ...

1 Describe a 'typical criminal', in terms of social class, gender, age and ethnicity.
2 Now describe a 'typical victim'.

The official measures of crime considered in the previous section give us a picture of offending and victimisation, in terms of the most common types of offences and trends in crime. However, they are also used to consider patterns of offending and victimisation in terms of social class, gender, age and ethnicity.

The 'typical criminal' and the 'typical victim' appear to be very similar:

working class, male, young and disproportionately likely to be black.

This has become a starting point for many theories of crime, which focus on explaining why individuals with these characteristic are most likely to be involved in crime. However, the patterns are slightly more complex than this, and many sociologists challenge them, not least due to the potential flaws in the measurement of crime already considered.

Social class

Offending

Sutherland (1949) pointed out that 'criminal statistics show unequivocally that crime, as popularly understood and officially measured, has a high incidence in the lower socio-economic class and a low incidence in the upper socio-economic class'.

Despite Sutherland's claim, it is surprisingly difficult to find data in the UK relating to the social class backgrounds of offenders. The evidence which does exist, for example, relating to the social characteristics of frequent young offenders, points to the disorganised and chaotic social backgrounds that are associated with poverty and deprivation. In 2002, the Social Exclusion Unit reported that many prisoners have a history of social exclusion, being more likely than the general population to have grown up in care, poverty, and to have had a family member convicted of a criminal offence. Despite a rate of unemployment of 5 per cent in the general population, the research showed that 67 per cent of the prison population had been unemployed prior to imprisonment, and 32 per cent had been homeless, compared to 0.9 per cent of the general population. Williams et al (2012) also found that other factors found more frequently in the prison population included: having run away from home; experiencing violence and/or drug and alcohol misuse within the family; regularly truanting from school; being excluded from school; and having no qualifications. Literacy and numeracy levels of prisoners are significantly lower than those found in the general population. For some additional evidence on the link between social deprivation and criminality, see the 2012 statistics for those in prison in the activity on page 73.

One consequence of evidence such as this is that most theories of criminal behaviour tend to focus on explaining working class criminality, basing their ideas on lack of status, money, opportunities and so on. However, information relating to the social class background of offenders may be more relevant in showing who gets caught than who commits crime.

Data from self-report studies tends to show that the difference between offending rates for working and middle class people is not as high as the figures above suggests. In their review of such data, Cavadino and Dignan (2001) point out that 'somehow between the commission of offences and the official responses of prosecution and punishment, the difference between the classes gets vastly magnified'. Reasons for this may include the types of offences committed, but also class biases operating at various stages of the criminal justice process. Evidence for such bias is explored further in the next section, as are explanations for working class criminality and for white-collar and corporate crime.

Victimisation

The British Crime Survey from 2010–11 showed that young households, lone parents and the unemployed are all more than twice as likely to be burgled as the average household and the unemployed are more than twice as likely to be the victims of violence as the average person. Young (1988) discussed the 'myth of the equal victim', suggesting that certain groups, such as the poor, are hit much harder when they become a victim of crime than other groups. This is supported by Kinsey's findings in the Merseyside crime survey (1984): the poor suffer more than the wealthy from the effects of crime. For example, a victim of burglary who is uninsured will be hit harder economically that a victim who has contents insurance. The poor are also more likely to be subject to 'multiple victimisation', as the many social problems they face increase their vulnerability to a range of crimes.

Gender

Offending

The police recorded crime figures consistently show that males commit around 80 per cent of all offences. Data from the Ministry of Justice shows that females accounted for only 18 per cent of arrests and 25 per cent of convictions in 2013. Although the number of offenders formally dealt with has been falling for both genders, it has been falling faster for females, meaning that these proportions are at their lowest in the past decade.

Official crime data suggests that the peak age for female offending is 15, younger than the peak age for males, at 18. Though girls may continue to offend in their teens, offending drops markedly after this whereas offending for males does not decline significantly until well into their 20s.

Gender may also intersect with social class. In 2010–11, female offenders were more likely than male offenders to be on benefits before and after their caution, conviction or prison sentence, whereas in the general population, males were more likely than females to be on benefits. This suggests that deprivation may have more of an impact of women's criminality than on men's.

The clear differences in patterns of offending in terms of gender have been challenged by those who argue that females get treated more leniently by the police and the courts. This view is known as the 'chivalry thesis' and will be considered in the next section, alongside the explanations for lack of female offending and explanations for why males may be more criminal.

Victimisation

Historically, the victimisation level for women has been lower than for men. The CSEW has shown each year since 1982 that fewer women are victims of crime than men. However, levels of victimisation for men have also decreased over the past five years according to the CSEW, and victimisation rates now differ little between men and women.

The types of crime men and women are victims of do differ. A higher proportion of men are victims of violence, but the perpetrator of the violence is more likely to be a stranger or acquaintance. However, women are twice as likely as men to have reported being a victim of non-sexual partner abuse and seven times as likely to have reported being a victim of sexual assault.

Activity: The meaning of a punch

1 Do you agree with Young that the meaning of a punch differs depending on the situation and the power relationship involved? Use the images to help explain you answer.

Males account for 7 out of 10 homicide victims, and they are most likely to be killed by a stranger or an acquaintance. However, over half of female homicide victims since 2003 were killed by a husband or partner, and on average, 2 women every week are killed by a husband or partner.

Young (1988) points out that the same crime does not have the same meaning or seriousness in all cases, and discusses 'the meaning of a punch' being very different in some situations that others, depending on the power relationships between the two parties. Such power dynamics are masked by the statistics.

Feminists often consider issues of domestic violence and female victimisation, and research suggests that the statistics on domestic violence vastly underestimate the problem. Hanmer and Saunders (1984) carried out unstructured interviews with women in one street in Leeds, and found that 20 per cent of the women there had been sexually assaulted and not reported it. Stanko (2000) found that over one 24-hour period, an incident of domestic violence was reported every second. Yet very few of these led to an arrest.

Walklate (2006) considered repeat victimisation and the reasons why women often remain in an abusive relationship. She found that many women are unable to leave, and by implication unlikely to report the abuse, due to various factors. These include the fact that they have nowhere to go, which is made worse when children are involved, and that some women lack economic independence. Psychological issues, such as self-blame, dependence and lack of confidence also play a part, and these may be key reasons why many incidents of domestic abuse go unreported.

Changes in patterns of gender and crime are discussed in more detail later in this chapter (see page 82).

Age

Offending

Evidence from police recorded crime figures suggests that young people are more likely to offend than adults. Although young people aged 10 to 17 are responsible for a minority of incidents of police recorded crime – 23 per cent of police recorded crime in 2009–10 – this represents a disproportionate amount of crime, given that 10 to 17-year-olds account for only about one in ten of the population above the age of criminal responsibility (currently 10 years old).

Gender differences can be seen in youth offending: males aged 10 to 17 were found to be responsible for 20 per cent of all police recorded crime in 2009 –10 and young women responsible for only 4 per cent. Juvenile offenders are more likely than adult offenders to receive a caution rather than a conviction for their first offence, with females (83 per cent) more likely to receive a youth caution than males (75 per cent) in 2013.

Despite these figures, McVie (2004) has argued that in reality, the relationship between age and offending is not quite so clear-cut. She points out that the data is often grouped into age-bands which may mask more precise trends. For example, Home Office data often groups everyone over 21 together, making it impossible to identify trends in adult offending, and the age groupings for teenagers often differ, making comparisons difficult. Additionally, different offences may have different 'peaks' in ages of offenders, but statistics often fail to break these down. For example, Soothill et al (2004), found the peak age of conviction for some crimes, such as burglary, to be around 16 or less, whereas motoring and drug offences peaked between 21–25 before declining.

Given the problems with police recorded crime statistics seen in the previous section, the age patterns in offending can be questioned. It may be that youth crime is more visible, thus appearing in the statistics more frequently than adult crime, which may be more likely to be undetected.

Explanations for the prevalence of criminal behaviour in the teenage years are put forward by subcultural theories, which are considered in the next section.

Victimisation

As with other social groups, it is often argued that the incidence of victimisation in terms of age is disproportionate to the fear of crime. For example, older people are more likely to fear crime, whereas young people are actually more likely to be victims of crime. Though evidence from the Islington Crime Survey (1986) supported this to an extent, Young (1988) argued that such fears are not as disproportionate or irrational as they may seem. In terms of the over forty-fives, the ICS found that they do have a lower crime rate against them than young people. However, when assault occured, they were more likely to be injured and to lose time off work, more likely to have an attack involving severe violence, such as kicking or use of a weapon, and the attack was therefore more likely to have a greater effect on their lives.

It is only recently that data on victims of crime under the age of 16 has been systematically gathered. Since January 2009, the CSEW has asked children aged 10 to 15 about their experience of crime. Based on CSEW interviews in the year ending June 2014, 12 per cent of children had been victims of crime. Of these crimes, the majority (56 per cent) were categorised as violent crimes, and most of the remaining crimes were thefts of personal property.

Activity

Age and patterns of crime

Item A

McVie (2004) concluded from her analysis of the Edinburgh Study of Youth Transitions and Crime, that there is a complex relationship between prevalence (the amount of young people involved in offending) and frequency (the amount of offences carried out by each offender). The evidence suggested that changes in frequency of offending had the most impact on crime rates in a given period, since prevalence remained fairly constant, and a small group of persistent offenders can have a marked impact on the crime statistics in a given period.

Item B

Young (1988) points out that considering victimization in terms of age alone misses the fact that it is the combination with other social factors such as gender and ethnicity which has the greatest impact on the likelihood of becoming a victim. For example, the Islington Crime Survey found that young, white females are 29 times more likely to be assaulted than those over 45, and 30 times more likely to be sexually attacked. The most dangerous age for women differs by ethnic group: it is the youngest age group for white women, the 25–44 age group for black women and the over 45 age group for Asian women.

1 Referring to Item A, explain what is meant by 'prevalence' and 'frequency' in terms of offending.
2 Consider possible reasons for the patterns of age and victimization and their link to gender and ethnicity.
3 Using your answers to the first 2 questions, and other material from this section, outline some of the difficulties in gaining accurate data on youth offending and on youth victimization.

Ethnicity

Offending

Statistics suggest that proportionally more people from black and Asian backgrounds are stopped and searched, arrested and charged, and sentenced to imprisonment, than their white counterparts. According to Ministry of Justice data, black people were stopped and searched seven times more than white people in 2009–10. In 2013, black people comprised 3.1 per cent of the population, but accounted for 14.2 per cent of all stop and searches. Asians comprised 6.4 per cent of the population, but accounted for 10.3 per cent of stop and searches.

The overall number of arrests decreased by 3 per cent in the five years to 2010, but arrests of black people rose by 5 per cent and arrests of Asian people by 13 per cent. Black people were arrested over three times more than white people in 2010. Bowling and Phillips (2006) point out that the Crown Prosecution Service is more likely to drop cases put forward by the police involving black suspects, suggesting that the police charge black people more frequently based on inadequate evidence, than they do with suspects from other ethnic groups.

Over the last few years there has been much public debate about levels of migration from Eastern European countries which are now part of the European Union. One concern which has been raised by some politicians and in the media is the high levels of criminality found amongst these groups. However, a report from the Association of Chief Police Officers in 2008 found that, despite newspaper headlines linking new migrants to crime, offending rates among mainly Polish, Romanian and Bulgarian communities were in line with the rate of offending in the general population. During the last fifteen years, whilst immigration from these countries has increased, the overall crime rate has fallen steadily, casting further doubt on such claims.

Victimisation

The 2012–13 CSEW shows that adults from mixed, black and Asian ethnic groups were more at risk of being a victim of personal crime than adults from the white ethnic group. This has been consistent since 2008–09 for adults from a mixed or black ethnic group; and since 2010–11 for adults from an Asian ethnic group.

Distinctions can be made between intra-racial and inter-racial crimes. Overall, the number of racist incidents and racially or religiously aggravated offences (inter-racial) recorded by the police decreased over the last five years from 2005. Home Office evidence from 2005 suggests that black people are five times more likely to be murdered than their white counterparts in England and Wales, but police records indicate that in about one in three gun murders, both victims and suspects are black (intra-racial).

Patterns of crime in a global context:

Getting you thinking ...

1 In what sense may activities in other countries be considered as 'crimes' affecting us in the UK?

Globalisation challenges our notions of 'crime' and 'the criminal', which have traditionally focused on national and cultural definitions of criminality and the policing of such activities in specific countries. Global crime transcends national borders and police forces, and is thus difficult to define clearly and to investigate and punish.

Global organised crime

Global or transnational organised crime is a growing concern, but is also a contested category of crime which is used in different ways. It may be used to refer to criminal activities themselves as well as those involved in the activities. One useful definition is 'the cross-border activities of organised crime groups arguably exploiting to their advantage increasing global interconnectedness' (Franko Aas, 2007).

Global criminal organisations are involved in a wide range of activities, including:

- drug trafficking
- human trafficking
- arms trading
- counterfeiting and extortion
- wildlife crime
- kidnapping
- corruption
- credit card fraud
- identity theft and other cyber crimes
- money laundering

The nature of the criminal organisations involved in such activities varies widely, from paramilitary and terrorist groups to gangs and from warlords to business cartels. Article 2a of the UN's Convention on Transnational Organised Crime defines an organised criminal group as a 'structured group of three or more persons existing for a period of time and acting in concert with the aim of committing one or more serious crimes or offences in order to obtain, directly or indirectly, a financial or other material benefit.' The convention also states that an offence is transnational if it is committed in, planned in and/or affects more than one state.

It is very difficult to provide accurate estimates relating to global organised crime, both due to difficulties in defining its scope, and because only a fraction of these criminal activities become known to law enforcement agencies every year. Some estimates give an idea of the scale of the problem. For example, in 2009 the United Nations estimated transnational organised crime to be an $870 billion business annually. This figure equates to six times the world's annual official development aid budget. Other estimates suggest that the world's shadow economy, including organised crime, could be as high as 10 per cent of global GDP.

The international response to the problem of transnational organised crime has been slow and is hampered by various factors. These include:

- the diversity of the groups and the range of activities involved;

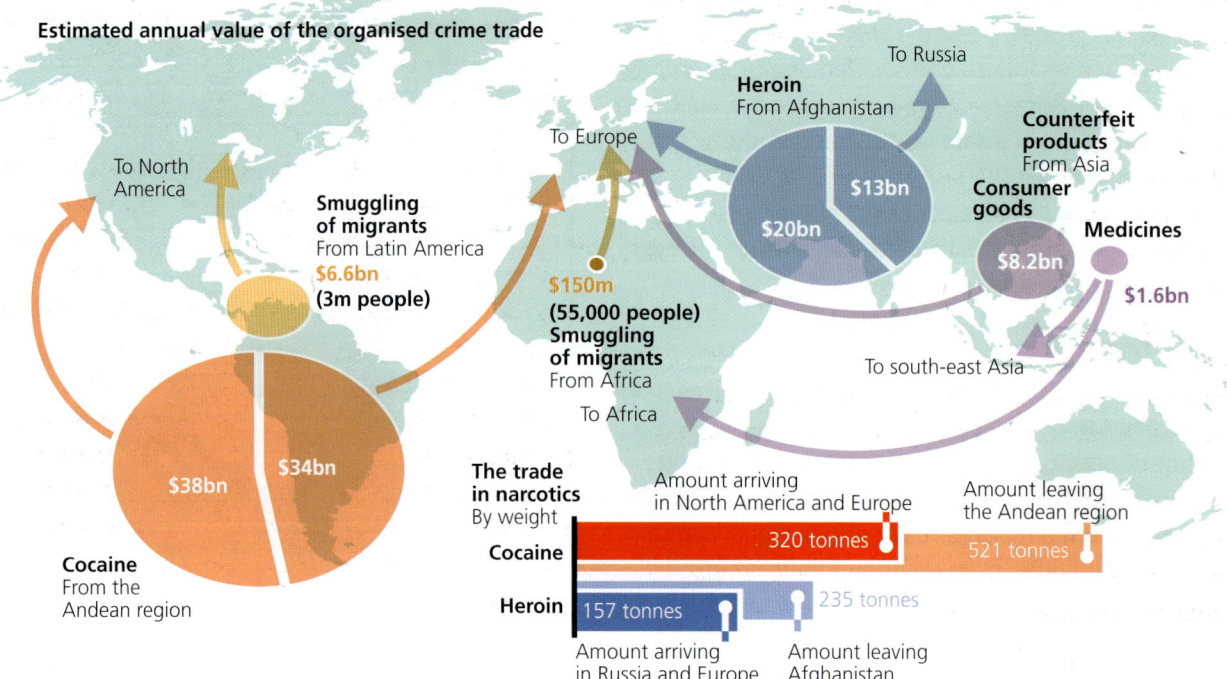

Estimated annual value of the organised crime trade

- difficulties relating to international co-operation;
- border issues and lack of common definitions;
- the increased trend towards state deregulation; and
- the lack of global attention at the expense of the threat of terrorism.

Criminal organisations have also taken advantage of new developments in communication and transportation, as well as increasingly open borders that facilitate the international movement of goods and services.

Peter Gastrow, from the International Peace Institute in New York, argued at an international conference on transnational organised crime in 2013 that the popular perceptions of organised crime, such as the stereotypical Mafia drug cartel with a Godfather boss, are out of date. Today's global criminal enterprises 'turn over billions of dollars and prey on every aspect of global society, fuelling conflict, destroying the environment, distorting markets, corrupting governments and draining huge resources from both'.

Gastrow suggests that a key problem is that state borders, which mean so much to governments, are irrelevant to the global criminal organisations, and this makes them very difficult to track and pursue. He predicts that increasing wealth gaps and skewed income distribution in the global economy will contribute to a growing demand for cheaper contraband goods and the expansion of criminal economies.

Castells (2000) sees organised crime groups as resembling business networks, which take the opportunity afforded by globalisation to link up with criminal groups in other countries. For example, to minimise risk and maximise profit, they may co-operate by basing their management and production in low-risk areas which lack regulation, whilst targeting their markets in more affluent areas.

However, this view of global co-operation is challenged by those who stress the relevance of 'glocal organised crime', which refers to the importance of the local context in which criminal networks function. This draws on Robertson's (1995) concept of 'glocalisation', referring to the intertwining of the global and the local, and the way in which local conditions impact on global phenomena. For example, though the drugs trade is a global criminal enterprise, the way it is organised in individual countries varies based on the political context, local demographics and culture, law enforcement issues and so on.

Activity: Global crime recap

1 Give examples to demonstrate the view that global organised crime is a contested concept.
2 Explain 3 reasons why the international response to global organised crime has been slow.
3 Explain the difference between 'globalisation' and 'glocalisation'.

Green crime

Green crime, or environmental crime, can be seen first and foremost as criminal activity which affects the environment in some way. Examples may include the dumping of toxic waste, fly-tipping and the poaching and trafficking of endangered species. Over the last 20 years, many new criminal offences which relate to the environment have been created. Some of these offences are committed on a global scale by large criminal organisations, and so there is an overlap between global organised crime and green crime. Additionally, because the planet is one unified eco-system, single-nation states have not got the power to deal with major environmental crime. Therefore green crime transcends political and national borders.

Franko Aas (2007) points out that, like organised crime, green crime demonstrates the intersection of the local and the global, as local environmental harm is often the product of a chain of geographically dispersed events and activities.

However, as with the study of corporate crime considered later in this chapter, what constitutes 'green crime' is debateable, and many 'green criminologists' also focus on legal activities which are seen as harmful to the environment. Thus, activities such as deforestation, CO2 emissions, and fishing are mostly legal but are seen as environmentally damaging and relate to the abuse of power in pursuit of profit. Critical criminologists, such as Marxists, would argue that the damage done by such activities far exceeds the damage done by 'street crime'. For example, consequences of state sanctioned activities often relate to the environment, even if it is only indirectly, according to Potter (2010). He gives the examples of food riots around the world as agricultural production has been given over to producing bio-fuels, and the fuel price protests by lorry drivers. Such 'crimes' demonstrate how the competition for scarce natural resources can lead to public unrest and disorder.

Green criminologists argue that crime should be considered in terms of 'harm', rather than in terms of the activities which those in power have defined as criminal. Even putting aside the 'harm' to the planet itself, the activities addressed by green criminology often cause much human harm. For example, millions of avoidable deaths around the globe are linked to preventable environmental problems, such as the absence of clean drinking water. Potter points out that it is nearly always the poorest people who suffer most from environmental harms, losing their livelihoods and way of life, or even their health and their lives, and the rich corporations responsible usually avoid any kind of criminal repercussions.

Carrabine et al (2004) classify green crimes into two distinct types, primary and secondary:

- Primary green crimes – are those crimes which directly inflict harm on the environment and, by extension, on people, because of damage to the environment. Carrabine recognises four main categories of primary green crimes: air pollution, water pollution, deforestation and species decline and animal rights.
- Secondary green crime – refers to actions committed as a response to the commissioning of primary green crime, such as attempts to cover it up by breaking environmental regulations or by dealing aggressively with protestors. Using criminal organisations to assist in the dumping of toxic waste would be an example. Additionally, State violence against oppositional environmental groups, such as Greenpeace, could be seen as a secondary green crime.

2.3 How can crime and deviance be explained?

Getting you thinking ...

1 How can criminality be explained?
2 Do the same explanations apply to all crimes and to all criminals?

Functionalism

One of the key aspects of functionalism is that the effect of things on individuals is not thought to be as important as the effect on society. So even behaviour which seems deviant and harmful to particular individuals may still be functional for society as a whole, if it serves a collective purpose.

The founder of functionalism, Emile Durkheim, saw crime as an integral part of a healthy society. He also felt that some crime and deviance was inevitable – a society would always have some deviance as people test the boundaries. For example, in a society with no other deviance ('a society of saints'), behaviour like sneezing or burping could become criminalised.

Value consensus, the majority in society sharing the same norms and values, is very important for society to function effectively and for social order to be maintained. If too many people do not learn these values, or have different values, it will leave society in a state of chaos, or 'normlessness', where there are no agreed rules. Durkheim called this a state of 'anomie' and thought it was a very damaging thing for society. This is why socialisation is so important for functionalists: to ensure that everyone learns the same norms and values, thus preventing anomie.

Promoting social solidarity: bringing together 'upright consciences'

Social solidarity refers to the sense of cohesion felt in society – all the members of a society feeling part of the whole. Certain events in a society which bring people together can be seen as promoting social solidarity. Examples would include national events such as royal weddings or births, sporting events such as the football World Cup or the Olympics, and also smaller scale events such as graduation ceremonies or family celebrations. Durkheim argued that crime is one of these events. He wrote that 'crime brings together upright consciences' and discussed the example of shared outrage about a scandal in a small town, which will lead to the expressing of a 'public temper', (Durkheim, 1960), thus promoting social solidarity – everyone is outraged together. The idea that all members of a community share a set of values, ideas of right and wrong, is referred to as the 'collective conscience'. This will lead a community to police itself, using sanctions to ensure that anyone who steps out of line knows it is wrong.

The collective conscience may be expressed through the shared sense of shock, outrage, horror, anger, fear, or grief that the public demonstrate after hearing about certain events. Examples may include reactions to war, natural disasters or other emergencies or tragedies, but also reactions to a deviant or criminal act by a member of society.

> **Quick question**
>
> Can you think of examples of when the British public have apparently shown a collective conscience?

Boundary maintenance and the promotion of social change

Members of any society or community must learn the boundaries of what is acceptable behaviour within that group. Crime and deviance facilitate this by showing members of society where the boundaries of right and wrong are, through publicly condemning and punishing those who stray beyond these boundaries. To ensure that this function of deviance is carried out, any deviance must be identified and punished. Such punishment will involve the agencies of social control – those institutions which identify and publicise deviance, and control it through the application of sanctions.

> **Quick question**
>
> You have come across the idea of social control, and ways in which social control can be formal and informal earlier in this chapter. Write a list of the agencies of social control, stating which are formal and which are informal.

Study

Wayward Puritans, Erikson (1966)

Erikson argues that members of a community will participate in confrontations with a deviant person who transgresses the community's boundaries. These confrontations may take the form of 'public degradation ceremonies'. These can range from public trials to the media coverage of crime. He notes that the decline of the very public punishment of deviants, in the form of public floggings or hangings, for example, happened at the same time as the development of newspapers, which took on a similar function. Subsequently, radio and television also took on this role of public condemnation, and today social media such as Twitter performs a similar role.

Boundaries are always shifting according to Erikson, and changes may occur which can be demonstrated through the relaxation of certain public reactions to previously 'deviant' behaviour. Thus another function of deviance, and societal reaction to it, can seen as helping society to progress by showing when a new value consensus is emerging. An example of this could be the changing attitude towards homosexuality in the UK. A change in the publicly expressed view towards homosexuality has led to a fairly swift shift from it being a criminal offence at the beginning of the twentieth century, to continued unequal treatment in terms of age of consent (which was not equalised until 2000), through to the introduction of gay marriage in 2014.

Applying and reviewing the functionalist views on deviance

1 Using the functions of deviance discussed below, suggest how each of the following behaviours could be seen as 'functional' for society. Each may perform more than one function:
   a) pornography
   b) people binge-drinking at the weekend
   c) football hooliganism
   d) drink-driving

2 Write down definitions of the following terms, using examples if possible:
   a) value consensus
   b) collective conscience
   c) anomie
   d) agencies of social control
   e) public degradation ceremonies

Anomie

For Durkheim and functionalists, a small amount of crime and deviance can prevent anomie, as long as it is punished. However, if a society allows too much crime and deviance without punishment, or if for some reason the value consensus breaks down (maybe if change in norms and values happens too quickly), this could result in a breakdown of social order and lead to a state of anomie, which threatens the stability of the whole society.

In each of the following examples, as normal order is suddenly removed and a state of anomie prevails, there may be an initial rise in deviance and criminality such as looting, violence and suicides:

● If there is a sudden change of government (a revolution, a coup or an uprising). For example: in Russia after Communism collapsed; in South Africa after the end of apartheid; and in Iraq after Saddam Hussein was removed.
● If there is a disaster which leads to the destruction of order. For example, in New Orleans after Hurricane Katrina or in New York after 9/11.
● If there is a major economic upheaval. For example, after the Wall Street Crash in 1929, or the more recent banking meltdown in 2008.

Quick question

Can you think of more examples which illustrate 'anomie' occurring in a society or community?

Deviance as a 'safety valve'

An additional function of deviance, suggested by some functionalists, is that it can act as a 'safety valve' – allowing an individual or group to 'let off steam' to prevent worse deviance. Davis' study of prostitution (1961) suggests that the goals of sexual behaviour in men are not inherently social, but that societies need to restrict the morally acceptable expression of sexuality to the family context to promote the bearing and raising children. This can lead to a conflict for many men which may lead to promiscuity or even rape. Davis thus argues that prostitution, far from being damaging to society, is providing a 'safe' outlet for these sexual tensions in a way which is less threatening to the family.

Evaluating Durkheim

Durkheim was the first sociologist to consider crime and deviance, and to look at its effects on society. His ideas about the balance between a functional and an anomic society have been very influential, and can be applied to real life examples. However, he did not explain why individuals actually commit crime – if we all share a value consensus, why do some people break the law?

So although Durkheim explains why we need deviance, he doesn't explain:
● why it happens,
● why some people do it more than others, or
● why different people are deviant in different ways.

Also, Durkheim doesn't consider the negative effects of deviance on individuals, such as victims of crime, or issues such as who creates the law, or who has power to evade the law – Marxists would challenge this.

Merton and strain theory

Merton (1938) is arguably the most influential sociologist to develop Durkheim's ideas, particularly using his concept of anomie. His ideas of anomie and the 'strain' that modern society's goals can create have influenced many other sociologists who would not all be seen as functionalists.

Merton argues that there are clear, culturally defined goals in any social structure, and there are also clearly defined means to achieve these goals, which are designed to regulate the behaviour of society's

It's not the taking part that counts, it's the winning!

Lance Armstrong, who won the Tour de France a record 7 times, but admitted to taking performance enhancing drugs in 2013.

1 How does Lance Armstrong support Merton's ideas?
2 Do you think that this attitude is prevalent in other sports? Give examples.
3 Can you think of examples from other areas of life which illustrate Merton's point about the goal of success being more entrenched into our culture than the legitimate means of achieving it?

members. Crime and deviance occur when the goals are emphasised more than the acceptable means. If alternative means to achieve the goal become more accessible, acceptable and even preferred by significant numbers in society, then anomie will occur. Thus Merton argues that in some societies there is a 'strain towards anomie', as the goal becomes more important than the means. He uses sport as an example: if the culture develops wherein winning is more important than fair play and sticking to the rules, then winning by any means becomes acceptable.

American culture provides Merton with a clear example of this strain, where the goal of success, and particularly money, has become entrenched and Americans are continually pressured to find ways of becoming financially successful and making more money. However, crucially, Merton argues that there is not as much emphasis on the legitimate ways to achieve the goal of success as there is on the goal itself. Merton accepted that those lower down in society would have restricted goals, (not all expecting to become millionaires) but even so, the socially acceptable channels do not always allow individuals to achieve success and are not sufficiently enforced. In these circumstances, individuals may turn to other means of achieving success, or lose faith in the system entirely.

Modes of adaptation

Merton argued that there were five different responses to goal of success, or 'modes of adaptation':

1 Conformity – will be the most common response to society's goals in a stable society. Thus most

people in America will work hard at school and in their job, to make as much money as they can in legitimate ways.

2 Innovation – will occur when an individual has internalised the goal (for example success) but has not fully internalised the acceptable means of achieving this. Merton argues that this can occur amongst middle class individuals, who are prepared to 'bend' the rules to make more money. However, it is those in the working class, who find the goal of success to be incompatible with their educational and employment opportunities, who are most likely to innovate, through criminal or deviant behaviour, to achieve success.

3 Ritualism – it is clearly unrealistic for many to continually strive for great wealth, thus the ritualist abandons, or at least scales down, the goal – lowering aspirations to achieve an equilibrium. Others may judge such a person as lacking ambition, or being 'stuck in a rut', thus they can be seen as deviant in a society of achievers.

4 Retreatism – those who struggle to achieve success may end up dropping out of the society which judges them and become retreatists. This may involve not working but also not participating in 'normal' life at all – often rejecting family and friends and pursuing self-destructive deviant behaviour.

5 Rebellion – the rebel may reject society's goals but replace them with alternatives, joining an organised movement which seeks a different type of society entirely, or which campaigns for a different cause.

Activity: Merton's modes of adaptation

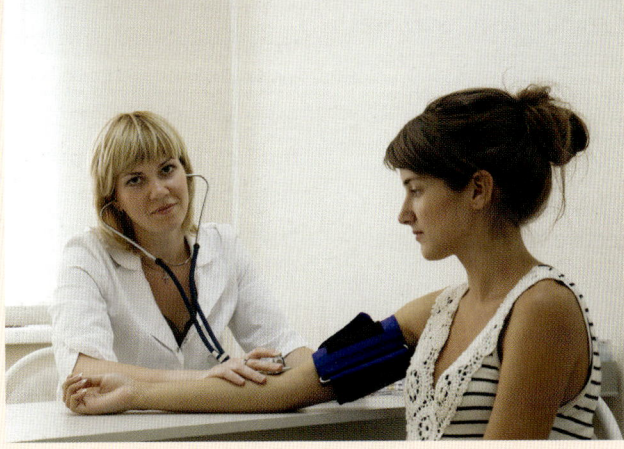

1 Identify which of Merton's responses are being illustrated by each of the pictures above.
2 Give at least one additional example for each 'mode of adaptation'.

Merton has been challenged for his assumption that the goal of financial success is universal in the USA. It could be argued that there may be many other goals (such as family and love) and many other reasons to display deviant behaviour. An individual may fall into several categories in different aspects of their life, for example, a bank manager, who is also a football hooligan!

Evaluating Merton: The slot machine analogy

In a Marxist critique of Merton, Laurie Taylor (1971) has likened Merton's analysis of individual modes of adaptation to playing a slot machine:

e)...................... play on and win fairly

d).................... cheat

c) .... play a different game

a)...................... play on mindlessly

b)...................... give up

But Taylor suggests that Merton hasn't asked the important questions

- Who put the machine there in the first place?
- Who's keeping all the profits?

1 Which of Merton's five modes of adaptation matches each of the responses to playing the slot machine given above?

2 How would a Marxist answer the two important questions Taylor poses?

Despite such criticisms, Merton's Strain Theory was very influential as a theory of crime which recognises that when an individual experiences strain or stress, crime is one potential response to this strain. This has been developed by subcultural theorists, with the key difference that whilst Merton focused on an individual's response to strain, subcultural theorists tend to see deviance as a collective response, in the context of a subculture.

Subcultural theories

The official statistics suggest that the typical criminal is young, male and working class. Subcultural theorists tend to accept this view of the 'typical criminal'. They focus on the influence of the peer group on young people and the norms and values which may form within subcultures to explain criminality. Subcultures formed by working class youths may normalise criminal and deviant behaviour as a response to the strains created by their social class and lack of opportunities.

Cloward and Ohlin (1961) also see deviance as a reaction to problems in achieving the values of mainstream culture, and are clearly influenced by Merton's strain theory. The deviant is unable to achieve valued goals (such as success and money) through legitimate means, and thus innovates, using illegitimate or deviant means to attain them. They argue that legitimate routes to valued goals are differently available, but so are the routes to these goals through illegitimate means. Access to 'criminal subcultures', through which gang members can access a hierarchy of criminal opportunity making money through criminal enterprises, is not available to all youths. In more unstable, disorganised areas, youths turn to violence and 'conflict subcultures' are formed to defend territory. Youths who are unable to access success through mainstream values or through joining criminal or conflict subcultures may withdraw from society's values altogether, descending into addiction and petty crime, becoming 'retreatists'.

Delinquent boys: the culture of the gang, Albert Cohen (1955)

Cohen focuses on delinquent subcultures, or gangs, which were prevalent in America's cities in the 1950s. He challenges the view that criminal activity is similar across the age-range, arguing that juvenile delinquency is uniquely non-utilitarian (not committed for profit), and associated with short-term hedonism (instant pleasure-seeking). He also recognises the acute pressures towards conformity to the peer group which youths feel, and how important their position in the group and their status in the eyes of others becomes. The achievement of status – 'respect in the eyes of one's fellows' – is paramount. Working class boys are aware of mainstream values, such as success at school, good qualifications, a good job and financial success,

and they understand that a middle class boy could get status if he achieved these things. However, a working class boy who clings to this value system will recognise himself as inferior compared to middle class boys. This creates a feeling of 'status frustration'.

In a delinquent subculture, status may be achieved via alternative criteria, such as being good in a fight. Those who perform successfully in terms of delinquent values within their subculture can gain status in the eyes of their peers, and can look down on the middle class boys who do not measure up to their status.

1 Which aspects of Cohen's ideas link to Merton's strain theory?
2 Do you agree that status is a more important goal for youths than financial success?

The role of subculture in the development of deviant values was also considered by Miller (1958). He argues that working class boys have their own 'focal concerns' (values) which have the potential to lead them into deviant behaviour. These are different to the values of middle class youths, this can help explain why levels of deviance are higher amongst the working class. The focal concerns of young working class boys include valuing freedom and excitement,

being in trouble, being tough and macho, and being smart and 'streetwise'. Conformity to this value system is more important to working class boys than middle class codes of conduct.

The views of Cohen, Cloward and Ohlin and Miller can all be criticised for the way in which they generalise about working class culture. In reality, working class styles are many and varied, and are subject to regional, ethnic and gender variations. Their ideas could also be seen as outdated.

'Badfellas', Simon Winlow (2001)

Item A

Criminality in the 'modern era'

'Denied access to criminal hierarchies, organised criminal apprenticeships and recognisable successful criminal role models, the youths of Sunderland's lowest income areas were also denied the possibility of fashioning a criminal career and were therefore pushed towards [violence].' (page 40)

Case Study: Tommy: '"That's what I liked: Big blokes being scared a you, everyone being nice to you and that … You know that feeling, just before a fight?...It's a good feeling … What else was I going to do, work in the shipyards all me life?"' (page 51)

Item B

The 'postmodern era'

'As the traditional structures have disappeared and as others lose their solidity, young men – particularly those from lower class backgrounds – find their

identities as men changing rapidly and influences upon those masculine identities arriving from a variety of new directions …' (page 67)

'Violence is certainly not out of reach and as a means of gaining status remains constant. However, it has now taken on new uses, meanings and interpretations and can be used as a tool with which one can fashion a criminal career.' (page 68)

Bouncers as an example of the criminal entrepreneur:

'... these individuals use their physical capabilities and standing amongst their peers, along with their occupation, to benefit themselves criminally and financially. For being a bouncer offers the criminal entrepreneur a number of avenues to exploit ...' (page 100)

1 In what ways do Winlow's findings regarding traditional working class criminality in Sunderland support Cloward and Ohlin's ideas?
2 In what ways do Winlow's points about the postmodern era challenge or modify Cloward and Ohlin's ideas?

An alternative view on subcultures and deviance comes from a radical, neo-Marxist perspective. For example, P. Cohen (1972) argues that the range of deviant, working class subcultures are an expression of contradictions within the parent culture. Examples may include the contradiction between traditional working class values and consumer culture, and the contradiction between upward social mobility and the marginalisation of the underclass. Some working class subcultures embraced consumerism and upward mobility, through their style which mimicked the middle class, for example mods. Others demonstrated more obvious resistance, such as skinheads. Cohen identified a link between the rise of such subcultures and a rise in levels of youth crime. Such delinquency is linked to territoriality and identity, but is also an expression of protest against the class situation the youths find themselves in. Further discussion of neo-Marxist accounts of subcultures and resistance can be found on page 66.

Cultural criminology

As seen in Winlow's study above, changes in society (from modern to postmodern) and the impact of this on working class communities may have affected criminality as well. More recent views on the influence of culture and subculture on crime have clear links back to the work of Merton, A.Cohen and Miller, as well as neo-Marxists, but modify and apply these ideas to fit the postmodern experience.

Cultural criminology brings a postmodern view to an understanding of delinquent subcultures, seeing them as expressions of identity, resistance and power struggle. Ferrell (1999) explains that cultural criminology stresses the 'energy of everyday life': crime is a result of anger, humiliation, exuberance, excitement and fear, rather than a rational decision-making process.

Katz (1988) argues that sociological explanations which focus on social characteristics such as social class, ethnicity and gender alone fail to take into account the ways in which people are drawn and propelled into crime, and the lure and authentic attractions which crime has. Many of those who fit the social characteristics of a typical criminal are not drawn into crime, so to fully understand criminality, we must understand its seductions – what makes a person give in to the temptation of crime, and what they are getting out of it at that moment? For example, he

suggests that a physical fight may be nothing more than a show of toughness. So crime is presented as having quite selfish and individualistic motivations. However, when Katz discusses crime as an expression of identity, for example being a 'badass', there are still links to ideas from subcultural theorists such as Miller (see above).

In his exploration of risk-taking behaviour, Lyng (2005) uses the concept of 'edgework'. This concept refers to exploring the edges that exist along cultural boundaries and undertaking activities which push and test those boundaries. Lyng argues that edgework can lead to intense emotions such as fear, anxiety and exhilaration, and by mastering those emotions the individual can feel a sense of control and accomplishment. Edgework is seen both as an escape from the constraints of modern society and as a way of coping and functioning in an increasingly complex postmodern society. These ideas have been applied to criminality, and can be linked to Katz's ideas about the seductions of crime and the sense of danger but also control which criminality may offer the perpetrator.

Quick questions

1 Can you think of examples of non-criminal risk-taking behaviour which illustrate Lyng's concept of edgework?
2 Give examples of criminal or deviant behaviour which edgework may apply to.

Cultural criminologists are also interested in power relations and the reactions to deviance from the media and the State, for example, the 'criminalization' of subcultural expressions of identity. This can be seen in reactions to nineteenth century hooligans, the moral panics surrounding mods and rockers, the public outrage created by punk and glam rock and the more recent concerns about gangsta rap. The role of the media in the social construction of crime and deviance is clear and, given the ever increasing role of the media in our lives, its influence on perceptions of crime should not be underestimated.

Ideas from many of these cultural and subcultural studies have been developed by Young (2003) to explain underclass criminality. Like Presdee, Young believes that working class deviance is about transgression, rebellion, risk-taking, anger and frustration. He argues that we live in a 'bulimic society',

Cultural criminology and the carnival of crime, Mike Presdee (2002)

Carnival has its historical roots as a cathartic ritual, though which hedonistic desires can be expressed and transgression (deviance) is celebrated. Most societies have some form of 'carnival', where a few times a year people can 'let off steam'. Presdee argues that in postmodern society, 'carnival' is a constant need and people live for the next opportunity to transgress – for example, girls' or lads' nights out and the binge drinking culture seen throughout the country every weekend. Those in power tolerate 'carnival' as a necessary safety valve, but are constantly trying to limit and control transgressive behaviour, since it is a threat to social order. Thus, the response of the authorities to deviance tends to be an increase in control.

However, Presdee argues that 'the creeping criminalisation of everyday life' provokes even more transgression. This is because one motivation to commit crime is the 'revolt against the mundane'.

Rules are broken because they are there. The 'risk' involved in deviant activity is what makes it appealing and is a challenge not a deterrent. Presdee gives the example of joyriding in Oxford, where the stealing and racing of cars became a regular ritual on one estate. The events were purely for pleasure, thrill and excitement, the stealing and driving abilities of those involved gained them status. The risk and danger further added to the thrill.

Those in power continually try to either criminalise or sanitise expressions of resistance. Activities which cannot be stamped out by use of the law and force are sometimes regulated and become 'mainstream', thus losing their appeal. Presdee cites the rave scene of the 1980s as an example of this.

1 Which aspects of Presdee's ideas link to functionalism? And which seem more linked to Marxism?
2 Apply Presdee's analysis to the growth of the music festival.

---

meaning a culture in which citizens are encouraged to 'worship success, money, wealth and status' but are 'systematically excluded from its realisation'. He discusses the 'intensity of exclusion' felt by the underclass, incorporating feelings of relative deprivation, but also resentment and humiliation.

Similar to Merton, Young uses the idea of 'anomie' to describe the contradictory feelings which today's society brings, describing it as 'the vertigo of late modernity'. He sees deviance as both an expression of exclusion and a desire for inclusion. These ideas are similar to those of Nightingale (1993), who describes the 'paradox of inclusion' experienced by young black youths, who turned to deviance to achieve the goals of mainstream society. Nightingale's ideas are discussed in more detail on page 87.

What do you think Young means by 'the vertigo of late modernity'?

As social mobility becomes entrenched and large sections of society move away from their origins through enhanced educational and career opportunities, those who are left behind in the inner-cities have to make sense of their failure. Katz and

Jackson-Jacobs (2004) argue that 'gangs make local attachments glorious', transforming the continuation of childhood friendships and hangouts into matters of pride – hence phrases like 'homeboy' becoming a badge of respect, rather than an insult. So gangs are a way for those who have failed to climb the social ladder to maintain status and respect.

Briefly explain the following concepts, and link them to the sociologist who used them:

1 Anomie
2 Public degradation ceremonies
3 Modes of adaptation
4 Status frustration
5 Focal concerns
6 Edgework
7 Carnival
8 Bulimic society

A general criticism of subcultural views is that they mainly seek to explain crimes committed by young, working class males. It could be that this crime is the most visible and the most focused on by the police, rather than the most prevalent. In developing subcultural ideas, cultural criminology clearly draws together ideas from functionalists, neo-Marxists and postmodernists to help explain criminality. However, it also draws on ideas about labelling and the social construction of crime. These ideas are most associated with interactionists, who look more closely at some of the criticisms outlined above.

Interactionism

Interactionists reject the idea that crime statistics are a realistic reflection of criminal activity. They argue instead that they are the result of a series of assumptions and judgements made by agencies of social control (such as the police).

This means that instead of seeking to explain why those with the social characteristics of a 'typical criminal' are more prone to commit crime, interactionists are interested in exploring how and why particular groups or individuals come to be defined as criminal or deviant in the first place, and how this definition affects their future actions.

> ### Study
>
> **Outsiders: Studies in the Sociology of deviance, Howard Becker (1966)**
>
> Becker argues that deviance is socially constructed:
>
> 'Social groups create deviance by making rules whose infraction constitutes deviance, and by applying those rules to particular people and labelling them as outsiders ... The deviant is one to whom the label has been successfully applied; deviant behaviour is behaviour that people so label.'
>
> He suggests that people who have been labelled as deviant cannot be studied to try to reach an explanation of their deviance, since some of those may have been wrongly labelled, and others who are deviant may not have been labelled at all. Becker is therefore 'less concerned with the personal and social characteristics of deviants than with the process by which they come to be thought of as outsiders and their reactions to that judgement'.
>
> He proposes that deviance is not a quality of some types of behaviour, but rather 'the product of a process which involves responses of other people to the behaviour'.

Master status and the self-fulfilling prophecy

Becker argued that the effects of the labelling process can be significant. A deviant label contains an evaluation of the person to whom it is applied. It can become a

'master status' which colours all other statuses and roles possessed by the individual. Others will respond to the individual in terms of the label and interpret any behaviours in relation to the label, and so the deviant identity becomes the controlling one for the individual.

> ### Activity
>
> **Master status**
> Consider the following behaviours:
>
> - Leaving an item in a trolley without paying for it when you go through the checkout
> - Gaining an A grade in a test
> - Talking to yourself at a bus stop
> - Watching some children playing on the beach
> 1 For each of the examples above, can you think of an example of a master status someone may have which would affect the way the behaviour is interpreted?

An important concept associated with labelling is the self-fulfilling prophecy. When an individual is labelled and reacted to in a particular way, they are likely to internalise (take on board) that label and it will affect their self-concept. They may then start to live up to the label, making decisions based on the deviant self-concept, which fulfil the assumption which has been made about them. Once a deviant label becomes a master status, it may be difficult for the individual to remain unaffected – he or she may be isolated from others and judged differently. This may mean that the individual will find it difficult to conform to many of society's other rules, such as holding down a job or having a relationship, and thus the specific deviant becomes a general deviant.

Becker further argues that a 'deviant career' may be commenced when an individual joins a deviant group or subculture. This group may rationalise, justify and support deviant identities and activities. Thus the individual will be more likely to see themselves as deviant – internalising the label. At this stage the 'deviant identity' becomes the controlling one – it will affect the individual's choices, lifestyle and self-concept. This notion of a deviant career is applied by Plummer (1996) to individuals who have been labelled as homosexual. This label becomes a 'master status' and the individual may internalise the label and start to pursue a 'homosexual career', which may involve joining a homosexual subculture, frequenting gay venues and becoming more camp.

The impact of public labelling

For Becker, behaviour only becomes deviant when it has been defined and labelled as such. He uses an example from anthropologist Malinowski (1966) to illustrate this point.

> **Activity**
>
> ### Malinowski and public shaming
>
> Malinowski (1966) describes an incident which occurred during his study of the Trobriand Islands in the South Pacific. Incest between cousins was seen as deviant, but in day-to-day life it was fairly commonplace and a blind eye was usually turned. However, one young man, who had a relationship with his cousin, was publically accused in front of the whole community by his rival. Suicide was seen as the only honourable course of action, and he threw himself from the top of a palm tree. Becker concludes that it is only when a public accusation was made that the behaviour became a serious issue.
>
> 1 Consider how the following contemporary examples may illustrate the example from Malinowski used by Becker:
>   a) The MPs expenses scandal, which first broke in 2009, when many MPs were found to have been routinely claiming expenses for things they were not entitled to.
>   b) Naming and shaming of celebrity deviants and deviant practices by companies (such as tax avoidance) via traditional or social media
> 2 Can you think of any more specific examples?

Like Becker, Lemert (1951) argues that societal reaction to behaviour is more significant than the behaviour itself. Using the example of alcoholism, he suggests that the reasons for drinking are many and varied, and less significant than the processes by which the drinking is identified and becomes an active part of the individual's identity.

Lemert uses the term 'primary deviance' to refer to deviant acts which are not publicly labelled. Many people may commit such acts, and they have little effect on the self-concept. Such behaviour is rationalised or dealt with as an acceptable part of the individual's lifestyle.

However, if the deviant behaviour is repetitive and highly visible, and if it attracts a severe societal reaction, it will begin to affect the individual's self-concept. Lemert states that 'when a person begins to employ his deviant behaviour or a role based on it as a means of defence, attack, or adjustment to

the.. problems created by the consequent societal reaction to him, his deviation is secondary.' Thus, secondary deviance is deviant behaviour which is consciously engaged in as an expression of a deviant self-concept.

> **Activity**
>
> ### Lemert and secondary deviance
>
> Lemert (1951) suggests that secondary deviance is unlikely to occur after the public labelling of just one deviant act, but rather is the result of a process:
>
> - Primary deviation
> - Social penalties
> - Further primary deviation
> - Stronger penalties and rejections
> - Further deviation, perhaps with hostilities and resentment towards those doing the penalising
> - Crisis reached in tolerance, formal action taken by the community
> - Strengthening of the deviant conduct as a reaction to the stigmatising and penalties
> - Ultimate acceptance of deviant social status
>
> 1 Lemert applies this process to an example of a schoolchild who starts off by playing a prank in class. Using his model, describe how this situation may evolve into secondary deviance?

Originally focused on explaining delinquency in young people, Matza (1964) argued that many youths will drift in and out of deviance. They do feel a moral obligation to obey the law, but may also feel pressure to pursue 'subterranean values', which challenge morally acceptable values (for example, excitement and risk-taking). When a youth commits a deviant act, he or she will use 'techniques of neutralisation' which justify the act and prevent a deviant identity from initially forming, enabling the youth to drift back to legitimate activities and to preserve their self-concept as a decent person. Matza proposes five techniques of neutralisation that individuals may use to justify their deviant behaviour:

- Denial of responsibility – arguing that the behaviour was not within the individual's control: 'It was not my fault'
- Denial of injury – arguing that the deviant behaviour did no harm: 'No-one got hurt'
- Denial of the victim – arguing that the victim deserved what happened: 'He had it coming'.
- Condemnation of the condemners – arguing that those labelling the behaviour are in the wrong, or are being hypocritical: 'They have got it in for me'.

- Appeal to higher loyalties – arguing that other values, such as friendship, family or profit were behind the behaviour: 'I was doing it to back up my mates'.

Matza suggests that most youths will eventually grow out of the drifting into deviance, as they take on adult responsibilities, though a few will start to internalise the deviant label and become habitual offenders.

> **Quick question**
>
> Can you recall any deviant activity you have been involved in? Did you use any of Matza's techniques of neutralisation to justify it?

The influence of the agencies of social control on the social construction of deviance

JOCK

Young (1971) looked at the societal reactions to drug taking amongst some alienated young people. He discusses groups of young people who faced a problem of 'anomie' and evolved into a Bohemian subculture, seeking out like-minded people and smoking marijuana as a solution to their problems. Powerful groups in wider society saw this subculture as a threat to their interests, and through the mass media and the criminal justice system, action was taken. Such societal reaction created new problems for the group, and the deviant behaviour actually increased.

This increase in deviance can be explained by the process of deviance amplification. Young presents different models of deviance amplification. For example, the increased deviance may be a result of increased isolation induced by the condemnation of the original deviance. Alternatively, it may be 'rebellion induced', as the deviants react angrily to the label and deviate even more. Young brings in the idea of the self-fulfilling prophecy as another aspect of deviance amplification. There is an imbalance of power between the social agencies defining the deviance (such as the media and the police) and the deviant group, which may lead to the group interpreting their own behaviour differently and accepting the public perception of them. This can lead to further deviance as the deviant label is internalised.

Cicourel (1968) was influenced by ideas from Lemert when he conducted his study of juvenile justice in two US cities. His research illustrates how the recorded crime statistics are often the result of a series of interactions and negotiations between the youths and the criminal justice system. He argues that the process of dealing with potential deviants involves the police and probation officers making judgements which are often based on pre-conceived ideas about what counts as suspicious or unusual. The decision about whether to arrest and charge a suspect is partially based on the appearance, manner and replies the suspect gives to the police. For example, if the individual is very apologetic and polite, no further action may be taken. Additionally, at the point of arrest, if the parents come to the station and convince the police that it will not happen again, then the individual may not be charged. Cicourel also found substantial differences between the two cities he studied, despite their similar size and socio-economic characteristics. One city, which employed more probation officers and kept more detailed records on offenders, had constantly high rates of juvenile delinquency. The other city fluctuated depending on media publicity and public concern. His conclusion is that the agencies of control and their policies operate to construct the official picture of juvenile justice in the USA.

> **Check your understanding**
>
> Briefly explain the following concepts, and link them to the sociologist who used them:
>
> 1 Master status
> 2 Self-fulfilling prophecy
> 3 Deviant career
> 4 Primary and secondary deviance
> 5 Techniques of neutralization
> 6 Deviance amplification

Evaluating interactionism

The ideas of interactionists, particularly in the 1960s, provided a challenge to the prevailing approach which appeared to blindly accept the official picture of the 'typical criminal' as fact, without questioning the processes and interactions underlying these statistics. Additionally, interactionism recognises that the simplistic division between deviants and non-deviants is unrealistic, and that everyone can be deviant at times, also highlighting the social construction and relativity of deviance.

However, interactionism has been criticised for failing to provide an explanation for the original deviant action, before the labelling process takes place. Interactionists such as Becker and Lemert may respond to this criticism with their suggestion that the majority of people may commit deviant acts which are never labelled, implying that no explanation for the initial deviance is really necessary.

Another challenge to interactionism is that it is deterministic – assuming individuals passively live up to their label. Some may fight to prove the label wrong, others, such as the British serial killer Harold Shipman, commit serious crime despite having no label. Thus it does not account for the deviant's other motives, such as status, financial gain, thrill or risk-taking. Plummer (1979) defends interactionism against this critique, arguing that interactionists do consider individual motivations, and some explore the ways in which a labelled individual may work to throw off the label.

A significant criticism of interactionist ideas is that they apply only to minor or particular types of deviance, such as youth crime, and perceived deviant lifestyles, such as homosexuality. It is less easy to explain serious crime using ideas of labelling – the idea that a killer only becomes 'deviant' once labelled is not convincing. However, Plummer suggests that there is a misconception of labelling theory at the basis of this criticism. Interactionists are not suggesting that societal reactions bring about the behaviour, but that labels can alter the labelled individual's self-concept and future decision-making.

Though they have much in common, Marxists have also challenged interactionist ideas. Neo-Marxists have argued that deviance can be a conscious act of resistance or rebellion, rather than a reaction to a label. However, interactionist accounts such as those described by Young do recognise this, but argue that societal reaction to this resistance will then further influence the deviant's behaviour. Another criticism is that interactionism fails to consider power structures in society, given its micro approach. Interactionists frequently refer to power, in terms of the power to label and avoid a label, and the power of the agencies of social control. However, Marxists argue that not enough attention is given to the social structure which provides this power.

Marxism

Unlike Functionalists, Marxists do not agree that crime and deviance function for the whole society. They argue that it is the powerful who benefit. Marxists look at issues such as the types of laws which are passed and enforced, and who benefits from these laws. Some Marxists also look at the way in which the capitalist system drives people to crime. Another key area of study is crimes of the powerful, including white-collar and corporate crime. This is looked at in more detail on page 75.

Marxism, ideology and social control

Marxists focus of the concept of ideology: a system of ideas and beliefs. The dominant ideology in society comprises the ideas which suit the powerful and their interests, and make sure the powerless stay in their place. This 'capitalist ideology' is presented as 'fact' and makes up our reality, so everyone in society accepts these ideas, and fails to question whether they are true, or represent our interests. Being socialised or 'brainwashed' into capitalist ideology is a major way in which the proletariat are controlled by the bourgeoisie.

Althusser (1970) argues that control of the proletariat is maintained through two sets of institutions. The Repressive State Apparatus (RSA) directly and obviously controls the proletariat, and comprises the government, the armed forces, the police and the criminal justice system – the formal mechanism of social control. The Ideological State Apparatuses (ISAs) control us more subtly, by socialising us into accepting the capitalist ideology. Examples of ISAs include the family, the media, education and religion – the informal mechanisms of social control. Althusser notes that whereas the RSA functions by violence, the ISAs function by ideology – and no class can hold power over a long period without exercising ideological control.

These ideas can be applied to crime and deviance: the ISAs are used to show us those who are 'deviant', as a warning, and also to divide us, keep us scared and therefore to justify the use of the RSA.

The examples of theft and murder are used by Box (1983) to illustrate how the concept of 'crime' is socially constructed by the powerful. Murder can be seen as 'avoidable killing', but there are many avoidable killings which do not get classified as murder. Box notes that 'we are encouraged to see murder as a particular act involving a very limited range of stereotypical actors, instruments, situations, and motives. Other types of avoidable killing are either defined as a less serious crime than murder, or as matters more appropriate for administrative or civil proceedings...' The people who commit legally defined murder are usually poorer and less powerful than those who commit other 'avoidable killing'.

Examples of 'avoidable killing' which are not constructed as 'murder' include deaths resulting from employers' acts of negligence or failure to give priority to environmental or health and safety risks, and from manufacturers' decisions not to properly test or recall dangerous products based on cost calculations. More specific examples of such 'criminality' are explored in the section of crimes of the powerful on page 75.

Power, crime and mystification, Stephen Box (1983)

Box (1983) directly links crime to social control. He argues that the official crime statistics are socially constructed and manipulated to criminalise the powerless. The idea that most criminals are working class and that crime is increasing are part of the capitalist ideology. This is used to scare us and to justify more control.

We are encouraged to believe that there is a crime problem, and this justifies an increase in policing and surveillance, greater powers of punishment and more prison places. The result of these controls seems to be an even higher crime rate, creating a culture of fear. The 'criminals' we are encouraged to fear are the typical criminals presented in the official crime statistics: young, male, working class and black.

Like other Marxists, Box accepts that this may have some truth, because these tend to be groups more affected by material deprivation and social exclusion, giving them more reasons to commit crime. He also accepts that controlling crime which harms ordinary individuals is desirable. However, Box argues that the whole idea of a 'crime problem' is part of the ideology of the powerful – an illusion to justify more control of those seen as a threat to the Capitalist system. This illusion also diverts our attention from the really serious crimes – those that cause avoidable deaths, injuries and deprivation.

For Box, the criminal law is a set of ideological constructs – tools and instruments designed to criminalise '... problem populations perceived by the powerful to be potentially or actually threatening the existing distribution of power, wealth and privilege'.

The real 'criminals' are the powerful themselves. They tell us criminals are evil, and crimes are committed by mentally unstable and uneducated working class people. This helps to disguise the fact that the powerful create the conditions for the offending of the powerless, and that the powerful are actually causing more harm in society than the so-called 'criminal classes'.

Quick question

Can you think of examples of money or property being taken from individuals against their will, which are not socially constructed as 'theft'?

Capitalism, alienation and criminality

Alienation is a concept used by Marx to describe the sense of powerlessness, lack of control and disconnectedness felt by the proletariat created by exploitation at work and capitalism. Marxists argue that alienation and the competitive conditions created by capitalism can drive people to criminality.

There is a causal link between crime and economic conditions according to Bonger (1916). Much crime is caused by poverty; hence during times of economic depression, crime rates amongst the poorer sections of society increase. Those living in poor conditions and in competition with one another for scarce resources will be driven to criminality.

Moreover, capitalism creates a climate of competition and inequality, due to an unequal distribution of resources. This promotes greed and individualism, rather than the co-operation and selflessness which may be found in more primitive societies. Materialism, false needs, racism, and the false masculinity of violence and domination are all related symptoms of the capitalist system. Thus capitalism directly creates crime due to desperation, but indirectly it also contributes to an increasing a sense of alienation and brutality, which leads to a further increase in crime.

Like other Marxists, Gordon (1973) argues that the focus of public fear, and governmental control, is on 'urban' or 'violent' crimes, with little attention being given to white-collar crimes, despite the harm that they do. He also points out that given the prevalence of crime in the USA, criminal behaviour seems to be the norm, rather than an aberration, citing a 1961 survey which found that 91 per cent of Americans admitted that they had committed acts for which they may receive custodial sentences. However, Gordon goes on to argue that crime is usually a rational response to the situations people find themselves in, and that capitalism, with its focus on competition for resources and inequality, creates the conditions in which crime is carried out. He uses the example of 'ghetto crime' in poor neighbourhoods, pointing out that legitimate jobs available to residents are insecure, low paid and often demeaning. In this context, criminality amongst the poor can be seen as a rational response to their situation. He links this to other criminality, such as corporate crime, and argues that the same analysis is true – in a competitive capitalist economy, corporate criminality as an attempt to maximise profits and beat the competition is perfectly rational.

Activity

Crime as a rational response to capitalism

'... this is the way you get your drug dealers and prostitutes ... They see that these things are the only way that they can compete in society, to get some sort of status. They realise there aren't any real doors open to them, and so, to commit crime was the only thing to do, they can't go back.'

Source: Arthur Dunmeyer, a black hustler from Harlem, quoted in Gordon (1973)

'I worked as a busboy for a week once. It was like being a pig in everyone else's slop. Why should I put up with that shit?... Doing crime is a lot more fun and pays a lot better.'

Source: Agnew (2006)

Kweku Adoboli was a 'rogue trader' who lost $2.3 billion for UBS Bank in 2011 through unauthorised trading. His defence argued that Adoboli had an excellent work ethic and sound motives for his actions, suggesting that the drive to make money for banks put pressure on traders to use any means possible to achieve that.

1 Using the examples given above, explain how crime be seen as a rational response to capitalism.
2 How would you criticise this view?

Check your understanding

Briefly explain the following concepts, and link them to the sociologist(s) who used them:

1 Capitalist ideology
2 Alienation
3 Repressive and ideological state apparatuses
4 Crime as a rational response to capitalism

In his review of the Marxist approach to crime, Chambliss (1975) summarises several points made by different Marxist criminologists. He argues that the structure of capitalism creates both the desire to consume and, for most, the inability to earn enough money to meet these consumption desires, highlighting a contradiction which can explain the lure of criminality. He points out that Marx himself recognised that crime takes some of the proletariat off the streets through incarceration, and employs another section of society in the control of criminality, reducing surplus labour. Chambliss also reiterates that criminal acts are located throughout the social class spectrum, but it is the enforcement of the criminal law which leads to the appearance that criminality is concentrated in the lower classes. The form which the criminality takes is directly related to the position and opportunities which relate to the individual: '... the drinking of the skidrow resident, the violence of the ghetto resident, the drug use of the middle class adolescent and the white-collar crimes of corporation executives ...'.

Evaluation of Marxist explanations

Marxists are often accused of being too extreme. It is possibly far-fetched to argue that the ruling class are all involved in a deliberate conspiracy to control and criminalise the lower classes. However, Marxists argue that even if it is not a deliberate conspiracy, the dominance of the powerful and their ideology operate in ways which benefit them and disadvantage the powerless.

Critics also cite examples of laws which do protect the rights of the powerless, such as laws against murder, theft and rape, but also health and safety regulations and human rights laws. However, as Box argues above, such laws are often framed and enforced selectively, and so still operate to advantage the powerful.

The argument from writers such as Bonger and Gordon, that capitalism creates crime, can be challenged by the point that most people obey the law, suggesting a value consensus. However, the selective enforcement of the law noted by Marxists suggests that crime is actually much more widespread than it appears. This is an idea taken up by neo-Marxists.

Neo-Marxism and radical criminology

Interactionism and Marxism clearly have much in common. Both suggest that criminality occurs throughout the social structure, but that those from the lower classes, and with less power, are more likely to be identified as criminals and arrested, charged and convicted. However, whilst interactionists focus on the process by which an individual comes to be labelled as deviant and its affect on their subsequent behaviour, Marxists look more at the reasons behind the inequality, and in whose interests the criminal justice system operates. Radical criminologists, who can be seen as a form of neo-Marxism, tend to combine these approaches.

The Saints and the Roughnecks, William Chambliss (1973)

Though generally seen as Marxist, in his observational study of two high school gangs, Chambliss identifies the differences in public perception of the boys' deviant behaviour, and how social class impacts on labelling and self-concept.

'The Saints' were eight young men from white upper-middle class families. They were constantly involved in deviant behaviour, including truancy, drinking and vandalism. Yet not one was officially arrested during the two year study. In contrast, another gang at the school, 'The Roughnecks', six boys from lower-class backgrounds, were constantly in trouble with police and community even though their rate of delinquency was similar.

The Saints were able to utilise their status and 'good reputation' in the school to negotiate their way out of classes, cheat on homework and tests, and gain higher grades that they deserved. They chose the sites of their weekend delinquency carefully, where they would not be recognised. In contrast, The Roughnecks were perceived as typical gang members, and subject to more community vigilance. The police were aware of their delinquency and looked for opportunities to arrest them.

Chambliss concludes that 'selective perception and labelling … means that visible, poor, non-mobile, outspoken, undiplomatic "tough" kids will be noticed, whether their actions are seriously delinquent or not. Other kids, who have established a reputation for being bright, disciplined and involved in respectable activities, who are mobile and monied, will be invisible when they deviate from sanctioned activities.'

1 What similarities can you see between Chambliss's study and Cicourel's study (see page 62)?

Birmingham University's Centre for Contemporary Cultural Studies (CCCS) produced much neo-Marxist analysis of deviant youth subcultures in the 1970s and 80s. Sociologists such as Hall and Jefferson (1976), P. Cohen and Hebdige produced accounts of 'spectacular' youth subcultures including teddyboys, mods, skinheads and punks. They focused on issues such as identity, style and societal reactions, whilst recognising the significance of the socio-economic conditions in which the youths were growing up. The CCCS studies argued that the attitudes and styles of each subculture could be seen as expressions of resistance against capitalist society and the class inequalities affecting their lives.

Style and attitude as resistance

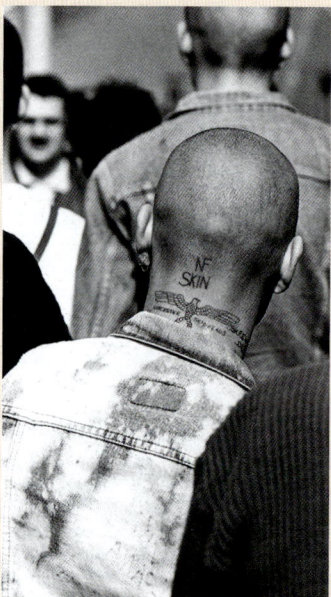

1 In what ways can the styles adopted by each of the subcultures shown be seen as a form of resistance against their social class situation?

Policing the Crisis, Hall et al (1978)

Hall et al's analysis utilises interactionist ideas on societal reaction to certain forms of deviance, such as labelling and the creation of moral panics, but it places this within the wider context of the social and economic conditions of the time.

The study recounts the moral panic about mugging in the 1970s. The term 'mugging' was first used by the British media in 1972, having previously only been used in America. Mugging does not actually exist as a crime – robbery would be the closest actual offence – and media coverage often quoted statistical increases which were impossible to verify given the lack of clarity about which crimes actually constituted 'muggings'. However, the term quickly entered the nation's vocabulary and, due to the focus of some of the early stories, it came to be associated with Black males. Rather than attempting to explain mugging itself, Hall et al are concerned with why British society reacted to mugging in such an extreme way, and at that precise time. They argue that crime, and the reaction to it, must be put into its historical and societal context if it is to be fully understood.

In the early 1970s Britain was experiencing an economic crisis, with high unemployment and a squeeze on wages. The conditions were creating unrest – there were strikes, student protests and widespread discontent, particularly in the inner cities. This affected the ability of the ruling class to govern by consent. They had to use force to control the crisis, clamping down hard on dissenters. Crime became the focus, justifying tougher policing. At the same time, racial tensions were stirred up in urban communities, as competition for jobs and resources was linked to immigration by some politicians. In this context, the hard-line reactions of the police and the courts to cases of mugging, coupled with sensationalist media reporting, created a moral panic and made a link between race and crime.

Hall et al argue that the 'black mugger' served as a scapegoat for the social problems of the day, and provided a distraction from the economic worries. At the same time tougher policing and control was justified and accepted by the public at large.

1 Can you think of any more recent examples of moral panics which may have distracted attention from wider social problems?

This combination of structure and action is developed more explicitly in *The New Criminology* by Taylor, Walton and Young (1972), in which they put forward a 'radical theory of crime'. They argue that a 'fully social theory of deviance' must consider the structure of capitalist society – the way it operates to the benefit of the ruling class – and at the individuals involved in social deviance – offenders, police, magistrates and judges – to consider how they interpret behaviour and actions.

A full social theory of deviance requires a Marxist understanding of the distribution of power in society, considering:

- the circumstances surrounding an individual's choice to commit a deviant act,
- the meaning of the act for the individual and
- any effects caused by societal reactions, including labelling and deviance amplification.

Like the CCCS, Taylor, Walton and Young suggest that an individual's class position, and the feelings of frustration this may create, may lead to the desire to resist and fight back against the capitalist system. The view of crime as a form of resistance has also been developed by Gilroy in relation to black criminality (see page 88). It is a source of criticism however, particularly from left realists, who call it a 'Robin Hood' thesis. They point out that most working class criminals commit crimes against other working class people, not as an act of rebellion against the capitalist state. However, resistance need not be a conscious act, but rather a result of anger and frustration that may end up being channelled into violence and other crime. Young became a key figure within left realism, and despite the above criticism, there are clear links between the two approaches. (see page 73).

Another radical study of crime produced by the CCCS which is influenced by this radical approach is Hall et al's Policing the Crisis.

By combining approaches drawn from both Marxism and interactionism, radical criminology opened up new perspectives in understanding crime and deviance. It was closely followed by another new approach, realism, which also drew on some older ideas but updated and adapted them to explain contemporary criminality.

Right-wing and left-wing views

Some of the newer theories of crime clearly align themselves to the political right or left. Before we consider them, it is important to understand what is meant by 'right-wing' and 'left-wing' views.

Right-wing views on society and crime

Right-wing views tend to focus on individual achievement and opportunity, believing that equality is not possible, or even desirable, in society and that talented people should be incentivised to work hard and should be rewarded accordingly. Thus, people will generally get what they deserve in life. They argue that the State should not intervene to support those who are struggling because everyone should take responsibility for their own actions.

When such views are applied to crime, the focus is usually on the bad choices which individuals make, and poor socialisation leading to the 'wrong' norms and values being followed. Thus right-wing thinkers would tend to blame the criminal or deviant for their actions, rather than blaming their circumstances or social inequalities. When considering solutions to crime they focus on tougher penalties but also on stricter forms of control.

We have already considered functionalist ideas on crime and deviance, and these would be seen as right-wing views. We will also be considering views from right realists and the New Right.

Left-wing views on society and crime:

Left-wing views see things very differently and tend to focus on issues of power and inequality in society. They argue that people at the bottom are victims of their circumstances, and that equality should be the goal of society. The state should intervene to share out the wealth and ensure everyone has equal chances.

The unequal system creates situations which may lead individuals into deviance and crime, thus left-wing views would blame the system rather than the individual deviant. Deviance could be a result of necessity or desperation, a reaction to labelling or unequal treatment or an act of resistance against inequality. Left-wing views also tend to argue that the law is not applied equally: 'crime' is defined and enforced by those with power.

Marxists are the main left-wing view of crime, but interactionists are also seen as left-wing, in their consideration of power and labelling, and radical criminology also takes a left-wing view. We will be considering views of left realists later in this section.

Right-wing views on crime: Control theory and the New Right

There are several newer right-wing views on crime and deviance. Sometimes these are all referred to as 'right realists' but actually there are differences between them. What they have in common is that they all share the general right-wing view of human nature, and are all influenced by Durkheim and functionalism.

Control theory

Instead of asking why people commit deviance and crime, Hirschi (1969) reverses the question to ask why most people do not.

Social bonds, Travis Hirschi (1969)

Hirschi's answer to the question of why people do not commit crime is that most people are too well-integrated into society and its norms and values and have too much to lose. He argues that it is those who do not have strong 'social bonds' who are more likely to commit crimes.

Hirschi's four 'social bonds':

Attachment – This relates to being attached to others in society, for example, family, friends and colleagues, and caring about them and about what they think. This would prevent many people from considering deviance, since violating the norms of society would go against the expectations that others have of you.

Commitment – This is about having responsibilities, such as a job, dependents, a house and possessions.

People obey rules for fear the consequences of breaking them. The risk is too great as they have too much to lose.

Involvement – This refers to being part of a community, a family, a workplace or a social group, and *'engrossment in conventional activities'*. People who are involved are too busy and occupied to consider deviance – they have a purpose.

Belief – This involves subscribing to a common value system within a culture, including religious beliefs, but also society's general morals or values. Such beliefs will be developed through socialisation and will prevent people from considering deviance, since they know it is 'wrong'.

1 Look back at your answer to the question above – do any of the reasons you gave correspond to those given by Hirschi?

Hirschi's argument is essentially that individuals with strong family and friendship networks, with responsibilities, who are engaged in social activities and who have a strong sense of morality, will be unlikely to commit crime. Statistics on the prison population tends to support Hirschi's ideas.

The New Right

The New Right view of criminality is largely put forward by Charles Murray. It is often included as part of right realism, but some of the conclusions and the policies suggested by the New Right do differ from other right realist ideas.

Murray argues that inadequate socialisation can lead young people from the 'underclass' to develop a culture characterised by dependency, lack of discipline and respect, criminality and laziness. He blames over-generous welfare payments for encouraging 'feckless' behaviour, and condemns the increase in single mothers raising young boys with no father in their lives, seeing 'illegitimacy' *as* a greater indicator of criminality than poverty alone. He suggests that girls without fathers may be emotionally damaged and search for a father substitute, often getting pregnant at an early age. Even more concerning is boys growing up without fathers, who '...tend to have poor impulse

control, to be sexual predators, to be unable to get up at the same time every morning and go to a job' (Murray 2005).

Murray and Herrnstein (1994) also consider the impact of cognitive ability, or intelligence, on criminal behaviour. Using IQ data, which has been subsequently challenged, they attempted to demonstrate that there is a correlation between low IQ and criminality. Even more controversially, they linked low IQ with race, though they did argue that white people with low IQ are also more likely to commit crime.

Evaluation of Murray's ideas

Murray's claims, that those in the underclass have a dependency culture and deviant values, have been challenged by many sociologists. For example, Gallie (1994) interviewed the long-term unemployed about their attitudes towards work. He found that most of the unemployed had a strong 'work ethic' and wanted to work, and there was no evidence of dependency culture. Similarly, Charlesworth's study of deprivation in Rotherham (1999) found that despite the clear effects which poverty had on people's physical and mental health, most still had strong moral values and did not commit crime, even though it would have been an 'easy option'.

Activity: Benefits Street

People protesting against 'Benefits Street' outside the Channel 4 offices.

In 2014, Channel 4 screened 'Benefits Street', a documentary claiming to show the reality of life on benefits, featuring one street in Birmingham. The show proved both popular and controversial, for the way in which it portrayed people dependent on welfare payments, showing many of those in the street committing crimes. Some of the participants complained that they had been misrepresented, claiming that they were originally told that the show was about the community spirit in deprived areas, and that the title was not mentioned to them. Many critics felt the show stigmatised those on benefits, with the leader of Birmingham City Council describing it as 'negative and simplistic'. He said that 60 per cent of Birmingham's poorest families who were claiming benefit were actually in work. One critic described the show as 'a medieval stocks updated for a modern format', and it was also dubbed 'poverty porn'. Channel 4 defended the show and has made similar programmes in other areas, though not all have welcomed the film makers. In Stockton, a banner reading 'Being poor is not entertainment' was put up. Grimsby MP Austin Mitchell asked the broadcaster to 'consider the ethics of ... demonising the poor and making poverty entertainment'.

1 Consider reasons why documentary makers may wish to make programmes such as those discussed above. What do you think Murray's opinion of such programmes may be?
2 How does the statistic used by the leader of Birmingham City Council challenge Murray's ideas?
3 How else can you criticise Murray's arguments about poverty and crime?

Young (2003) challenges the distorted picture presented by the New Right as a 'sociology of vindictiveness', that seeks to 'punish, demean and humiliate' those at the bottom of society. He argues that certain sections of society, such as teenage mothers, beggars and immigrants, are portrayed as contributing to the problems of society quite disproportionally to their actual impact. Young suggests that these groups are an 'easy enemy' and become scapegoats.

The evidence on which Murray and Herrnstein's ideas on IQ are based is questionable, since IQ tests are challenged as being culturally biased. Additionally, the assumption that there is a causal link between IQ and crime based on the IQ of people in prison fails to consider that other factors, such as poverty, may be influencing both IQ and criminality. The link to race can also be challenged – the criminal justice system is criticised as institutionally racist, and those from ethnic minorities may be more likely to be arrested, charged and sentenced more harshly, not due to IQ but due to racism.

Realist criminology

Realist ideas in criminology arose in the 1970s and 1980s and can be split into right realism (sometimes called 'new realism') and left realism (sometimes called 'radical realism'). As 'realists' they do share some basic ideas:

- Realists tend to accept the 'typical criminal' shown in the police recorded crime figures as a starting point for their explanations of crime. Though these statistics may be flawed and even inaccurate, they do reflect real crimes.
- Realists challenge some of the traditional theories for being too 'idealistic' and romanticising the criminal.
- Realist views share a concern about the 'corrosive effects which crime can have on communities' (Matthews and Young, 1992), focusing on the 'lived reality of crime' and its effects on victims and communities.
- They challenge traditional theories for being too remote and offering no practical solutions. Both types of realism offer practical policies to address crime rates.

However, there are clear differences between realists. Right realists take conventional definitions of crime for granted, focusing almost exclusively on 'street crime', whereas left realists, whilst recognising the importance of street crime to many people, do seek to challenge this narrow view of crime and consider white-collar crime and global crime as well. In attempting to explain crime, right realists, in common with other right-wing views of crime, still tend to put the blame on the individual offenders, focusing on solutions which will control such people. However, left realists focus more on social injustices, inequalities and relationships between the police, wider society and offenders, and can thus be seen as part of radical criminology.

Right realism

Wilson (1975) challenges mainstream criminology, particularly Marxist criminology, for being based on ideology rather than facts, for example with its over-emphasis of white-collar crime. He argues that the morals of society must be upheld, and implies that trying to understand and thus justify criminality is not desirable.

Wilson suggests that long-term trends in crime can be accounted for primarily by three factors:

1 Young males are the group most likely to commit crime, since they are temperamentally aggressive and tend to have short-term horizons. Thus, shifts in the age-structure of the population will increase or decrease the crime rate, as greater or fewer numbers of young males are around.

2 There may be changes in the benefits and the costs of crime at different times, due to accessibility, the economy, the availability of jobs and so on, which will change the rate at which crimes occur, especially property crimes.

3 Broad social and cultural changes in society, reinforced through the family, the media and religion, may influence general norms and values, which may in turn affect the extent to which certain 'at risk' individuals are tempted into deviance or are willing to conform.

Wilson argues that these factors are largely uncontrollable, so no government can actually prevent crime at source. He does not believe that poverty is the root cause of crime, pointing out that many poor people do not commit crime. Thus, attempts to redistribute wealth, for example, are costly, unfair and will do little to reduce crime. Crime can only be addressed by enforcing the law. Wilson places less emphasis on the severity of punishment and more stress on the certainty of capture: if a criminal does not believe he will be caught, the punishment is irrelevant as a deterrent.

Thus, the environment plays a key role in creating a 'culture' of order and acceptable behaviour. If social order is clearly maintained, then individuals will not be tempted to participate in deviant behaviour and if the police are visibly clamping down on crime, a culture will be created where other residents also report crime more and are involved in informal social control. However, if there is an impression that no-one cares, and that disorder is prevalent, then even previously law-abiding people may see it as acceptable to join in with deviant behaviour.

Additionally, Wilson and Kelling (1982) argue that the community will change its behaviour in the face of low level disorder, 'staying indoors' more and 'not getting involved', which will tend to escalate the likelihood that crime will start to flourish, with no one to challenge it. This can lead to the development of urban decay and crime will start to flourish. Those who can, will move away and an area may go into a downward spiral. They argue that once an area has a criminal culture there is little point trying to police it. A foot patrol becomes useless in a very crime-ridden area – police should spend efforts elsewhere where they can make a difference. Those areas at the tipping point should be identified, where order can be restored with a visible police presence. Right realist solutions to criminality are explored more fully in the next section, on page 93.

Broken Windows, Wilson and Kelling (1982)

Wilson and Kelling based their ideas on psychology experiments and a study into policing in Newark, New York in the mid-1970s. The police study, as a response to public opinion, experimented with increasing police foot patrols, or 'bobbies on the beat' as it is described in the UK. The local residents, after a five-year programme of increased foot patrols, indicated that they felt much safer and that crime had reduced. The police officers on patrol had a better relationship with the residents, and had taken on an 'order maintenance' role, addressing low-level deviance such as public drunkenness, rowdy behaviour and begging.

The psychology studies Wilson and Kelling considered demonstrated the 'broken windows' phenomenon – when a derelict building has one broken window, the others will soon follow. The principle is that when people identify a building or property as derelict and uncared for, they will see it as acceptable to further vandalise it. Wilson and Kelling report an experiment by the psychologist Zimbardo, who left an abandoned car in a middle class area and a similar one in a more run-down area. The second car was vandalised quite quickly, and in a few days had been completely stripped. The first car was not touched, until Zimbardo returned and smashed one of the car's windows. After that, others quickly followed suit, and within a few hours the car had been destroyed. For Wilson and Kelling this demonstrated that once communal barriers have been broken down, deviance can happen anywhere. In applying this more widely, they suggest that 'untended behaviour' leads to a breakdown of community controls. So in relation to the Newark experiment, the presence of the police and their ability to address low-level disorder created an orderly environment less conducive to crime.

1 Apply this analysis to your own experience of litter. In what environment may you be more likely to drop a piece of litter? In what context would you definitely not litter?

Broken windows

Item A:

Item B

The UK riots in August 2011

A Home Affairs Committee of MPs looked into causes of riots which took place in many parts of the UK in August 2011, and concluded that:

'The single most important reason why the disorder spread was the perception, relayed by television as well as social media, that in some areas the police had lost control of the streets.

What ultimately worked in quelling the disorder was increasing the number of police officers on duty and flooding the streets with police.'

Source: Home Affairs Committee Report 19 December 2011

1 Explain how Item B illustrates Wilson and Kelling's argument
2 How do Wilson and Kelling's ideas link to Durkheim's concept of anomie? Use Item A and Item B to explain links between the two ideas.

In his earlier work, Wilson (1975) stated that 'wicked people exist'. Wilson and Herrnstein (1985) also emphasise that there is a biological element to criminal behaviour. They challenge the (left-wing) criminologists who seek to deny the importance of individual characteristics, such as impulsiveness or temper, arguing that some people do have a predisposition for criminality. These 'criminal' traits in some individuals will be heightened if they lack proper socialisation. In a strong nuclear family, criminal tendencies may be suppressed, as the right norms and values are taught. However, some families, such as single-parent families or those which lack a commitment to society's norms and values, may not provide the important socialisation needed.

These ideas are close to those of the New Right and put the blame for criminality squarely on the individual, their biology and their upbringing. Indeed, Herrnstein worked with Murray on ideas about IQ and criminality (see page 70). Thus some of the same criticisms levelled at the Murray and the New Right are also applicable to Wilson's right realist argument.

However, the main challenge to right realism is that it plays down the causes of offending, focusing instead on the failures in social control and punishment. Young (1992) argues that deviance and control cannot be studied independently of each other, as they are parts of the same equation.

Left realism

Young (1986) argues that it is important for left realism to navigate between the two extremes often found in criminology: the hysteria about the underclass, media driven moral panics and the over-policing of crime in certain communities (characterised by New Right and right realist views); and the denial of the severity of street crime and its impact (characterised by 'left idealists' such as Marxism and radical criminology). Left realists accept that white-collar and corporate crime are significant, and they do question people on these in their research. However, they argue that 'left idealists' overemphasise these types of crime to the exclusion of other crimes. Left realists also accuse left idealists of having a romantic view of the criminal as a victim of circumstances, or a misunderstood rebel – they call this the 'Robin Hood' thesis.

> **Quick question**
>
> Where in this chapter have you already come across Young's ideas?

According to left realists, there has been a *real* and significant increase in levels of street crime, and the fear surrounding such crime. This cannot all be explained by biased policing or moral panics. The 'perception' of crime as a problem has a significant effect on people's lives and behaviour, especially in certain areas. For example, in the second Islington crime survey it was found that 80.5 per cent of people saw crime as problem affecting their lives. Women were found to be particularly affected, with many not going out after dark due to fear of crime.

The square of crime

Matthews and Young (1992) see the notion of the 'square of crime' as an important reminder to criminologists that crime arises at an intersection. Any understanding of the roles of the offender and the victim must be supplemented with an understanding of the role of public opinion and informal control, expressed through the media, the influence of peers, the community, the family and so on. The fourth element is the role of the State, in the form of the formal agencies of social control, such as the government, police and criminal justice system. These last two clearly intersect, since public sentiment can drive government policy and police practice, and vice versa.

In their recognition of the social construction of 'crime' and the role of individual interpretations and structural processes, left realist ideas are similar to the radical criminologists considered above, and Young acknowledges this. However, left realism focuses on victims more than other radical views.

CRIMINAL JUSTICE SYSTEM	CRIMINAL OFFENDER
GENERAL PUBLIC	VICTIM OF CRIME

1 Consider the example of a street robbery, where a middle-aged female was threatened with a knife and her bag was stolen.
2 Produce an analysis of this 'crime' from the four points of the 'square of crime' shown above. For example, consider:
   a) What would the event mean to each agent, and what response may they have to it?
   b) How will the response of each affect the other three agents?

Left realist explanations for crime

Study

What is to be done about Law and Order? John Lea and Jock Young (1993)

Lea and Young explain crime in terms of three concepts:

- **Relative deprivation** – This concept relates to feelings of deprivation which people may experience when they compare themselves to others in their society. It used to be assumed that as societies became wealthier, crime rates would fall. However, the reverse has proved true, and the concept of relative deprivation can help to explain this. In wealthy countries, the gap between the 'haves' and the 'have-nots' is vast, and we are continually encouraged to strive for more and to judge ourselves against those more successful than ourselves. Relative deprivation may be fuelled by the media, which shows us what others appear to have, and promotes materialism and false needs. It can be linked to Young's concept of the 'bulimic society' (see pages 58–9).
- **Marginalisation** – This concept refers to those on the edges or margins of society, who lack clearly defined goals, involvement and representation in society. Those who are marginalised, or socially excluded, may feel abandoned and frustrated, experiencing economic, social and political deprivation.

- **Subculture** – This is used to refer to a group with a shared set of norms and values, developed as a response to the norms and values of wider society, which may be unachievable. The formation of subcultures is linked to relative deprivation and marginalisation, as those who share a sense of deprivation and frustration will develop lifestyles which allow them to cope with this problem.

Though they are left-wing, Lea and Young are influenced by subcultural theorists such as Cohen and also by Merton. So ideas such as anomie, strain and status frustration can be particularly applied to those who are relatively deprived, marginalised and operate in subcultures.

However, left-wing influences can clearly be seen in Lea and Young's analysis, which sees the social and economic circumstances of the individual, rather than their upbringing and choices, to be the key causes of criminality.

1 Consider some common crimes. Do the three concepts put forward by Lea and Young provide a convincing explanation for these crimes?
2 Can you think of any crimes which cannot be explained in these terms?

The exclusive society

In later work, Young (1999) developed the concepts of relative deprivation and marginalisation, focusing on the way in which society economically excludes increasing numbers of people, and drawing a link between social exclusion and crime. Referring to Hutton's view of the '40:30:30 society' (40 per cent secure employment, 30 per cent insecure employment, 30 per cent marginalised/idle/poverty), Young argues that as economic exclusion increases, this leads to social exclusion, the breakdown of communities and families and an increase in crime and disorder. This can create a culture of fear, which can lead to scapegoating and even more social divisions. Young is concerned that this breakdown in consensus is leading to a less tolerant society, with harsher reactions towards the excluded and the deviant. This lack of tolerance partially comes from the right-wing of sociology, and what Young calls the 'sociology of vindictiveness'.

Despite their use of victim surveys, left realists are challenged for their lack of evidence on the motives of offenders themselves. Some also question how 'new' their ideas are – left realism can be seen as merely an extension of radical criminology. What distinguishes realist criminology is its focus on practical solutions,

and some of the 'solutions' presented by left realists, such as addressing the fundamental inequalities in society, can be seen as decidedly 'unrealistic'.

There are clear distinctions between right and left realists. By explaining crime in terms of deprivation and exclusion, left realists are focusing on the impact of society and inequalities on individual behaviour. In contrast, the right realists are focusing more on the socialisation and norms and values of offenders. This distinction is demonstrated clearly in the different solutions to crime that each view puts forward. These are considered in detail on page 91.

Check your understanding

Briefly explain the following concepts, and link them to the sociologist who used them:

1 Social bonds
2 The underclass
3 Broken windows
4 The sociology of vindictiveness
5 The square of crime
6 Relative deprivation
7 Marginalisation

Section summary

Make a copy of the following passage and fill in the blanks, using the words given below

In attempting to explain criminal behaviour, sociological theories can be broadly split into right-wing and _____ views. All explanations attempt to explain the link between social class and offending rates, and subcultural theorists also particularly focus on issues of age.

Right-wing views include more traditional theories such as _____, which focuses on the functions of crime in reinforcing _____ and acting as a _____, and on the concept of strain, when the socially accepted goals become more important than the socially accepted means of achieving them. These ideas are particularly associated with _____, and he has influenced subcultural views such as those of Cohen and _____, but also newer right-wing views such as _____.

Left-wing views are generally influenced by _____, but interactionists also address issues of power and control, rather than focusing on _____ as right-wing sociologists do. Radical criminologists have combined aspects of these two left-wing theories, and concept of the _____ has been developed by left realists to demonstrate this 'complete' approach to understanding crime.

Though the right and left-wing divide seems clear, _____ has clearly been influenced by both approaches, combining ideas of _____ and status with an awareness of structural inequalities.

cultural criminology, Marxism, safety valve, left-wing, square of crime, Merton, anomie, boundaries, right realism, socialisation, Cloward and Ohlin, functionalism

---

Crimes of the powerful: White-collar crime and corporate crime

White-collar crime is often taken to refer to crime committed by professionals in the course of their employment. However, it is a problematic concept

with a vague meaning and is used by different groups of sociologists to refer to different activities, from an employee stealing paper clips from work to a multi-national corporation knowingly taking health and safety risks to maximise profits.

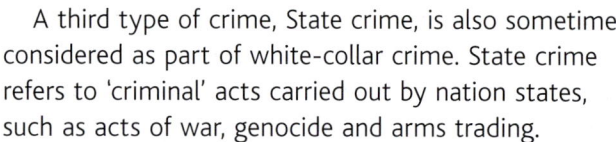

Some of the activities often considered under the heading of white-collar crime are not actually criminal offences, but could or should be seen as criminal, according to some Marxist sociologists, such as tax avoidance or price fixing.

White-collar crime was originally defined by Sutherland (1949) as 'a crime committed by a person of respectability and high social status in the course his occupation'. Thus it would not include an upper-class person who stabs his enemy – since this is not occupational, and would also not include those in the criminal underworld running protection rackets – since they lack the respectability and status Sutherland mentions. Croall (2001a) challenges the use of the word 'crime' in Sutherland's definition, given the earlier point that some activity is not technically criminal, and also questions whether the status of the person is always important, since it may be the position of trust which they hold which causes the harm. An alternative definition, given by Croall is 'an abuse of a legitimate occupational role that is regulated by law'.

However, it is helpful to recognise that those considering white-collar crime are often considering two distinct types of crime:

1 Occupational crime – crime committed by employees in the course of their jobs, for example, stealing from or defrauding an employer;
2 Corporate crime – crime carried out by businesses or corporations, often motivated by a desire to increase or protect profits.

A third type of crime, State crime, is also sometimes considered as part of white-collar crime. State crime refers to 'criminal' acts carried out by nation states, such as acts of war, genocide and arms trading.

White-collar crime is very difficult to estimate and investigate. People in powerful positions are able to use their financial and political power to escape arrest and conviction, which could explain the under-representation of white-collar crime in the official statistics. It is also unlikely to appear in victim surveys. Victims of crimes such as fraud may be unaware of their victimisation, and if a company is the victim of employee white-collar crime it may decide not to publicise the matter even if it becomes aware. Other crimes, such as corruption, are often seen as 'victimless', though arguably the public at large are the eventual victims. For example, prices often rise to cover losses caused by white-collar crime.

Marxists argue that the criminal law is a tool of the ruling class, and thus the powerful actually create the law to serve their own interests, criminalising activities which they see as undesirable whilst allowing other activities, which may be even more damaging to the general population, to continue. The powerful are also able to manipulate the public perception of criminality. For example, Box (1983) points out that the way society defines criminality focuses on working class criminals. So what we see as 'theft' would be more likely to involve a working class shoplifter, rather than a company charging high prices, or a bank charging people to use their own money. Thus he argues that white-collar crime is not 'socially constructed' as crime, and is given less focus than crimes committed by the powerful, even though they ultimately cause more harm to society.

Illustrating Box's point, Tombs (1999) analysed deaths at work caused by employer activity. He found a total of 1,316 fatal injuries in the period 1994–95, including 36 fatalities from the supply or use of flammable liquids and 877 fatalities associated with driving in the course of employment. Occupationally caused fatal illnesses such as asbestosis and lung disease produced a further 1702 deaths. He concludes that the scale of unlawful workplace deaths 'vastly outweighs the numbers of recorded homicides', which stood in that year at 834 homicides in England, Wales and Scotland.

Goldstraw-White (2010) found that even those convicted of white-collar crimes often do not see themselves as 'real criminals'. She conducted semi-structured interviews with 41 offenders imprisoned for white-collar crimes, such as fraud and tax evasion. Though the value of their offences ranged from £18 million to £100 million, she found that many did not accept that they had done anything wrong, distinguishing themselves from other inmates. They felt morally justified in what they had done, and stressed that they did not 'hurt' anyone, resisting the label of criminal.

Risk plays a large part in white-collar crime according to Friedrichs (1996). Though the chances of being caught and punished are very low, such activity does involve a calculated gamble, which may be part of the appeal. However, he also points out that corporate decision making often involves a cost-benefit analysis, in which the possible risks of cutting corners (for example, in terms of the safety of workers, customers and the general public) are weighed against the additional profits which may be generated. Though weighing life against profit can be seen as fundamentally immoral, Friedrichs argues that such calculations play a central role in business.

Activity

Examples of white-collar crime

Item A

The Bhopal disaster involved a gas leak at the Union Carbide chemical company in Bhopal, India in 1984, which killed at least 3,787 people, and caused 10's of thousands of serious and permanently disabling injuries. There were allegations that the leak was caused by the company cutting corners in their health and safety precautions. In June 2010, seven ex-employees, including the former UCIL chairman, were convicted in Bhopal of causing death by negligence and sentenced to two years imprisonment and a fine of approximately $2,000 each. The company ended its responsibility for the clean-up in 1998, but the site remains contaminated.

Item B

General Motors were found to have dangerously positioned the fuel tank on their Chevrolet Malibu cars in the 1970s, causing a high risk of fire. Evidence was discovered showing that GM knew about the risk, but conducted a cost-benefit analysis, calculating that with 500 fuel-led fatalities per year, their payout in compensation would be less than if they recalled all the cars – saving them $6.19 per vehicle. At a civil trial for compensation from one victim's family, $4.8 billion was awarded in punitive damages by a jury. This was later reduced on appeal by a judge. A similar issue involving the Ford Pinto car was uncovered in the 1970s and there was evidence that they too conducted a cost-benefit analysis, also deciding against a recall.

Item C

The 2010 BP disaster was the largest accidental marine oil spill in the history of the petroleum industry. The explosion killed 11 platform workers and injured 17 others. The spill caused extensive damage to marine and wildlife habitats, and to the region's fishing and tourism industries. An internal investigation found that managers had misinterpreted data that told them a blowout was imminent on the very day the disaster happened. The investigation has also suggested that the team leader overseeing the project ignored warnings about weaknesses in cement outside the well which could have prevented the gas from escaping.

1 Do the above examples amount to crime in your opinion? Which 'crimes' have actually been committed?

2 Were those responsible punished adequately?

3 Is the 'cost-benefit' analysis undertaken by corporations justifiable in a profit driven economy?

Explaining white-collar crime

To undertake this activity you will need to have considered the explanations of crime covered earlier in this chapter.

Item A

Rogue trader

Nick Leeson was a trader for Barings Bank, personal bank to the Queen. From 1992, he made unauthorised speculative trades that at first made large profits for Barings, earning Leeson a huge bonus. However, when he started making losses, he covered it up and took even more risks to try to recoup the money. By the end of 1992 the losses exceeded £2 million, which ballooned to £208 million by the end of 1994. Leeson left a note reading 'I'm sorry' and fled Singapore.

Losses eventually reached £827 million, and after a failed bailout attempt, Barings was declared insolvent. Leeson was jailed for 6 ½ years.

1 Apply each of the following to explain why individuals such as Nick Leeson may commit white-collar crime:
   a) Merton – strain theory (anomie)
   b) Cohen – status
   c) Lyng – edgework
   d) Young – relative deprivation and the bulimic society
   e) Matza – techniques of neutralisation
   f) Gordon – a rational response to capitalism
   g) Sutherland and Cressey – differential association

However, despite evidence about the prevalence of and harm done by crimes of the powerful, realists argue that, in reality, what ordinary people care about and are frightened of is street crime. Thus, Marxists could be accused of over-emphasising the importance of white-collar crime, rather than accepting the 'fact' that most criminals are from the working class.

Explanations for white-collar crime:

- **Personality based approaches** – Psychologists argue that certain personality types can be linked to success in business, but they may also be linked to criminality. For example, successful people are likely to be ambitious, but also possibly unscrupulous and prepared to tread on others to reach top. This lack of personal morality may explain why successful people may also sometimes 'cross the line' and commit white-collar crime.

- **Differential Association** – Sutherland and Cressey's (1955) theory of differential association relates to the frequency of exposure to deviant definitions, which can affect an individual's tendency to follow a deviant path, as he or she learns 'appropriate' responses to different situations. Criminal practices may become the cultural norm amongst people in some businesses, thus the white-collar criminal may not see him or herself as deviant at all, but see the behaviour as appropriate in the context of the workplace culture.

Other explanations for crime considered previously tend to relate to working-class crime, for example, status-frustration, subculture, poverty and inequality. These do not seem to apply to white-collar crime – or do they?

Explaining the relationship between gender and crime, including feminist explanations

Are women getting away with offending?

Pollak (1950) argued that the idea that males commit significantly more crime than females is a myth, caused by the differences in the types of crimes committed and the differences in the perception and treatment of male and female offenders. There is a biological element to his analysis, as he suggests that women are compelled by their physiology to commit certain crimes: their hormones and menstrual cycles cause emotional disturbance and low self-esteem. He also claims that women are biologically more devious than men, given their need to conceal menstruation, fake orgasms and the requirement for them to have a passive role in society. They use their home environment to conceal their crimes and women prefer professions like maids, nurses and teachers so that they can engage in undetectable domestic crime.

Women also manipulate men to commit crime for them – they are often the mastermind and beneficiary, but avoid arrest since male partners take the blame. Pollak additionally suggests that chivalry within the criminal justice system results in more lenient treatment of female offenders. Though much of Pollak's argument has no basis in evidence, the 'chivalry thesis' has been put forward by several criminologists, suggesting that females are 'getting away with' their offences

The chivalry thesis: differences in the treatment of male and female offenders

The chivalry thesis is the argument that the male-dominated criminal justice system has a paternalistic and indulgent attitude towards women, seeing them as vulnerable, child-like and not fully responsible for their actions. This may lead male police officers to let females off with warnings or cautions, or charge them with lesser offences, and may lead male judges and magistrates to sentence female offenders more leniently.

There is some evidence to support the idea of chivalry within the criminal justice system – female criminals do tend to receive more lenient sentences from the courts for certain types of offences. For example, Speed and Burrows (2006) found in their review of sentencing for shoplifting cases in 2004–5 that male offenders were twice as likely to receive a custodial sentence as female offenders (30 per cent, as against 15 per cent).

However, chivalry can be challenged as too simplistic. Klein (1973) argues that the concept of chivalry is racist and classist, founded on the notion of women as 'ladies', and that this only applicable to middle class white women, who are the least likely to come into contact with the criminal justice system in the first place. Heidensohn (1986) suggests that female offenders who conform to the expectation of feminine behaviour, by crying or showing maternal love, may be treated more 'leniently' than males, but those who do not are treated more severely. Carlen (1983) points out that a female's role as a mother is also taken into account much more than a male's role as a father in sentencing – which can lead to the appearance of leniency, since many female offenders have children.

Courts take into account various factors when sentencing any offender. Mitigating factors operate in the offender's favour and may reduce the sentence, for example, a lack of previous offending, a guilty plea or personal circumstances. Aggravating factors have the opposite effect, and may increase the severity of a sentence. These may include a lack of remorse, a prior history of offending and the use of a weapon. Though Farrington and Morris (1983) found some empirical evidence that women did receive less severe punishments, they also found that female offenders are far more likely to be first-time offenders, to plead

guilty and to have committed a less serious form of the relevant offence; they stole smaller or fewer items, used less violence, and so on. They concluded that female offenders are not being treated any differently from males when mitigating factors are taken into account. Hedderman and Gunby (2013) found, in their interviews with judges and magistrates involved in sentencing, that there was an awareness that female offenders often have much more complex problems. One magistrate pointed out that much female offender crime is related to their relationships with men, including domestic violence and single-parenthood. The fact that these mitigating factors are taken into account when sentencing may be completely appropriate, and not evidence of 'chivalry' at all.

Activity

Chivalry in the criminal justice system?

In the five years from 2009 to 2013, males were more likely to be given an immediate custodial sentence than females. The differences can be largely attributed to the different types of offences males and females, with females more likely to commit the less serious offences.

Female offenders were less likely than male offenders to have any previous cautions or convictions throughout the 10 years from 2003 to 2013, with a third of females and only a fifth of males being first-time offenders in 2013.

In 2013, for the offence categories of 'theft, dishonesty and fraud', and 'assault and public order offences', female offenders were more likely than males to have mitigating factors applied to their sentence, such as the appearance of genuine remorse and the offender having caring responsibilities. Males were generally more likely than females to have aggravating factors applied, such as being a member of a group or gang and evidence of pre-planning or pre-meditation.

Source: Ministry of Justice (2014)

1 In what ways does this evidence support the chivalry thesis?
2 What other explanations, apart from chivalry, does the evidence suggest may account for differences in sentencing for male and female offenders?

On the other hand, there is evidence that, far from the lenience suggested by the chivalry thesis, females may be treated more harshly than

Female offenders – mad or bad?

Item A

Procek (1980)

Procek (1980) argues that the approach by the criminal justice system to understanding and dealing with female criminals is always psychological. An explanation of depression is more acceptable for a female than aggression, whereas for men it may be the other way round. Female crime is also over-sexualised – linked to menstruation, the menopause and hormones. Conversely, male sentencing tends to focus on environmental and social factors, for example, a male offender having lost his job, having difficult family circumstances, being provoked or being influenced by friends.

Item B

Sentencing case-studies

1989: Kiranjit Ahluwahlia was originally convicted of murder and sentenced to life imprisonment for the murder of her husband, who had physically and psychologically abused her for years. Her conviction was eventually overturned on the grounds of diminished responsibility, though provocation was rejected as a defence at her original trial.

1991: Joseph McGrail received a suspended sentence for kicking his wife to death. He pleaded provocation on the grounds that she was an alcoholic and swore at him. The judge said the dead woman 'would have tried the patience of a saint'.

2008: Joanne Hill, a mother who drowned her disabled daughter in a bath was convicted of murder and sentenced to life in prison, after a jury rejected her defence of diminished responsibility. Hill had a history of mental health problems dating back 15 years.

1997: Joseph Swinburne was sentenced to 200 hours community service after successfully pleading provocation as a defence to stabbing his wife 11 times when she told him she was leaving him for another man.

1 Consider the case-studies in Item B. In what ways do they support or refute the arguments put forward by Procek in Item A, the chivalry thesis, and the argument that female offenders are treated more harshly than their male counterparts?

---

their male counterparts in some circumstances. For example, behaviour which would be seen as 'high spirits' in boys is seen as abnormal and unacceptable in girls, and thus teenage girls are sometimes subject to stricter sanctions for relatively minor transgressions. Chesney-Lind (1989) argues that female deviance tends to be 'sexualised' – attributed to a lack of morality, being 'easy' and 'out of control'. Though female delinquency has received little attention from criminologists in comparison to male delinquency, historically the labelling and interventions into the lives of female delinquents in the USA had a significant impact on lives of many young girls. In her research into US courts in the nineteenth and early twentieth century, Chesney-Lind found many more girls than boys were sent to 'training schools', and girls were charged with 'waywardness' or 'immorality' based on their sexual behaviour.

When women do commit serious offences, especially if they are violent and/or involving children, they are going against female stereotypes. These women are often demonised by the media, and presented as 'monsters', devoid of any feminine characteristics – this is sometimes referred to as the 'evil woman' theory. The media portrayal and public perception of Myra Hindley, the Moors Murderer, is a good example. Despite her death in prison in 2002, in the public mind she arguably remains more notorious and hated than Ian Brady, her co-defendant, even though it is widely accepted that he was the driving force behind the pair's killings of five children in the early 1960s. It has been suggested, for example by her biographer Jean Ritchie, that if Hindley had played her part in the original trial differently, renouncing Brady and showing more emotion and remorse, she may have been treated less harshly by the court and the media.

Biological explanations for gender differences in criminality

Early criminologists often explained crime and deviance in terms of biology, and these explanations were also applied to the difference in levels of male and female criminality.

Though recognising the impact of social conditions on criminality, Lombroso (1898) argued that biological anomalies were a more significant indicator, seeing the habitual criminal as halfway between 'the lunatic' and 'the savage'. He claimed that most women are genetically less inclined towards criminality, showing a natural passivity and not possessing enough intelligence or initiative to break the law. However, the female 'born criminal', though few in number, could be especially savage. By studying the physiology of female criminals, he concluded that they possessed genetic anomalies, showed masculine traits and a lack of maternal instinct.

Thomas (1907) argued that men and women possess essentially different personality traits. Men have more active natures and women are more passive, impacting on their tendency to criminality. In a later work (1923) Thomas argued that women require more social approval and affection than men. The socially acceptable way of achieving this involves accepting domesticity, and this is the path which middle-class women take. Poor females, who lack socialisation and morality, may refuse to take on a submissive role, but may instead use their sexuality for emotional gain: '*The beginning of delinquency in girls is usually an impulse to get amusement, adventure, pretty clothes, favourable notice...*'. Critics have suggested that, like Pollak, Thomas was expanding on the biblical myth of the scheming and manipulative woman, and showed ignorance of the extreme economic hardships facing the deprived women he described.

In opposition to these early accounts of female criminality, most sociologists consider the expectations of society and the process of socialisation to have a more significant impact on criminality than any 'natural' traits.

Functionalist explanations: Sex-role theory

Functionalists focus on socialisation, particularly within the family, as an explanation of the higher levels of male criminality, and by implication, the lower levels of female criminality. Sex-role theory contends that boys and girls are socialised differently, resulting in boys becoming more delinquent. Sutherland (1949) stated that there are clear gender differences when it comes to socialisation. Firstly, girls are more supervised, taught to be more passive and domesticated and are more strictly controlled. Boys are encouraged to take risks, and to be ambitious, extrovert, tough and aggressive. Therefore, boys have more opportunity and inclination to commit crime. If some women do become deviant, it may be because they have been socialised in more masculine ways, maybe as tomboys or with brothers.

Parsons (1955) believes that there are clear and obvious gender roles within the nuclear family. The father performs the 'instrumental' role which requires him to be the leader and provider, whilst the mother performs the 'expressive' role of giving emotional support and socialising children. Girls are socialised into more submissive and caring behaviour compared to boys, which is less conducive to deviance. Additionally, girls have a readily available female role model at home (their mother) whereas boys have less access to their male role model as traditionally the father was out at work for most of the time. Parsons argues that the young male child experiences 'status anxiety' and has difficulty identifying with the correct sex – this can lead to exaggerated masculine behaviour and frustration, which may be channelled into delinquency.

Feminist explanations

Much feminist work on explaining female offending rates has focused not on why some females *do* commit crime, but why the majority *do not*. Such feminist views also focus on socialisation, so to an extent their ideas may seem similar to the views of functionalists. However, the feminist views also highlight the controls placed on women and girls in patriarchal society which prevent them from having the opportunities which may lead to criminality. Feminists see this as a form of patriarchy, rather than as a desirable reinforcement of 'natural' roles.

Smart (1976) looked at the stricter socialisation and control over girls within the family. These controls on how often, and when, girls are allowed to go out, and where and with whom they are allowed to go, are fed by exaggerated fears about safety. Stranger sex attacks are very rare, and boys are actually more likely to become victims of physical attacks, but parental fear leads to girls and women becoming prisoners in their own homes.

For males, crime can be seen as role-expressive – an extension of the male role of protector, provider and dominant aggressor. However, for females, crime is role-distorting – going against their expected role of nurturer and carer. Women have more to lose if they do deviate – they not only risk prosecution and punishment, but also disapproval and being seen as 'unfeminine', whereas a male criminal is still thought of as a true man. So a female deviant is 'doubly deviant'.

Women and social control, Frances Heidensohn (1996)

Heidensohn argues that women experience four forms of control, which tend to lead to conformity rather than deviance:

- At home: through their role as housewife and mother, in terms of the expectations of nurturing, the constraints placed on women's activities and the 'supervision' which women are placed under;
- In public: via notions of 'reputation', the male monopoly of violence and fears of victimisation, and through expectations of 'a woman's place' and men's control of the public domain;
- At work: through the dual burden of the housewife role and that of waged worker, and through their subordinate roles in the workplace itself;
- In social policy: such as welfare and benefits provisions which tend to reinforce women's position as primary carers.

Females are particularly controlled through familial ideology. A woman's expected primary role is arguably still that of housewife and mother. In fulfilling this role, women play a key part in maintaining social order, by socialising the next generation and supporting their husbands, providing a comfortable refuge which will limit the delinquent activities of men as well. Any deviation from this domesticated role will risk labelling and more sanctions for breaking the role as well as the deviance itself.

Activity

Women and social control
Controlling girls though sexual reputation

The policing of women through sexual reputation starts in adolescence, where a girl's sexual reputation is a constant source of debate and gossip between boys and girls, as well as between teachers and social workers.

The crucial point about the label 'slag' is that it is used by both girls and boys as a deterrent to nonconformity. No girl wants to be labelled as a 'slag'. The effect of the term is to force girls to submit voluntarily to a very unfair set of gender relations.

Source: Adapted from Lees, S. (1989)

Controlling women though the family

'Marriage and domesticity provide powerful controlling mechanisms to ensure the good behaviour of adult women. They are all the more powerful since they can largely be imposed with the willing, even eager, acquiescence of women themselves.'

Source: Adapted from Heidensohn, F. (1996)

1 In what ways would Lees' points about control of girls' sexual behaviour potentially affect levels of crime and deviance amongst girls and women?
2 Lees' research was carried out in the 1980s – do you think a double standard about acceptable sexual behaviour for girls and boys still exists?
3 What link may there be between Lees' points about control of adolescent girls through sexual reputation and Heidensohn's point about women eagerly accepting the control of marriage and domesticity?

However, Carlen (1987) has challenged and developed control theory, arguing that it is important to explain why some women do commit crime, despite such patriarchal control. She argues that the costs of criminal behaviour will usually outweigh the benefits for women, since most women conform to notions of respectable womanhood expected by society, making both a 'class deal' and a 'gender deal'. Thus, the women most likely to become offenders are those who may have been brought up outside the familial ideology which reinforces the gender deal (for example, those brought up in the care system), and women who are marginalised in terms of education and employment, and thus cannot fulfil the class deal. Such women may feel they have little to lose.

Recent changes in rates of female criminality

With the rise of the female liberation movement and the increase in female opportunities, the logic of the sex-role and control theories considered above would imply that we should start to see an increase in female crime. Females are out in the public sphere more now, with fewer restrictions on their behaviour, and have different role expectations.

Sisters in Crime: The Rise of the New Female Criminal, Freda Adler (1975)

Adler pointed out that there had been and would continue to be an increase in female crime. She cites 'liberation' as the main cause – as females achieve equality this leads them into more 'masculine' behaviour. On one level she argues it is about opportunity. As women leave the domestic sphere, they may have more opportunities to commit crimes such as embezzlement and fraud. Additionally, in the workplace, the traits encouraged in males which may lead to criminality, such as assertiveness, aggression and risk-taking, will apply to female employees too.

Adler uses international statistical evidence from the 1960s to show female crime increasing at a much faster rate than male crime, though this increase only applied to property rather than violent crime.

There has been some support for Adler's ideas in regard to a change in acceptable behaviour for young females today. For example, Jackson (2006) found that there seems to be more prevalence and acceptance of 'laddish' behaviour from girls. Denscombe (2001) found that the teenage girls he studied were adopting traditionally 'male' values, such as being hard, being in control and risk-taking.

However, many have criticised Adler's 'Liberation thesis'. Her statistical evidence has been challenged; since female crime rates were so low, even small rises in female crime would lead to large percentage increases, which may appear more significant that they are. Her prediction that the increase would continue at a much faster rate than for male crime has been largely shown to be inaccurate, since 40 years later male crime remains significantly higher in both the US and the UK. For example, according to Home Office crime statistics for England and Wales, prosecutions and convictions fell for both genders between 2009 and 2013. Summary (minor) offence prosecutions saw a larger drop for males whereas indictable (serious) offence prosecutions saw a larger drop for females. In 2013, males still accounted for 82 per cent of arrests and 75 per cent of convictions in England and Wales.

The notion of successful females committing crimes in the workplace, driven by ambition and aggression, is not supported by evidence. Common female crimes such as prostitution and shoplifting are not driven by liberation, but by poverty and oppression. Poor and marginalised women in the USA are more likely to be criminals than 'liberated', middle-class women according to Chesney-Lind (1997). She did find some evidence of females branching into more traditionally 'male' offences, such as drugs offences. However, far from being evidence of liberation, this was linked to economic and social issues facing young women, including gender expectations, and young women were often introduced to drugs by male family members or partners. James and Thornton (1980) found that women prisoners were most likely to be from impoverished and uneducated backgrounds, and were mostly unaware of women's liberation, which mainly benefitted middle-class women.

However, Adler argued that women's liberation has affected all women, whether they are aware of it or not, since it created changes in society's expectations and opportunities for women, regardless of whether a woman identified herself as a feminist or not.

Challenging Adler's prediction regarding an increase in female criminality, Gelsthorpe (2006) considers the 150 per cent rise in the numbers of women in prison in England and Wales, which occurred between 1994 and 2004. She argues that this is only partly related to an increase in female criminality during this time. Women still commit different types of crime to men (for example, more property related than violent crime), and they still commit crimes much less frequently than men. Thus, the increase in women in prison does not necessarily reflect an increase in criminality amongst women, but more a shift in sentencing policy. This may be more about a decline in 'chivalry' and a change in society's perception of women, rather than a change in women's perception of themselves.

Masculinity: why do males commit more crime?

Some of the sex-role based explanations considered above suggest that because the expectations for women are limited to motherhood and marriage, there is less pressure on them to achieve success, so they may have less need to commit crime. They will also have fewer opportunities for crime in the domestic context. Conversely, the pressure on males to be the breadwinner, provider and protector may be a trigger for criminality.

Messerschmidt (1993) looks at hegemonic masculinity and the pressures on males to accomplish this. Hegemonic masculinity emphasises competitive individualism, aggression and violence in relation to authority and control. Drawing on ideas from Cohen (see page 58), Messerschmidt argues that young males experience their world collectively, emphasising the importance of the school and the peer group, and argues that youth crime is a way of 'doing masculinity', especially when other resources are unavailable. Depending on the age and class of the male, he may accomplish his masculinity in different ways, some of which may be deviant and/ or criminal. For older males it may be by being a successful breadwinner or by beating his wife. For youths it may be by gaining a reputation for violence, by being the hardest one in the gang, by number of sexual conquests, by drinking or by taking part in dares or pranks.

Similarly, Mosher (1991) characterises hegemonic masculinity as 'hypermasculinity', referring to its dangerousness and acceptance of violence. A poor, jobless youth may display his masculinity, and thus enhance his status, through sexist banter, wearing gang-style clothing, or by carrying a gun.

Young males have a tendency to reproduce the existing versions of masculinity they are exposed to while growing up, according to Baird (2012), thus explaining the violent gang culture prevalent in much of inner-city America. However, he argues that whether young males embark on violence and gang-membership as a path towards masculinity depends on the availability of family support and their ability to form 'socialisation spaces' away from the street corner, avoiding the 'gang male role model system'.

The 'crisis of masculinity', which is alleged to have occurred through the decline of industrial jobs, may have led working class males towards more violent behaviour to accomplish their masculinity, as their traditional breadwinner role has been taken away. Winlow (2001) considers this in his study of working class masculinity in Sunderland, arguing that mass unemployment in the 1980s left many young males in the North East without a breadwinner status, and violence became more significant as a way of expressing masculinity. He also suggests that new masculine careers, including drug dealing, protection rackets, dealing stolen goods, and 'security', demonstrate how criminality has become an 'entrepreneurial concern': a way of making money.

Check your understanding

Briefly define the following terms and give an example of each:

1 Chivalry thesis
2 Role expressive
3 Role distorting
4 Status anxiety
5 Liberation thesis
6 Hegemonic masculinity
7 Hypermasculinity

Explaining the relationship between ethnicity and crime

Getting you thinking ...

1 What different explanations for the over-representation of some ethnic minorities in the police recorded crime figures can you think of?

The police recorded figures suggest that African Caribbean males commit more crime than their white counterparts, and that Asian crime rates are increasing. The sociological debate surrounding such patterns of criminality has been divided between those who accept that certain ethnic groups are more criminal, focusing of the reasons for this, and those who highlight racism within the criminal justice system as an explanation for these patterns. However, other analyses, such as that of left realists Lea and Young (1993), accept that these two views are not mutually exclusive, and that whilst there is some convincing evidence that black males in particular may experience discrimination in the criminal justice system, there may also be higher rates of criminality amongst this group.

Discrimination and racism within the criminal justice system

The interactionist concept of labelling can be applied to explain the high levels of arrest and conviction rates for black males. Anderson (1990), in his study of policing in a neighbourhood of Philadelphia, argues that the police tended to assume white people were middle-class and trustworthy, whereas black people were lower class and criminal. This 'colour-coding' often worked to confuse race, age, class and gender issues as well as ignoring individual behaviour according to Anderson. He describes how police officers would stop, harass and abuse young black males on the street on a regular basis, though most had done nothing to deserve it. The responses of the black males varied – some went to lengths to defer to the police and even dressed differently to try to avoid suspicion, but most saw it as inevitable and just part of life in their neighbourhood.

Hall (1999) considered the issue of policing and race relations in the two decades between the Scarman Report of 1982 and the McPherson Report of 1999. The Scarman Report was the official response to racial violence and rioting in some British cities in the early 1980s. The McPherson Report concluded the official inquiry into the murder of the black teenager Stephen Lawrence in 1993 and the subsequent police investigation. The Scarman Report officially recognised, for the first time, that social and economic disadvantages faced by ethnic minority groups could create a disposition towards violent protest, but also highlighted the issues relating to the policing of such communities, endorsing more Racial Awareness Training programmes. Hall argues that these recommendations were only partially implemented and not fully supported by the Government or the police. Further riots followed in the mid-eighties, and police tactics became ever more aggressive in dealing with them. In such a climate, Hall finds the flawed police investigation into Stephen Lawrence's murder scandalous, but unsurprising. Hall welcomed the conclusion of the McPherson Report, regarding institutional racism in the Metropolitan Police force, as a step forward in recognising and addressing some of the problems. However, he concludes that until individuals are held more accountable for their actions, not much will change. Supporting this conclusion, Phillips and Bowling (2002) argued that despite the McPherson

Report, ethnic minority neighbourhoods were still over-policed with military style methods.

Institutional racism and police culture

Institutional racism refers to racism within the social processes and practices of an institution. It has been widely applied to the police, and a related concept is 'police culture', sometimes referred to as 'police occupational culture' or 'cop culture'. This refers to a shared set of norms, values, attitudes and practices, which develop amongst the police, and which in turn affect the way in which they carry out their duties. Another related concept is 'canteen culture' which refers more to the attitudes and values exhibited by the police in their off-duty socialising. It has been suggested that police and canteen culture may include a normalisation of racist attitudes. For example, Smith and Grey's (1985) report for the Policy Studies Institute highlighted the explicit and accepted racist language of the officers they were observing.

Holdaway began his research into police culture as a serving officer in the 1970s. He discusses the 'racialisation' of policing (1996), arguing that routine and mundane police work and relationships can take on a racial 'framing', through which people and events are seen in a way that prioritises race when it is not relevant or ignores race when it is. Consequently, police officers may inadvertently act in racist ways without completely realising it.

Policing necessarily involves the exercising of discretion by individual police officers in the use of their powers. Chan (1997) argues that inappropriate use of such discretion has led to the over- and under-policing of particular types of both offenders and victims. A similar point is made by Bhilox (1983), when he states that most policing is directed at the excluded in society, who are often young, poor and black. The police pursue policies of 'differential deployment' (concentrating policing on areas where the targeted reside) and 'methodological suspicion' (routinely suspecting only a limited proportion of the population). This can have a negative impact on ethnic minority communities, who may feel a sense of injustice which can lead to further conflict. Scraton (1985) similarly sees the police as an occupying force imposed on working class and ethnic minority communities. They impose law which reflects ruling class interests, and black criminality is part of a 'culture of resistance', formed as a response to racism.

Is there still racism within the police force?

In 2003, a BBC Panorama investigation, 'The secret policeman', was broadcast, in which journalist Mark Daly went undercover in the Greater Manchester Police training centre. His secretly filmed footage showed examples of extreme racism amongst the new recruits, both towards other trainees and later towards victims and suspects from ethnic minorities. When the programme aired it caused an outcry and led to several police officers being sacked.

Recent examples suggest continued racism in the police. For example, the 2012 incident caught on a mobile phone in which a police officer used the 'N'

word to a black suspect. The police shooting of Mark Duggan in 2011, seen as the trigger for the subsequent riots, was also perceived as evidence of police racism, and has been compared to several well-publicised police shootings of unarmed black males in the USA, including Michael Brown and 12-year-old Tamir Rice in 2014, and Tony Robinson in 2015.

1 Are allegations of racism within the police force still relevant today in your view? Use evidence to support your answer.
2 What more needs to be done to address the issue of institutional racism in the police?

Sentencing and the courts

Court data shows differences in the sentences issued to people of differing ethnicities. Hood (1992) provided convincing evidence to show that race affects sentencing, demonstrating that when all other variables were taken into account, black men were 5 per cent more likely to be imprisoned than white men, and in some courts the difference was even greater. More recent evidence suggests that things have not changed significantly. A higher percentage of those from ethnic minority groups were sentenced to immediate custody than from the white group in 2010, and black people received the highest average custodial (prison) sentence length, at 20.8 months, with White people receiving the lowest average, at just 14.9 months. The most common sentence outcome for white and mixed ethnic group offenders was a community sentence, whilst for black, Asian and Chinese or other offenders the most common sentence outcome was immediate custody. Between 1993 and 2003, the white prison population increased by 48 per cent, but the black prison population increased by 138 per cent and Asian prison population increased by 73 per cent. Such evidence suggests that there is institutional racism within the criminal justice system as a whole, not just within the police, but within the justice system generally.

Evaluating institutional racism as an explanation of the relationship between ethnicity and crime

Many would argue that the differences in crime rates cannot all be down to institutional racism within the criminal justice system. Police recorded crime statistics

for London from 2010 showed that, though 12 per cent of men in London are black, 54 per cent of the street crimes, 46 per cent of knife crimes and almost half of gun crimes were thought to have been committed by black men by the Metropolitan Police. This is largely based on the victim identifying their attacker as black, and many of these victims were black themselves. Thus the police would justify more stop and searches and arrests on this basis. Waddington et al (2004) have argued that the apparently higher levels of police stopping and searching young black and Asian males is not necessarily evidence of racism. They consider other factors such as the 'availability' of people from certain ethnic backgrounds in public places and the age profile of those from ethnic minorities. Waddington et al's research suggests that black and Asian males were not treated disproportionately by the police, since the amount of times they were stopped and searched was in line with their proportion of the 'available population'.

Many sociologists accept that individuals from certain ethnic groups are committing more offences, which are more serious and thus deserving of longer sentences. Though partially accepting this, Glynn (2014) considers reasons for the persistent reoffending amongst black males and barriers to desistance from crime. He argues that the belief that criminal justice processes are inherently racist, and the promotion of racist stereotypes creates a defiant reaction amongst some black males. Crime becomes a way of 'getting back' at a society which has rejected them. Thus racism within the system may not just give the perception of higher crime rates amongst black males, it may also cause increased criminality. This idea is explored further below.

Explaining higher levels of criminality within some ethnic groups

To explain the higher crime rates amongst some ethnic groups, the influence of culture and subculture are often considered, as well as issues relating to deprivation, exclusion and racism.

Study

On the Edge, Carl Nightingale (1993)

Nightingale considered explanations for the high levels of criminality and violence amongst young black males in Philadelphia. He argues that in addition to factors such as poverty, unemployment and racism, the culture of conspicuous consumption and the glorification of violence which pervade American culture are key factors. Black youths in America consume the mainstream culture though the media like everyone else and buy into the dominant values of consumerism and money and power. However, turning to deviant ways of achieving these goals, such as violence and crime, is an understandable response in light of their economic and racial exclusion from more legitimate paths.

Nightingale discusses 'the paradox of inclusion', in which the desire to be part of the mainstream culture which excludes them drives the desire for success, designer labels, and the American lifestyle. However, poverty and racism inevitably mean that violence and criminal behaviour is the only available route to 'success'.

This 'paradox' is also illustrated in Bourgois' (1995) study of Latino and African-American drug dealers in New York's El Barrio area. He discusses the 'anguish of growing up poor' in the richest city in the world, arguing that this creates an inner-city street culture in which deviant practices become the norm and are a way of surviving and gaining respect. Bourgois argues that dealing drugs is a 'rational' career choice for ambitious and highly motivated youths in comparison to the existing on welfare or a minimum wage job.

Quick question

Which sociologist considered in a previous section saw crime as a 'rational choice' in capitalist society?

Similar ideas can be applied to explain higher levels of black criminality in the UK, though many researchers have been reluctant to focus on culture as an explanation for minority ethnic criminality, perhaps being overly conscious of contributing to pervasive racial stereotypes. A report from the Home Affairs Select Committee of the House of Commons in 2007 concluded that a range of factors contributed to high levels of criminality amongst black youths; most notably: entrenched poverty, educational underachievement, high numbers of school exclusions, family conflict and breakdown linking to a high proportion of single-parent families, and lack of positive role models.

According to Pitts (2008), since the 1990s Britain has witnessed a rise in violent youth gangs and associated gang-related street culture. In particular minority ethnic young people have found themselves 'immobilised' at the bottom of the economic ladder and cut adrift from the values of mainstream society. This acute marginalisation has created a response of frustration and rage, and in this context, gang membership and violence have become normalised. Gunter (2008) considers the importance of subculture in explaining crime amongst young black males in east London. He highlights the significance of 'road culture' and 'badness' on young black people's identities, experiences and lifestyle choices. Road culture is influenced by black youth culture that is played out in public settings 'on the road' (streets and housing estates). Young people involved in 'badness', characterised by violent behaviour, criminal activity and low-level drug dealing, are referred to as 'living on road', and gain respect.

Combining the two approaches – how racism can create resistance and criminality

Lea and Young (1982, 1983) in a left realist analysis of the link between race and crime, criticise the moral panics which have surrounded 'black crime', such as the way the media have focused on mugging and linked it to ethnicity in the past. For example, they challenge the headline from the Sun newspaper on 23rd March 1983, which read 'BLACK CRIME SHOCK: Blacks carried out twice as many muggings as whites in London last year'. They point out that 'mugging' is actually not a distinct criminal offence, so statistics are not clear and may include a vast range of different incidents which are brought together in a misleading way to form a newsworthy headline. Additionally, no reference to the ethnicity of the victims in such incidents is made, or to potential biases on the part of the police. These ideas can be linked to Hall et al's study of coverage of black mugging (see page 67).

The Myth of Black Criminality (1982), Police and Thieves (1982a) and Steppin' out of Babylon – Race, Class and Autonomy (1982b), Paul Gilroy

Gilroy considers the history of race relations as a significant factor in explaining criminality amongst some ethnic groups. Both British Asians and African Caribbeans originate from former colonies of Britain and carry 'the scars of imperialist violence', according to Gilroy. Resistance to such imperial rule created a culture of resistance in the colonies, and in Britain similar techniques to resist exploitation were used. For example, in the scenes of inner-city rioting in the late 1970s and early 1980s, in places such as Southall and Brixton, black and Asian communities consciously hit back against police harassment, racially motivated attacks and discrimination. Thus, he sees ethnic minorities as defending themselves against a society that treats them unjustly.

Gilroy challenges those seeking to blame black culture, generational conflict or even deprivation for higher rates of black criminality. Gilroy argues that the 'myth of black criminality' serves a political agenda, allowing the 'alien immigrant' and the 'black mugger' to personify crime. It is fuelled by racist police practices, targeting black communities. The media contribute to this myth by stereotyping black males, which leads to more public labelling and justifies more control.

However, Lea and Young also challenge those who dismiss any link between race and crime as 'merely' evidence of racism in the criminal justice system. Though accepting that this racism exists, as realists they argue that higher crime rates amongst certain minority ethnic groups are real and need to be understood. Racial discrimination will lead to an acute awareness of 'unnecessary injustices', and in addition, some sections of black and Asian communities in the UK are particularly affected by unemployment and deprivation. Lea and Young discuss the ways in which a minority of the oppressed groups in any industrialised society are 'brutalised' into criminality, thus suggesting that race and class combine to partially explain patterns of offending. Additionally, they point out that most crime is 'intra-racial' rather than 'inter-racial', and thus also 'intra-class', furthering their argument that issues of race are not necessarily central to criminality, but issues of social class often are.

These arguments about deprivation and social class being the key indicators of criminality can also help to explain why some ethnic groups (such as those of Indian or Chinese origin) have much lower crime rates than others, which is hard to reconcile with the idea of a racist criminal justice system, but more understandable when social class is taken into account.

However, Palmer (2013) challenges arguments which see race as a secondary factor to social class, suggesting that they place too little emphasis on racial discrimination within the criminal justice system and ignore real distinctions between the identities and experiences of white and black working-class youths. She argues that because of the multiple disadvantages faced by young, black males, it cannot be assumed that they commit crime for the same reasons as young white males, since race and racism must be taken into account. Her own research, conducted with black residents of an inner-city London neighbourhood, supports several of the explanations considered above. For example, wider culture and the media impacted on the aspirations of the black youths she studied, who made references to feelings of 'relative deprivation' and 'unnecessary injustices'. However, Palmer's respondents also referred to a lack of discipline within families, and feelings of being let down by their community as well as education and wider society. Like Gilroy, she also feels that 'group histories' have an impact on the ways in which individuals make sense of their world. Palmer concludes that whilst racism may not be a direct cause of crime, its impact on how young, black males see themselves and other black people is a relevant factor.

Ethnic identity and criminality

'"Ever since I've been growing up, I've seen my Black community divided … I share skin complexion with them but as far as the Black community is in my eyes, we're just a sea of lost, confused and insecure people and everything we do is dictated to us … through the media and through the lack of education … we just follow whatever we see."'
Marcus, one of Palmer's young respondents,

'"When you watch [TV] all you see is materialistic things, you get me? 'I got a girl, I got a car, I got this,

Activity (continued)

I got that' and nobody is not sharing. That's what they teach you on TV, nobody ain't sharing ... If you're a child that was hanging around a crowd of black youths when you was growing up, then normally you'll get into just hustling of drugs and try and obtain the image."'

Robert, another of Palmer's young respondents,

Source: Palmer, S. (2013)

1 Read the comments from two of Palmer's respondents, above. Can you see links between what they say and any of the other explanations for criminality you have considered?

2 In what ways might the experience of young black working-class males differ from that of young white working-class males?

Asians and crime

Crime levels amongst British Asians have, until relatively recently, been disproportionately lower than or similar to those of white people. This has been linked to strong family values and socialisation within Asian families, and to them not fitting in with the police stereotype of 'criminals' – unlike those from African Caribbean backgrounds.

However, since the Home Office tends to classify 'Asians' in one category, which includes those of Indian, Pakistani and Bangladeshi backgrounds, who may have very different social class and cultural backgrounds, FitzGerald and Sibbitt (1997) have argued that this has long masked different crime patterns within these groups. Despite this, crime rates amongst young Asian males have been increasing significantly in recent years. Similar explanations to those relating to black males some years ago, relating to age-profile and socio-economic factors could partially explain this increase.

Bowling, Parmar and Phillips (2003) highlight the 'pliability' of stereotypes of Asian people, demonstrating that previous conformist perceptions of Asians, and particularly Muslims, have altered. They suggest that the stereotypes previously assumed to explain law-abiding behaviour, relating to strong sense of community, family and religious values, are now thought to promote criminal and deviant activity amongst Asian youth. Similarly, Abbas (2004) argues that the stereotype of the 'passive Asian' has given way to a climate of 'Islamophobia' following 9/11 and more recent terrorist scares. For example, evidence suggests that the stopping and searching of Asians by the police has increased significantly in recent years. Current concerns about 'radicalisation' have led to claims about the targeting of young Muslims by the police and harsher punishments being issued by the courts.

Activity

Punishing radicalised Muslims

Yusuf Sarwar and his friend Mohammed Ahmed, both 22 and from Birmingham, flew to Turkey in May 2013. They joined up with rebels in Syria, where Yusuf told his mother he was assigned as a kind of ambulance driver, picking up dead bodies, and he soon wanted to come home.

'My son is not a terrorist, he didn't make bombs, he didn't kill anyone, he tried to help. He did a stupid thing and when he realised this he wanted to come home.'

His mother went to the police and said she was told they would help her get her son home. When the two men returned to Heathrow in January 2014 they were arrested and detained in Belmarsh high security prison. In December 2014 Yusuf and Ahmed were sentenced to prison for 12 years and eight months each. The judge said they had 'willingly, enthusiastically and with a great deal of purpose, persistence and determination embarked on a course intended to commit acts of terrorism'.

Yusuf's mother said that she felt betrayed by the police and courts over the length of his prison term. 'The police say 'mothers come forward', you can trust us, we will help. But now they will see what happened to my son. What kind of person would go to the police if they think their son will get 12 years in prison? Nobody wants to do that. I did not want that.'

The family intend to lodge an appeal against the sentencing.

Adapted from '"Police betrayed me," says mother of imprisoned British jihadi' by Tracey McVeigh, 6 December 2014, in *The Guardian*

1 What do you think was the justification for this sentence? Do you think it was too harsh?

2 What effect may cases such as this have on:
   a) the way the police perceive young Muslims?
   b) the way Muslims perceive the police and criminal justice system?

Check your understanding:

Briefly define the following terms and give an example of each:

1 Institutional racism
2 Paradox of inclusion

3 Myth of black criminality
4 Culture of resistance
5 Unnecessary injustices
6 Islamophobia

2.4 How can crime and deviance be reduced?

Getting you thinking ...

People in areas of social deprivation are having their lives blighted by crime.

Imagine you have just formed a new government and you have a choice about your budget. You can spend the money tackling poverty (increasing benefits, improving education, retraining unemployed, improving facilities and so on), or you can spend the money on more police officers, CCTV, better street lighting, and a whole range of other anti-crime measures.

1 What effect would each choice have on crime?
2 Which would you do, and why? (Think about cost, but also popularity and effectiveness.)
3 Which approach do you think would be favoured by those from the right-wing and by those from the left-wing?

Left-wing policies on crime reduction

Crime prevention

Left-wing views see the social structure as the main cause of crime, focusing on issues such as inequality, deprivation and social exclusion. Their approach to crime prevention is therefore long-term, focusing on structural changes to tackle the social causes of crime. This may include pursuing policies such as:

- Reducing income inequalities, for example through a more redistributive taxation policy, raising the minimum wage and increasing benefits
- Raising the living standards and quality of life for poorer families, for example, by building more affordable and social housing and improving leisure and recreational facilities in deprived areas.
- Reducing unemployment, for example through investment in apprenticeships and training initiatives.

- Improving education and training opportunities and reducing educational inequalities, for example, through compensatory educational schemes.

Punishment

There are two main approaches to punishment:

1 **Retribution** – which aims to making the offender pay or suffer for what he or she has done, and can be seen as a **punitive** approach, or form of revenge.
2 **Rehabilitation** – or reform, which aims to reintegrate the offender back into society, having addressed the causes of the offending.

Right-wing views tend to support retributive justice strategies, whilst left-wing views focus more on rehabilitation.

To understand the rehabilitation approach to justice, it is useful to consider the affect of a punishment of the offender and their self-concept.

Crime, shame and reintegration, John Braithwaite (1989)

Braithwaite discusses two types of 'shaming' which can be created through punishment:

Disintegative shaming, which is prevalent in the traditional retributive framework of justice. This involves the labelling and stigmatisation of the offender, affecting their self-concept: 'You are a bad person'. This can be linked with Becker's idea of 'master-status' (see page 60), and the self-fulfilling prophecy, and Braithwaite argues that it is likely to lead more reoffending.

Reintegrative shaming, in contrast, focuses on the offender's behaviour, rather than the offender themself: 'You did a bad thing'. The aim is to reaffirm the offender's membership within the law-abiding society, encouraging remorse by making offenders face up to the consequences of their actions. This approach avoids labelling, and seeks to explore ways in which the offender can make amends and avoid making the same mistakes in the future.

Left-wing views, such as left realists, would favour 'reintegrative shaming' (see the Study above). They argue that helping the offender to address the issues which caused the offending and to recognise the damage that their offending has done to the victim and the wider community are the best way to prevent reoffending. This approach may include the promotion of more community sentencing, such as unpaid work and treatment programmes for addiction or mental health problems. Such sentences have much lower reoffending rates than custodial sentences, arguably because they address the causes of the original offending. Another left-wing approach to punishment, which has gained momentum and popularity in recent years around the world, is restorative justice.

Restorative justice (RJ) is an approach which recognises the impact of offending on the victim, the community and the offender themself. This can be related to the concept of the square of crime (see page 73). This approach recognises that both offenders and victims of crime benefit by taking an active role in the justice process. In addition, by encouraging offenders to take responsibility for their actions, both the victim's and offender's personal needs are addressed, so RJ can be characterised as an inclusive as opposed to exclusive approach.

According to Braithwaite (2004) '... restorative justice is about the idea that because crime hurts, justice should heal. It follows that conversations with those who have been hurt and with those who have afflicted the harm must be central to the process.' Restorative justice programmes that foster dialogue between victim and offender show a high rate of victim satisfaction and offender accountability, and also show considerable success in reducing reoffending.

RJ can be seen as a set of principles, rather than a particular practice, and its forms vary. Some restorative justice schemes replace a custodial sentence with a community based one, and may allow the victim and/or the community to have a say in what happens to the offender. This may be more appropriate for minor offending, and has been particularly pioneered in the area of youth offending. At the other extreme are interventions involving more serious offenders who are already serving custodial sentences. Victims may be asked if they wish to embark on restorative justice, which usually involves a face-to-face meeting with the offender, in a controlled setting. The victim has the opportunity to explain to the offender the impact their crime has had, and the offender is encouraged to consider their reasons for offending. Such programmes are becoming more common, and have even been used in serious crimes such as rape and murder.

Control

Left-wing approaches to the control of crime tend to focus on relationships between the police, the criminal justice system, and the community and other agencies.

- **Policing** – Left realists Lea and Young (1993) challenge what they see as flaws in current policing. They argue that the public lack confidence in the police and believe them to be prejudiced. This stems from a drift which has been seen towards 'military policing' (conflict policing), rather than consensual policing. A vicious circle is created, particularly in some communities, where military policing leads to less co-operation with the police, which in turn leads to even more military style tactics.
  Lea and Young argue that the relationship between the police and the community needs to be improved, by 'minimal policing', characterised by trust and co-operation. The 'over-policing ' of certain crimes, such as minor drug offences

Activity

Restorative justice in action

Item A

An example from the USA

The Red Hook Community Justice Court has transformed crime rates in Brooklyn, New York, including more than 75 per cent reductions in homicide, robbery, burglary and assault in the two decades to 2011. One of the key principles is a commitment to preventing the incidence of crime by tackling the issues at source. To achieve this, the court runs a number of unconventional initiatives, such as community mediation sessions and leadership training for local teenagers. 'Punishments' can involve direct compensation to the victim, such as cleaning up graffiti or returning stolen property, or indirect compensation such as voluntary work in the community.

Item B

An example from the UK

Since 2011 in Surrey, all but the most serious youth crimes are referred to a panel of police and youth support workers who decide whether the young person should go to court, be given a caution or a youth restorative intervention (YRI). If the recommendation is a YRI, a police officer or youth support worker will speak to both the offender and the victim to discuss whether they are happy with this approach rather than court.

Since they were introduced, more than 3,000 cases – 70 per cent – 80 per cent of crimes committed by young people – have been dealt with through a YRI. According to an independent analysis, YRIs have reduced reoffending by 18 per cent, and 1,160 fewer young people have received a criminal record.

1 Why do you think offending and reoffending rates appear to have been reduced through using these approaches?
2 Both these initiatives focus on youth offending – why do you think restorative justice is particularly appropriate for young offenders? Would it also work for adult offenders?
3 What problems may there be with schemes such as these? Are they appropriate in all cases?
4 If you were a victim of crime, would you be willing to consider restorative justice? Why or why not? Visit www.restorativejustice.org.uk and look at some of the case studies outlined under 'Restorative Justice in Action' to help you decide.

and delinquency, is part of the problem and other crimes, such as domestic violence, racially motivated crime and white-collar crime, are 'under-policed'.

- **Multi-agency working** – Another left-wing policy is the promotion of more co-operation between the agencies in society which affect and control individuals' behaviour. The police, the local council, social services, the media, religion, community groups, the school and education authorities and the family all have roles to play in improving the 'moral context' in which crime is committed. Lea and Young argue for a more co-ordinated approach between these agencies, including more communication regarding individuals and families seen to be 'at risk' of offending and/ or victimisation, allowing for early interventions. Recent examples, such as the sexual exploitation and abuse of vulnerable young people within gangs and institutions, suggest that failures in communication between such agencies can have serious consequences.

Evaluation of left-wing policies

The long-term crime prevention strategies outlined above can be challenged as being unrealistic and ineffective in practice. Murray (1994) points out that the USA attempted such policies in the 1960s and 70s, including pre-school socialisation programmes and programmes that provided guaranteed jobs for young people without skills and on-the-job training. He argues that such policies were all 'notorious failures' which did not produce long-term group results that survive scrutiny. The long-term nature of such schemes also means the likelihood that they will be fully funded and followed through by successive governments is slim.

Limitations of restorative justice include the fact that it relies on the co-operation of all parties, and thus more formal justice systems will always still be needed in cases where this co-operation is not forthcoming. However, Marshall (1998) points out that the majority of individuals offered the chance to participate indicated that they would like to do so, and later failures to carry out agreements reached are actually much lower than failures to pay court-ordered fines, for example.

In 2001, the UK government funded a seven-year research programme looking into the effectiveness of restorative justice. In her report, Shapland (2008) found that the majority of victims chose to participate in face-to-face meetings with the offender, and 85 per cent of victims who took part were satisfied with the process. There was a significant decrease in the frequency of reoffending and cost savings of up to £9 per £1 spent on RJ were seen.

However, there are those who see RJ and other rehabilitative approaches to punishment as a 'soft option', and there is public support for more and longer custodial sentences and a more retributive approach to punishment, which is supported by the right-wing views considered below.

Left realist views of community policing have been challenged by Gilroy (1982) as being simplistic, and under-estimating the deliberate racist strategies which he argues underpin the policing of some communities.

Right-wing policies on crime reduction

Prevention

Clarke (1980) argues that criminality is usually a conscious choice, and the criminal opportunities available and the likelihood and the potential consequences of being caught are significant factors affecting criminality. A right realistic approach to crime prevention focuses on making crime more difficult to commit and making capture and punishment more likely.

- **Situational and Environmental crime prevention** – The concepts of situational and environmental crime prevention are often used interchangeably, but situational crime prevention can be seen as specific measures making particular crimes harder to commit or capture more likely, whereas environmental crime prevention can be seen as wider measures, generally relating to the public environment, which can make any deviant behaviour less likely.

A key situational crime prevention technique is 'target hardening'. This refers to the increasing of the security surrounding the 'targets' of crime, such as houses, cars and other property. This may be achieved through installing alarms and better locks and encouraging safer practices, such as locking cars at petrol stations.

Specific examples of target hardening show success in the reduction of certain crimes. Clarke (1980) cites the following examples:

- Theft from telephone boxes was virtually eliminated when aluminium coin boxes were replaced with steel ones which were harder to break into.
- Car thefts were reduced dramatically in Germany when steering column locks were made compulsory on all cars in 1963. An updated example of this could be that newer cars today have built in security devices as standard, which greatly reduces thefts.

Environmental crime prevention measures include the design of public housing estates and town centres, street lighting and the use of CCTV. Security professionals and town planners are aware of environmental crime prevention, and often focus on the concept of 'defensible space'. Areas are designated as 'public', 'semi-private' or 'private', with the recognition that public areas are the most vulnerable to crime, since no-one has direct responsibility for them, and surveillance and control is more difficult.

Surveillance is another important environmental crime prevention measure. This can be direct, through the use of CCTV or security guards, or more subtle, such as using clear rather than opaque doors and barriers in flats, and minimising closed spaces. The use of CCTV continues to increase in the UK, and the British Security Industry Authority (BSIA) estimated in 2013 that there is one surveillance camera for every eleven people in the UK.

Another environmental crime prevention strategy is improved lighting. Studies suggest that this can have a significant effect on crime reduction, both directly by making deviant activities more visible and thus discouraging them, but also indirectly, as more people are encouraged out onto the streets, since they feel safer, further reducing criminal opportunities. For example, Painter and Farrington (1999), in their study in Stoke-on-Trent, showed that the incidence of crime decreased by 43 per cent in the experimental area where street-lighting was improved. Additionally, rather than displacing crime to less well-lit areas, they found a 'diffusion of benefit', since crime also decreased in the adjacent area.

Punishment

Right-wing criminologists generally favour harsh and punitive sentences, pursuing the aim of retributive justice, often based on the idea that the punishment must fit the crime.

Longer prison sentences and harsher prison regimes have been popular policies in recent years, particularly in the USA. The 'three-strikes and you're out' policy, involving life imprisonment with no parole (release) for

Activity

Surveillance – a good or a bad thing?
Item A

The benefits of surveillance

Councillor Hazel Harding, Leader of Lancashire County Council and Chair of the Local Government Association Safer Communities Board, suggested that:

'CCTV is very popular with law-abiding members of the public who see it as a preventative and feel much safer ... There are some good examples of how CCTV has helped perhaps not always to prevent but certainly to detect crime and as such it has been very useful ...'

Source: House of Lords Constitution Committee (2009)

Item B

The risks of surveillance

The increasing use of surveillance technology – including body-worn video, drones and number plate recognition systems – risks changing the 'psyche of the community' by reducing individuals to trackable numbers in a database, the government's CCTV watchdog has warned.

Surveillance Commissioner Tony Porter said the public was complacent about encroaching surveillance and urged public bodies, including the police, to be more transparent about how they use smart cameras to monitor people.

He is nervous about the 'burgeoning use of body-worn videos [BWV]', not just by the police but by university security staff, housing and environmental health officers – and even supermarket workers: 'It changes the nature of society and raises moral and ethical issues ... about what sort of society we want to live in ...'

1 What are the arguments in favour of and against the increased use of surveillance technology as a method of crime prevention?

a third offence, even if relatively minor, was introduced in America in the 1990s. This policy has contributed to a quadrupling of the US prison population, the second highest per capita in the world. It was mimicked by a watered-down version, involving mandatory minimum sentencing, in the UK, though human rights legislation means that such sentences were rarely upheld.

As well as deterrence and retribution, a key role in harsh penalties lies in the shaming and stigmatisation of the behaviour, which acts as a form of public denunciation. This links to functionalist ideas of 'degradation ceremonies' and their role in reinforcing the collective conscience and the acceptable boundaries of behaviour (see page 52). On a practical level, imprisoning offenders for life takes them off the streets and means that issues of rehabilitation and reoffending become irrelevant. Murray argues that this is a choice which has to be made – incarcerating large sections of the population is inevitable if crime rates are to be reduced. For more on Murray's ideas, see the Activity on page 95.

Right realist Wilson (1975) disagrees somewhat with the above views on retributive punishment, because he feels that the certainty of capture is more of a deterrent than the potential harshness of the sentence. He suggests that if potential offenders do not believe they will be caught, then the potential penalty becomes largely irrelevant. Certainty of capture must be achieved by changing the role of the police, as described below.

Quick question

Which do you think would be more of a deterrent against committing crime: a harsher penalty or a greater certainty of capture?

Control

Right-wing ideas on social control are linked to the crime prevention approaches discussed above, such as increased surveillance. Other direct forms of control involve more direct police and State interventions into community and family life.

- **Policing, order maintenance and zero tolerance** – The view of policing put forward by right realists such as Wilson and Kelling (1982) (see page 72), involves prioritising the police's role in 'order maintenance', for example by increasing foot patrols. Their ideas seem to be supported by the Chief Inspector of Constabulary for England and Wales, Tom Winsor, who set out his ideas for policing in 2013. He argues that the police should focus more on preventing crime than catching criminals and that a greater focus on targeting would-be offenders and potential crime hotspots will save money and reduce crime.

'Zero tolerance policing' is a related policy, which refers to the aggressive policing of minor and anti-social crime, including littering, vandalism, drugs offences, begging, prostitution and graffiti to 'clean up the streets'. For example, tackling vandalism immediately, to show that it is not tolerated, re-emphasises shared norms and values and reinforces the certainty of capture. The theory is that the incidence of more serious crime will then be reduced as social control is increased and a law-abiding culture is reinforced.

This policy was famously pursued in New York in the 1990s. Zimring (2011) showed that between 1990 and 2009 the homicide rate in New York declined by 82 per cent, and rates for other crimes also fell dramatically. It is difficult to prove how much of this decline is directly attributable to zero tolerance policing strategies. However, the combination of zero tolerance policing, situational crime prevention strategies and harsher punishments is widely argued to have had a significant effect on crime rates in several US cities.

- **The welfare state and the family** – Another approach to controlling crime, associated with the New Right, focuses on the family and the benefits system. Murray (1984, 1990) argues that an over-generous welfare system encourages 'feckless' behaviour, and prevents families and individuals from taking responsibility for their actions. He argues that benefits should be cut, and that if families cannot afford to bring up their children, then they should be adopted. Extreme versions of these ideas include compulsory sterilisation programmes, a form of eugenics. Murray argues that stigmatisation can also be very effective, involving the community sanctioning reckless behaviour rather than tolerating it.

Evaluation of right-wing policies

Right-wing policies are often criticised for not addressing the underlying causes of crime. Simon (1988) points out that 'changing people' is difficult and expensive, which can explain why policy-makers have abandoned this approach, focusing instead on restricting people's movements and actions. However, because the original causes have not been addressed, if such restrictions are relaxed, crime will increase again. Additionally, any apparent crime reduction may just be a form of 'displacement'. This is the idea that because the criminal behaviour's causes have not been addressed, it will just be 'displaced' (moved) to somewhere else. Clarke (1980) accepts this risk may apply in some cases, but argues that some crime will be prevented completely by removing the temptation. He also points out that the public, police and politicians are largely in favour of situational and environmental crime prevention measures.

The growing trend towards social control is portrayed by Cohen (1985) as catching-up more and more people in *'ever-larger nets of ever-finer mesh'*, as punishment extends from prison through the community, and the variety of sanctions keeps on growing. Davis (1994) presents a similarly bleak picture of segregated cities and a culture of fear created by the right-wing influenced policies discussed above, leading to a form of social engineering which may have 'ominous racial overtones'.

However, given the blight on deprived communities caused by crime, some argue that more control is a price worth paying. Additionally, a common response to concerns about increasing control is that those with nothing to hide have nothing to fear. However, CCTV in city centres, security patrols in shopping malls, expanded electronic data collection and strengthened asylum and immigration controls target the innocent as well as the guilty according to Hudson (1997).

Harsh punishments, such as the death penalty, are also challenged. Though it is often argued that they act as a deterrent, there is little evidence to support this. Jurisdictions which use the death penalty generally have higher crime rates than those which do not. As seen above, reoffending rates following custodial sentences are generally much higher than for more rehabilitative sentencing options.

Activity: Policy into practice

The Troubled Families Programme

The coalition government launched the Troubled Families Programme in 2011, aimed at turning around the chaotic lives of thousands of families in the UK, in which poor parenting, abuse, violence, drug use, anti-social behaviour and crime have become generational patterns. Local authorities operate targeted interventions on a 'payment by results' basis. Such interventions may involve treatment for addictions, parenting programmes, and support for adult family members to get into work.

The original target was to get 120,000 troubled families in England to turn their lives around by 2015, getting children back into school, adults back to work and reducing youth crime and anti-social behaviour. At the beginning of 2015, the government suggested that over 105,000 families had been helped. Though approximately £440 million has been invested in the scheme, the government argues it has saved the taxpayer £1.2 billion, due to reduced costs in terms of crime, health, housing and benefits.

Despite such apparent success, concerns have been raised about the label 'troubled families', how 'turning around' families can be measured, and whether initial progress will be maintained once support is withdrawn. Some local authorities have also warned that the continued squeeze on their budgets puts such programmes at risk.

1 Which of the approaches to crime reduction does this policy seem to exemplify?
2 What are the strengths and weaknesses of this policy as an approach to crime reduction?

Check your understanding

Briefly explain the following policies, and link them to the right-wing or left-wing approach to addressing crime:

1 Situational and environmental crime prevention
2 Multi-agency working
3 Retributive justice
4 Consensual policing
5 Public degradation ceremonies
6 Zero tolerance
7 Restorative justice

Section summary

Make a copy of the following passage and fill in the blanks, using the words given below

Right-wing and left-wing approaches to solving the problem of crime reflect the different _____ for crime that each view presents. Since left-wing views look at _____ causes of crime, and see the need to consider the role of society, the community and the _____ in their explanations, their policies of crime reflect this. For example, addressing inequalities in society and fostering better relationships with the _____ and the community are both policies promoted by left realists. _____ justice, which promotes the _____ of the offender, and sees the victim as a key part of the healing process, is another policy clearly influenced by left-wing ideas.

Section summary (continued)

Conversely, right-wing views focus more on control, arguing for _____ policing and _____ justice. They see criminals as being responsible for their own actions, and seek to make criminality a less appealing choice. _____ crime prevention, making it harder to commit crime, is therefore an important right-wing policy.

Both approaches can be challenged, and whereas left-wing views are sometimes seen as too _____ and soft to make any real difference, right-wing views can be challenged as failing to tackle the _____ of crime. It could be argued that a combination of both approaches is the most effective approach.

situational, underlying causes, retributive, explanations, long-term, police, restorative, victim, zero tolerance, structural, rehabilitation

Practice questions

1 Outline patterns and trends in green crime and global organised crime [10]
2 Identify and evaluate right-wing policies on crime reduction [20]
3 Outline and assess subcultural explanations of crime and deviance [40]

Chapter 3

Education

3.1 What is the role of education in society?

Getting you thinking ...

1 In a group consider the reasons why education is now seen as essential for all children in modern societies. Refer to the pictures but also use your own ideas.

2 Note down a list of all the possible functions or purposes of education.

Functionalism

Functionalists argue that in advanced industrial societies, like the UK, a range of specialised institutions have evolved. Each institution carries out specific functions which link into the functioning of other institutions in order to make society run smoothly. For example, primary schools are linked to families which perform the function of primary socialisation, preparing children to go on to the secondary stage of socialisation at school. Schools also prepare pupils for the world of work so are also linked to the needs of economy.

Durkheim: education and social solidarity

Moral education

The French sociologist Emile Durkheim argued that all societies needed to create a sense of social solidarity in their members. By this he meant a feeling of unity and belonging based on shared beliefs and values. In pre-industrial societies social solidarity was created by people sharing common experiences as part of families and through shared religious beliefs and rituals. In industrial societies individuals come from more diverse backgrounds so education plays a vital role in instilling a sense of a shared culture and identity in the younger generation. Durkheim saw the teaching of history as particularly valuable because it encourages young people to take pride in their country and its culture and achievements, however, this could also be encouraged by studying subjects such as literature, music or religious studies.

The division of labour

For Durkheim, education was not only about instilling shared values into children but also about preparing young people for the world of work in industrial societies. In pre-industrial societies children typically learned the skills they required as adults from parents or other family members as they would follow the same occupation as their family. However, in industrial societies there is a more complex division of labour; individuals can choose from a wide range of specialised jobs and will not necessarily follow in their parents' footsteps. Schools therefore provide the specialist skills and knowledge required of an industrial workforce which parents themselves may not be able to provide.

Evaluation of Durkheim

Durkheim's approach helps to explain how education has become so much more important in industrial societies where compulsory education for all children has become the norm. However, the idea that education is based on shared values can be seen to be increasingly problematical in multicultural societies like Britain. In the past Christianity provided a common set of values which was emphasised in aspects of schooling such as acts of worship in school assemblies and religious education based on Christianity. However, few schools now conduct truly religious assemblies and religious education encourages an understanding of different faiths. It is therefore more difficult to see how education in Britain creates a sense of social solidarity.

Criticisms of functionalism

- **Whose values?** – Marxists would question the view that education reflects a set of beliefs shared by the majority of society, arguing that the values emphasised by schools are ones which benefit capitalist employers. For example, pupils are encouraged to be obedient workers by the discipline of school.
- **Meritocracy** – The view that education is meritocratic is questioned by many sociologists who point to evidence that some pupils fail to achieve not because of lack of ability but because they are disadvantaged by social background factors such as social class or ethnicity.
- **Education and work** – It can be argued that far from schools teaching pupils the skills they need to perform their jobs in an industrial society, as claimed by functionalists, schools put too much emphasis on traditional academic subjects and fail to focus on the practical and social skills required in the workplace.
- **Globalisation and common culture** – The view that part of the role of education is to transmit a common culture based on a shared sense of national identity can be seen as outdated as young people will increasingly compete for jobs in a global society. Rather than focusing on national values, education may need to prepare young people to live in societies based on greater cultural diversity.

Contemporary relevance of functionalism

Functionalist theories fell out of fashion among sociologists and educationalists from the 1970s onwards. However, in recent years there has been a growth in concern among politicians and some educationalists about the need for education to transmit the shared values of UK society. This can be seen in the introduction of citizenship education by the Labour government in 2002 (see Item C in Activity on page 110). More recently the Al Madinah free school, an Islamic primary school in Derby raised concerns because it appeared to be following a very conservative Islamic approach to education, for example segregating girls and boys in class, expecting all teachers to wear Islamic dress and only offering Arabic as a modern language. The school was eventually closed in 2014 after an 'inadequate' rating by OFSTED. Critics of the school argued that state funded schools should reflect broader British values such as democracy and multiculturalism. In this sense the concern of functionalists that education should be a unifying force bringing together pupils from different social backgrounds continues to have some relevance in the 21st century.

The school as a social system, Parsons (1961)

Talcott Parsons (1961) is an American sociologist who argued that education has three main functions in modern industrial societies like the USA.

A bridge between school and work – Parsons argued that while the family remained the main primary agency of socialisation (see page 85) education has taken over the main responsibility for secondary socialisation and acts as a bridge between the family and world of work. Parsons argued that in the family children are treated in terms of particularistic values, parents judge their children according to values that apply to them alone. A child may not learn to talk or walk before other children their age, they may not be better looking than other children but to their parents they are still the best child in the world. In the wider society individuals are judged by universalistic values, values which are applied to everyone, for example in judging which applicant is best for a job. Schools help children to make this transition, for example as children move into secondary school they are increasingly assessed according to universalistic values, for example through exams.

Education and value consensus – Parsons also sees schools as socialising young people into the value consensus of society. He argues that in American society there are two key values which children must learn:

- **Individual achievement** – This is learned through competing with others and rewarded with praise from teachers, higher grades and educational qualifications. This prepares young people for the world of work where they will have to compete with others to achieve.
- **Equality of opportunity** – Schools reflect the values of American society based on a belief that everyone has an equal chance of success. Schools reflect this by encouraging all pupils to succeed. This is reflected in British schools which usually have an equal opportunities policy emphasising that all children irrespective of gender, ethnicity, social class or disability should be treated equally and given equal opportunities.
- **Role allocation** – Parsons, in common with other functionalists such as Kingsley Davis and Wilbert Moore (1945), argues that an important function of education is selecting and grading pupils for their future roles in society. Schools are seen as operating on the principle of meritocracy, rewarding the most talented and hard-working students with higher grades and better qualifications. This in turn ensures that employers can identify the most able individuals are identified and recruited them to fill more important positions on the world of work.

Evaluation – Parsons' theory offers a useful insight into the inter-relationship between educational institutions and other institutions such as families and economic organisations. Most sociologists would also accept that education plays an increasingly important role in preparing young people for the world of work. However, functionalist sociologists have been heavily criticised (see page 99).

Activity

The functions of education

Item A
Primary school

Item B
Sitting exams

(continued)

Item C

Citizenship education

Until relatively recently pupils in British schools did not have lessons in citizenship. However, there was widespread concern that citizens are not sufficiently aware of their rights and responsibilities and do not understand the way in which the political system works. As a result the Labour Secretary of State for Education David Blunkett asked Professor Bernard Crick and an advisory group to produce a report on citizenship education in English schools which was published in 1998.

Blunkett called for the implementation of Crick's recommendations saying, "We must provide opportunities for all our young people to develop an understanding of what democracy means and how government works in practice – locally and nationally – and encourage them to take an active part in the lives of their communities. Linking rights and responsibilities and emphasising socially acceptable behaviour to others, underpins the development of active citizenship."

Critics, including Chris Woodhead, the then Chief Inspector of Schools, were concerned that schools would neglect the academic basics in favour of lessons in political literacy.

In 2002 citizenship was made a compulsory part of the national curriculum for 11–16 year olds and a new AS Level in Citizenship was introduced for post-16 students. In Citizenship students are expected to develop a broad knowledge of their rights and responsibilities as citizens, the functioning of the political system and an awareness of topical events and how to find information about current affairs. Moreover there is an expectation that students will be actively involved in school and community activities.

More recently the coalition government undertook a review of the national curriculum and many feared that citizenship education would be cut from schools. However, in 2013 under pressure from David Blunkett and other supporters of citizenship education, Michael Gove the Secretary of State for Education announced that citizenship would remain part of the compulsory national curriculum.

1 How might Items A and B illustrate Parsons' idea that schools represent a bridge between the particularistic values of the family and the universalistic values of the wider society?

2 To what extent does this reflect your own experience of education?

3 Study Item C. Why might it be argued that citizenship education represents an important means of transmitting the shared values of a democratic society to the next generation?

4 To what extent do you think that educating young people as future citizens is an important function of the education system?

Marxism

Althusser: Education as an ideological state apparatus

The French philosopher Louis Althusser (1972) argues that the main role of education is to persuade young people to accept their place in the capitalist system. Capitalist societies are very unequal and challenges to it could cause conflict and instability. Althusser argues that the ruling class manage to keep this in check not so much through force as by ideological control. He suggests that there are a number of institutions he calls ideological state apparatuses (ISAs) which have this purpose. In the past, organised religion was the main means by which people were persuaded to accept their place in society. Today the mass media and education have taken over as two of the key ISAs.

Althusser argues that education transmits capitalist ideology in two ways:

- it teaches young people that capitalism is normal and natural, despite its inherent inequalities and injustices. Schools do little to encourage young people to question or criticise the existing society.
- by selecting and grading pupils for unequal positions in society, schools makes inequality appear fair and legitimate. Pupils who fail or leave with few qualifications are seen as doing so due to their own lack of ability or motivation rather than the fault of a society where some pupils have much better educational opportunities than others.

Schooling in capitalist society, Bowles and Gintis (1976)

American sociologists Samuel Bowles and Herbert Gintis (1976) argue that the main role of education is social reproduction in other words education ensures that the inequalities of the existing capitalist society are reproduced in each new generation. Schools do this by ensuring that each new generation of workers are socialised to accept their future place as obedient workers in the capitalist economy. They also ensure that most children end up in a similar class position to their parents, in other words working class children end up in working-class jobs and middle-class children in middle-class jobs.

School and work – Bowles and Gintis argue that in order to prepare young people for work the organisation of schools is closely modelled on that of workplaces, what they call the correspondence between school and work. They argue this correspondence principle can be seen in a number of aspects of schooling in America.

- **Discipline** – Schools encourage punctuality, hard work and obedience and they discourage creativity, independent thinking and critical awareness. This helps to create the kind of obedient workers who follow instructions required by capitalist employers.
- **Motivation by external rewards** – In the workplace most workers gain little satisfaction from their jobs and are motivated by external rewards such as pay. This corresponds to the way schools motivate pupils by the prospect of external rewards, like educational qualifications, rather than because they actually enjoy learning.
- **Hierarchy** – Schools are based on a hierarchy of ranks, for example lower school students, sixth formers, teachers, senior teachers and head teachers. This prepares pupils for the workplace where they will have to accept the authority of those above them, for example supervisors or managers.

The way knowledge is organised and presented to pupils is known as the curriculum. For Marxists and indeed many other sociologists, the hidden curriculum is just as important. This is based on schools teaching pupils to think and behave in certain ways, for example through systems of discipline and school routines. For Bowles and Gintis it is the hidden curriculum which instils values such as hard work and obedience into pupils.

The myth of meritocracy – Bowles and Gintis argue that the idea of meritocracy put forward by functionalists is a myth used to justify inequalities in capitalist society. Pupils are encouraged to believe that everyone has an equal chance and that those who succeed do so on merit. In reality, they argue, pupils from the working class and ethnic minorities have much lower chance of success because the system works against them. By fostering this belief, those who fail in education are encouraged to accept dead-end jobs and low pay because they feel they deserved to fail because of their own lack of ability or effort.

Bowles and Gintis carried out research in New York schools to support their arguments. They found that the students who gained the highest grades were often not the most intelligent but were hardworking, dependable and obedient to teachers. Bright students were often rebellious, critical and questioned the teachers' authority so were awarded lower grades. Bowles and Gintis also found that it was white middle-class students who most often fitted the image of the ideal student for teachers and who were rewarded with the best grades.

- **Evaluation** – Marxist theories of education gained a lot of support from sociologists as they helped to explain class differences in educational attainment. A range of sociological research shows that there is only a loose link between pupil's abilities, for example, intelligence as measured by IQ tests, and their performance in education, whereas educational achievement is closely related to social background factors such as class, ethnicity and gender. This calls into question the functionalist ideas of meritocracy and equality of opportunity. However, Marxists have also been heavily criticised in their turn.
- **Influence of the formal curriculum** – Bowles and Gintis focus heavily on the influence of the hidden curriculum in socialising pupils into conformist and obedient attitudes. However, critics point out that, particularly in the UK, many subjects in the formal curriculum – such as history, media studies and indeed sociology – encourage students to look at society critically.
- **Resistance to the hidden curriculum** – Some Marxists such as Willis (see page 103) have argued that working class students do not simply passively accept their place in society in an obedient manner but show little respect for school rules or teachers' authority, this hardly fits with Bowles and Gintis's picture of schools creating a docile workforce.

- **The relative autonomy of the education system**
Bowles and Gintis and Althusser imply that the education is largely controlled by the ruling capitalist class and responds to their needs. In reality the UK education system until recently was controlled by local education authorities (LEAs) representing local councils elected by ordinary people. Moreover, employers have often complained that the education system does not produce the kind of workers they are looking for. For example schools are accused of focusing too much on academic or irrelevant subjects and not prioritising basic skills, such as numeracy and literacy, or on vocational skills which have a direct relevance to the workplace. The education system therefore enjoys relative autonomy or a degree of independence from the control of employers.
- **Changes in the workplace** Bowles and Gintis's theory can also be seen as out of date in respect to how workplaces are organised in the twenty-first century. There are far fewer jobs in factories which simply require workers prepared to do boring repetitive jobs without question. The biggest growth has been in the service sector in professional and managerial jobs thus many employers now look for workers who are capable of team working or taking decisions.

The contemporary relevance of Marxism

In defence of Bowles and Gintis it could be argued that some changes in the English education system have actually made it resemble their description more closely. For example, after 1988 the government took away the ability of teachers, schools and LEAs to determine their own curriculum and imposed a national curriculum (see page 167) which emphasised subjects which were seen as most relevant to the needs of employment such as maths, English and science. Subjects which might encourage students to question society critically, such as sociology, were not included in the national curriculum.

Some sociologists also argue that educational institutions are increasingly being run along the lines of capitalist businesses. They highlight the increasing marketisation (see page 155) and commodification of education (see Item C on Rikowski's work on page 104) as evidence of this trend. In light of this, Bowles and Gintis's claim that schools correspond to the organisation of capitalist workplaces may be relevant today.

Study

Learning to labour, Willis (1977)

A study by the British sociologist Paul Willis (1977) attempted to overcome some of the weaknesses of the Marxist approach to education. Willis studied 12 working-class boys who he calls 'the lads' in their last year and a half at school and their first months at work. Willis used a variety of methods associated with an ethnographic approach to research, including participant observation inside and outside school, group discussions, informal interviews and diaries. In this respect Willis draws on interpretivist approaches to research, trying to view the world of the lads through their eyes and quoting extensively from his recordings of his discussion with them to illustrate their viewpoints. However, in his analysis of his data Willis also draws on the Marxist concept of social reproduction and subtitled his book 'Why working class kids get working class jobs'. In this sense Willis can be described as offering a neo-Marxist approach to education.

The counter-school culture – Willis describes the lads in his study as a counter-school culture because they appeared to oppose the values of the school and their teachers in many respects. For example, the lads attached no value to academic success or qualifications and looked down on other boys who wanted to be successful describing them as 'ear oles' or 'lobes'. The lads avoided doing any work at school and invented elaborate schemes and excuses to get out of lessons or avoid studying. The main priority for the lads was what they called 'having a laugh' which involved playing practical jokes and undermining the authority of teachers.

For the lads masculinity was associated with earning a wage in a physical job and many of the boys already had part-time jobs. Smoking, drinking alcohol and avoiding wearing school uniform were also ways in which they asserted their adult status and resisted the authority of teachers. While the 'ear'oles' looked forward to getting jobs with prospects the lads could not wait to leave school and earn cash, albeit in relatively low paid jobs, for example in factories or on construction sites.

Willis argues that many of the elements of the counter-school culture such as resistance to authority, sexism, the status of manual labour and the importance of 'having a laff' are derived from shop-floor culture, the culture of manual working class males more generally. When Willis studied some of the boys as they moved into the world of work he noticed a similar attitude among adult manual workers and suggested that 'having a laff' and other forms of resistance are ways of dealing with the monotony of work and subjection to authority whether in school or in the workplace.

Resistance and social reproduction – While many Marxists see schools as effectively brainwashing pupils into being docile workers, Willis shows that if this is the intention of education it is remarkably unsuccessful. The lads engage in a process of resistance, not just against school but against the whole capitalist system. Willis suggests that to some extent the lads see through the ideology of capitalism, they are all too aware that the system is far from meritocratic and the dice are loaded against working-class boys like themselves. At the same time he points out that the attitudes and behaviour of boys like the lads actually condemn them to failure and ending up in jobs in which they will be exploited. At the end of the day the lad's resistance changes nothing in capitalism but simply reinforces the process of social reproduction.

Evaluation – Willis's study was highly influential on the sociology of education and unlike many Marxist accounts is based on detailed research and evidence. Willis also encouraged many subsequent studies which looked at what actually goes on inside schools from the point of view of pupils themselves, particularly why some pupils reject the idea of success in education and form anti-school subcultures (see pages 129 and 146).

However, there are some weaknesses in Willis's study:

- His sample consisted of only 12 boys in one school so could not be said to be representative.
- He tends to present a view that pupils are polarised into pro and anti-school subcultures. Subsequent studies have suggested the reality is more complex with many pupils accepting some elements of school life and resisting or rejecting others, meaning that there are a variety of different school subcultures or approaches to dealing with school life (see also pages 129–31).
- It has been suggested that Willis's account is now rather dated. In the 1970s it was possible to leave school at 16 and find a manual job relatively easily with few qualifications. This is much less true today with higher levels of youth unemployment and fewer unskilled manual jobs available.

Activity

Globalisation and privatisation of education
Item A

A city academy

Lord Harris, former treasurer to Conservative Party leader Margaret Thatcher, and carpet empire magnate, has sponsored nine London City Academies. Academies are schools which have been removed from the control of local councils and are often sponsored by private businesses, although they still receive the majority of their funding from central government (see also page 158 and pages 160–2).

Item B

Opposition to 'privatisation' of education

Students and others protesting against tuition fees in universities. Many opponents saw this as a step towards the privatisation of higher education.

Item C

Globalisation and the commodification of education

Glen Rikowski (2002) argues that far from changes in society meaning the Marxist approach to education is outdated, if anything it is more relevant than ever. Rikowski argues we are undergoing a process of globalisation whereby capitalist businesses are operating not just within nations but in an international market where capital, production processes and even workers are moved around the world to wherever businesses can make the biggest profits. Part of this process involves gradually removing control over institutions such as education, health and social services from governments and transforming them into commodities which can be bought and sold by businesses in the same way as groceries or mobile phones.

Rikowski argues that education has been increasingly organised on business lines, for examples services to schools such as cleaning and catering are organised by private companies and schools themselves are organised like private businesses competing with other schools for customers as education has become marketised (see also page 155). While this process began in the 1980s with the educational reforms of the Conservatives, he argues the Labour government of 1997–2010 also played its part, for example in creating academies, taking more schools out of the control of local authorities and moving them closer to being part of the private sector of education.

Rikowski argues that this process has been slow and almost unnoticed by many people but is moving education in Britain (and indeed in other countries) towards being run by private businesses at a profit. He fears that the future could be one where rather than schools being run as a service by the state providing an essential right for all they will become simply another type of capitalist business organised for profit. However, he argues that teachers are in a position to resist this

process as they are the ones who produce the labour power or future workers needed by capitalism. He calls on teachers to stand up for social justice, equality and solidarity and to challenge capitalism in their teaching.

Critics of Rikowski argue that while there has been a trend towards school being run on business lines this is a long way from schools being run for profit by global capitalism and that this is unlikely in the foreseeable future.

Adapted from Rikowski (2002 and 2005)

1 Why might it be argued that academies such as those referred to in Item A represent a step towards education being run by private business?
2 Why might some individuals and groups, such as the protestors in Item B, be opposed to what they see as the privatisation of education?
3 In what ways does Rikowski in Item B present a Marxist view of education?
4 What evidence is there for and against Rikowski's arguments?

Social democratic approaches

Social democratic theories heavily influenced government educational policies between 1944 and 1979. Social democratic approaches have some similarities with functionalism. But, whereas functionalism is a sociological approach which seeks to explain the role of education in industrial societies, social democratic theory is more concerned with shaping government educational policies to ensure that everyone has an equal chance to succeed in education. The influence of social democratic approaches is discussed further later in the chapter but some of the main themes of this approach are summarised below.

Equality of opportunity

Like functionalists, social democrats believe in equality of opportunity in education and meritocracy. However, they argue that the education system in Britain still has a long way to go to achieve this. Anthony Halsey (Halsey et al 1961, Halsey et al 1980), one of the leading social democratic thinkers demonstrated how after the 1944 Education Act (which was supposed to have provided equal opportunity for all) class differences in education persisted with middle-class children achieving better qualifications and being more likely to go to university than working-class children.

Wastage of ability

Social democratic theorists argue that good educational opportunities should be a right provided by the state to all children, not just those wealthy enough to pay for a private education. They argue that there is a massive wastage of ability because many bright working-class children's talents are not recognised or harnessed by the education system.

Education and economic growth

Like functionalists, social democrats argue that modern industrial societies need a more highly trained and specialised workforce and they see the education system as providing this. They generally favour increased government spending on education as they argue this investment will create long term benefits in terms of a more highly qualified workforce which will enable British employers to compete more effectively with other countries.

Evaluation

Social democratic approaches have had considerable support from sociologists who point to a range of evidence that working-class children are still disadvantaged in the British education system (see pages 114–117).

Social democratic approaches have also influenced government policies, for example from 1965 onwards Labour governments attempted to promote the comprehensive school system of secondary education (see page 165) because they argued it was more likely to offer equality of opportunity than the selective system which appeared to favour middle-class children by selecting far more of them through the 11+ exam for grammar schools.

Between 1997 and 2010 the Labour government also invested heavily in expanding higher education with the aim of ensuring that eventually half of all school leavers went on to some form of higher education. This was based on the idea that the UK could only compete in a global economy if it had a highly skilled workforce.

Although social democratic approaches have had more influence on mainstream educational policy than for example Marxism, they have been criticised by both Marxists and New Right thinkers.

- Marxists argue the social democratic approach does not go far enough. While they recognise inequalities in the education system, their solutions mainly involve reforms within the education system. For Marxists the underlying reason for inequalities in education is the way education is shaped by the needs of the wider capitalist system. Until that is replaced by a more equal socialist society there is little hope that the education system can offer equal opportunities for all children.
- New Right thinkers argue that it is the influence of social democratic thinking on educators which

is the problem in the education system. They argue that schools have been too obsessed with ensuring that all children have equal outcomes. They argue that there will always be inequality in educational achievement, instead government policies should focus on raising standards for all children.
- Some studies have also questioned the assumption that spending more money on education leads to economic growth (see for example, Alison Wolf (2002) in the Activity below).

The contemporary relevance of social democratic approaches

Social democratic approaches to education represent the main alternative to the New Right influenced approach adopted by the coalition and Conservative governments since 2010. The New Right approach involves breaking-up the comprehensive education system and replacing it with a variety of specialist schools, academies and free schools. Social democratic critics argue that this will mean a move away from an education system based on equality of opportunity. They suggest only middle-class families will be able to exploit the new system based on parental choice and competition for places at the highest achieving schools. (See for example Stephen Ball in Item C in the Activity on free schools page 109).

Activity

Debates about education and the economy
Item A
The economic benefits of higher education

A review of research into the economic benefits of investing in education for the Department for Business Innovation and Skills suggests the role of Higher Education (HE) in improving economic growth and competitiveness is widely acknowledged. It is clear that individuals with a university degree tend to have a significantly higher wage rate than those without. Graduates, on average, are paid 70–180 per cent more than workers without formal educational qualifications.

Their analysis suggests that the accumulation of graduate skills contributed on average 0.1–0.7 percentage points per annum to average labour productivity growth over the period 1994–2005. The lowest contributions were found in Germany, with relatively high contributions in Japan, the UK, Sweden and Spain.

The UK has a world-class system of higher education, and is home to 10 per cent of the world's top 100

universities. While higher education has expanded significantly between 1982 and 2005 and has continued to expand since 2005, the share of the workforce holding a university degree in the UK remains below that in Finland, the US, Japan and Canada in 2005, suggesting that there may still be room for further expansion.

Over the period 1994–2005, the share of the workforce with a university education in the UK rose from 12 to 18.9 per cent, or increased by 57 per cent. The study's estimates suggest that this will have raised the level of productivity in the UK by 11–28 per cent in the long-run. Over the same period, average labour productivity in the UK increased by about 34 per cent, suggesting that at least a third of this can be attributed to the accumulation of graduate skills in the labour force.

Adapted from Holland et al (2013)

Item B
Does education really have economic benefits?

Alison Wolf argues an unquestioning faith in the economic benefits of education has brought in huge amounts of wasteful government spending. In short she concludes: 'The simple one-way relationship which so entrances our politicians and commentators – education spending in, economic growth out – simply doesn't exist'.

Wolf argues that employers are certainly using education when they hire but she suggests that education may be serving essentially as a simply way of ranking, screening and selecting people in a mass society. As for linking growth in education and economic success, she explores the 'tiger' economies of the Far East and finds no definitive linkage. Switzerland is not notable as a big spender on education but nobody would deny its economic wealth: and, likewise, the US has supposedly an appalling school system, but appears to do well

economically. Indeed she asserts 'we definitely over-educate', especially in terms of the UK now producing so many graduates.

Adapted from Palfreyman (2002)

1 What evidence is presented in Item A which suggests that government spending on higher education brings benefits to the UK economy?
2 How might this support the social democratic view of the role of education in society?
3 What criticisms does Alison Wolf make of this view in Item B?
4 Why does Wolf argue that employers may still obtain some benefit from the way the education system operates?

New Right approaches

Social democratic approaches dominated government educational policy in the period after the Second World War. However, the election of a Conservative government under Margaret Thatcher's leadership in 1979 changed this. The Thatcher government was strongly influenced by New Right or neoliberal approach to politics and economics and this could be seen in their educational policies (see pages 154–7). Like social democratic approaches, New Right ideas are a form of ideology informing government policies on education rather than a sociological theory of education.

Reduction in state control

The New Right argued that the nanny state was controlling people's lives too much and called for individuals to be able to use their own initiative and enterprise. For example, they argued that schools were stifled from running their own affairs because of excessive interference by bureaucrats in local education authorities (LEAs).

Reduction in government spending

The New Right also argued that a lot of government expenditure was wasteful and called for a reduction in spending and taxation. For example, they argued that by reducing the power of LEAs, less money would be spent on administrators, educational advisors and support services, allowing school to use funding to directly benefit pupils.

Marketisation and competition

New Right thinkers believe that goods and services are best delivered through a competitive market. For example, supermarkets have to compete on price, quality and customer service in order to attract consumers and make a profit and this means they have to be very efficient at what they do or go out of business. The New Right believe public services should be organised on the same principle, rather than one organisation (for example the local education authority) providing all educational services in an area there should be a choice of providers (for example different types of schools) competing with one another in an education market. This would drive up standards in all schools and colleges as they seek to attract more customers.

Vocationalism

One way in which the New Right agree to some extent with social democrats is that education can help to support economic growth. However, the New Right argued that UK governments have in the past put too much emphasis on academic education some of which has little relevance to the world of work. The New Right called for a greater emphasis on vocational education, for example courses which directly train students in skills they can use in the workplace.

Evaluation

Sociologists in general have not been enthusiastic about the impact of New Right policies on education and have offered a range of criticisms of them.

- **Educational markets are unfair** It would appear parents who are themselves highly educated and well off are in a much better position to take advantage of parental choice in education. For example, middle-class parents tend to ensure they get their children into schools with a good reputation and may even pay extra to buy a house in the catchment area of a successful school.

- **Selection by schools** Although the New Right promote the idea of parental choice, problems arise when some schools are over-subscribed. In these circumstances school are likely to adopt some form of selection, for example faith schools may give preference to children who practice a particular faith and some schools may make use of some kind of entry exam or other assessment. It is likely that in these circumstances schools will select pupils who are most likely to be successful and they are more likely to come from middle-class backgrounds.

- **Raising standards** Levels of attainment in terms of GCSE and A Level pass rates have certainly improved in England and Wales but it is not clear that this has been due to the introduction of more competition between schools. Critics also argue that it is middle-class children's attainment which has improved most leading to a widening of class inequalities; for example, the proportion of working-class children going to university has only increased slightly compared to a much larger increase in access to higher education for middle-class children.

- **Narrowing the aims of education** Some critics argue that the New Right have turned schools and colleges into exam factories which focus purely on maximising the number of students who gain qualifications. Students themselves have also been encouraged to adopt an individualistic competitive outlook where the only thing that matters is their own success. In this process educational institutions have lost sight of other important aspects of education, for example learning to co-operate with others and developing skills such as creativity, critical thinking and self-awareness.

The contemporary relevance of New Right approaches

New Right approaches have had considerable influence on educational policies in the last 30 years and their supporters would argue they have proved successful. For example, the proportion of pupils leaving school with qualifications such as GCSEs has increased and a growing number of young people go on to university. The New Right would also argue that parents and students now have much greater choice about schools; rather than standard local comprehensive schools, there is a choice of different schools, for example specialising in arts, sciences, sports or technology, along with academies and free schools.

Although New Right ideas have met with considerable opposition from some teachers and educationalists, this approach has remained the dominant influence on education policy since 2005.

Activity

The debate over free schools

Item A

Free schools

In 2010 the Coalition government announced that anyone could apply for government approval to set up a new form of school known as a free school which would receive funding from the state but would be free from direct government control. Some free schools have been set up by existing schools, charities and religious organisations but some have been established by groups of parents who are simply dissatisfied with existing educational provision in their locality. Free schools have greater freedom to decide their own curriculum than traditional state schools and do not have to employ qualified teachers. Supporters of free schools argue that they will offer parents and children alternatives to existing state schools and help to drive up standards in education.

Experiments in education: Are free schools the research and development wing of state education?

Activity (continued)

Item B

An example of a free school

Toby Young, a journalist, helped to set up West London Free School (WLFS) – a four-form entry secondary in Hammersmith, London. He argues that the strongest argument for free schools is that they provide a protected space within the state sector where teachers and educationalists can try out new things, he calls it 'the research and development wing of state education'. He argues that by allowing schools like the WLFS to innovate and experiment we can eventually discover more effective ways of teaching and learning and thus drive up standards in all schools.

Children at WLFS receive what Young describes as a 'classical liberal education'. Regardless of background or ability, all pupils are expected to study a core of academic subjects – English language, English literature, maths, history, geography, divinity, Latin, French, physics, chemistry and biology – complemented by plenty of art, music, drama and sport.

Young suggests that the early signs for the school are good. Their 'classical liberal' formula is popular with local parents. The school had nine applicants for every place in 2012, making it the most oversubscribed state secondary in Hammersmith. The intake is not just white, middle class: approximately 28 per cent of the year 7s are on free school meals and between 30 and 40 per cent are black, Asian or minority ethnic. Roughly 25 per cent of all the pupils – year 7s and year 8s – have special educational needs (SEN) and 50 per cent have English as an additional language.

The school is therefore a fairly typical mix for an inner London comprehensive and, so far, there's no evidence that any pupils are struggling to cope, including those with statements of SEN. The school has not needed to permanently exclude any pupils and in a parental satisfaction survey 100 per cent said they'd recommend the school to others. The year 7 girls' netball team came second in the local league and roughly two-thirds of the first cohort of 120 children are learning a musical instrument. An important plus point is there's no attainment gap between those children on free school meals and others. When the school assessed the year 8s in 2012 they discovered that girls on free school meals are outperforming every other cohort.

Adapted from Young (2012)

Item C

A critique of the marketisation of education

Professor Stephen Ball, a sociologist of education, is also a leading critic of what he calls the 'marketisation of education'. Ball argues the English education system has been broken up and fragmented by both New Labour and the coalition government. He argues that education has been taken backwards to the situation before the 1870 Education Act (when the state first provided education for all) as a coherent system of state education is replaced by 'a patchwork of uneven and unequal provision' including free schools and academies of various kinds, faith schools, studio schools and university technical colleges.

Ball also argues that instead of schools being run by democratically elected local councils they are increasingly controlled by 'an incoherent and haphazard jigsaw of providers – charities, foundations, social enterprises and faith and community groups – monitored at arm's length by the central state'.

While these changes have been pursued in the name of parental choice, Ball argues that in reality parents have no direct, local participation or involvement their children's education. Parents are more like customers of electric or water companies able to choose to change providers but having no control over those who provide their services. How much choice parents have also depends of where they live, while in some areas there may be a choice for example of different academies or free schools in many rural areas this choice does not exist.

Ball suggests there is no room for those parents who just want to send their child to a good local state which is part of their community and history. He concludes by pointing out that 'parents can choose the school they want, or not, but communities cannot – unless they open their "own" free school'.

Adapted from Ball (2013)

1 In what ways does the introduction of free schools fit in with the New Right approach to education?
2 What arguments in favour of free schools are put forward by Toby Young in Item B?
3 What criticisms are made of New Right approaches to education by Stephen Ball in Item C?
4 Using information from all the Items and elsewhere evaluate the value of free schools as an addition to the English education system.

Feminist approaches

Feminists have campaigned for equality in education for 200 years. In the nineteenth century women fought to gain admittance to British universities and were able to study at most universities by 1900, although in very small numbers. However, Cambridge University did not allow women to qualify for degrees until 1948. Even in the 1970s about twice as many males as females gained university places. Girls' education often focused on preparing them for a role as wives and mothers, for example girls were encouraged to take subjects such as cookery, needlework and home economics and discouraged from taking sciences and practical subjects such as woodwork and metalwork.

As recently as the 1980s feminist Dale Spender (1983) described women as invisible in education arguing that the curriculum was male biased with limited attention being paid to the role of women in history, sciences or the arts. Spender also showed that boys tended to receive more attention and encouragement from teachers.

While Marxists have highlighted how the hidden curriculum prepares young people for their future class positions in society, feminists argue that the hidden curriculum also operates to reinforce gender inequalities. Males and females may not only study different subject in the formal curriculum but there may also be hidden messages in the way school are organised, for example in many schools and colleges more of the senior teachers and headteachers are male while jobs such as cleaners and catering staff are mainly performed by females implying that it is normal for women to carry out more subordinate roles.

Similarly, Marxists argue that education is concerned with the process of social reproduction ensuring that class inequalities are perpetuated in each new generation. Many feminists see schools acting as agencies of gender socialisation, in order to reproduce relationships of domination and subordination between males and females.

Evaluation

Thanks to campaigns and research by feminists there have been major changes in education in the last 30 years. Many of the more obviously sexist aspects of education have disappeared from the British education system: girls can now study the same subjects as boys and teaching materials have been rewritten to remove sexist images, for example pictures of scientists at work showing only men. Most schools now have equal opportunities policies and teacher training encourages them to treat both sexes equally and to have the same expectations of boys and girls. From this perspective feminism has made a major contribution to equality of opportunity in education.

Some commentators, however, argue that feminism has been so successful that it is now no longer relevant, if anything it is boys who are now under-achieving (see page 147). It can also be argued that feminists focus too much on gender inequalities when the evidence suggests that differences between social classes in educational achievement are far more of an issue than those between females and males.

The contemporary relevance of feminism

Many feminists argue that their ideas remain relevant to education today. Feminists argue that girls achieving better, on average, better than boys has not removed hidden forms of sexism and sexual discrimination in education. The article in the activity below by a 17 year old girl offers some examples. Girls are also still under-represented in certain subjects at A Level and university level, notably maths, some sciences and some technology subjects (see Item B in the activity on page 142).

Chapter 3 Education

Activity

Do girls still need feminism?

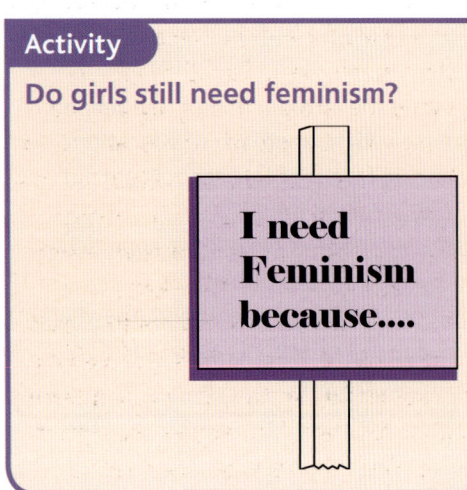

The Guardian newspaper gave a voice to Jinan Younis a sixth former at a school in Altrincham after she received online abuse for trying to start a feminist society.

I am 17 years old and I am a feminist. I believe in gender equality and am under no illusion about how far we are from achieving it. Identifying as a feminist has become particularly important to me since a school trip I took to Cambridge last year.

Activity (continued)

A group of men in a car started wolf-whistling and shouting sexual remarks at my friends and me. I asked the men if they thought it was appropriate for them to be abusing a group of 17-year-old girls. The response was furious. The men started swearing at me, called me a bitch and threw a cup of coffee over me. For those men we were just legs, breasts and pretty faces. Speaking up shattered their fantasy, and they responded violently to my voice.

Shockingly, the boys in my peer group have responded in exactly the same way to my feminism. After returning from this school trip I started to notice how much the girls at my school suffer because of the pressures associated with our gender. Many of the girls have eating disorders, some have had peers heavily pressure them into sexual acts, others suffer in emotionally abusive relationships where they are constantly told they are worthless.

I decided to set up a feminist society at my school to try to tackle these issues. However, this was more difficult than I imagined as my all-girls school was hesitant to allow the society. After a year-long struggle, the feminist society was finally ratified.

What I hadn't anticipated on setting up the feminist society was a massive backlash from the boys in my wider peer circle. They took to Twitter and started a campaign of abuse against me. I was called a 'feminist bitch', accused of 'feeding [girls] bullshit', and in a particularly racist comment was told 'all this feminism bull won't stop uncle Sanjit from marrying you when you leave school'.

Our feminist society was derided with retorts such as, 'FemSoc, is that for real? #DPMO' [don't piss me off] and every attempt we made to start a serious debate was met with responses such as 'feminism and rape are both ridiculously tiring'.

It's been over a century since the birth of the suffragette movement and boys are still not being brought up to believe that women are their equals. Instead we have a whole new battleground opening up online where boys can attack, humiliate, belittle us and do everything in their power to destroy our confidence before we even leave high school. If you thought the fight for female equality was over, I'm sorry to tell you that a whole new round is only just beginning.

Adapted from 'What happened when I started a feminist society at school', *The Guardian*, 20 June 2013

1 Why does the young woman who wrote this article argue that girls and women still need feminism?
2 How would you evaluate her argument?

Liberal and radical approaches

Many of the theories of education considered so far argue that an important role of the education system is to prepare young people for the world of work and serve the needs of the economy. This view is questioned by the liberal view of education (not to be confused with the neoliberal view put forward by the New Right). The liberal approach goes back to the middle ages and was espoused in the nineteenth century by thinkers such as John Henry Newman and Thomas Huxley. They argued that education should be for its own sake and develop students as rounded human beings with a broad knowledge of many different subjects. In the USA the idea of a liberal education can still be seen in many university courses where, rather than specialising in one or two subjects, students are encouraged to pick courses from a wide range of disciplines.

Education in the UK has arguably moved away from this liberal ideal as there has been more emphasis on vocationalism in education. This is the view that what is learned in education must be of relevance to the world of work. In higher education this can be seen in greater prominence being given to vocational degrees which directly prepare students for their future careers (for example Events Management or Journalism) rather than purely academic degrees (such as English Literature or Philosophy).

Illich: Deschooling society

Some writers on education have attacked both this traditional liberal approach and vocational approaches to education and argued for a more radical approach as to how people are educated. Ivan Illich (1973) argues that we should deschool society by getting rid of schools and other institutions of formal education altogether. Illich argues that qualified teachers are not the best people to undertake education but rather people with knowledge, skills and enthusiasm for a particular area. He advocated the development of learning webs, whereby people who wanted to learn something would be put in contact with people who wanted to teach something so they could then learn together in an informal way. Illich argues that other people should not dictate to us what we need to learn but we should learn what we find interesting and useful.

On the face of it Illich's ideas seem to have some similarities to the idea of free schools advocated by the New Right but his ideas go much further as he wishes to abolish schools altogether, not simply replace one kind of school with another. Illich's ideas are in fact much closer to Marxism as he too sees education as a means of control and a way in which young people are socialised into accepting an unequal and institutional society by learning in hierarchical and rule bound schools.

Critics of Illich argue that his ideas are impractical and utopian and many educationalists would argue that trained and expert teachers are best qualified to deliver education. There would be no guarantee that Illich's proposed learning webs would ensure that everyone received the education they needed in order fulfil their role as adults in the kind of industrial society we live in.

Activity

An alternative approach to schooling

Summerhill School is an independent fee paying British boarding school in Suffolk that was founded in 1921 by Alexander Sutherland Neill. He believed that the school should be made to fit the child, rather than the other way around. Summerhill is run as a democracy and rules are made at meetings three times a week which everyone can attend; staff and students all have equal votes. The school is run according to Neill's principle of 'freedom, not licence' meaning that you can do what you like as long as it does not harm others. Pupils can choose what lessons, if any, they attend, although they may come in for criticism from their peers if they miss lessons and impede the progress of others. Classes often contain pupils from a range of age groups and pupils can take exams whenever they feel ready for them.

Summerhill had some influence on the progressive education movement of the 1960s where many educationalists advocated a more 'child-centred'
approach, allowing children to choose what they wanted to learn and learning through discovery rather than formal teaching. Critics however, argue that Summerhill prepares young people poorly for a society where individuals cannot always choose what they want to do and fails to adequately prepare pupils for formal educational qualifications. Summerhill's philosophy also seems very much at odds with the direction of mainstream education in the UK where the curriculum is increasingly laid down by central government and there has been pressure on teachers to abandon progressive ideas of education and to return to more traditional teaching methods.

1 What differences are there between the way pupils are educated at Summerhill and the way you have been educated?

2 What are the advantages and disadvantages of the approach to education pioneered by A.S. Neill at Summerhill?

Activity

Summary of perspectives on the relationship between education and the economic system

Copy out this table on a large sheet of paper and write a brief summary in each box.

	Functionalist	Marxist	Social Democratic	New Right
How does this approach see education preparing young people for the world of work?				
What criticisms (if any) does this approach have of how the education system does this?				
What are the key concepts associated with this approach?				
What are the main criticisms of this approach?				

Section summary

Make a copy of the following passage and fill in the blanks using the words given below.

.... theories focus on the benefits which education provides to society. They argue that education has important functions in modern industrial society, these include creating a sense of .... or shared values amongst members of society, acting as a bridge between the .... of the family and .... of the wider society and achieving a process of .... or sorting and grading to ensure that young people are placed in the jobs which are most suited to their talents and abilities. Such theories also see education as teaching children important skills needed in the workplace which cannot be taught by parents because in industrial societies there is a complex .... meaning that people do many different specialised jobs and do not always follow in their parents' footsteps.

This view of education is rejected by .... theories. Such approaches argue that education is an .... which simply socialises children into the ideas and beliefs of the ruling class. Such approaches also reject the idea that education is based on the principle of .... or achievement based on ability and hard work but rather is based on a process of .... whereby most children end up in a similar social class position to their parents. Some Marxists point to the .... between school and work, for example the hierarchy in schools reflects the hierarchy between bosses and workers in the workplace. Other Marxists point out that not all working class children meekly accept their position in capitalist society but there is .... against the discipline imposed by schools and employers in the form of ...., for example, pupils who refuse to conform to school rules.

.... theories of education are concerned with trying to develop policies to ensure equality of opportunity in education. They argue that harnessing the talents and abilities of all children will have benefits for the .... as well as creating a fairer and more equal society.

This approach is opposed by .... theories which argue that focusing too much on creating equality in education has meant standards in education have fallen. Such approaches advocate the .... of education whereby schools are encouraged to compete like private businesses. They also encourage the development of .... education in order to ensure that young people develop skills which are directly relevant to the world of work.

.... theories focus on gender inequalities in education. They argue that we still live in a .... or male dominated society. For example, schools still play a part in ...., teaching girls and boys different roles in society.

.... theories reject the idea that education should focus on preparing young people for work and suggest it should develop young people into rounded human beings. Ivan Illich takes this even further and calls for a process of .... so that people can learn what they want to learn from anyone willing to teach them rather than being forced to learn from teachers and educational experts.

correspondence, counter-school cultures, deschooling society, division of labour, economy, feminist, functionalist, gender socialisation, ideological state apparatus, liberal, marketisation, Marxist, meritocracy, New Right, particularistic values, patriarchal, resistance, role allocation, social class reproduction, social democratic, social solidarity, universalistic values, vocational

3.2/3 Inequalities in education

Social class and education

The expansion of state education since the late nineteenth century has meant that education has gone from being the privilege of the well-off to a right to which all children are entitled. Since the 1940s state education has been based on the idea of equality of opportunity for all children. Despite this, sociological research over the last 70 years has shown that class differences in achievement in education have persisted, despite numerous attempts by different governments to reduce them. While differences based on gender and ethnicity have been reduced in the last twenty years those based on class have narrowed only slightly.

Measuring class and attainment

Measuring class and educational attainment is not straightforward. Traditionally sociologists have adopted a positivist aproach using quantitative or statistical data in order to show a correlation between the social class of children (usually based on parents' occupations) and attainment at different stages in education (for example the percentage of children achiving 5 A*-C grades at GCSE). Quantitative data can also be used to explain class differences in attainment, for example in order to establish correlations between class and other variables, for example the amount of interest and support demonstrated by parents for their children's education. Interpretivists have argued this kind of approach fails to understand the meaning which education has for different groups of children. They have tended to make use of qualitiative data often gathered from in-depth ethnographic studies of small groups of pupils in order to understand their experiences of education in much greater detail.

One useful source of secondary data for sociologists in the past was the Youth Cohort Studies, a series of government sponsored longitudinal surveys based on large samples begun in 1985 which followed young people in England and Wales through education. These provided useful data on how young people from different social classes fared at different stages in their education. Unfortunately since 2011 the government has discontinued the Youth Cohort Survey and the Department for Education no longer produces data on class and educational achievement.

UCAS (the organisation) which handles applications to universities also used to collect data on the social class background of university applicants but has also discontinued this. It now only collects postcode data which gives only a very rough guide to the social background of candidates. (The last set of data from UCAS based on social class from 2008 are shown in the Activity below.)

Activity

Social class and educational attainment

Note: Young people in these tables are classified by the occupations of their parents using the NS-SEC classification (the social classification used for many official government statistics).

Item A

Attainment at 16 and 19 by social class

	Level 2 by age 16	Level 3 by age 19
Higher professional	83	77
Lower professional	76	71
Intermediate	62	56
Lower Supervisory	51	44
Routine	44	38
Other/not classified	37	35

Percentage of young people achieving Level 2 and Level 3 qualifications by social class, 2010

- Level 2 qualifications include GCSEs and BTEC intermediate
- Level 3 qualifications include A Levels and BTEC national

Source: Department for Education, (2011)

Activity (continued)

Item B

Social class and higher education

	Higher managerial and professional	Lower managerial and professional	Intermediate	Small employers and own account workers	Lower supervisory and technical	Semi-routine	Routine
Under 21	22.5	30.4	13.9	7.8	4.6	14.7	6.1
21–24	10.3	24.7	17.8	5.8	3.4	28.2	9.8
25–39	8.5	25.9	20.3	5.5	3.0	29.5	7.4
40+	11.0	27.4	19.3	5.8	2.7	29.0	4.9
Total	**20.4**	**29.6**	**14.7**	**7.4**	**4.4**	**17.0**	**6.5**
per cent in the population according to 2011 Census	10.3	20.8	12.7	9.4	6.9	14.1	11.1

Social class of applicants accepted to degree courses by age, 2008 (percentages)

Source: UCAS annual datasets 2008 and 2011 Census

Item C

Class differences in entry to top universities

Cambridge University, one of the 24 establishments in the elite Russell Group

According to the report by John Jerrim of the Institute for Education in London children with parents in professional or managerial jobs are more than three times more likely to attend a top university than working-class students, even when they have earned the right grades. The research published by the Sutton Trust showed that the wide gap in attendance between the two groups was only partly due to academic ability. The report suggests that 27 per cent of the difference in admissions between the social classes in England was not due to differences in academic ability.

'Although academic achievement is an important factor, a substantial proportion of the elite university access gap in each country remains unexplained," Jerrim wrote. "This suggests there are significant numbers of working-class children who, even though they have the academic ability to attend, choose to enter a non-selective institution instead.'

Adapted from Adams (2013)

1 Study Item A. What class differences are apparent in the educational attainment of young people at:
   a) age 16
   b) age 19?
2 Study Item B. Compare the percentage of people going to university from different social classes with the percentage of the population in each social class. Which social classes are over-represented and which are under-represented in terms of going on to study degree courses at university?
3 Why does Item C suggest that social class not only affects a person's chances of going to university but also affects what kind of university they are likely to go to.
4 What explanations can you offer for the class differences in education shown in Items A-C?

Free school meals and attainment

While the government no longer publishes official statistics on social class and educational attainment it does produce data comparing children receiving free school meals with other children. Parents of children aged over 7 who receive free school meals (FSM) have to be in receipt of one of a number of state benefits such as income support or universal credit. FSM is therefore a useful indicator of children who come from the the lowest income families and can be used to assess how far poverty and low incomes affect children's chances in education.

FSM is, however, a fairly crude measure of class and education and focuses only on children at the bottom of the income scale. It does not differntiate between children who are not on free school meals by social class. There are also children from poor homes who either do not qualify for FSM (for example because their parents are in employment) or whose parents do not claim FSM even though they are entitled to.

Activity

Comparing the attainment of FSM pupils and other pupils

Item A

How FSM pupils perform at different stages in education

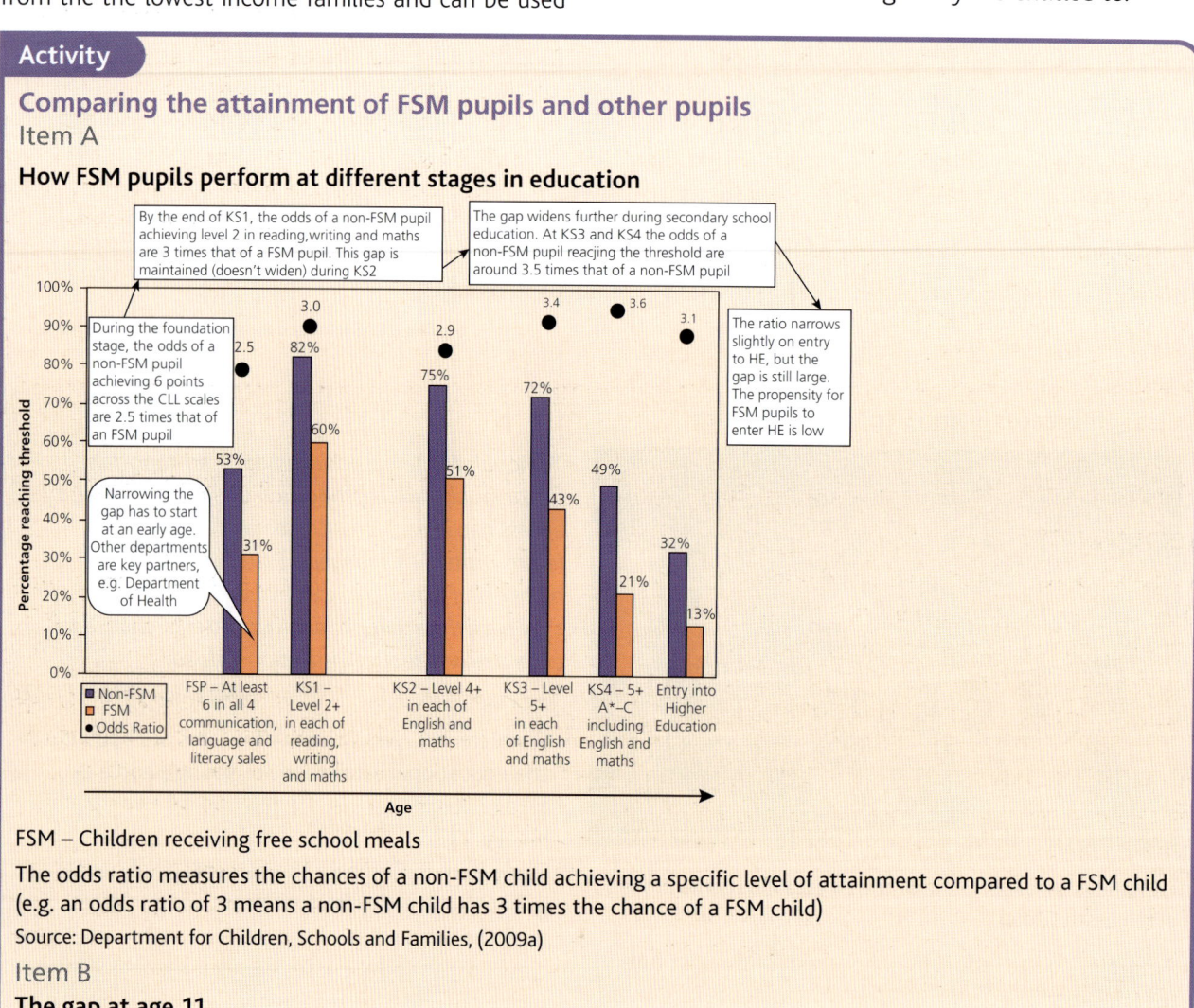

FSM – Children receiving free school meals

The odds ratio measures the chances of a non-FSM child achieving a specific level of attainment compared to a FSM child (e.g. an odds ratio of 3 means a non-FSM child has 3 times the chance of a FSM child)

Source: Department for Children, Schools and Families, (2009a)

Item B

The gap at age 11

Attainment at age 11 in England

Source: Sippitt, A. (2014)

Activity (continued)

Item C
The gap at GCSE

Percentage point attainment gap at GCSE between non-FSM and FSM students

	2006/07	2007/08	2008/09	2009/10	2010/11
5 or more grades A*-C at GCSE and equivalent	27.1	26.7	24.0	20.3	18.4

FSM – pupils receiving free school meals

Source: Department for Education (2012)

1 Examine Item A. How do FSM children fare compared to others on tests of communication, language and literacy (CLL scales) in the reception stage of primary education?
2 According to Item A, how does the gap in attainment between FSM children and others change as they move through the stages of the education system?
3 Why is it suggested that narrowing the gap has to start at an early age?

4 What do Items B and C suggest has happened to the gap between FSM and other children in attainment:
  a) at age 11 (end of key stage 2) ;
  b) at GCSE (end of key stage 4)?
5 Suggest possible reasons why children in receipt of free school meals achieve less in education than others.

Material factors and educational attainment

A number of sociologists have investigated how far low incomes or lack of money are a factors in the lower educational attainment of poorer children such as those receiving free school meals. These are often refered to as theories of material deprivation.

Smith and Noble: Barriers to learning

Teresa Smith and Michael Noble (1995) argue that low incomes can create a number of barriers to learning:

- Lack of funds to pay for school uniforms, school trips, transport to and from school, classroom materials and textbooks meaning children can be bullied or fall behind with schoolwork.
- Children from low-income families suffer more ill-health affecting attendance and performance at school.
- Being unable to pay for private tuiition or private education.
- Being less likely to have access to a computer with internet access, educational toys, books and space to do homework in a comfortable well-heated home.
- The marketisation of schools may further disadvantage poorer children as they are more likely to be concentrated in more unpopular schools with poorer resources.

Using data from the UK, Jo Blanden and Paul Gregg (2004) confirmed that there was a direct relationship between income and educational attainment: they calculated that a one third reduction in income from the mean (a reduction of around £140 per week) increases the probability of a child getting no A*–C grades at GCSE by around 3–4 percentage points, and reduces the chances of achieving a degree by a similar amount.

Material factors and access to higher education

Some sociologists have argued that the increase in tuition fees for universities and the replacement of student grants with loans (which have to be repaid) has discouraged poorer students from going on to higher education. Claire Callender and Jon Jackson (2005) carried out a survey of nearly 2,000 prospective higher education students and found evidence that debt aversion (fear of getting into debt because of requiring a student loan) was discouraging some students from lower income backgrounds from applying to university.

In 2012 there was a sharp rise in tuition fees with many universities charging as much as £9,000 a year. This was followed by a 10 per cent drop in applications to universities. It would appear that it is students from poorer backgrounds who are most likely to be deterred from going to universities by higher fees.

Evaluating the impact of material factors

While material factors almost certainly affect educational attainment it is hard to know how much impact they have. It is very hard to disentangle material factors from what sociologists call cultural factors, for example the level of education of parents and how much encouragement and support they are able to give children. A study by the Department for Children, Schools and Families (2009b) *Deprivation and Education* points out that material and cultural deprivation often go hand in hand thus poorer children may lack books and educational toys in their homes or have poor diets causing ill health because of low incomes but they are also likely to have less educated parents who are less likely to know how to stimulate their intellectual development or to have high aspirations for their children.

Material factors also seem to have more impact on some social groups than others. For example in terms of educational achievement two of the most successful minority ethnic groups in the UK are Indians and Chinese. Among the children of these groups there is far less difference between the achievement of free school meal children and others than in the white population. This suggests that some groups manage to overcome the disadvantages of material deprivation more than others, for example by having high expectations and aspirations for their children.

Activity

Material factors and education
Item A

Material deprivation (left) appears to put poorer children at a disadvantage in education. Middle-class children (right) are more likely to have computers, books and space to do homework.

Item B
Income and access to material resources

Note: The data below were collected from research for the Joseph Rowntree Trust based on a large scale longitudinal study of children as they moved through the education system.

The study classified children according to SEP quintiles which are based on measures of the economic position of families, including income, occupational class of mothers and fathers and housing tenure. The population is divided into quintiles or groups of 20 per cent ranked from richest to poorest.

Activity: Material factors and education (continued)

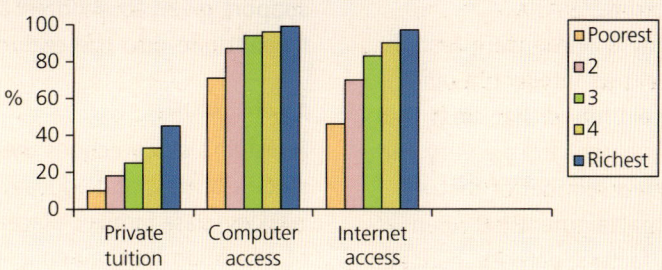

Access to material resources by SEP quintile (at age 14)

Adapted from Chowdry et al (2010)

Item C

The cost of extra-curricular activities

When my children were younger I vowed that I would never become one of those parents constantly ferrying their offspring to music lessons, sports clubs and other activities. But it's hard to resist the pressure to offer your children at least some of the opportunities their peers are enjoying so here I am, writing cheques and trying to work out if we can also squeeze karate in this term.

So far I haven't made use of private tuition – another paid for out of school activity that is surprisingly common in my neighbourhood. Where we live, on the outskirts of London, parents are willing to pay upwards of £30 an hour for a tutor to help their child with school work or prepare for entrance tests to secondary schools. As new polling from the Sutton Trust shows 23 per cent of young people report having tutoring, a figure that rises to 37 per cent in London.

Participation in enrichment activities, which are sometimes offered free by schools, is more common. My children are part of a large majority who enjoy after school clubs like choir, Brownies or sports. Sutton Trust polling finds 76 per cent of parents report that their child participated in a regular extra-curricular activity in the past 12 months. But this figure varies significantly by social and economic status. As you might expect, it's those from the most advantaged backgrounds who are most likely to take part in activities and also have the most money spent on them.

35 per cent of households earning more than £52,000 a year have paid fees for extra-curricular activities for their children in the past three months, compared with only 9 per cent households earning less than £14,000 a year. In other words, a child from the richest fifth of families is four times more likely to enjoy paid for extra-curricular activities than one from the poorest fifth. And the amount spent on these activities also varies by social class. 22 per cent of parents with professional or administrative occupations reported spending £500 or more on one child in the last year, compared with just 10 per cent of those with manual or routine jobs.

Adapted from Selvarajah (2014)

1 Using the pictures in Item A and any other evidence explain how material factors might help to explain class differences in educational attainment.

2 What evidence is shown in Item B that access to certain material resources is linked to social class and income?

3 In what ways might access to extra-curricular activities such as those in Item C be dependent on the incomes of parents?

4 Why might being able to access the resources in Item B and the activities in Item C help children to be more successful in education?

Cultural factors and educational attainment

Many sociologists argue that class differences in education have their origins in a child's home background. While the material factors discussed in the previous section are important in this respect, cultural factors focus on social class differences in norms, values and attitudes to education.

Feinstein: Social class and parental support

Leon Feinstein (2003) used data from two longitudinal surveys to analyse factors affecting children's success in education. These were the National Child

119

Development Study (which followed children born in one week in March 1958) and the British Cohort Study (which followed children born in 1970).

In the British Cohort Study children were tested at different ages to monitor their intellectual and educational progress. Feinstein found that class differences in ability were apparent from a very early age. Feinstein suggested that a number of factors accounted for differences in attainment between children, including material factors, parents' education and the quality of the schools children attended, however, class differences in parental interest and support were the most significant factor. This was measured by teachers' assessments of how much interest parents showed in their children's education.

Feinstein argues that pre-school programmes such as the Sure Start scheme initiated by the Labour government in 1998 (see page 169) are one way of overcoming the disadvantages faced by working-class children, however, he argues that the additional support given to children by these programmes needs to continue into the early years of primary schooling.

Evaluation

Feinstein's study echoes the conclusions of many older studies of class and education which suggested that working-class families place less value on the importance of education for their children and tend to have lower aspirations for them. These attitudes and values are therefore passed on to children in their socialisation. Although, Feinstein does not use the term himself, some studies have suggested that working-class children suffer from not only material deprivation but also cultural deprivation. This implies that working-class children lack adequate preparation for education in the way they are socialised by parents and are disadvantaged as a result.

Activity

Home background and educational achievement

Item A

The importance of parents in children's education

If parents were not successful at school themselves, if they are not confident with the written word ... then they are unlikely to be confident in this kind of activity. When their children have homework involving comprehension, research or working in a foreign language they may feel a gap between wanting to help and knowing the best way to do so. This is not to say that computers, homework clubs, relatives and advice cannot get round these obstacles, but they are obstacles nevertheless, and ones not experienced by parents who are say accountants or managers. These obstacles are increased if parents have low levels of literacy themselves.

Source: Adapted from Gaine and George, (1999)

Item B

Class differences in home background

Note: The item below is based on a longitudinal study by the Joseph Rowntree Foundation. It examined the involvement of parents in their children's education and compared different income groups or SEP quintiles (five groups ranging from the richest 20 per cent to the poorest 20 per cent of the population).

Expectations for education:

Richer parents tend to have higher expectations for their children's education than poorer parents. For example, four out of five parents in the top SEP quintile think that their child is likely to apply to university, compared to just over half of parents in the bottom SEP quintile at age 14.

Family interactions:

Parents in the top SEP quintile are more likely to help their children with their homework, are more likely to get involved in school activities and more likely to share family meals with their children than parents in the bottom SEP quintile.

Source: Adapted from Chowdry et al, (2010)

Item C

A homework club

Homework clubs have been started to help children who might otherwise struggle.

Activity (continued)

1 Using information from Items A and B and elsewhere, explain why the home background of middle class children is likely to give them an advantage in education over working-class children.

2 To what extent do you think organisations such as homework clubs (see Item C) and pre-school education can help to compensate children for lack of support and encouragement by parents?

3 Evaluate how far the fact that working-class children are on average less successful at school than middle-class children is due to the attitudes of their parents.

Critics of Feinstein argue that some of his statistics may not be valid measures of what they aim to quantify. For example, parental interest is measured in terms of teachers' perceptions of their interest which may not be accurate. For example some parents may appear to teachers to be unconcerned about their children's progress because they do not discuss it, for example at parents' evenings. However, parents who themselves had a bad experience of school may be reluctant to approach authority figures such as teachers. Middle-class parents may be more confident and articulate in discussing their child's progress and therefore come across as more interested.

A study by Gillian Evans (2007) of a working-class council estate in south London adopted a qualitative methodology, using methods such as participant observation and informal interviews in order to immerse herself in the local community. She found working-class parents very much wanted their children to do well at school but, unlike middle-class parents, tended not to use what she called formal-learning-type skills in the way they cared for their children. These would include counting, shape and colour recognition and speaking and writing. As a result working-class children are less prepared for school and never catch up with their middle class peers. However, Evans rejects the idea of cultural deprivation. She argues for a social variation model as she argues that working-class methods of bringing up children are not inferior but simply different.

Bernstein: speech patterns

British sociologist Basil Bernstein (1961, 1970, 1972) suggested that differences in the way social classes use language are at the root of class differences in education. Bernstein identified two codes of speech which he termed the restricted code and the elaborated code.

The restricted code is a kind of shorthand speech which everyone uses in situations where they are talking about things which are familiar, whereas the elaborated code is a more complex form of speech which does not rely on knowledge of what is being discussed to understand meanings. These speech codes should not be confused with people using different accents, dialects or forms of slang.

Bernstein argues that working-class people tend to mainly communicate using restricted code while middle class people find it easier to switch between codes depending on the situation. He suggests that schools necessarily have to use elaborated code as education 'is concerned with the transmission and development of universalistic orders of meaning'. Thus, teachers have to be able to explain things which are unfamiliar using descriptive language and pupils have to use elaborated code when discussing things in lessons or answering exam questions. As a result working-class children start school with a disadvantage over middle-class children who are already used to using both codes of speech. Bernstein argues that class differences in language have their roots in the kind of speech parents use in their working lives and how they in turn socialise their children.

Evaluation

Bernstein's theory had a huge influence on educationalists and focused teachers on the importance of developing complex forms of language in all pupils. However, in a famous article 'Education cannot compensate for society' Bernstein (1971) argued that it is difficult for schools to compensate for inequalities which are rooted in the wider society.

Bernstein's ideas have also attracted a range of criticisms:

- Bernstein's definition of social class is vague, for example sometimes he refers to the working class in general as using the restricted code and sometimes only the lower working class. Many sociologists today argue that it is too simple to divide society into two distinct classes with two different forms of speech as implied by Bernstein's theory.

- The evidence on which Bernstein bases his theory is based on a very small amount of possibly unrepresentative research.

- Bernstein appears to imply that working-class forms of speech are inferior and some have accused him of adopting a form of cultural deprivation theory. However, Bernstein has strongly denied this, describing working-class speech as having 'warmth, vitality, simplicity and directness'.

Social class and language

Item A

Two codes of speech

Bernstein showed four pictures to five-year-old boys and asked them to describe what was going on. Here are two examples of the stories told by the boys.

They're playing football and he kicks it, and it goes through there. It breaks the window and they're looking at it and he comes out and shouts at them because they've broken it. So they run away and then she looks out and she tells them off.	Two boys are playing football and one boy kicks the ball and it goes through the window. The ball breaks the window and the boys are looking at it, and a man comes out and shouts at them because they've broken the window. So they run away and then that lady looks out of her window, and she tells the boys off.

Source: Adapted from Bernstein, B. (1973)

Item B

Restricted code or non-standard English?

William Labov, an American linguist, wrote a famous article 'The logic of non-standard English' questioning whether black working-class speech was inferior to the standard English spoken by educated middle-class people. Labov argues black speech is actually more colourful and descriptive and should be treated as a 'non-standard' form of English with its own grammatical rules and conventions. The problem, according to Labov, is not the restricted speech of black working-class people but the insistence by teachers and the education system that the only correct form of speech is that used by the middle class.

Source: Adapted from Labov, W. (1973)

1 Study Item A. Which story would Bernstein describe as being told in restricted code and which would be described as in elaborated code. Explain your answer by identifying features of each code in the stories.

2 Study Item B. How could Labov's arguments be used to question the view that working class-forms of speech are inferior to those of educated middle-class people.

3 Should teachers try to encourage all pupils to communicate in standard middle class English or should schools encourage children to simply express themselves in whatever forms of English they feel most comfortable with.

Cultural capital theory, Bourdieu (1971, 1974, 1984)

The French sociologist Pierre Bourdieu developed an approach to social class and education which has had considerable influence on studies of education in Britain. Bourdieu rejects the idea of cultural deprivation which implies that working-class culture is inferior to middle-class culture and lays the blame for the educational under-achievement of working-class children on their parents' failure to adequately socialise them and encourage them to succeed at school.

Bourdieu instead lays the blame on the educational system and indeed on the whole capitalist society. Drawing on Marxism, Bourdieu argues that the main role of the education system is cultural reproduction in other words ensuring that the culture of the dominant classes is passed on to the next generation. Bourdieu rejects the idea that this culture is actually superior to working class culture, it is simply defined as superior because it is associated with the most powerful and high-status groups in society.

Bourdieu argues that knowledge of the culture of the higher social classes confers what he calls cultural capital, a form of social advantage which can be translated into wealth and power. Pupils from upper-class backgrounds possess this cultural capital because they have been socialised into it by their families and by attending elite schools (such as public schools in England). Middle-class children also grow up in a culture which is closer than that of working-class children to the dominant culture so also possess a degree of cultural capital.

Bourdieu suggests that family background leads to the development of a particular habitus, a set of cultural expectations which guide the individual in making choices in life and in what is regarded as normal reasonable behaviour. Cultural capital consists in part of certain forms of knowledge but also of what Bourdieu calls 'intangible nuances of manners and style' this might include ways of talking, and tastes in music, clothing, leisure pursuits, food and many other aspects of culture. For example, members of the dominant class are likely to have an understanding of aspects of high culture, such as classical music, fine art or literature, while the working class place more value on popular culture, such as pop music, entertainment TV programmes or popular sport such as football.

Bourdieu argues that the education system gives more status to forms of knowledge which are associated with the dominant class. Success in education therefore depends of possessing cultural capital so that children can display the cultural understandings associated with the higher social classes. He suggests that an important role of the education system is the social function of elimination. By this he means that the forms of assessment (such as exams) used in the education system serve to eliminate working-class children because they are constantly defined as not having the right cultural knowledge to succeed. However, many working-class children drop out of their own accord thorough a process of self-elimination; they know the system is rigged against them and give up the struggle to succeed long before they finish their formal education.

Bourdieu therefore concludes that the real function of education is not to provide equal opportunities for all but to ensure a process of social reproduction whereby children from the higher social classes succeed and the privileges of the dominant class are legitimated by their success in education. Thus Bourdieu's theory has many similarities to other approaches influenced by Marxism such as Bowles and Gintis or Willis

Evaluation

Bourdieu's theory of cultural capital has been hugely influential on a range of research on education and other aspects of culture His approach overcomes some of the problems of cultural deprivation theories which imply that working class culture is inferior to middle-class culture. Bourdieu also points to ways in which the power and status of social class influences what is considered worthwhile knowledge in education and indeed society more generally. For example, the skills and knowledge of a motor mechanic are probably far more useful if your car has broken down than those of a professor of philosophy yet the academic knowledge of a philosopher carries more status than the practical knowledge of the mechanic, at least in the higher social classes.

Bourdieu's theory has also attracted criticisms:

- The concept of cultural capital is rather vague and difficult to measure, although Sullivan's study (in the Activity below) is an attempt to operationalise it for research purposes.
- While Bourdieu acknowledges the importance of material factors or what he calls economic capital, some critics argue that he gives insufficient importance to these in his theory.
- Bourdieu's concept of social reproduction exaggerates the extent to which children end up in the same social class as their parents. For example the Oxford Mobility Study revealed there had been considerable upward social mobility by children from working-class backgrounds into higher social classes.

Activity

Research into cultural capital

Item A

A test of cultural capital theory

Alice Sullivan carried out a survey based on questionnaires to children approaching school leaving age in four schools in England. She based the social class of children on the highest status job of their parents and the cultural capital of the parents on their educational qualifications. The cultural capital of the children was measured by a number of factors including:

- The books they read (e.g. whether they read more complex fiction).
- The TV programmes they watched (e.g. whether it included documentaries and more sophisticated drama as opposed to soap operas and game shows).
- Whether they played a musical instrument.
- Attendance at museums, art galleries, theatres and concerts.
- A test of knowledge of cultural figures and vocabulary.

Sullivan then attempted to see if there was any correlation between student scores in terms of cultural capital and their GCSE results. She found attendance at cultural events and playing music had little effect but factors such as watching sophisticated television and knowledge of cultural figures were associated with better results.

Sullivan found that it was middle-class children who had most cultural capital and they were also more successful in terms of GCSE results. However, she also points out that there were significant differences in educational attainment between the social classes which could not be attributed to the effects of cultural capital. She suggests that material resources and educational aspirations may be other important factors which account for the greater success of middle class children.

Source: Adapted from Sullivan, A. (2001)

Item B

The importance of mothers' cultural capital

Diane Reay carried out interviews with mothers of 33 children at two London primary schools. She found that the working-class mothers worked just as hard towards ensuring their children's success in education as the middle-class mothers. However, what really counted was the cultural capital possessed by the middle-class mothers.

Middle-class mothers tended to be better educated themselves and were more knowledgeable about how the educational system operated. They used their cultural capital to help children with homework and had the confidence to tackle teachers and demand the best for their children.

Middle-class mothers also had more material capital which meant they could employ domestic help, such as cleaners, giving them more time to help their children. They could also afford private tuition to boost their children's success.

Source: Adapted from Reay, D. (1998)

Item C
Cultural capital and higher education choices

Kings College, Cambridge University. Working-class students may not apply to universities like Cambridge because they feel 'out of place'.

Diane Reay, Miriam David and Stephen Ball did research on a sample of students from six different schools and colleges in and around London. They gave a questionnaire to 502 students, ran focus groups and carried out 120 in-depth interviews.

Reay et al argue that Bourdieu's concept of habitus is very relevant because the habitus of working-class children leads them to see elite universities such as Oxford or Cambridge as 'not for the likes of them'. Young people of different social classes develop a view of themselves based on their class background and tend to seek out universities which are likely to be inhabited by people like them.

By contrast young people who have attended private schools tend to have a detailed knowledge of the premier league of universities acquired from family, friends and school. According to Reay et al, unlike working-class students, they have a 'confidence, certainty and sense of entitlement' which leads them to choose top universities. Working-class students often exclude themselves from applying to these universities, even when they have the ability, in order to avoid the risk of academic and social failure.

Source: Adapted from Reay *et al*, (2005)

1 Study Item A. How did Sullivan demonstrate in her research that there was a link between social class, cultural capital and educational success?
2 Why do you think Reay's research in Item B suggests that the cultural capital of mothers is more significant than that of fathers in children's educational attainment?
3 How does Reay et al's research in Item C suggest the concepts of cultural capital and habitus are relevant to understanding class differences in higher education?
4 With reference to all three Items explain why material factors as well as cultural factors may be important in ensuring educational success?

School factors and educational attainment

In the last two sections of this chapter we examined two sets of factors which help to explain class differences in educational achievement: material and cultural factors. Both of these sets of explanations focus on the influence of factors in a child's home background on how they fare at school. Some sociologists have argued that focusing on the home background ignores the importance of processes taking place within schools. This argument has been most fully developed by interactionist sociologists but their ideas have also influenced other sociologists to undertake small-scale and in-depth research inside schools.

Interactionism is an interpretivist approach to sociology and tries to understand how individuals interpret and define situations as they interact with others in daily life. Interactionists argue that individuals develop a self-concept or view of themselves which is based on how others react to them. In the context of education this suggests that how pupils interact with teachers and fellow students can shape their identities and self-concepts which can in turn influence their educational attainment.

The influence of teachers' expectations on pupils

Study

Deviance in classrooms, Hargreaves et al (1975)

A study of education which illustrates many of the ideas of interactionism is *Deviance in Classrooms* (1975) by David Hargreaves, Stephen Hester and Frank Mellor. They carried out interviews with teachers and classroom observations in two secondary schools and noted how students came to be typed or classified. They draw on the interactionist approach of labelling theory which argues that how we are labelled by others affects the way we see ourselves.

Hargreaves et al argue that when they meet new students teachers classify them in a number of stages:

- **Speculation** – This involves teachers making guesses about students based on factors such as appearance, willingness to conform to discipline and how likeable they are.
- **Working hypothesis** – Based on their interaction with students the teachers develop a theory about what kind of child each student is.
- **Elaboration** – This hypothesis is tested in the classroom and either confirmed or rejected based on teachers' experience.
- **Stabilisation** – The teacher feels she/he knows the student and tends to interpret everything about the student in terms of how they have been typed. Thus if a student has been labelled as deviant (e.g. as a troublemaker) then it will be difficult for the teacher to see their actions in a positive light.

Study

Examination setting, Gillborn and Youdell (2001)

A number of other studies have developed the ideas of Hargreaves and his colleagues and have suggested that working-class pupils are far more likely to be typed negatively by teachers. For example, in a study of two London secondary schools David Gillborn and Deborah Youdell (2001) found that teachers tended to allocate pupils to sets or ability groups based on how students had been typed. Rather than relying on objective measures of ability such as test results, teachers tended to use a 'common sense' understanding of ability to allocate students to sets. Working-class students were often perceived by teachers as disruptive, lacking in motivation or lacking parental support and so were labelled as being of 'lower abillity'. This led to teachers having lower expectations of them and often entering them for foundation level GCSE exams where they were unable to achieve higher grades. Gillborn and Youdell's study therefore gives support to the view that teachers' expectations can contribute to class inequalities in attainment.

Study

Class and teachers' expectations, Dunne and Gazeley (2009)

Mairead Dunne and Louise Gazeley (2009) carried out a study which collected quantitative and qualitative data from 22 teachers in 9 state secondary schools in England. Their findings confirm the interactionist perspective which suggests that teachers tend to judge pupils not only by ability but also by factors related to social class. Of the 88 pupils who were identified as 'underachievers' 70 per cent came from working-class homes. Teachers tended to comment positively on middle-class parents and their support for their children while working-class parents were often seen as hostile to the school and unconcerned about their children's behaviour. Teachers often made negative predictions concerning outcomes for working-class students such as poor educational achievement, unemployment, unskilled work, crime and early pregnancy. Working-class pupils on the other hand perceived teachers behaviour towards them as negative, for example, complaining that teachers shouted at them and failed to explain things clearly, as reasons for their lack of motivation. Dunne and Gazeley conclude by arguing that judgements about social class underpinned teacher's perceptions and labels.

Evaluation

There have been many studies which have supported the idea that teachers' expectations affect how pupils perform at school and that these expectations can be linked to children's social class background. Although few sociologists today would describe themselves as interactionists, the concepts they developed such as; self-concept, labelling and self-fulfilling prophecy, are still used by many sociologists. Similarly the qualitative methods pioneered by interactionists based on detailed ethnographic research inside schools have been widely adopted.

However, the idea that pupils necessarily accept and live up to the labels placed on them has been questioned by some researchers. For example, Margaret Fuller (1984) carried out a small-scale study of a group of working-class black girls in a London comprehensive school. They felt that teachers held a number of negative stereotypes about them linked to them being female and black. However, the girls refused to live up to the expectation that they would fail. Instead they worked hard to prove their teachers wrong and tried to ensure they were successful at school.

The effects of ability grouping

In the 1940s and 50s pupils in many schools were streamed by ability. This involved placing all students in the same stream or ability group for all subjects. In the 1960s and 1970s many progressive educationalists advocated mixed ability teaching whereby pupils of different abilities were taught in the same group. It was argued that this avoided the negative labelling associated with placing pupils in lower streams. Although many schools still use mixed ability groups some sociologists have noted a re-emergence of ability groupings, particularly in secondary schools. However, students are now

---

Activity

The self-fulfilling prophecy

In the 1960s Robert Rosenthal and Leonora Jacobson carried out a famous experiment in an elementary school in California. They tested all the children in the school with an IQ test (a type of intelligence test) at the beginning of the experiment and then selected 20 per cent of the pupils at random as an experimental group. The teachers did not know that these children had been selected purely randomly and were told that they should expect rapid intellectual progress from these pupils. After a year, Rosenthal and Jacobson returned to the school and tested all the pupils for IQ. The pupils in the experimental group had on average made more progress than the other students in the school.

Rosenthal and Jacobson did not observe the interaction between teachers and pupils. They simply speculated that the teachers had somehow communicated their higher expectations to the chosen pupils through their manner, tone of voice and degree of friendliness and encouragement. In fact, their study is based on a positivist type experiment using statistical data to compare an experimental group (the supposed 'intellectual spurters') and a control group (the rest of the school). This is in contrast to most interactionist studies of education which adopt a more interpretivist approach, typically using methods such as in depth interviews and classroom observation to produce detailed qualitative accounts focusing on small groups. Nevertheless, their conclusion that 'teachers' expectations can significantly affect their student's performance' is in line with the findings of many more recent qualitative studies of classroom interaction. Sociologists refer to this as a self-fulfilling prophecy, a process where labelling someone in a certain way actually causes them to live up to the label and fulfil the prophecy made about them.

Source: Adapted from Rosenthal and Jacobson (1968)

1 In a social scientific experiment researchers typically compare an experimental group who have been subjected to a variable with a control group who are identical in every respect except for the one variable. In Rosenthal and Jacobson's study what was:
   a) the experimental group;
   b) the control group;
   c) the variable they wished to study?
2 What effect did Rosenthal and Jacobson conclude this variable had on the experimental group?
3 How might each of these points be used to criticise Rosenthal and Jacobson's experiment?
   a) Some psychologists argue that IQ tests are a poor guide to children's intellectual ability.
   b) Rosenthal and Jacobson did not directly observe what went on in the classroom.
   c) The effect of teachers' expectations was only found in younger children in the first two years of school and no consistent difference between the control and experimental groups was found among older children.

typically setted rather than streamed. Setting involves placing students in different ability groups for different subjects. Thus a student might be in set 1 for maths but in set 3 for English.

Mixed ability versus setting

Supporters of ability grouping argue that it allows more able to students to be stretched while allowing less able students to work at their own pace. On the other hand supporters of mixed ability argue that setting by ability can become rigid meaning that it is difficult for students in lower sets to move up even when they start to show they have more ability. In relation to social class studies such as Gillborn and Youdell (see page 127) suggest that bright working-class and ethnic-minority pupils are often placed in lower sets because of their behaviour or assumptions teachers make about their ability and once placed tend to live up to a self-fulfilling prophecy.

Gillborn and Youdell argue that setting tends to place working-class and ethnic-minority students at a disadvantage. However, a larger scale study by Judith Ireson, Susan Hallam and Clare Hurley (2001)

compared 45 comprehensive schools some using mixed ability, some partial setting for some subjects and some setting for at least four subjects. They found that in relation to maths, science and English (the subjects where setting is most commonly used) the amount of setting between Years 7 and 11 does not appear to have any effect on GCSE attainment. Another study by William and Bartholomew (2004), however, found that pupils in higher sets for maths gained some advantage but that those in lower sets were disadvantaged. This would tend to support labelling theory's suggestion that setting can help to create a self-fulfilling prophecy.

Pupil subcultures

A number of studies of education have suggested that pupils are not only affected by teachers' expectations and the organisation of schools but also but their peer groups. Students tend to form what sociologists call pupil subcultures; within a school there are different groups of pupils with different norms, values and attitudes.

Study

Conformists and delinquescents, Hargreaves (1967)

One of the earliest studies of pupil subcultures was carried out by David Hargreaves (1967). While teaching in a single-sex secondary modern school, he observed that there were two main subcultures; a conformist subculture, consisting of boys who worked hard, followed school rules and tried to achieve success; and a delinquescent subculture, consisting of boys who rejected the values of the school. For these boys status was achieved not through academic success but through rebelling against school for example by smoking, fighting, avoiding wearing uniform and messing around in lessons. Drawing on interactionist theory, Hargreaves argued that the labelling process had helped to create the delinquescent subculture

which was much more prevalent in the lower streams than the upper streams. Boys in the lower streams had not only failed the 11+ exam and thus ended up in a lower status secondary modern school (rather than a grammar school for the more able) but they had then been assigned to a lower stream, effectively writing them off as failures. Hargreaves argues that such boys suffered a sense of status frustration and thus created an anti-school subculture where they could gain status amongst their peers, for example as a tough fighter or as someone willing to risk breaking rules.

Hargreaves study was supported by a number of subsequent studies which focused on the idea of pro-school and anti-school subcultures. For example Willis's study (see pages 103–4).

Study

Differing pupil strategies, Woods (1979)

Other studies, however, have suggested that pupils' attitudes are more complex than suggested by the idea of two opposing subcultures. Peter Woods (1979) for example notes that some pupils move between conformity and rebellion to school rules, sometimes depending on which lesson they are in. Pupils also

conform and rebel in a variety of ways using different strategies to survive school. For example, some apparent conformists are ritualists who behave well but have little motivation to succeed while some rebellious students are not particularly confrontational but may reject school tasks in favour of gossiping or doing their hair.

Differing working-class male subcultures, Mac an Ghaill (1994)

Maírtín Mac an Ghaill (1994) identified a number of male peer groups among Year 11 students in a largely working class comprehensive in the west Midlands.

- **Academic achievers** – These represented the pro-school group who mainly followed the rules and were keen to achieve success in terms of qualifications. They tended to be placed in top sets and mostly came from skilled working-class backgrounds.
- **Macho lads** – These were similar to Willis's 'lads' in outlook. They rejected the authority of teachers and school and developed an anti-school subculture based on acting tough, having a laugh and looking after your mates.
- **New Enterprisers** – They wished to achieve success at school but only in subjects which they saw as having vocational relevance, such as business studies and computing and were less keen on academic subjects which they saw as less relevant to the world of work.
- **Real Englishmen** – These boys came from more middle-class backgrounds and tried to cultivate an attitude of effortless superiority. They felt it was 'uncool' to take advice from teachers and although many of them eventually achieved good results they tried to appear as if they did little work towards this.

Mac an Ghaill's study thus tends to suggest that alongside pro and anti-school subcultures there are other peer groups which may have more mixed attitudes towards schooling.

Social class and subcultures

Many studies of subcultures suggest there is a link between pupils' social class and their attitudes towards schooling. Some studies such as Willis argue that the attitudes of anti-school groups originate in the shop floor culture of working-class males, although groups such as 'the lads' then recreate their own version of this culture in the school. Others like Hargreaves put more emphasis on the labelling process and teachers' attitudes which lead to pupils becoming polarised into opposing subcultures as they move through secondary school. For Mac an Ghaill it is a combination of factors, for example, setting and the teacher-pupil relationship which resulted from this helped to encourage anti-school subcultures. However, he also points to pupils' position in the working-class as a factor since working-class boys from more skilled backgrounds appear to be less likely to form oppositional subcultures than those from poorer backgrounds.

Evaluation

Recent studies of subcultures have tended to explore how other factors such as gender and ethnicity are also important in the formation of pupil subcultures and it can be argued that some of the older studies neglect girls and ethnic minority pupils and focus mainly on white working-class boys. Nevertheless, peer groups and subcultures can be seen as an important factor in explaining class differences in attainment as most studies have suggested that it is poorer working-class children who are most likely to form peer groups which hold anti-school attitudes and values.

School subcultures

Note: This extract is based on research for a doctoral thesis by Sumi Hollingworth

Eden Hill sixth form featured a tight-knit group of students, who often spent their time outside the school gates smoking. The group were predominantly white girls and boys from more middle-class backgrounds. They wore a sort of London hipster style but with elements of the 'preppy' style of American college 'grads'. The other prominent clique was the 'football crowd'; a looser-knit group of minority ethnic boys: this group is where the black (Caribbean and African) boys tended to be found.

Subcultures are not just groups of people of the same race, class and gender. Subcultures involve people performing the characteristics associated with these attributes. For example, the football crowd performed a certain 'black, working-class masculinity'. This involved a passion for football; what they referred to as 'loudness' and 'jokes,' ascribed to black Caribbean culture; and prioritising sport and sociability over their academic studies.

An 'exception' was Tristan, a white British boy who loved football and was actually at the centre of the football crowd. Indeed, Tristan performed this black working-class masculinity so well that he admitted people often assumed he wasn't white.

Activity (continued)

Exceptions such as Tristan might lead us to think that social mixing is happening. But these performances do not carry an equal value, which means that not everyone is equally able to access the different groups.

To elaborate, in the context of an academic sixth form, such as Eden Hill school, the rebellious cigarette-smoking outside the school gates by the white, middle-class group was read differently by the school authorities to the 'laddish' behaviour of the football crowd. This smoking outside of the school gates in full view of the public, was turned a blind eye to. On the other hand, the school did prioritise dealing with another type of 'bad' behaviour: the 'rowdy' behaviour of younger students waiting at the bus stop after school, on a bus route taken predominantly by black students. Despite the fact there had been no complaints, the school council decided that a school behaviour officer would patrol the bus stop after school.

So while the black students' presence is read as aggressive, the smokers' group are able to use their whiteness as a resource to offset their bad behaviour. Their style has them read as middle class and academically high achieving, whether or not the individual members of the group are high attaining or not. Consequently, their bodily presence outside the school gates is actually a selling point, rather than a threat.

Source: Adapted from Hollingworth, S. (2014)

1 What do you think Hollingworth means when she suggests that subcultures involve a performance? Use examples from the extract to illustrate this.
2 How did the school react differently to the behaviour of the 'smokers' compared to the 'football crowd'? How can this be explained?
3 How might the following sociological concepts be applied to understanding the findings of this study?
   a) labelling
   b) pupil subcultures
   c) social class
   d) ethnicity
   e) masculinity

Section summary

Copy and complete the diagram

Copy the diagram below onto a large sheet of paper. Fill the bottom row of boxes with a brief summary of each type of explanation. Don't forget to include key studies and concepts relevant to that explanation.

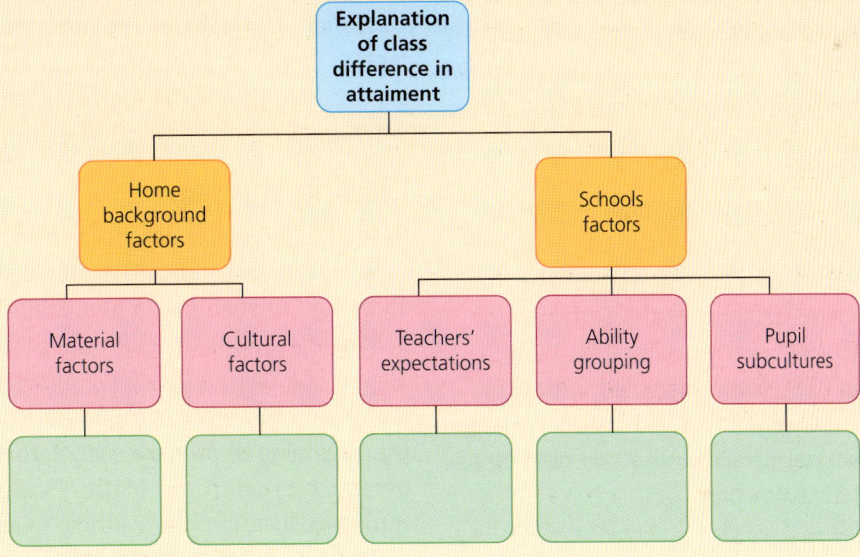

Ethnicity and Education

Measuring ethnicity and attainment

Measuring the relationship between ethnicity and educational attainment is difficult. One of the biggest problems is how pupils are classified into ethnic groups. Up until the 1980s studies often lumped together different groups into one category, for example Indian, east African, Asian, Pakistani and Bangladeshi groups were often simply included under a single heading as Asian. More recent studies have used much more specific classifications, usually based on categories used in official statistics. Even here there are still problems, for example statistics are often based on how parents record their children's ethnicity when registering them for school which may not always be an objective form of classification.

Older studies of ethnicity and education were also often based on small samples, sometimes focusing only on certain areas of the country. In recent years the Department for Education (DfE) has collected national statistics about educational attainment of all children in England Wales which are broken down by ethnicity and these provide more representative and reliable data (see Activity on page 133).

GCSE

Data based on GCSE results shows that Chinese followed by Indian pupils are the best performing ethnic groups. Interestingly, Bangladeshi students who were achieving below the national average in 2007/08 were achieving slightly better than white students by 2011/12. This may reflect the success of efforts to improve attainment in certain London boroughs where Bangladeshi communities are concentrated. Of the main ethnic minority groups, black Caribbeans and to a lesser extent Pakistanis have lower than average attainment, although both groups have gradually closed the gap with white student in the last few years. Until recently very little data was collected about Gipsy, Roma and Irish Traveller (GRT) children but the DfE data shows them to be achieving far less than all other ethnic groups.

Post-16 attainment

While some ethnic minorities still continue to perform less well than their white counterparts in GCSEs at the age of 16, data based on 19-year-olds suggest that many ethnic minority students catch up at the sixth form or college stage. In terms of Level 3 qualifications (which include A Levels and BTEC National qualifications), with the exception of Gypsy, Roma and Traveller young people, white student have the lowest attainment by age 19 (see Item B in Activity on page 133).

Higher education

Ethnic differences in terms of entry to higher education have narrowed considerably in recent years. A study by Helen Connor and her colleagues (2004) found that people from ethnic minorities are more likely to take HE qualifications than white people, however, on average all minority ethnic groups do not do as well in degree performance as white students. Ethnic minorities are also more likely to go to the newer (post 1992) universities which generally have a lower status than the older more established universities.

While Indian and Chinese groups are the most likely to take the traditional 'A' level route to higher education and are better qualified as higher education entrants, black ethnic groups, particularly black Caribbean, are generally older on entry, with a wider range of entry qualifications than the average, often gaining their qualifications by studying at further education colleges rather than at school.

Gender and ethnicity

Within all ethnic groups there are gender differences in educational achievement with females achieving higher than males in every ethnic group at all levels of education. However the gap between the sexes is wider in some groups than others. For example, in 2010/11 among black Caribbeans 82.6 per cent of girls but only 72.2 per cent of boys achieved 5 or more GCSE grades A*-C compared to 95.0 per cent of girls and 90.6 per cent of boys from Chinese backgrounds.

Social class and ethnicity

Class remains one of the most important social factors in educational attainment and in general terms ethnic minority groups with a higher proportion of middle-class people, such as Indians, also perform better in education. However, as the next section on material factors demonstrates social class and economic factors can be seen to assume a greater importance among white pupils than among some ethnic minorities.

Closing the gap

Examining final attainment in terms of GCSE results or university entry provides only a partial picture. A study by Christian Dustmann, Stephen Machin and Uta Schönberg (2008) based on the Millennium Cohort Survey (a longitudinal study) shows that children from many minority ethnic groups start off achieving less at the beginning of primary school, for example in terms of tests on English and Maths. However, as they move through education many ethnic minority children catch up or overtake their white co-students. Dustman et al comment that the 'catch-up (or overtaking) is most striking for Bangladeshi and Chinese pupils, for whom the gain exceeds 20 per cent.' The only group for which they did not observe a narrowing of the achievement gap in primary school was black Caribbean pupils.

White British underachievement

In the past much of the research on ethnicity and education focused on the under-achievement of ethnic minorities, especially African Caribbean pupils and to a lesser extent Pakistanis and Bangladeshis. Some more recent studies have started to suggest that it is poor white British children who are the most significant group of under-achievers. For example, a large-scale study based on the Pupil Level Annual Census and the National Pupil Database by Geeta Kingdon and Robert Cassen (2007) found that nearly half of all low achievers were white British males and that low achievement was strongly associated with eligibility for Free School Meals. In view of this some researchers have suggested that it is social class rather than ethnicity which is the most significant form of disadvantage in relation to education in the UK today.

Activity

Ethnicity and educational attainment

Item A

Percentage of pupils achieving 5 or more GCSEs at grade A* to C

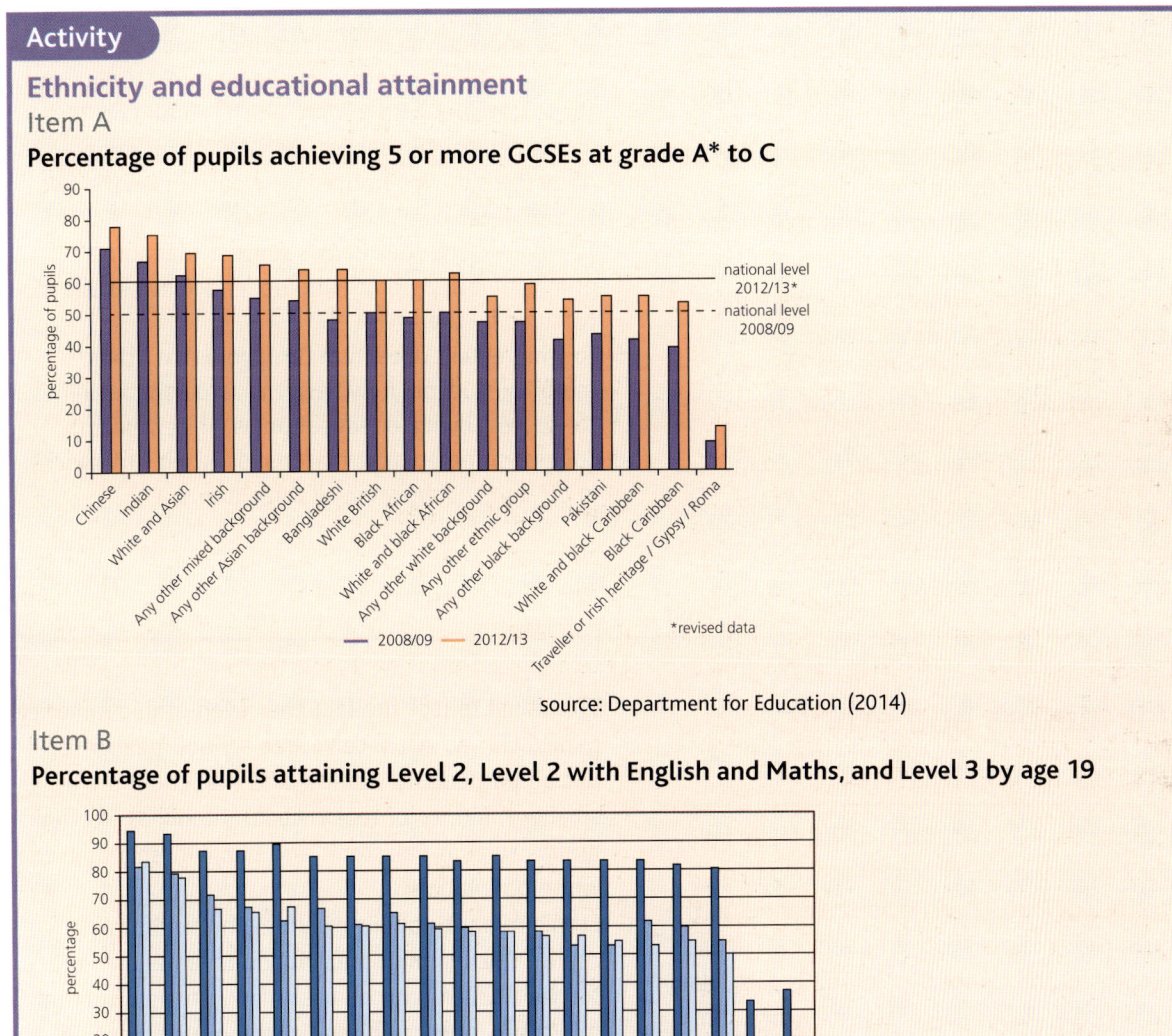

source: Department for Education (2014)

Item B

Percentage of pupils attaining Level 2, Level 2 with English and Maths, and Level 3 by age 19

source: Department for Education (2013)

Item C

According to the Race for Opportunity Report, in 2007–08, 16 per cent of students from the UK studying for degrees were from a black, Asian or ethnic minority background compared to 14.2 per cent of the 18–24-year-old age group as a whole.

While ethnic minorities are over-represented in universities overall they only made up 14.1 per cent of the total of students at the 20 leading Russell Group universities. London universities, including the London School of Economics (LSE), King's College London, Imperial College and University College London, were the best-performing Russell Group universities for the recruitment of ethnic minority students.

Outside London, only the universities of Birmingham, Manchester, Nottingham and Warwick seem to attract a representative proportion of the UK ethnic minority population. Only 1 in 10 students accepted by Oxford and Cambridge universities are from minority ethnic groups (11.1 per cent and 10.5 per cent respectively) Chinese and mixed ethnicity students were better represented at Oxbridge than average but those from all other ethnic minority groups were under-represented.

The research revealed that British Indians were the largest ethnic minority group in UK universities in 2007–08 at 3.3 per cent compared to 2.7 per cent of the total population of 18–24-year-olds. They were followed by black or black British Africans (3.2 per cent) who have almost tripled their university presence in the last 12 years. British Bangladeshi and British Pakistani students were still the most under-represented groups within UK universities.

Source: Adapted from Sellgren, S. (2010)

1 According to Item A in 2011/12 which ethnic groups achieved significantly above the national average and which achieved significantly below the national average for 5 GCSEs grades A*-C?
2 According to Item A which groups improved their attainment most and least between 2007/08 and 2011/12?
3 Item B shows the attainment of 19 year olds and covers both Level 2 qualifications (which includes GCSE and equivalent qualifications) and Level 3 (which includes A Levels and equivalents). Compare these statistics with Item A which is based on attainment of 16 year olds, what similarities and differences do you notice in the patterns in the two sets of data?
4 To what extent does Item B suggest that some ethnic minority groups who under-achieve at age 16 catch up by the age of 19?
5 To what extent does Item C suggest that ethnic minority students now have the same opportunities for success in higher education as white students?
6 Suggest some possible reasons for ethnic differences in attainment shown in all three items.

Material factors and ethnic differences in attainment

Some sociologists have argued that material factors play a role in ethnic differences in educational attainment. According to Lucinda Platt (2007) ethnic minorities in the UK have much higher levels of poverty and much lower rates of employment than white people. This is particularly true of Pakistanis, Bangladeshis and black Africans. On the face of it, material factors ought to be a major source of disadvantage for children from these minority ethnic groups. However, statistics for different ethnic groups show much smaller differences between pupils eligible for free school meals (FSM) and others in most ethnic minorities than white pupils (see chart on page 135).

Two possible explanations of these patterns can be offered:
1 The differences in material factors between FSM pupils and others in ethnic minorities may be smaller than the differences in the white population.

This could reflect the fact that even ethnic minority pupils who do not receive free school meals may not be particularly well-off and that there are a smaller minority of really wealthy families in ethnic groups such as Pakistanis and Bangladeshis than the white population.
2 Ethnic minority pupils may use their cultural capital to overcome material disadvantages. Tariq Modood (2004) argues that many parents in ethnic minorities, particularly Indians and African Asians, have more cultural capital than one would expect given their occupations. This reflects the fact that immigrants often take jobs for which they are under-qualified even though they have good educational qualifications from their country of origin. If we accept Modood's argument then for minority ethnic pupils cultural factors may assume a greater importance than material factors in explaining educational attainment.

Activity

Poverty, ethnicity and educational attainment

Item A

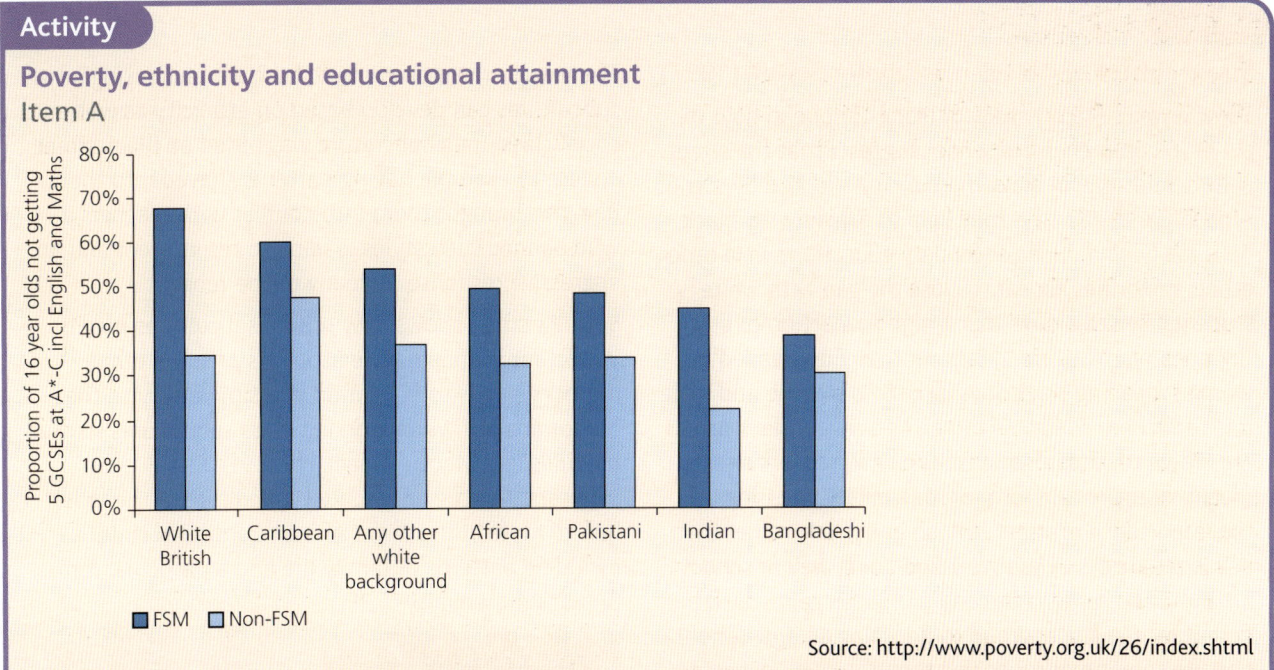

Source: http://www.poverty.org.uk/26/index.shtml

1 Study Item A above. How could this data be interpreted to show:
   a) that material factors may have an impact on educational attainment at GCSE?
   b) that low incomes appear to have more impact on attainment in some ethnic groups than others.

2 How could the difference in attainment between white British pupils eligible for free school meals and minority ethnic pupils eligible for free school meals be explained?

Cultural factors and ethnic differences in attainment

Archer and Francis: Aspirations of Chinese parents

Support for the importance of cultural factors in some minority ethnic groups comes from a small scale study by Louise Archer and Becky Francis (2007) of Chinese parents and students in London schools. Chinese students are the highest achieving ethnic group in the English education system and according to Archer and Francis this reflects the fact that both working class and middle class Chinese parents invest considerable time money and energy in their children. Even poor working-class parents who have little education themselves have high aspirations for their children.

Strand: Attitudes of white British pupils compared to ethnic minorities

Another study by Steve Strand (2008) based on a much larger scale longitudinal survey of over 1,500 young people found that white British working-class students (of both sexes) and black Caribbean working class boys had the lowest attainment at 16. Strand argues that even relatively poor recently arrived immigrant groups such as Portuguese, Pakistanis and Bangladeshis often see education as a way out of poverty. White working class families by contrast may have experienced poverty and unemployment for up to three generations and do not necessarily believe education will change anything.

Strand admits that this argument fails to explain the low attainment of black Caribbean boys where he suggests both parents and pupils have high aspirations. Here he argues that in school, factors such as teachers' expectations may provide a better explanation of low attainment.

Ethnicity and language

Some studies have suggested that children from minority ethnic backgrounds may be disadvantaged if English is not their first language. Children from Bangaldeshi and Pakistani households in particular may grow up speaking languages such as Bengali, Urdu or Punjabi. However, research by Dustmann et al (2008) suggests that as children from most minorities where English is a second language appear to catch up with white pupils as they progress though school, this does not appear to be a disadvantage in the long run. Interestingly they found that black Caribbean pupils make smaller progress than any other ethnic group even though for most of them English is their first language.

Street culture and black masculinity, Sewell (1997)

Tony Sewell's (1997) study of black Caribbean boys in a 11–16 comprehensive school suggests that the street culture and style of black masculinity adopted by some African Caribbean boys may help to explain why black boys fall behind during secondary education while other ethnic minorities appear to close the gap with white students. Sewell argues that a high proportion of black Caribbean families are lone parent families headed by women meaning black boys lack the discipline and male role model provided by a father. As a result, black boys are drawn towards a gang culture which emphasises a macho or aggressive form of masculinity, focusing on the importance of street fashion and music rather than academic success. Hard work and doing well at school are defined as effeminate and such boys gain status and acceptance in a peer group by adopting an anti-school posture sometimes modelling themselves on gangsta rappers or Jamaican 'yardies'.

Sewell suggested that in the school he studied there were four main groups of black students and only a minority the 'rebels' fitted into the subculture described above.

- **Conformists** At 41 per cent these were the largest group. These pupils tried to use education as a route to success and rejected the form of masculinity adopted in black street culture.
- **Innovators** The next largest group (35 per cent) were more anti-school and were suspicious of teachers but tried to keep out of trouble. They wanted to achieve success but disliked the process of schooling.
- **Retreatists** These were a small minority (6 per cent) of loners who kept themselves separate from other students. Many of them had special educational needs.
- **Rebels** This was the group which most strongly adopted a macho form of black masculinity. At 18 per cent they were a relatively small minority of black pupils. These students rejected both the norms of school life and the value of educational qualifications arguing that racism would prevent them achieving high status jobs even if they were successful at school.

The rebels are an example of how anti-school subcultures can develop based on ethnicity as well as social class. Their subculture was based on black street styles, for example having patterns shaved into their hair, this brought them into conflict with teachers who banned such styles leading to resentment and an aggressive response by many of the rebels.

Sewell's study shows how school subcultures may be important in shaping the attitudes of some ethnic minority pupils to education in a similar way to the predominantly white working-class subcultures studied by Willis and Mac an Ghaill. However, Sewell also suggests that the anti-school subculture of the rebels has its roots in the wider African Caribbean culture including patterns of family life and a particular form of black masculinity.

1 In what ways might the young men in the picture above represent a similar form of black masculinity to the style adopted by the rebels in Sewell's study?
2 To what extent does Sewell's study suggest that most black students were part of an anti-school subculture?
3 In what ways might Sewell's study be seen as offering a cultural explanation of the lower attainment of black male students?
4 What other explanations might sociologists offer?

Evaluation

Sewell's is a small scale ethnographic study focusing on one school which is possibly unrepresentative. Although Sewell is himself from a black Caribbean background and has set up projects to help black students who have been excluded from mainstream education, he has been accused of misrepresenting black culture and blaming African Caribbeans for their own underachievement. Critics argue this diverts attention from the real problem which is racism in the education system and the wider society.

In Sewell's defence it can be argued that he acknowledges racism as a problem and highlights how in some instances discrimination by teachers exacerbated the anti-school attitude of the Rebels. Sewell also tried to counter the negative stereotypes of black students by showing that only a minority were Rebels and that the largest group were in fact Conformists.

Some support for Sewell's arguments was given by Adolph Cameron, head of the Jamaican Teachers' Association. Speaking in 2011 at an event in the UK, he said that black schoolboys can choose to perform poorly to avoid undermining their masculinity. In Jamaica, where homophobia was a big issue, school success was often seen as feminine or 'gay'. He was concerned the same cultural attitude was affecting African Caribbean male students in the UK. He said: 'Education ... takes second place to notions of entrepreneurship as, predominantly our young men, get involved in the informality of what has been called a 'hustle culture'... Boys are more interested in hustling, which is a quick way of making a living, rather than making the commitment to study. This is supposed to be a street thing which is a male thing.' (quoted in Richardson, 21 October 2011).

The under-achievement of African Caribbean boys has been attributed by many sociologists to racism in the UK education system but it seems unlikely that racism could explain the underachievement of boys in Jamaica where the vast majority of both pupils and teachers are black. In view of this it could be argued that cultural factors could be a significant influence on the attitude of African Caribbean boys to education in both Jamaica and the UK.

Vincent et al: Attitudes of black middle-class parents

A study by Carol Vincent and her colleagues (2013) shows how class and ethnicity need to be considered together in studying education. They studied black middle-class parents who had high aspirations for their children, often making efforts to meet teachers and insisting on high standards from their children. While such parents often had a considerable degree of cultural capital, for example from carrying out research to improve their own understanding of education they still found that many teachers had an assumption that they knew less about education than white parents and were seen to be less interested in their children's education.

School factors, ethnicity and attainment

A number of sociologists argue that rather than being disadvantaged by home background ethnic minority pupils are disadvantaged by institutional racism within the education system. The concept of institutional racism implies that ethnic minority students are treated less favourably than white students but this is not simply due to the prejudice of a minority of racist teachers but rather an unconscious and often unintended bias in the way the whole education system is organised without sufficient consideration for the needs and interests of children from ethnic minorities.

One example of this is the accusation from some commentators that British schools have an ethnocentric curriculum, in other words one which focuses on the culture of white British people. Examples of this might include teaching western European languages but failing to include ethnic minority languages, focusing on white culture in literature, art and music at the expense of other cultures and failing to recognise the contributions of other nations and cultures in history, for example, the influence of Muslim mathematical and scientific discoveries on the European renaissance or the part played by troops from British colonies in the two World Wars.

Against this it could be argued that there has been a much greater emphasis on multi-cultural education in most British schools in the last twenty years, stressing the equal status of all cultures. Examples would include the purging from textbooks of negative images of minority groups, teaching about religions other than Christianity in religious studies and the celebration of Black History Month by many schools.

Gillborn and Youdell: Teachers' expectations of black pupils

A number of studies have suggested that teachers have lower expectations of ethnic minority pupils, especially black Caribbean students. For example, in an ethnographic study of two London comprehensive schools David Gillborn and Deborah Youdell (2000, 2001) argue that teachers have racialised expectations of different ethnic groups. They point out that few teachers in their research are openly racist, in fact many teachers are passionately committed to challenging racial inequalities, however, despite this, the processes operating in schools often worked against black students. Black students themselves stated in interviews that they felt disadvantaged and that teachers blamed them more than white students for disciplinary problems and that control and punishment of black students was given a greater priority than academic concerns.

One problem according to Gillborn and Youdell is that pressure on schools to achieve higher success rates in terms of 5 or more higher grade GCSEs has led to a system of educational triage whereby teachers are encouraged to focus on students who are on the borderline of achieving 5 grade Cs or above. Those who are certain to succeed and those who are unlikely to succeed are given less priority in terms of teaching and additional support. Unfortunately, black students are often perceived by teachers as being in the final category meaning that teachers' low expectations become a self-fulfilling prophecy.

More recently David Gillborn (2011) has argued that the introduction of the Ebacc or English baccalaureate benchmark, which requires pupils to achieve A*-C grades at GCSE in maths, English, two science subjects, a foreign language, and either history or geography will only make this situation worse. In 2010, black Caribbean pupils were less than half as likely (6.8 per cent in total) to achieve the grades in subjects necessary for the Ebacc, compared with white British pupils, while only a handful of Traveller or Gypsy/Roma pupils in the whole country met the Ebacc standard.

Mirza: Teachers and black girls

A study by Heidi Mirza (1992) of 198 15–19 year olds in two comprehensive schools in south London broadly supports Gillborn and Youdell's arguments. Mirza argues that there is myth of underachievement for black women. She found that most of the girls she studied were confident in their own abilities but felt that teachers put them down and did not give them a chance to prove themselves.

Mirza suggests that a few of the teachers she observed were overt racists, however, a greater problem was teachers who tried to be 'colour blind' and so ignored the issue of racism in schools. Other teachers were more actively anti-racist but failed to really understand the needs of black students or were patronising towards the black girls, for example, telling them that they knew what was best for them. Like Gillborn and Youdell, Mirza argues that black girls were often denied opportunities not because they lacked ability but because of the low expectations teachers had of them. Despite this negative labelling, Mirza argues that most black girls were concerned with academic success and worked hard to achieve it.

Mac an Ghaill: Young, gifted and black

Mairtin Mac an Ghaill (1992) carried out a small scale ethnographic study of 25 black and Asian students studying at a sixth form college. Like many of the other studies considered in this section he emphasises how aspects of social class and gender are linked to issues of racism and ethnicity. Nearly all the students he interviewed spoke of the pervasiveness of racism in British society generally, although they disagreed over its extent within education.

Student responses to schooling varied considerably and were to affected by their gender, class and schools they had formerly attended. Interestingly the students who felt most strongly they were victims of racism and negative labelling were not necessarily the ones who had the most negative attitudes towards education. Like a number of other studies this suggests that the notion of a self-fulfilling prophecy in relation to ethnic disadvantages in education is too simplistic. For example, one black girl who had attended a private school described the other girls as 'racist snobs' but suggested this just made her more determined to prove they were wrong about black people. An Asian male who had attended an inner city school where there was a strong anti-academic culture suggested that teachers simply did not expect them to do well but pointed out that 'it's just as bad for white kids in many ways'.

Most of the students in the study had achieved success by a variety of survival strategies. Some girls used what Mac an Ghaill calls resistance within accommodation whereby they would band together to help one another get good marks but resisted conforming to school rules in terms of dress, appearance and behaviour. Others tried to get friendly with teachers who they knew were supportive and attempted to avoid racist teachers in order to avoid conflict.

Evaluation

Mac an Ghaill's study has the merit of showing that we need to adopt complex multi-facted explanations of how class, gender and ethnicity interact in student's experiences of education. His approach in many ways fits in with other ethnographic studies influenced by an interpretivist approach, such as Mirza or Gillborn and Youdell. Such studies also highlight the way in which schools may contribute to the disadvantages faced by some groups in education because of institutional racism within the education system.

Such approaches have been heavily criticised. For example Peter Foster, Roger Gomm and Martyn Hammersley (1996) argue that research has 'failed to establish that discrimination against black students occurs on any scale in the allocation of students to courses or through the effects of allocation.' (Foster et al, 1996). Foster et al argue that often such studies base their arguments on very limited evidence, for example, of one or two cases of allegedly discriminatory behaviour. Much of the research in this area is based on ethnographic studies of small possibly unrepresentative samples.

On the other hand it can be argued that there is a body of such studies carried out over many years which all point to evidence of racism and discrimination in education and this is hard to ignore. In a recent study Keith Davidson and June Alexis (2012), two leading black educationalists, are unequivocal about where the blame lies when it comes to black children's attainment arguing that 'It is the education system that is underperforming'.

Activity

Differences in school discipline between ethnic groups

Item A

A study of one school

David Gillborn carried out a study over two years of what he called 'City Road' comprehensive school. When observing lessons he found that African Caribbean boys were reprimanded much more frequently than white or Asian students for the same offence, for example chatting in class. He also carried a quantitative analysis of the school's detention books and found that although pupils of other ethnicities were more likely to be punished for breaking school rules, a disproportionate number of African Caribbean pupils had received detentions for offences which were based on the teacher's interpretation of the pupil's attitude or intent, for example black boys' behaviour was frequently seen as a challenge to teacher's authority even though no school regulation had been broken.

White teachers were often suspicious of the style of dress and speech of African Caribbean boys, interpreting them as strategies of resistance rather than as simply cultural differences. Some boys were even reprimanded for adopting a perceived 'black' style of walking. In contrast the cultural differences of Asian pupils were not perceived as threatening and they were largely treated the same as white.

One consequence of the perceived unfairness of the treatment of African Caribbean boys was for them to draw together and form anti-school subcultures in opposition to the school. They would form all black 'cliques' which emphasised a pride in their ethnicity and their physical prowess and would respond in a confrontational manner to teachers when they felt themselves to be treated unfairly. In some cases such confrontations led to permanent exclusion of black students from school. More frequently badly behaved students were contained in smaller groups by the school and not entered for examinations.

Gillborn also focused on a few highly motivated black students who did achieve success at 'City Road'. He points out that they only did so by making considerable efforts to avoid confrontations with teachers and to actively work at dispelling the negative image staff had of them. Such boys also had to distance themselves from other black boys often losing friends in the process and facing ridicule from their peer group.

Source: Adapted from Gillborn, D. (1990)

Item B
National statistics on school exclusions by ethnicity

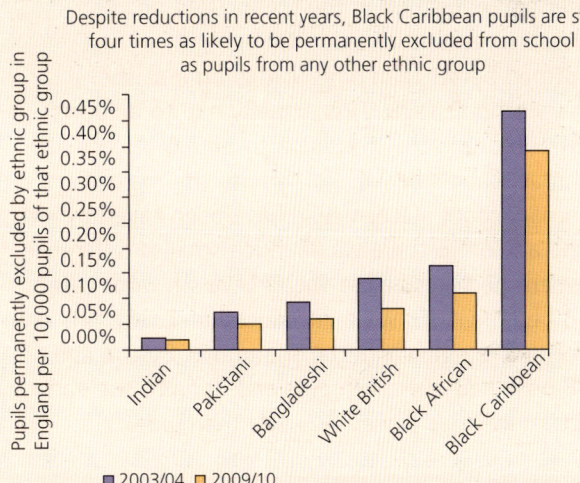

Despite reductions in recent years, Black Caribbean pupils are still four times as likely to be permanently excluded from school as pupils from any other ethnic group

Pupils permanently excluded by ethnic group in England per 10,000 pupils of that ethnic group

■ 2003/04 ■ 2009/10

Source: http://www.poverty.org.uk/27/index.shtml

Item C
Ban on 'black' hairstyles ruled illegal

A court ruled in 2015 that a London school's decision to ban hairstyles it says have become associated with gang culture was an example of 'unlawful, indirect racial discrimination which is not justified'. The case was a victory for the family of African Caribbean teenager 'G', who wears his hair in cornrow braids as part of a family tradition. The judge, Mr Justice Collins said that in future the school authorities must consider allowing other boys to wear cornrows if it is 'a genuine family tradition based on cultural and social reasons'. Even though the family's application for judicial review was successful, G, now 13, does not wish to return to the school, which he left in tears on his first day.

Adapted from *The Daily Telegraph*, 7 February 2015

1 Study Item A. What evidence of discrimination against African Caribbean boys was found in Gillborn's study.
2 What problems might there be with the validity, reliability and representativeness of a study of one school such as that in Item A?
3 How might Item B be used to support Gillborn's claim that African Caribbean boys are unfairly subjected to greater discipline in schools than other groups?
4 What other explanations could be given to the patterns of school exclusions shown in Item B?
5 Study Item C. To what extent would you agree that schools banning cornrow hairstyles is a form of racial discrimination?

Gender and education

Gender differences in attainment

Up until the 1990s much of the research on gender and education in the UK focused on the 'underachievement' of girls although girls in fact performed better than boys at this time at the primary school stage. Girls actually had to achieve a higher score in the 11+ exam to obtain a place at grammar schools because otherwise the majority of grammar school places would have been taken by girls. By the age of 16 there was a much smaller difference between the sexes and in the O Levels (exams taken at 16 before GCSEs were introduced in 1988) girls only performed marginally better than boys. By the age of 18 boys had overtaken girls and up until the early 1990s more boys passed A Levels than girls.

GCSEs

All this began to change in the 1990s. From 1990 onwards the gender gap between girls and boys obtaining 5 or more GCSE grades A* to C widened from 7.6 percentage points in 1990 to 10.6 in 2002. Although the gap had narrowed to 7.0 percentage points by 2010/11, it had increased again to 8.8 by 2013/14 (DfE data from various years). Girls performed better than boys in all subjects in 2013/14 with the exception of Maths where boys did fractionally better. Although girls have maintained their lead over boys at GCSE it is worth noting that both girls and boys have increased their attainment over the last thirty years and boys are now doing better than girls were only a few years ago.

Activity

Item A

Percentage of girls and boys achieving 5 grades A*–C at GCSE 1989–2014

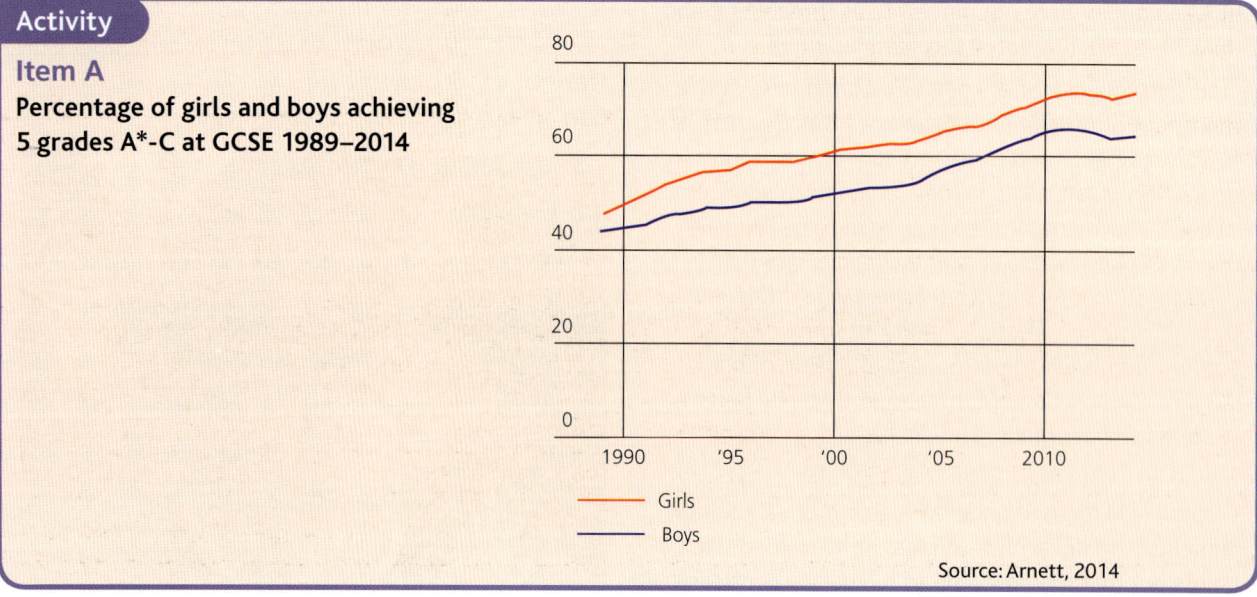

Source: Arnett, 2014

Activity (continued)

Item B

Percentage of pupils achieving key stage 4 indicators by gender. England, 2013/14

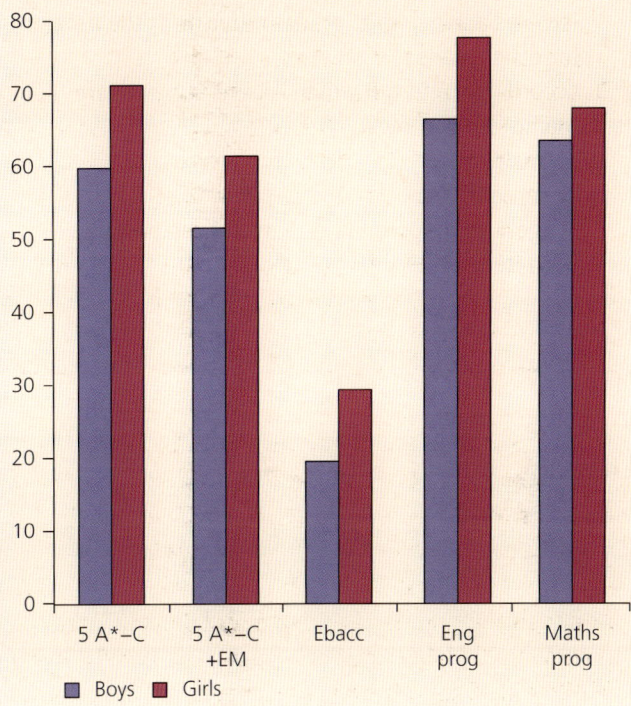

Boys ■   Girls ■

- 5 A*–C + EM = Percentage achieving 5 or more A*–C grades including English and Maths.
- Ebacc = Percentage achieving the English Baccalaureate qualification (higher grades in English, maths, a science, a foreign language, and either history or geography).
- Eng prog = Making expected progress compared to key stage 2 SATs in English.
- Maths prog = Making expected progress compared to key stage 2 SATs in Maths.

Source: DfE (2014) GCSE and equivalent attainment by pupil characteristics, 2013 to 2014

1. According to Item A how has the percentage of girls and boys achieving 5 or more grades A*–C changed since 1989?
2. How has the gap between girls' and boys' attainment at GCSE changed since 1989?
3. Compare the progress made by girls and boys in English and Maths according to Item B.
   a. In which subject (Maths or English) is there a bigger gap in progress between girls and boys?
   b. How would you explain this?

A level

Since 1995 females have overtaken males in the percentage attaining A level grades A to E. In 2012/13 females achieved higher scores on average across all Level 3 qualifications (A Levels and equivalents).

- In 2012/13, the average point score per student achieved by females by the end of key stage 5 (KS 5) was 740.3 compared to 706.4 for males.

- In addition, the average point score per entry by the end of KS5 was 217.4 for females compared to 209.6 for males
- However, males attained more top grades at A level. 13.0 per cent of males achieved three A* or A grades by the end of KS5 compared to 12.1 per cent of females (DfE 2014)

Activity

Gender and A Level results

Item A

Percentage of entries achieving GCE A Level by grade, 2014

	Number of entries	A*	A*-A	A*-C	A*-E
Male	349,462	8.6	25.8	73.8	97.5
Female	417,253	7.9	26.1	78.7	98.4
All	766,715	8.3	26.0	76.5	98.0

Source: Joint Council for Qualifications

Item B

Gender participation rate for selected A Level subjects, 2014

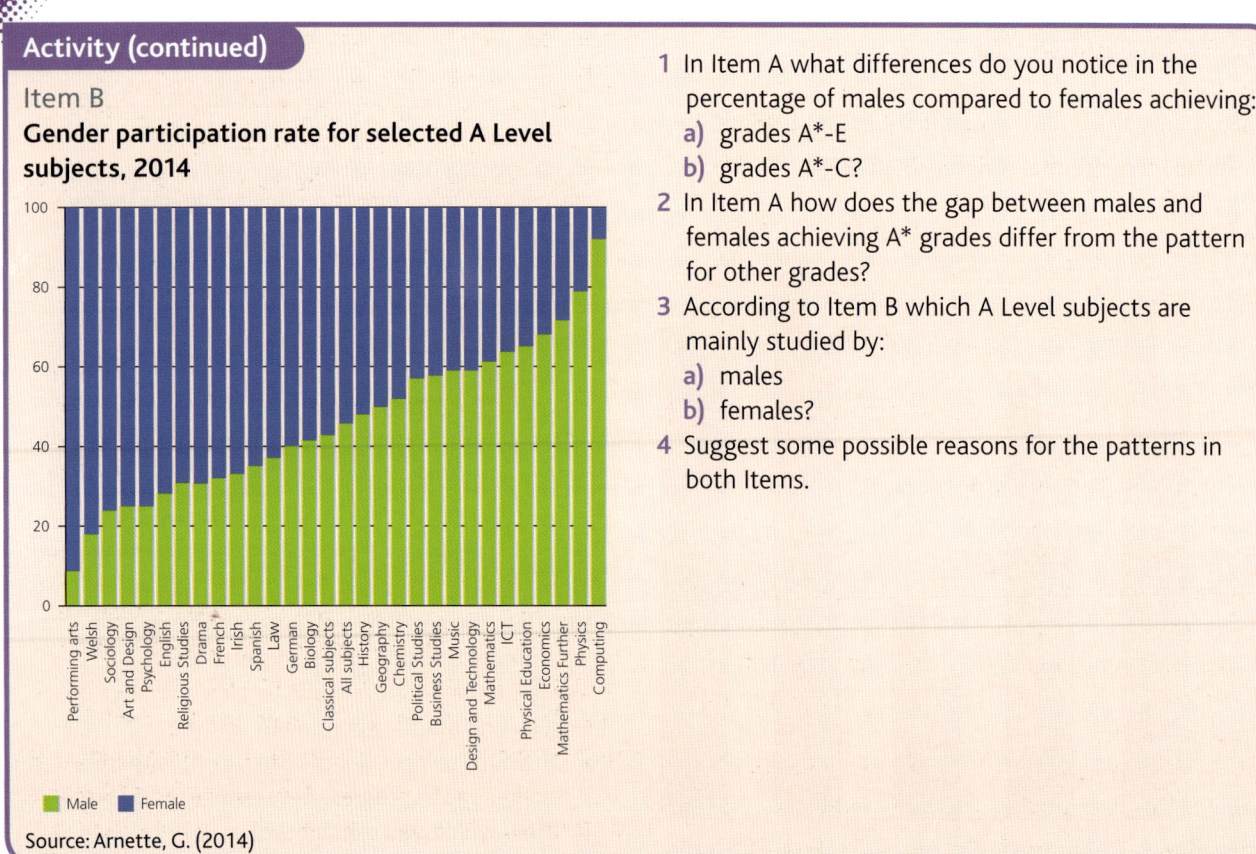

Male ☐   Female ☐

Source: Arnette, G. (2014)

1. In Item A what differences do you notice in the percentage of males compared to females achieving:
   a) grades A*-E
   b) grades A*-C?
2. In Item A how does the gap between males and females achieving A* grades differ from the pattern for other grades?
3. According to Item B which A Level subjects are mainly studied by:
   a) males
   b) females?
4. Suggest some possible reasons for the patterns in both Items.

Higher education

In the 1970s women made up only about a third of students in higher education but by the end of the 1990s the proportion of females outnumbered males. In 2014 the gap was at a record level with nearly 58,000 more women than men being accepted to study at UK universities. Women have also overtaken men in some areas which were traditionally male dominated, for example in 2014 there were 5,000 women and only 3,800 men accepted to study medicine and dentistry. On the other hand in most STEM subjects (science, technology, engineering and maths) men are still over-represented, for example in engineering and computer science.

The growth in women studying in higher education coincided with the growing gap between girls and boys in attainment in schools in GCSEs and A Levels. It also reflects the increase in available places particularly following the reorganisation of higher education and establishment of new universities after 1992. More of the additional places created in universities appear to have been taken up by women than men.

Students in higher education in the UK by gender

Year	Males	Females
1970/71	416,000	205,000
1980/81	526,000	301,000
1990/91	588,000	491,000
2000/01	934,000	1,126,000
2010/11	1,090,000	1,411,000
2013/14	1,010,035	1,289,090

1. How has the proportion of female to male students studying at universities changed since 1970?
2. How would you explain this change?

Source: *Social Trends*, 2007, 2011 and HESA https://www.hesa.ac.uk/stats

Are females outperforming males?

On the face of it females are now outperforming males at every level of education, however, this is an over-simplification. Looking at exam results and entry into higher education overall females are ahead and have been for at least the last twenty years, however, the following points should be noted.

- Only some boys are underachieving, particularly white working class boys and African Caribbean working-class boys.
- Some groups of girls are underachieving, particularly white working-class girls.
- The gender gap has actually decreased in recent years, particularly at A Level and also in terms of entry to higher education.
- Although gender is an important factor in education it is less of a source of inequality than class (which appears to have over five times the effect of educational attainment) and ethnicity (which has twice the effect).
- Some feminists also point out that there are still areas of education where females are disadvantaged, for example, in terms of subject choice fewer females study traditionally male subjects, such as STEM subjects, especially at A Level and university.
- It can also be argued that subtle forms of sexism still exist in education, for example boys tend to be more dominant in the classroom and the playground and girls may find their confidence is undermined by sexual harassment and teasing from boys. For example, in an observational study Becky Francis (2005) found that boys gained status in the classroom by adopting 'laddish' or 'class clown' roles in order to dominate classroom interaction. This resulted in boys gaining more of the teachers' attention and girls and quieter boys being more marginalised.

Explanations of the improvement in girls' achievement

Changing attitudes

A study by Sue Sharpe (1976) of working-class teenage girls in London schools in the 1970s found that their main priorities for the future were 'love, marriage, husbands and children'. Sharpe (1994) returned to the same schools in the 1990s and repeated her research and found girls were much more concerned with jobs and careers. By the 1990s girls did not assume they would be able to rely on a husband for economic support and saw education as the main route to financial independence.

A more recent study by Becky Francis and Christine Skelton (2005) similarly found that the majority of pupils in both primary and secondary schools saw their future identity in terms of their careers, rather than seeing employment as simply a stopgap before marriage. Francis and Skelton also found that girls, especially in middle-class families, were under increasing pressure from parents to achieve exam success.

Changes in the job market

The changing attitudes of girls and women reflect a change in employment opportunities for women. In 1971 53 per cent of working-age women were in employment and this had risen to over 67 per cent in 2014. In the same period male employment fell, reflecting a decline in jobs in manufacturing industries which traditionally employed large numbers of males. In contrast, the service sector which employs more women has expanded and an increasing number of these jobs require degree level qualifications. Many girls now have positive role models in the form of mothers and other female adults who are full-time earners. Girls' higher aspirations and concern for economic independence are also more realistic in view of the greater job opportunities for women.

Feminism

Changes in opportunities for women have come about partly because of campaigns by the women's movement in the 1960s and 1970s. This led to improved legal rights for women such as the Equal Pay Act (1970) and Sex Discrimination Act (1974) and also meant that many women who would not consider themselves feminists today take for granted that they should expect equal rights with men. Madeleine Arnot (1999) points to a growing number of female teachers in secondary schools who have disseminated feminist ideals to girls and acted as positive role models, dispelling girls' fear of success and showing that being too clever would not make them unattractive to men.

Individualisation

Some sociologists have linked changes in the attitudes of women and girls to Ulrich Beck's (1992) theory of risk society. He argues that we are moving into an era of second modernity in which society is characterised by greater risk and uncertainty. This can be seen in greater concern about the risks of divorce and relationship breakdown and also of loss of jobs. Along with this sense of risk people have become more individualised, meaning that they are more concerned about their own personal needs and are more self-sufficient and self-reliant, this is particularly apparent in the attitudes of women who Beck sees as 'setting the pace for change'. The changing attitudes of young women to education and employment mentioned above can be seen as part of this process. Young women are putting their own financial independence first and are more wary of the risks associated with marriage and economic dependence on a husband.

Differences in socialisation and behaviour

Traditionally the socialisation of girls tended to emphasise preparation for traditional feminine roles such as being a wife and mother and caring for others. This may be changing as parents encourage girls to have higher aspirations. However, research by Geoff Hannan (2000) suggests that while boys relate to peers by doing, girls relate to one another by talking. This starts from an early age and means that girls develop language skills which are essential for success in education much earlier than boys.

Girls appear to mature earlier than boys. In the past it was assumed that boys would catch up in secondary school but this no longer seems the case. It appears that girls work harder and are more motivated than boys. According to Joe Burns and Paul Bracey (2001) girls put more effort into homework and unlike boys are prepared to draft and redraft assignments.

Changes within the education system

Most of the explanations discussed above link changes in the achievement of girls to changes in the wider society. However, some sociologists have pointed to important changes in the education system itself which have affected girl's achievement.

- **Emphasis on coursework** – The introduction of GCSEs in 1988 put greater emphasis on coursework and it has been argued that this benefited girls as they tend to be more organised and better at completing work by deadlines. However, in recent years there has been a shift back to greater emphasis on assessment by final exams in both GCSEs and A levels and this does not seem to have greatly benefited boys.
- **Feminisation of education** – In 2010 statistics released by the General Teaching council showed that in a quarter of primary schools there were no male teachers while even in secondary schools female teachers now outnumber males. While many feminists argued that schools in the past were not 'girl friendly' it has been suggested that education is now geared much more to the needs of girls with boys lacking positive role models in the form of male teachers. However, a study by Christine Skelton and her colleagues (2006) of a sample of Year 3 classes and their teachers found that most pupils and teachers rejected that idea that matching the gender of pupils and teachers would produce any real benefits. Moreover, many teachers tried hard to cater for the interests of both boys and girls and used different approaches to manage their relationships with girls and boys because they were aware of the argument that boys and girls might have different educational needs.
- **Positive action to boost girl's achievement** – Such changes may have helped girls but were not an intended consequence of the policies of governments or schools. However, since the 1980s there have also been deliberate attempts to boost the attainment of girls. For example schemes such as GIST (Girls into Science and Technology) and WISE (Women into Science and Engineering) have encouraged more girls to study male dominated subjects. Most schools have adopted Equal Opportunities Policies which commit them to treat girls and boys equally.
- **Feminist research** – Research demonstrated the extent to which girls were disadvantaged in a variety of ways, for example in the expectations of teachers and in the curriculum and teaching materials which often reflected traditional assumptions about gender roles. As a result most schools have made considerable efforts to eliminate sexism in the classroom.

Under-achieving girls

Note: The idea that girls are now out-performing boys tends to conceal the fact that many girls are still under-achieving. This is highlighted by the two studies summarised below.

Hyper-feminine girls (left) and ladettes (right) can be seen as forms of feminine identity which reject the importance of academic success.

Item A:

Hyper-feminine girls

A study by Louise Archer and her colleagues demonstrated that girls can form anti-school subcultures as well as boys. In their study of working class girls in London comprehensives they found that many girls saw educational success as irrelevant and planned to leave school at 16, often intending to work in the retail sector. The girls spent much of their time entertaining themselves by disrupting the school system. Many of the girls also adopted a sexualised hyper-feminine identity. This entailed putting far more time and effort into their hair, make up and appearance than into school work. For such girls being sexually attractive was an important source of status in their peer group and a means of avoiding ridicule and social exclusion. However, their resistance to rules about school uniform also often brought them into conflict with teachers and led to them being stereotyped as less able academically.

Adapted from Archer et al (2007)

Item B

Lads and Ladettes

Carolyn Jackson made a study of Year 9 pupils and found that the academic pressure inherent in the current education system was encouraging many students to simply opt out of competing because of a fear of failure and not wishing to appear stupid. Such students cultivated an attitude of being 'too cool for school'. For these pupils achieving status in their peer group has become more important than academic success. Appearing unconcerned about failure also offers the advantage that when some pupils are successful they can appear 'geniuses' as they have done so without apparently doing any work.

Jackson's study links to a range of other studies of 'laddish' anti-school subcultures among boys but she also found what she refers to as a ladette culture among girls. Such girls rejected the traditional 'good girl' model of femininity and instead adopted a more assertive and 'sassy' image which did not go well with working hard. Teachers in fact often found ladettes harder to cope with than lads because of the way in which they challenged traditional ideals of femininity. Jackson sees adopting a ladette identity as partly a response to new role models for young women, for example female celebrities who adopt more traditionally masculine behaviours such as heavy drinking.

However, she sees girls as adapting to the same pressure as boys where both sexes are forced to choose between competing academically with the constant fear of failure and trying to fit in socially into peer groups where working hard is labelled as a sign of being 'uncool' or a 'geek'.

Source: Adapted from Jackson, C. (2006)

1 In what ways do the studies summarised in Items A and B suggest that educationalists should be concerned about the under-achievement of some girls as well as some boys?
2 What explanations do Archer and Jackson offer for under-achievement by certain groups of girls?

Why are boys achieving less well?

A crisis of masculinity

Some sociologists such as Mairtin Mac an Ghaill (1994) argue that the decline of male jobs in manufacturing industry has led to a crisis of masculinity. In the past working class males found their identity and status as wage earners performing manual jobs which required physical strength. Such jobs have decreased in the last forty years and been replaced by more feminised jobs in the service sector. Traditional masculine roles are therefore under threat and many working class boys feel uncertainty about their future roles, often perceiving qualifications as a waste of time. For some boys alternative ways of achieving masculinity have become more attractive, for example laddish behaviour and anti-school subcultures.

Lad culture

Sociological research since the 1960s has demonstrated the existence of working class male anti-school subcultures (see discussion of Hargreaves 1967, Willis 1977 and Mac an Ghaill 1994 on pages 129–30). Some more recent studies have suggested that the laddish behaviour characterising such subcultures is now more widespread among not only working class but also some middle-class boys and even some girls. However, laddish behaviour remains more of an issue among boys and helps to explain why boys are less committed to academic success than girls.

Boys' attitudes

Some studies have suggested that boys are often over-confident about their own abilities and do not see the need to work hard to ensure success. Becky Francis (2000) also notes that boys also often have career ambitions, such as professional footballer, which are both unrealistic and less likely to require academic success. Girls on the other hand are more likely to focus on schoolwork as they have realistic aspirations but also ones which require academic qualifications.

Evaluation

From the 1990s onwards there was growing concern in the media and among politicians about the 'problem of boys' under-achievement'. In 2006 a senior Labour politician, Gordon Brown, warned about the prospect of 'a wasted generation of boys' (*The Guardian* 13 October 2006). However, many feminists question why there has been this concern over boys' under-achieving when for decades nobody seemed concerned about girls achieving less than boys.

Some sociologists such as Amanda Coffey (2001) suggest this amounts to a moral panic, an over-reaction by society to a small problem which is blown out of proportion by the media. Coffey argues that such fears reflect wider concerns about an alleged fall in educational standards and loss of traditional masculine identities. In reality, the attainment of both sexes in education is improving. Moreover, focusing on gender differences alone ignores important differences within each gender, for example those based on class and ethnicity.

Activity

Boys and reading

Boys' underachievement in reading is a significant concern for schools across the country. In a National Literacy Trust survey, 76 per cent of UK schools said boys in their school did not do as well in reading as girls. 82 per cent of schools have developed their own strategies to tackle this.

- The issue is deep-seated. Test results consistently show this is a long-term and international trend. Boys' attitudes towards reading and writing, the amount of time they spend reading and their achievement in literacy are all poorer than those of girls.
- Boys' underachievement in literacy is not inevitable. It is not simply a result of biological differences; the majority of boys achieve in literacy and are fluent readers.
- The Boys' Reading Commission has found that boys' underachievement in reading is associated with the interplay of three factors:

- The home and family environment, where girls are more likely to be bought books and taken to the library, and where mothers are more likely to support and role model reading;
- The school environment, where teachers may have a limited knowledge of contemporary and attractive texts for boys and where boys may not be given the opportunity to develop their identity as a reader through experiencing reading for enjoyment;
- Male gender identities which do not value learning and reading as a mark of success.

Source: Adapted from National Literacy Trust (2012)

1 Why is boys' lack of achievement in literacy a cause of concern to both the government and schools?
2 What explanations are offered as to why boys are less skilled at reading than girls?
3 How might the fact that boys lag behind girls in reading ability be related to broader gender differences in educational attainment?

Educational inequalities in a global context

The global 'gender apartheid' in education

Although there are still gender differences in education in the UK these are relatively insignificant when compared to some other parts of the world. Some feminists have argued that girls and women are so disadvantaged in some countries that a situation of gender apartheid exists. The term gender apartheid refers to the economic and social sexual discrimination against individuals because of their gender or sex. It is a system enforced by using either physical or legal practices to relegate individuals to subordinate positions. In terms of education, this means that girls and women are denied the same educational opportunities as males and in some cases are denied the chance to receive an education at all.

The UN Millennium Goals

One of the United Nations' Millennium Development Goals was to 'eliminate gender disparity in primary and secondary education, preferably by 2005, and in all levels of education no later than 2015'.

However, the UN's own data based on household surveys from 61 developing countries shows that among the poorest households girls are more likely to be excluded from education than boys. In sub-Saharan Africa, only 23 per cent of poor, rural girls complete their primary education (UN 2014). In Yemen, 92 per cent of the poorest young women have not completed primary school, compared to 47 per cent of the poorest young men (World Inequality Database in Education http://www.education-inequalities.org)

Perspectives on 'gender apartheid'

Some feminists have criticised the UN for doing too little. Ann Elizabeth Mayer (2000) argues that while organisations such as the UN have condemned racial forms of apartheid (such as that found in South Africa up until 1994) gender apartheid has been largely ignored; UN members have been reluctant to impose sanctions on countries guilty of gender apartheid as they did on South Africa during the era of racial apartheid. On the other hand other feminists have such as Ann Russo (2006) argue that the campaign to open up educational opportunities to women and girls in Afghanistan following the US-led invasion in 2001 was simply an excuse to justify American 'empire building'.

It can also be argued that the concept of gender apartheid is based on a modern western liberal view of education and gender roles. From this perspective accusing societies of educational gender apartheid is based on a western inability to understand other cultures.

Measuring gender inequalities in education

Different measures can be used to assess the degree of gender inequality in education globally. A simple but crude measure is the level of illiteracy (being unable to read and write) as illustrated in Item A in the Activity on page 149. In many countries literacy rates for females are much lower than for males.

Another way in which the UN measures gender inequalities in education globally is by the Gender Parity Index (GPI) this is based on a calculation of the ratio of girls to boys enrolled at different levels of education. Gender parity in education is reached when the GPI is between 0.97 and 1.03. Most western countries have a GPI of close to 1.00 showing that almost equal numbers of males and females are enrolled in education.

Gaining an education has enormous benefits for women in developing countries. An extra year of primary school boosts girls' eventual wages by 10–20 per cent and an extra year of secondary school by 15–25 per cent. A girl in Africa who receives an education is three times less likely to contract HIV and AIDS (VSO, 2011).

Reasons for gender inequalities

According to UNESCO (United Nations Educational Social and Cultural Organisation) there are a number of factors in poorer countries which restrict girls' opportunities for education.

- **Constraints within families** – In many countries girls are expected to take on domestic responsibilities while boys often receive preferences when choices have to be made regarding education.
- **Constraints within society** – These include pressure for early marriage, the threat of sexual harassment and violence to girls outside their own homes and religious and cultural beliefs against educating girls.
- **Policies of school systems and educational practices** – School systems in countries of all kinds are not always empowering for girls. They may not be sensitive to girls' needs in the curriculum, in guidance and counselling services, teaching methods and there may be a lack appropriate female role models.
- **Benefits of education** – Even when girls achieve parity in access to education or academic performance, this parity does not always lead to

equal benefits of education, especially in the job market of developed countries (UNESCO, 2012).

Evaluation

UN statistics can be criticised as they are based on official statistics, some of them collected in poorer countries where surveys may be unreliable. Also statistics on levels of literacy or enrolment in education may not tell the full story, for example, girls may be enrolled in education but be educated separately from boys, or be taught a curriculum which primarily prepares them for traditional domestic roles or for unskilled work, such as in agriculture.

It can also be argued that focusing on gender inequalities in education ignores other forms of inequality which affect children's educational opportunities globally. For example, children of primary-school age from the poorest 20 per cent of households are over three times more likely to be out of school than children from the richest 20 per cent of households. Disparities in school participation linked to place of residence also persist. Rural primary-school-aged children are twice as likely to be out of school compared to their urban counterparts. In some countries, such as Mongolia, GPI data shows more girls than boys in education this reflects the fact that boys are often taken out of school at an early age to start work.

The concept of global gender apartheid in education tends to suggest that this is a world-wide phenomenon. In reality opportunities available to girls and women are much more restricted in some countries than others. Women appear to be most disadvantaged in parts of the Middle East and Sub-Saharan Africa while in many Southern Asian countries there has been significant progress towards opening up education to girls.

There are some countries where conservative religious groups have attempted to close down any opportunities for girls to be educated. For example, in parts of Northern Pakistan the Taliban have tried to ban girls going to school. In 2012, 15 year old Malala Yousafzai was shot by gunmen on her way to school for campaigning for girls' education. Nevertheless, she recovered and in 2013 made a speech to the United Nations General Assembly and was subsequently awarded the Nobel Peace Prize.

In northern Nigeria an armed Islamist group called Boko Haram has carried out attacks on a number of schools. They have demanded that all western style schools should be closed meaning that girls would be denied any education. In 2014, they drew international condemnation by kidnapping more than 200 schoolgirls from the town of Chibok, saying they would treat them as slaves and marry them off. There is therefore still a long way to go before women and girls across the world enjoy equal rights in education with males.

Activity

Global gender inequalities in education

Item A

Youth literacy rates for boys and girls.

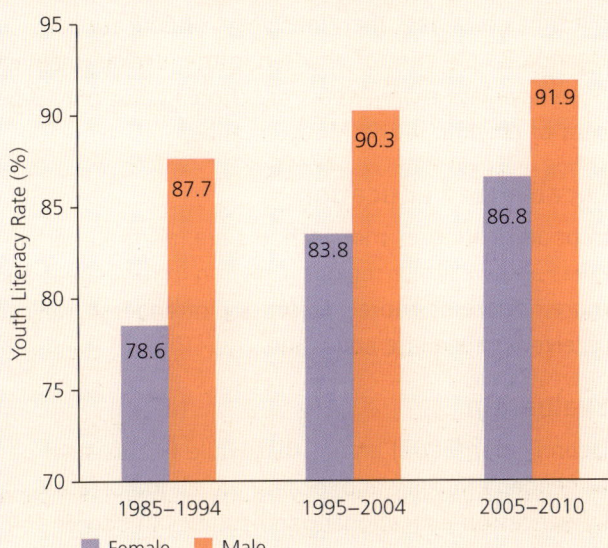

Youth Literacy Rate (%)

- 1985–1994: Female 78.6, Male 87.7
- 1995–2004: Female 83.8, Male 90.3
- 2005–2010: Female 86.8, Male 91.9

■ Female   ■ Male

Sources: http://educateachild.org/explore/barriers-to-education/gender

Item B

Girls' education in Afghanistan

The fields of Bamyan province are dotted with people at this time of year, heads down digging in the earth. It's potato harvest time and children are helping too – as they have done for centuries. But one thing has changed: many of the young girls working with their families are also going to school for the first time.

In between dropping fist-sized potatoes into a bucket, 10-year-old Hamida says that, until last year, 'I'd never been to school.' She is one of 3.2 million girls now getting an education in Afghanistan, according to UNICEF. It's a dramatic rise from 2001 when the US-led invasion brought to an end the Taliban ban on girls going to school. The female literacy rate has tripled – but at around 13 per cent, it is still one of the world's lowest, a sign of how far Afghan girls and women have fallen behind in the past three decades of conflict.

Educating Afghanistan
● Girls in education – 3.16 million
● Boys in education – 5.16 million
● Girls not in education 2.4 million
● Boys not in education 1.6 million
● Adult literacy (+15 years) 39 per cent
● Female literacy (+15 years) 13 per cent

Source: UNICEF

Outside Kabul and other big cities progress in girls' education is more patchy. Most Afghans still live in rural areas, where poverty, conflict and conservative attitudes are more likely to keep girls and women at home. Of the 4.2 million Afghan children not getting any education, UNICEF estimates 60 per cent are girls – and most live in rural districts and the southern and eastern provinces where NATO-Taliban clashes have been most fierce. These are also the heartlands of the Pashtuns, the ethnic group from which the Taliban emerged and who have always had the most conservative views of a woman's role.

Back in her Bamyan village, Hamida still has a lot of work to do in the family home, helping look after her younger siblings as well as in the fields. But six days a week now, she makes the 2km walk uphill to her local school perched on a mountainside. 'There was no school in my time,' says her mother – only 30 years old. 'My daughter wants to be a doctor. May God help us, so her dreams come true.'

Source: Adapted from North, A. (2012)

1 According to Item A, what trends are there in levels of literacy for both girls and boys between 1985 and 2010?

2 What difference is apparent in levels of literacy between girls and boys and how is this changing?

3 With reference to Item B assess the extent to which the concept of 'gender apartheid' is relevant to understanding the educational opportunities available to girls in Afghanistan.

The disparity in educational provision around the world

In addition to gender inequalities in education around the world there are also a number of other types of inequality in education globally.

Poverty and education

- Children in poor countries are less likely to attend school and if they do attend school may only do so for a much shorter period of time than in most western countries. Children who attend school for less than four years can be defined as in education poverty according to WIDE (World Inequality Database on Education).
- Within poor countries the poorest children are least likely to receive education
- In the poorest countries children are less likely to be taught by trained teachers, for example in Equatorial Guinea, Senegal, Angola, Benin, South Sudan and Guinea Bissau less than 50 per cent of primary school teachers are teacher trained (UNESCO).
- In poorer countries children are less likely to go on to secondary or tertiary education. For example, in Sub-Saharan Africa the enrolment rate for higher education is only seven per cent compared to 29 per cent worldwide (British Council, 2014). In such countries opportunities to go to university are often confined to the wealthiest groups with poorer children having little or no chance to access higher education.

Ethnic inequalities

There are inequalities between ethnic groups and tribes in many countries globally. For example, in Thailand where nationally only 8 per cent of children have less than four years of schooling 90 per cent of children of Myanmar and 54 per cent of children from hill tribes have less than four years of education. In Uganda 83 per cent of children in the Ngakaramajong tribe have less than 4 years of schooling but only 3 per cent of children in the Munyoro tribe.

Locality and education

In poorer countries more schools are located in urban areas and wealthier regions. Children in rural areas and more remote or poorer regions are often least likely to receive an adequate education.

Evaluation

Deon Filmer (2007) argues that while factors such as gender, ethnicity and locality are all important influences on educational opportunities in poorer countries, poverty is by far the most significant factor holding many children back. He points out that in countries where not all children complete education poverty is usually the strongest factor associated with non-completion.

Country	% never attended national average[1]	% never attended poorest children[1]	% never attended wealthiest children[1]	% less than 4 years education[2]	Mean years of education[3]
Niger	59	79	–	80	1.50
Liberia	56	72	31	39	5.28
Chad	55	89	25	69	2.79
Somalia	53	89	10	72	1.91
Mali	52	63	21	78	2.02
Guinea	45	62	16	67	3.11
Burkina Faso	43	65	–	69	2.78
Afghanistan	40	56	16	69	3.08
Guinea Bissau	38	56	15	52	4.08
Pakistan	36	64	12	36	5.91

Indicators of educational inequality in selected countries

1 Percentage of children aged 3–6 years above primary school entrance age who have never been to school

2 Percentage of the population living in education poverty (with less than four years of education for the age group 20–24 years)

3 Average number of years of schooling attained for the age group 20–24 years.

Source: World Inequality Database on Education

Activity

Case studies in global education

Item A
Education in the Democratic Republic of Congo

Fighting has been going on between government troops and various armed factions in the Democratic Republic of the Congo since 1994. The chances of children going to school are heavily influenced by whether they live in a conflict zone, and whether they are rich or poor.

Almost all children aged 7–16 in the capital city, Kinshasa, have been to school, whether male or female. In the conflict-affected region of Katanga, the richest children have a similar chance of going to school as those in Kinshasa. But one in three of the poorest children have never been to school. The poorest girls in Katanga are the worst off of all: 44 per cent have never been to school, compared with 17 per cent of boys in the region. Overlapping inequalities create even greater disparities. The poorest young women in conflict-affected areas suffer the worst disadvantages: almost nine out of ten in Katanga do not have basic skills that can be gained through completing primary school.

Source: Adapted from UNESCO (2013)

Item B
Education in Bangladesh

Bangladesh has made great progress in education. In 2011, only 6 per cent of those aged 7–16 had never been to school. Progress has been exemplary in the way it has benefited poor girls and boys in disadvantaged areas. In 2004, 38 per cent of poor children in Sylhet had never been to school. By 2012, only 17 per cent were in this position. The country's successful programme of paying cash to parents whose daughters attend school has resulted in it being one of the few low-income countries to have more girls in school than boys.

Despite Bangladesh's tremendous progress in getting children into school in recent years, there remains a legacy of young people who have not completed primary education. In 2011, while 56 per cent of the poorest youth had not completed primary school, the same is true for only 10 per cent of the richest. In almost two thirds of districts the dropout rate from education is over 30 percent. They have difficulty acquiring quality teachers and 97 per cent of pre-primary and primary students are in overcrowded classrooms.

Source: Adapted from UNESCO (2013) and L. Steer *et al* (2014).

Item C
Education in Sweden

The Swedish educational system is a system that attempts to make sure every child has an equal chance to succeed. One way that Sweden is accomplishing these goals is by making sure every child can go to day care affordably. Of the total cost of childcare, parents pay no more than 18 per cent for their child; the remaining 82 per cent is paid for by various government agencies and municipalities. 97.5 per cent of children age 1–5 attend these public day-care centres. Also, a new law was recently introduced that states that all four and five year old children can attend day care for free. Since practically all students, no matter what their socioeconomic background, attend the same day-care centres, equalisation alongside educational development begins early and in the public sphere. Furthermore, parental leave consists of 12 months paid leave (80 per cent of wage). This results in the privilege and affordability of staying home and bonding with one's child for the first year of life. Due to this affordability, less than 200 children in the entire country of Sweden under the age of 1 are placed in child care.

Inequality in the educational system is further diminished by providing all Swedish citizens and legal residents with the option of choosing which school they want their children to be placed in, regardless of what neighbourhood they reside in or what property taxes they pay. Additionally, the Swedish government not only provides its citizens with a free college education, but also with an actual monthly allowance for attending school and college. Together, these privileges allow for all Swedish children to have access to the same resources.

Source: Adapted from Bjornberg and Dahlgren (2003)

1 What kinds of educational inequalities within the Democratic Republic of Congo are shown in Item A?
2 What evidence is shown in Item B to suggest that poor countries like Bangladesh can make progress in improving educational opportunities for all children?
3 What difficulties might exist in improving educational opportunities in a country like Bangladesh?
4 Study Item C. Suggest reasons why the Swedish education system is more successful than that of England in creating equality between different groups?

Make a copy of the following passage and fill in the blanks using the words given below

One of the main forms of inequality of opportunity in education is based on _____ which is usually defined in terms of the income and occupation of a child's parents. Some sociologists argue such inequalities in education are rooted in a child's home and family background. Some studies have emphasised the importance of _____ factors in explaining differences in achievement. This explanation focuses on the disadvantages created by low incomes; poverty may mean some children lack books, computers, space to study or even a balanced diet all of which might help children in their education.

Other sociologists emphasise _____ factors; these are linked to the attitudes and values parents pass on to their children and the extent to which they encourage their children to have high aspirations. Bourdieu rejects the idea that working-class culture and language are inferior and argues that the higher social classes simply have more _____ or familiarity with forms of knowledge and style which are defined as correct and worthy of status by the dominant class.

Other sociologists argue that class differences in education are created by processes within schools. They argue that there is a process of _____ whereby teachers classify students in types, for example 'troublemakers' or 'less able'. The practice of dividing students into ability groups or _____ can also contribute to this; working-class pupils are more likely to be placed in lower sets and so live up to the lower expectations of teachers. Pupils are also influenced by their peers in school and working-class pupils, especially boys appear to be more likely to become part of _____ meaning that they reject ideas of academic success and instead engage in rule breaking and disruptive behaviour.

Sociologists are also interested in differences in education based on _____ or cultural groupings. Some of the explanations relating to such differences are similar to those relating to social class. Cultural explanations may also be relevant as some minority ethnic groups such as Chinese appear to have very high _____ for their children who are the highest achieving group in the UK. It has been argued that other minorities are disadvantaged by their cultural background, for example, Sewell argues that African Caribbean boys develop a form of _____ based on street culture which rejects the value of academic success.

Many sociologists, however, argue that ethnic differences in educational attainment are linked to the existence of _____ in schools. This suggests that the whole education system creates an unconscious bias against some ethnic minority children. One example is that it is argued there is an _____ curriculum in many schools whereby white culture is given more priority in what students learn than minority cultures. Some schools have tried to counter this my developing _____ which emphasises the positive contribution of minority cultures to British society. It is also argued that the concept of labelling is relevant to some ethnic minorities because teachers have _____ meaning that they are likely to expect more from white pupils and certain ethnic minorities such as Chinese and Indians while having lower expectations of groups such as African Caribbeans.

The third main form of inequality in education is gender. Feminists argue that there is _____ in the education system and that in the past this often meant that teachers had lower expectations of girls. However, today females are outperforming males at most levels of education. Beck argues that there has been a process of _____ which means that girls put more emphasis on their personal needs rather than traditional social expectations such as getting married and having children.

Other sociologists have focused on why boys have fallen behind girls. One explanation is that we have seen the _____ of education whereby schools are now better adapted to the needs of females rather than males, for example most teachers are now female, especially in primary schools. Some sociologists have even argued that young men are now suffering a _____ due to a loss of traditional male jobs in manufacturing and greater uncertainty about what it means to be a man. One reaction may be that some boys are reasserting traditional forms of masculinity in the form of _____ whereby young men define academic interests such as reading and doing well in exams as effeminate.

However, it is not only boys who reject education some sociologists have pointed to groups such as _____ girls who emphasise perfecting their physical attractiveness at the expense of academic success and _____ who behave more like boys, behaving in an aggressive manner.

3.4 How has the UK education system changed?

There has never been a single education system in the UK; Scotland and Northern Ireland have always had separate systems from England and Wales. Wales was given its own devolved government in 2006 with powers over education and its system has since diverged from England, for example there is more emphasis on comprehensive schools at secondary level rather than a diversity of schools as in England. Wales also chose to reject the reforms of A Level qualifications due to take effect in England from 2015 onwards. In this section we will focus mainly on the English education system, however, even in England there has always been diversity in how education is organised between different areas of the country.

Stages of education

In most of the UK education is organised around a number of stages.

- **Early years education** – Education is not compulsory until the age of 5 but before this age many children attend nursery schools which are run both by local authorities and private providers. In England three and four year olds are entitled to 570 hours of free pre-school education a year.
- **Primary education** – Many children start primary school aged four and the National Curriculum Year 1 begins at the age of five. In most parts of England children transfer to a secondary school aged 11 at the end of Year 6 but in some areas there are middle schools taking children from 8 to 12 or 9 to 13.
- **Secondary education** – This covers education from ages 11 to 16, though many secondary schools also have a sixth form which take students up to the age of 18.

- **Further education** – Young people born since 1997 are now expected to take part in some kind of education or employment with training until the age of 18. Further education covers a very diverse range of education and training after the age of sixteen. It includes sixth form colleges which take pupils from the ages of 16 to 19 focusing on similar qualifications to school sixth forms. Further education colleges take students over the age of 16 including adults of all ages. They may offer academic courses similar to sixth-form colleges but also focus on vocational education and training, including students who are in employment who may attend college on a part-time basis.
- **Higher Education** – Up until 1992 higher education was provided by a range of institutions including universities, polytechnics and colleges of higher education. Since then all higher education institutions have been converted into universities. Most students attending universities are studying for first degrees, however, some students go on to take higher degrees, such as masters or doctorate degrees.

Different types of school

As well as different types of schools and colleges at different stages, there is also considerable diversity within stages, this is most apparent in the range of secondary schools now found in England.

- Independent schools – These are schools which are not controlled or funded by the state. Originally all schools were independent but since 1870 the state has gradually assumed responsibility for the education of most children; currently only around 7 per cent of children attend independent schools. Because independent schools receive no government funding most charge fees, though some offer free places or scholarships to pupils selected on ability. Top independent schools can charge £30,000 a year or more.

- **Comprehensive schools** – Since the 1970s most state secondary schools in England and Wales have been comprehensive schools which means they take children of all social backgrounds and do not select children by ability.
- **Grammar schools** – Grammar schools were part of the tripartite system of secondary education which existed in most parts of England and Wales from the 1940s to the 1970s (see page 129). Entry to grammar schools is based on an exam called the 11+ which aims to select only the most able and academic children. In the 1960s and 1970s most local authorities moved to comprehensive education and most grammar schools were forced to either become comprehensives or independent schools.
- **City Technology Colleges** – These are a form of secondary school set up by the Conservative government in the 1980s. They are based on a partnership between government and private businesses and aimed to offer education based on the national curriculum but with a strong emphasis on technology, maths and science. Only 15 such schools were built and all but three of these have now converted to become academies.
- **Academies** – Academies were originally developed by the Labour government from 2000 onwards to replace what were seen as failing comprehensive schools. The coalition government has encouraged all secondary schools to become academies and by November 2013 there were 3,444. Unlike traditional comprehensives, academies are not controlled by local education authorities but are directly funded by central government. Some academies are sponsored by businesses, charities, religious groups or other educational institutions. Academies have much greater freedom than traditional comprehensives to run their own affairs including more control over their curriculum, staffing and budgets.
- **Free schools** – Free schools are an extension of the idea of academies developed by the coalition government since 2010. Groups of parents, educational charities and religious groups can apply to set up entirely new schools with government funding. Free schools have even more freedom to run their own affairs than academies and are in effect independent schools with government funding.
- **Faith schools** – Before 1870 most education in the UK was provided by religious bodies. As the state took over education these were mostly

absorbed into the state system but church schools were allowed to maintain their distinctive religious ethos. In allocating places faith schools may give preference to children brought up within their religious faith. About a third of state schools in England are faith schools, predominantly Church of England, followed by Roman Catholic with smaller numbers of Jewish, Muslim, Sikh and Hindu faith schools.

- **Specialist schools** – From 1997 onwards the Labour government encouraged the development of specialist secondary schools moving away from the idea of comprehensive schools which catered for all types of children towards schools which emphasised specialist skills while still teaching the national curriculum. Most of the early specialist schools focused on technology, business and enterprise, engineering, mathematics, computing or science but more recently other specialisms such as sports, humanities and music have emerged. Specialist schools are permitted to select up to 10 per cent of their intake on aptitude in their specialism.
- **Special schools** – These are schools catering for pupils with Special Educational Needs (SEN), these may include severe physical disabilities, learning difficulties and behavioural difficulties. In recent years governments have encouraged a policy of inclusion, meaning wherever possible children with SEN should be educated in mainstream education.

Conservative reforms of education 1979–1997

Up until the 1980s virtually all state schools were funded and controlled by local education authorities (LEAs) linked to local councils. Most secondary schools were comprehensive schools taking pupils of all abilities and offering a broad education which aimed to cater for the aptitudes and interests of every child. Although there had been debates about education between the main political parties (for example many Conservatives had opposed the abolition of grammar schools which selected bright children using the 11+ exam) both political parties had broadly accepted the framework of education established after the Second World War which was largely based on social democratic ideas of equality of opportunity for all children.

In 1979 a Conservative government led by Margaret Thatcher was elected. They rejected the post-war consensus on education and instead aimed to apply the ideas of the New Right to education as well as other public services.

New vocationalism

The Conservatives argued that the existing education system was failing to produce young people with the skills required by industry. Comprehensive schools were seen as focusing too much on academic and general education and failing to provide young people with vocational skills which could be used in the workplace. By the early 1980s youth unemployment was increasing fast and the government blamed this on the lack of employment skills among school leavers.

The government's solution was to introduce the Youth Training Scheme (YTS) in 1983, initially as a one year scheme for unemployed school leavers. Young people were required to undertake training with an employer and also received vocational training in colleges and training centres, though these did not necessarily lead to qualifications or guarantee permanent jobs. Critics of YTS argued that the scheme simply offered second class training for trainees and cheap labour for employers. While on schemes young people were not counted as unemployed so the scheme was also seen by opponents as a way of reducing youth unemployment statistics.

Another strand of new vocationalism was the introduction of National Vocational Qualifications (NVQs) from 1986 onwards. These were designed to offer a more coherent set of qualifications relating to skills in the workplace (for example, in engineering, retail or hairdressing). Unlike GCSEs and A levels, NVQs were designed so trainees could be assessed by demonstrating their competencies or skills under workplace conditions.

Subsequently General National Vocational Qualifications (GNVQs) were introduced as qualifications which could be studied in schools and colleges rather than in workplaces. These qualifications in areas such as Business and Health and Social Care were broader than NVQs and assessed a mixture of academic and vocational skills. These were later replaced by Vocational A Levels.

NVQs and GNVQs aimed to raise the status of vocational qualifications and make them equivalent to academic qualifications. For example Level 2 NVQs are seen as on a par with GCSEs and Level 3 with A levels. However, critics argue there is still an academic-vocational divide in education with vocational qualifications being seen as second best.

Marketisation of education

One of the key ideas of the New Right is that services planned and delivered by the state (such as education) are often expensive and inefficient. Services delivered by market forces (such as those offered by private businesses) are seen as much more efficient and responsive to consumer demand.

The Conservatives sought to develop these principles in reorganising the education system. While schools and colleges would remain funded by the state they would become more like private businesses competing with one another for customers and having to ensure they were efficient and profitable if they were to survive. The Conservatives introduced formula funding whereby the funding of schools was largely based on the number of enrolments. Successful schools attracted more pupils and therefore more funding. Local educational authorities were seen as bureaucratic and ineffective and the Conservatives aimed to give greater control to schools while at the same time making them more accountable to central government for their performance.

The 1988 Education Reform Act

This Act was the most important reorganisation of education in England and Wales since 1944. It aimed to replace the locally planned and co-ordinated system of education with a national system which also offered more diversity and choice to parents and schools at local level. The key to this was the establishment of a market in education. Key elements of this were as follows.

- **Parental choice** – Comprehensives offered little parental choice; most parents were obliged to send their children to the school attached to their catchment area. Under the Education Reform Act (ERA) open enrolment was introduced giving parents the right to choose their child's school and schools' budgets were based on the number of pupils they could attract. The aim was that schools would become like businesses competing for customers and this would raise the standards of all schools.

- **Diversity of schools** – To further increase choice the Conservatives introduced new types of schools, City Technology Colleges (see above) and Grant Maintained (GM) Schools. Schools were allowed to opt out of the control of the LEA and manage their own budgets, curriculum and staffing by becoming grant maintained schools. They were in many ways the precursors of today's academies. This represented a significant move away from the comprehensive idea of 'one size fits all' towards the range of diverse and specialist secondary schools which are found today.

The national curriculum

The national curriculum was a key element of the Education Reform Act (1988) (ERA). While the Act gave many schools more freedom to run their own affairs, it also imposed a standard curriculum on all schools. For the first time ever central government dictated to teachers exactly what they should teach. The national curriculum was divided into four key stages with standard assessment tests (SATs) at the end of each key stage to measure children's progress. GCSEs were introduced to replace O Levels and CSEs as the main qualification at the end of key stage 4. The national curriculum also dictated what subjects pupils should be taught and even how much time should be allocated to each one. The national curriculum included the core subjects of English, maths and science plus seven other foundation subjects.

The national curriculum can be seen as an extension of new vocationalism in that it emphasised the subjects which the government saw as most relevant to the needs of work while subjects seen as less vocationally relevant such as art, music and sociology were marginalised. The national curriculum was also an important part of the marketisation of education as the results of SATs and GCSEs were intended to provide parents with information to help them choose between schools.

League tables

From 1992 onwards secondary schools were obliged to publish the results of their SATs, GCSEs and A Levels and from 1997 primaries also had to publish their SATs results. The government then published league tables of schools' results, ranking schools in terms of their performance. This was intended to encourage competition between schools and raise standards as high performing schools were likely to attract more pupils and hence increase their budgets.

Critics, however, argued that league tables were not a fair reflection of the quality of education in different schools. They only measured test and exam results and told parents little about other aspects of a school, for example its pastoral care or sporting and extra-curricular activities. League tables also disadvantaged schools in more deprived areas and those with large number of children from ethnic minority groups. These might be very good schools but they were unlikely to achieve similar results to schools serving white middle-class catchment areas.

OFSTED

State schools had always been subjected to government inspection but in 1993 the Office for Standards in Education (OFSTED) was set up with the job of carrying our more rigorous inspections of each school every four years and producing reports providing further information to parents and the government on the performance of schools.

Evaluation of Conservative policies

- **Standards** – Supporters of the Conservatives' educational policies argued that they did much to raise educational standards which were seen to have declined following the introduction of comprehensives in the 1960s. Certainly from the 1980s onwards the proportion of school leavers gaining qualifications increased, although it could be argued that this was simply a continuation of a trend which had been going on throughout the twentieth century.
- **Choice** – Many parents welcomed the introduction of open enrolment as it allowed more choice about their child's schooling. Research by Sharon Gewirtz and her colleagues (1995) found that schools which were under-subscribed were under increasing pressure to give parents what they wanted. However, Gewirtz et al argue that all too often this simply meant that schools made greater efforts to attract more academically able students, often spending more money on marketing rather than improving the support given to less able and SEN students. Moreover, the parents who benefited most from open enrolment were those who were most skilled and motivated at taking the time to research the options available, most frequently well-educated middle-class parents. One consequence of this was that the Conservative reforms may have simply widened inequalities of opportunity between poor children and those from wealthy backgrounds.
- **Vocationalism** – The reform of vocationalism certainly produced greater coherence in vocational qualifications in the form of NVQs and GNVQs. This was also reflected in schools offering a wider range of courses with a vocational element such as the CPVE (Certificate in Pre-vocational Education) and BTEC qualifications which were more suitable for students who did not wish to pursue more academic courses. However, critics argued that many such qualifications were never seen by employers as having the same worth as GCSEs and A Levels. Similar criticisms were directed at schemes such

as YTS. Dan Finn (1987) argued that the scheme had more to do with depressing the wage levels of young workers, reducing youth unemployment and keeping unemployed youths off the streets where they might cause crime and disorder than offering quality training which led to real jobs.

Activity

The National Curriculum

Item A

The curriculum 1904 and 1988

The 1904 curriculum (regulations laid down what subjects should be taught but not what should be taught in each subject)	The national curriculum 1988
English language English literature Mathematics Science Drawing Geography History One language Due provision for manual work and physical exercise (Housewifery in girls' schools)	**Core subjects: 30–40 per cent of the timetable** ● English ● Mathematics ● Science
	Non-core subjects: 50 per cent of the timetable ● Art ● Geography ● History ● Languages (modern foreign languages) ● Music ● PE (physical education) ● Technology
	Optional subjects: 10-20 per cent of the timetable ● Religious education
	Other requirements ● Sex education ● A broadly Christian act of daily worship ● Citizenship (added in 2003)

Members of the Women's Land Army during the Second World War. It can be argued that the traditional view of history embodied in the national curriculum ignored women's role in history.

Item B

Debates about the national curriculum

The national curriculum has been criticised by teachers for being over-prescriptive (trying to control too much of what is actually taught), bureaucratic (involving a huge increase in paperwork), increasing the burden of assessment for pupils and teachers, and responsible for squeezing other worthwhile educational experiences out of the curriculum – for example GCSE sociology.

Moreover, there have been disagreements over the content of the national curriculum subjects. For example, there has been a long-running dispute over what aspects of history should be included. Successive government ministers have intervened to put forward a particular view of history, stressing traditional approaches. This ignores elements of history (for example, women's role in history) that are important in a multicultural society such as Britain.

Postmodernists would also argue that, given the fragmented and diverse nature of postmodern societies, in which individuals have many conflicting educational needs, the attempt to impose a common curriculum on everyone is unlikely to meet those needs. To present a national curriculum that is supposed to encompass everything a child in Britain should know is an enterprise doomed to failure. All information, according to postmodernists, is shifting and precarious. What is today's 'knowledge' is tomorrow's 'falsehood'.

Adapted from Lawson et al (2010)

1 Compare the curriculum for 1904 with the national curriculum of 1988 (Item A). What similarities and differences do you notice?
2 To what extent would you agree with the argument that the national curriculum represented a return to a very traditional curriculum?
3 What are the advantages of establishing a common curriculum for all pupils and ensuring that they are assessed using the same national tests?
4 Using Item B and any other arguments and evidence summarise the main criticisms of the national curriculum as it was laid down in 1988.

New Labour and education 1997–2010

It might be expected that when Labour came to power in 1997 they would reverse many of the reforms initiated by the Conservatives. However, the new prime minister, Tony Blair had rebranded his party as New Labour and aimed to follow what he called the Third Way which involved neither the free market policies of the Conservatives nor the socialist approach of old Labour. This was reflected in Labour's education policies which were in many ways a mixture of social democratic and New Right ideas.

Social democratic approaches

One of Labour's main priorities was to tackle what they called social exclusion. This focused on a variety of ways in which less advantaged groups such as the poor, the unemployed and ethnic minorities were excluded from opportunities available to more privileged members of society. A key aspect of this was improving educational opportunities for children from such groups. This can be seen in a number of Labour policies.

- **Sure Start** – This scheme, started in 1999, provided pre-school children and their families in disadvantaged areas with a variety of support, including play centres, home visits, help with childcare and courses for unemployed parents to assist them in getting back to work. An evaluation of Sure Start by the DfE (2010) found that mothers in Sure Start areas reported a more stimulating home environment and better physical health for their children but concluded that the benefits were 'modest'.
- **Education Action Zones** – (EAZs) were set up in 1998 to raise motivation and attainment in deprived, low-income inner city areas. Representatives of parents, schools and businesses in 72 of the EAZs were given £1 million to spend in each area on whatever they prioritised to improve education, for example homework and breakfast clubs and work related courses.
- **Excellence in Cities (EiC)** – gradually replaced EAZs and gave extra funds to education authorities in inner city areas to boost attainment for students from low income backgrounds, for example through programmes for gifted students, learning mentors and low-cost home computers. EiC achieved some success, for example the percentage of pupils achieving five or more A* to C grades increased by 11 percentage points in EiC schools compared to around 5 percentage points in other schools.
- **Academies** – were originally set up by Labour to replace 'failing' comprehensive schools in inner city areas. Academies can been seen as following social democratic ideas in that they attempted to boost the attainment of children in the most deprived areas and narrow class and ethnic inequalities in education. However, academies could also be seen as a continuation of the Conservatives' policy of moving more schools outside the control of LEAs and replacing standard comprehensives with a greater choice of secondary schools.
- **EMAs** – Labour aimed to increase the number of 16–18 year olds in education and training as it was particularly young people from more disadvantaged background who were most likely to drop out of education at the age of 16. One policy to support this was the introduction of Educational Maintenance Allowances (EMAs) in 2004 which

offered a weekly cash allowance to young people from low income families who remained in education. Research done in 2004 by the Institute for Fiscal Studies and Loughborough University found staying-on rates improved by 5.9 percentage points among those who were eligible. This effect was most pronounced amongst boys whose parents were unemployed or employed in unskilled or semi-skilled manual jobs, the group with lowest staying-on rates.

- **Higher Education (HE)** – Labour also expanded access to higher education as the class gap in participation in HE had been steadily widening. Labour aimed to ensure that at least half of school leavers went on to HE, including many more from poorer social backgrounds. To fund the extra places Labour introduced tuition fees in 1998 and replaced student grants with loans that had to be repaid. However, under Labour the gap in participation rates between social classes actually widened as most of the additional university places were taken up by students from the higher social classes.

New Right approaches

Some of Labour's other policies can be seen as extensions of the Conservatives' marketisation approach to education.

- **Specialist schools** – In 2001 Alistair Campbell, Tony Blair's press spokesman declared the end of the 'bog standard comprehensive'. Labour not only introduced academies as an alternative to LEA run comprehensives but began to develop specialist schools (see page 165). By 2007 over 75 per cent of all secondary schools in England were specialist schools.

- **Performance targets and league tables** – Labour continued the regime of testing via SATs and inspection by OFSTED initiated by the Conservatives and set performance targets for improvement in schools in a bid to continue to raise standards. They also continued to use league tables to assess schools' performance, though the league tables based on examination results only were replaced with ones which included measures of value added, for example measuring how far pupils progress between starting at a school and leaving.

- **Vocational education and training** – In 1998 Labour introduced the New Deal for Young People. 18–24 year olds who had been out of work for six months were provided with personal advisors who guided them through different options which might assist them in returning to work. The scheme had some success, 46 per cent of participants entered employment but critics argued unemployment was falling anyway and that this was a more important factor. Labour also extended the range of NVQ, including a Level 5 award which was equivalent to a degree. GNVQs were rebranded as Vocational GCSEs and Vocational A Levels.

Evaluation of Labour policies

Labour introduced a number of social democratic influenced policies aimed at reducing inequalities in education and these may have had a modest effect in helping young people from more deprived social groups. However, critics argue that Labour's continuation of New Right inspired marketisation policies tended to have the opposite effect and increase inequality of opportunity in education as suggested in the passage below.

Activity

Labour education policies
A critique of New Labour policy
It has been suggested that while Labour introduced many policies aimed at monitoring and raising standards in schools, it has dispensed with very little of what the Conservatives initiated. While the Conservatives were at the forefront of market forces, choice and competition in education, Labour was responsible for taking these mechanisms further.

Geoffrey Walford (2005) pointed to contradictions with policy initiatives that on the one hand, were aimed at reducing inequality and providing better opportunities for the disadvantaged and, on the other encouraging diversity and the development of markets.

Labour also developed extensive use of target-setting at all levels to plan and monitor change, for example schools were given targets for improving their exam results. The setting of targets may be helpful when used by individuals to guide their development but may become tyrannical when the target becomes the overriding reason to action. Measurement by targets may encourage teachers and head teachers to hide damaging information and to boost favourable figures. For example, by concentrating on small numbers of pupils to improve test results, such as raising those just below GCSE C grade to just above it, other pupils or different aspects of school life may be neglected.

Labour's encouragement of academies and specialist schools led to greater choice in education but as Stephen Ball (2008) pointed out middle-class parents are able to operate a system based on choice to their advantage to ensure their children receive the 'best' from the system. Schools in the areas chosen by large numbers of middle-class parents tend to perform well and are oversubscribed. Those that cannot make the choices that help them to escape, the poorer more deprived geographical areas remain in schools deserted by the middle class. These become 'sink schools', less likely to attract extra resources and teachers. In these ways the development of an educational market helps to reproduce social inequalities.

Source: Adapted from Bartlett and Burton (2012)

1 How might the growth of specialist schools be seen as an aspect of the marketisation of education?
2 Summarise the main criticisms of Labour's education policies discussed in Item B.
3 What arguments could be put forward in support of Labour's education policies?

Coalition education policies 2010–15

In 2010 a coalition government came to power supported by the Conservative and Liberal Democrat parties. Of the six government ministers in the Department for Education, five were Conservatives so the Conservatives were the dominant influence on education policy during this period.

Tackling inequality of opportunity

The coalition announced that they wished to turn schools into 'engines of social mobility' and that they wished to help children 'overcome the accidents of birth and social background'. Part of this entailed the creation of new types of schools to help raise standards for all children. The coalition also introduced the pupil premium in 2011. This was an additional payment given to schools for every free school meal child enrolled. In theory, this money should be used by schools to boost attainment amongst the poorest children, however, many head teachers felt it merely made up for cuts elsewhere in education funding.

The coalition made a number of cuts in spending which affected education, including Labour plans to build new schools, cuts to local government which meant that some Sure Start centres had to be closed and the scrapping of the EMA scheme (which was replaced by a much cheaper scheme of bursaries for low income students). It was significant that the proportion of 16–18 year olds staying on in full-time education fell slightly for the first time since 2001 when EMAs were abolished in 2010.

Further diversity and choice

Despite these apparently social democratic aspirations the policies pursued by the coalition strongly reflected the New Right approach which had dominated Conservative policies up to 1997. The coalition extended the idea of diversity and choice by hugely expanding Labour's idea of academies as an alternative to standard comprehensives and also developed free schools as another alternative. The Department for Education suggests that such schools would be more responsive to local needs and will help to drive up standards in education.

- **Academies** – Labour had already established the idea of academies but they were mainly designed to replace under-performing secondary schools in areas of social disadvantage. Under the coalition all schools, primary and secondary, were given the right to convert to academy status. Sponsored academies were those which had been instructed to become academies by the Department for Education, usually because they were designated as in need of improvement. Converter academies were those which had chosen to become academies, in most cases because the schools felt they would be financially better off. Between 2010 and 2014 the number of academies increased from 203 to nearly 4,000 with over a third of these being primary academies. Around two thirds of secondary schools are now academies with more preparing to convert.

A study by Becky Francis, Merryn Hutchings and Robert De Vries (2014) of academies for the Sutton Trust suggests that on average, the improvement in GCSE results for disadvantaged pupils in sponsored academies was greater than the average for mainstream schools between 2011 and 2013. However, there was enormous variation between academy chains, with only 16 out of 31 exceeding the figure for all mainstream schools in 2013. The report suggests that the most successful academies have been those benefiting from effective sponsors such as charities, business organisations or more successful schools where under-performing schools can receive support to improve. Often one sponsor supports a chain of academies who can work together to support one another. However, not all academies have the benefit of such sponsorship and even some of those which do have performed less well than the average for maintained schools run by local authorities.

- **Free schools** – The first free schools opened in 2011 and they represent an even more radical form of marketisation than academies in that they are in effect independent schools funded by the state. Free schools have even greater freedom to design their own curriculum and teaching styles than academies and do not even have to employ qualified teachers. Although free schools are subject to Ofsted inspections they do not have to follow the national curriculum but have to teach English, maths and science. (some of the debates about free schools are examined in more detail in Activity on page 119).

Higher education

In 2012 the Coalition raised the maximum tuition fees which universities could charge from £3,290 to £9,000 per year. The Coalition argued this was necessary to fund the growing number of students going on to higher education. However, in June 2012 applications to English universities were down by 10 per cent compared to much smaller falls in Scotland, Wales and Northern Ireland where home students were not required to pay fees. Applications may have fallen partly because of a fall in the number of 18 and 19 year olds in the population. However, the Independent Commission on Fees (2012) concluded that many young people were put off applying to university because of fear of debt. Currently the average student leaves university with debts of around £44,000, though many graduates on lower incomes are only required to repay a fraction of that amount.

Evaluation of coalition policies

The main thrust of the coalition's education policies has been an extension of the policies to increase choice and drive up standards followed by the Conservative and Labour governments. For supporters of this approach, this has been a real success providing parents and children with a range of alternatives to traditional comprehensive schools run by local authorities.

Like Labour, the coalition has attempted to increase attainment in areas of social deprivation and this has had some success in reducing some class and ethnic inequalities in achievement. For example, the gap between free school meal pupils and others has narrowed at both the age of 11 and in terms of GCSE results. Ethnic inequalities have also decreased with some groups such as Bangladeshi and black African overtaking white British pupils in terms of GCSE results between 2009 and 2013.

Many of the criticisms of the coalition's policies reflect earlier concerns of the trend to marketisation of education under the Conservatives and Labour.

- **Reforms of education are ideological** – Like the Conservatives in the 1980s the Coalition are seen by their opponents as bent on removing power from local education authorities and teaching professionals who are seen as too left-wing and committed to the comprehensive system.
- **Loss of democratic control over education** – Moving more and more schools out of the control of LEAs means that democratically elected councils no longer govern schools. Instead free schools and academies are run by a range of charities, businesses and religious groups which are not subject to the same accountability to local communities. In theory giving schools greater freedom to run their own affairs can be seen to be democratic but in practice the Secretary of State for Education in London increasingly decides educational policy which critics argue means that power in education is actually more centralised rather than devolved down to schools and teachers.
- **Greater inequality** – Middle-class and better educated parents will be better equipped to take advantage of a system based on choice to secure places at the best schools for their children while changes such as scrapping EMAs and increasing university tuition fees seem to be at odds with the coalition's expressed desire to improve opportunities for poorer students.

The debate about academies

Item A

Ark–an example of a successful academy chain

Ark is an education charity and one of the country's top-performing academy operators. Our network comprises both new-start and transition schools that have become Ark academies. Our aim is to create outstanding schools that give every Ark pupil the opportunity to go to university or pursue the career of their choice. Ark runs a chain of 31 academies in London and other parts of the country, of these 14 are primary academies.

To embed core subjects and make time for enrichment, many of our schools run a longer school day. Others are open at weekends and during school holidays, offering revision and master classes as well as residential stays, day trips and summer schools. In all our schools, every hour of every day is devoted to children learning and no time is wasted.

Ark has a track record of success. Around 90 per cent of our schools which have been inspected by Ofsted are rated as good or outstanding – compared to a national average of 80 per cent, and we out perform national GCSE attainment in English and mathematics as well as key stage 2 to 4 progress. 57 per cent of our pupils gained five or more GCSEs graded A* to C including English and maths compared with a national average of 52.6 per cent. In our primary academies, our 7-year-olds exceed national average attainment in reading, writing and maths.

One example of a successful Ark school is Burlington Danes Academy in West London whose predecessor school was in special measures. The academy, which opened in 2006, received a grade of 'outstanding' from Ofsted in 2013.

Source: Adapted from http://www.arkschools.org/

Item B

Criticisms of academies

The main reason so many schools are converting to academies appears to be money. A survey of head teachers in 2011 revealed that 46 per cent had converted their school to academy status or were intending to do so. Three quarters of these suggested they were making this decision for financial rather than educational reasons. Becoming an academy boosts the income of a school by roughly 10 per cent or more.

The Conservatives justify the academy programme in terms of 'empowering local communities but it actually puts a great deal of power in the hands of the Secretary of State for Education in London. Critics argue the reforms are undemocratic because nobody apart from the Education Secretary can actually stop the process of schools which were formerly controlled by local councils becoming academies. One example is Downhills Primary School in Tottenham, north London where, despite protests from parents and the local community, the government went ahead and approved the school's conversion to an academy.

The success stories among academies such as the high performing chain of schools set up by Ark schools have been given a lot of publicity by the Department for Education but they are less keen to publicise the failures. For example, Birkdale High School in Southport, Merseyside only converted to an academy in August 2011 but was graded 'inadequate' and placed in special measures by Ofsted inspectors in March 2012. Similarly, only two years after opening, Sir Robert Woodward Academy in Lancing, West Sussex went into special measures. It would appear that converting a school to an academy does not guarantee its academic success.

Source: Adapted from Hasan, M. (2012)

1 What evidence is there from Item A to show that moving schools to academy status can raise standards in education?

2 Many academies have been established in areas of social deprivation where in the past educational attainment has been very low. How might it be argued that academies may be a means of reducing class and ethnic differences in educational attainment?

3 Summarise the criticisms of academies put forward in Item B?

4 How would you evaluate the expansion of academy schools since 2010?

The impact of educational policies on class, gender and ethnic inequalities in education

Social class

Equality of opportunity Government policies have explicitly tried to reduce social class inequalities in educational achievement ever since the 1944 Education Act laid down the principle of equality of opportunity in education. The subsequent development of comprehensive schools by Labour governments in the 1960s and 70s attempted to take this further. Despite this, class inequalities in education have remained deeply entrenched in Britain and there have been only marginal reductions in differences in attainment at all levels.

Competition and choice Policies based on choice and competition in education were initiated by the Conservatives in the 1980s but continued under subsequent Labour and coalition governments. Critics argued that the focus on raising standards across the board in education has been at the expense of concern about inequalities affecting disadvantaged groups. However, particularly under Labour, policies such as Sure Start, Education Action Zones and Educational Maintenance Allowances did show some modest success in improving outcomes for poorer children by focusing additional resources on inner city areas and pupils from low income families. Under the coalition after 2010 the introduction of the Pupil Premium and opening of new academies in areas of educational disadvantage has also been seen by some as helping to narrow inequalities in educational opportunity.

Criticisms of educational reform Sociologists influenced by Marxism, however, argue that attempts to reduce social class inequalities purely by changing the education system are doomed to failure. The causes of such inequalities of opportunity lie in the fundamentally unequal nature of British society and the fact that the education system has always been designed around the culture and interests of the higher social classes. Only a much more radical attack on economic inequalities and redesigning the education system to meet the needs of diverse groups and children rather than capitalist employers would produce real equality of opportunity. Against this, some New Right thinkers such as Peter Saunders argue that pursuing equality of outcomes in education is unrealistic as children are not equal in terms of ability so some groups of children will always perform better than others. From this perspective all that the education system can do is provide the best opportunities for all children.

Gender

In the last thirty years a number of policy intitiatives have attempted to boost the attainment of girls and break down gender divisions in education. Examples of these include:

- **GIST (Girls into Science and Technology) and WISE (Women into Science and Engineering)** These schemes encouraged female students to opt for courses and careers in science, technology and engineering which have traditionally been male dominated, for example by arranging female scientists to visit schools as positive role models, arranging work experience opportunities in these fields for girls and providing non-sexist curriculum materials and careers advice.
- **Single sex classes** Some schools have experimented with single sex classes in subjects like maths and science, meaning that girls can undertake practicals, ask questions and join in discussions without having to compete with boys who may dominate such lessons. However, the evidence supporting the success of such approaches is very inconclusive.
- **The National Curriculum** The imposition of science along with maths and English as a core subject meant that for the first time girls were obliged to study science up to GCSE level, although with the exception of Biology fewer girls still study sciences at A Level than boys.
- **GCSEs and coursework** The emphasis on coursework in GCSE (until more recent changes) has been seen by some sociologists as favouring girls as it is argued girls are better at working consistently over a long period, though this has been disputed. Given that there has been a shift back to more emphasis on exam based assessment in both GCSEs and A Levels and this has not unduly affected the gender gap in attainment; coursework may not advantage girls as much as has been claimed.
- **Concerns about boys** While policy initiatives in the 80s and 90s tended to focus on girls'

underachievement, the concern of governments and schools in recent years has turned to boys. For example a report for the DfES by Mike Younger, Molly Warrington and their colleagues (2005) reviewed a range of initiatives being implemented by schools to boost boys achievement, for example giving more importance to speaking and listening as a means of supporting writing and more integrated use of ICT so that quality presentation can be more easily achieved, and drafts amended with more ease. Some schools have also had success with mentoring for under-achieving students while others had developed a central focus on the Arts across primary schools, with artists-in-residence schemes, poetry weeks, dance sessions run by professional dancers, and drama productions which allocated lead roles to disengaged boys.

Gender inequalities in education have arguably been reduced much more than those of social class and ethnicity in recent years. However, to what extent this is due to government policies or even initiatives within individual schools can be questioned. For many sociologists the improvements in girls' attainment reflects changes in the wider society. Similarly the under-achievement of some boys can be linked to ideas of masculinity deeply rooted in the culture of the white working-class as well as some minority ethnic groups.

Ethnicity

Multicultural education Up until the 1970s ethnic inequalities in education were not given much attention by educational policy makers, it was assumed that children of immigrants would gradually become integrated into British society and ethnic differences would disappear. The Swann Report (DES, 1985), however, emphasised the importance of multicultural education and argued that both minority ethnic and white children needed to learn to appreciate the cultural diversity of British society. As a result from the 1980s onwards many schools began to adopt multicultural approaches to education, for example making pupils more aware of different forms of music, religious beliefs, languages and food.

Anti-racist education Some educationalists argued that much multicultural education ignored the issue of institutional racism in the education system and

called for a more radical approach known as anti-racist education, involving vigorous opposition to racist attitudes and practices. However, David Gilborn (2008) argues that neither Conservative nor Labour governments were ever really committed to anti-racism in education, although it gained some support in a few left-wing local authorities. Gilborn in fact argues that after 2001, following terrorist attacks in the USA and UK, and riots in cities such as Bradford there was increasingly an 'aggressive majoritarianism' in the stance of the UK government which he sees as based on Islamophobia (fear of Muslims). Government policies moved away from multiculturalism towards a demand that ethnic minorities should assimilate more into white British society.

Supporters of the development of academies and free schools argue that they have achieved some success in boosting educational attainment in deprived inner city areas which often include large numbers of minority ethnic children. For example, the attainment of Bangladeshi children has improved significantly relative to other groups, including white children, in recent years largely due to improvements in schools in the East End of London where the majority of this community is located. However, a report for the Runnymede Trust by Debbie Weekes-Bernard (2007) suggested that the emphasis on marketisation and parental choice in education in recent years had not benefited pupils from ethnic minorities as it was mainly white middle-class parents who were best able to use the choices of schools available for the benefit of their children.

Conclusion

In all three areas of inequality debates about educational policy are strongly influenced by ideology. For example, social democratic approaches have tried to use education as a form of social engineering to create equality in society but have perhaps been unwilling to tackle the material and cultural inequalities in the wider society which hold back disadvantaged groups. Similarly the concern of the New Right with competition in education has in many ways emphasised the idea of winners and losers in education meaning that all too often it is children from already disadvantaged backgrounds who are defined as the losers.

Section summary

Make a copy of the following passage and fill in the blanks using the words given below.

In the 1980s the idea of one type of school for all children which had been supported by the _____ approach to education began to be questioned by the _____ approach which had a strong influence on Conservative government policies at that time. The Conservatives introduced policies based on _____ of education, meaning that schools and colleges were encouraged to compete and run themselves on the lines of businesses. One example of this was the introduction of _____ to schools where parents could in theory choose to send their child to any local school of their choice. The 1988 Education Reform Act also introduced the _____ which laid down what teachers had to teach together with _____ to measure how successfully children had reached their targets in learning at each key stage. Schools were ranked in terms of their results in _____ to further encourage competition and with the aim of raising standards. Another aspect of the Conservatives policies was _____ which aimed to improve the quality of education and training related to skills for work. Examples of this included the introduction of the _____ for unemployed school leavers and _____ which aimed to provide a coherent set of qualifications for workplace skills which would be on a par with academic qualifications.

After 1997 the New Labour government put more emphasis on policies to tackle _____ aiming to improve the education and training opportunities available to poorer and disadvantaged young people. To help pre-school children Labour introduced _____ which set up centres for disadvantaged children and their families. Labour also targeted extra funding into education in poorer inner city areas with schemes such as _____ and _____. To encourage children from lower income families to stay on in education after 16 they were offered a weekly cash incentive called _____. Labour however also continued aspects of the marketisation in their education policies, widening the choice of secondary schools by encouraging _____ for example business and arts schools. They also introduced _____ where under-performing schools were taken out of the control of local authorities and sponsored by other educational institutions or educational charities.

Since 2010 the coalition government has mainly followed New Right ideas in education encouraging not only secondary schools but also _____ to become academies and introducing the idea of _____ whereby groups of parents of charities can set up new schools independent of government control but with state funding. However, the coalition also aimed improve educational attainment among children from poorer backgrounds, for example by offering extra funding in the form of the _____ to schools for children entitled to free school meals.

academies, Education Action Zones, Education in Cities, Educational Maintenance Allowances, free schools, league tables, marketisation, National Curriculum, National Vocational Qualifications, New Right, open enrolment, primary schools, pupil premium, social democratic, social exclusion, specialist schools, Standard Assessment Tests, Sure Start, Youth Training Scheme

Practice questions

In what ways does a child's ethnicity influence his or her educational attainment?	[10]
To what extent are boys now under-achieving in education compared to girls?	[20]
Assess the extent to which policies of marketisation of education have helped to improve educational opportunities for all children.	[40]

Chapter 4

Religion, belief and faith

Option 3 Section B

Religion, belief and faith

Content

1 **How are religion, belief and faith defined and measured?** Defining religion, faith and belief; different types of religious institutions and movements, measuring religion, faith and belief.

2 **What is the role of religion, belief and faith?** Theoretical views of the role of religion, belief and faith for the individual and for society; theoretical views of the relationship between religion and social change.

3 **What are the patterns and trends of religion, belief and faith?** Patterns and trends in relation to social class, gender, ethnicity, age; religion, belief and faith in a global context.

4 **Is secularisation occurring?** Debates on secularisation in relation to religious belief, religious practice, power and influence of religion in society; theoretical views on secularisation; religion and social policy.

4.1 How are religion, belief and faith defined and measured?

Getting you thinking ...

> "I belong to no religion.
>
> My religion is love.
>
> Every heart is my temple."
>
> –*Rumi*

A quote from Rumi

1 What do you think Rumi meant when he wrote about religion in this way?

2 Write a list of words that you would use when discussing the meaning of religion.

3 How would you define religion?

4 Write a list of the similarities and differences between the terms religion, faith and belief as you understand them.

Defining religion, faith and belief

Sociologists have defined religion in different ways and these competing definitions have led to different sociological ideas about the role of religion for the individual and society. They have also resulted in sociologists forming different views about the impact of religion on social change. Smart (1988) offers an understanding of religion as consisting of a number of different dimensions. These dimensions can be seen as contributing to a definition of religion which can apply to different religions traditions from different cultures and societies.

Study

The seven dimensions of religion, Smart (1998)

Ninian Smart (1998) offered a definition of religion as consisting of seven dimensions –

1 **The Practical and Ritual dimension.** In this dimension religious adherents engage in practices or rituals such as religious worship. Smart argues that some rituals are very elaborate and some are quite simple but that they share characteristics that mean that they belong to this dimension.

2 **The Experiential and Emotional dimension.** This dimension refers to all of the personal experiences that occur within religious traditions, including the dramatic religious experiences of key figures such as Jesus or the Buddha. The dimension also includes the ways in which religious people are affected emotionally by participating in their faith.

3 **The Narrative or Mythic dimension.** In this dimension religious people share stories that shape their lives and their communities. Examples might be stories from the Qur'an in Islam or the story of the life of Guru Nanak in Sikhism. Some stories are thought to be real historical events that actually happened. Also included in this dimension are stories that would not be considered by some to be historically accurate such as the parables of Jesus.

4 **The Doctrinal and Philosophical dimension.** In this dimension, religious people share beliefs about life and the world. Such beliefs would inform their understanding of reality and guide action. Some religious traditions are seen as having detailed and elaborate beliefs (such as Roman Catholic Christianity which holds strong beliefs about the role of the Virgin Mary), while other traditions have fewer doctrines and beliefs (such as the Religious Society of Friends or Quakers).

5 **The Ethical or Legal dimension.** In this dimension, members of religions seek to abide by rules, guidelines and ideals that shape their lives and behaviours. Such rules might be very clear and specific or they might be more general and function as inspiration for behaviour without being too precise. An example might be the Decalogue or 'ten commandments' within Christianity, or the 613 mitzvot in Judaism.

6 **The Social and Institutional dimension.** In this dimension, religious traditions develop patterns of organisation that can shape social life and people's experience of religion. The institutional structures associated with churches, denominations or sects are included in this dimension.

7 **The Material dimension.** This dimension includes physical, artistic objects, such as religious paintings or icons and religious buildings such as Mosques, Gurdwaras or Cathedrals.

Smart argues, therefore, that religion is not just about belief or ritual but that there is much more to it. He also argues that secular world views such as nationalism or Chinese Communism could be understood using his seven-fold scheme. This leads to the conclusion that the study of religion should include aspects that would never, normally, be considered religious (like Chinese Communism). The value of Smart's scheme is that it encompasses the complexity of religion and the fact that not all specific examples of religion will emphasise all the different dimensions to the same extent. Another value is that the seven dimensions can be used to interpret the wide variety of religious phenomena that exist in the world.

1 Using Smart's theory about the different dimensions of religion, consider how you might go about conducting sociological research into religion. For example, what sort of research methods might you choose to investigate dimension 1 (The Practical and Ritual dimension)?

2 What sociological research methods could you use to investigate dimension 2 (the Experiential and Emotional dimension)?

3 Would the methods be different for each dimension? List reasons for your answers.

4 What problems might you encounter? Write a list of the difficulties that might be associated with researching religion as Smart presents it.

Defining religious belief

Sociologists try to distinguish between religious belief and religious faith. Religious belief can be defined as the type of belief that is characteristic of views held by a religious person. For some religious people, key beliefs will centre on ideas about God and human destiny. For example, a Christian might report that she believes in God, Jesus and life after death in 'heaven'. However, for other types of religious people, such as Buddhists from the Theravada tradition, there is no belief in God and ideas about life after death are very different from Christian ones. Buddhist beliefs about human destiny centre on the idea of 'rebirth'. These variations suggest that religious beliefs are relative to the particular religions that are being investigated and defined by them.

It can be argued that religious people usually have beliefs about life and the world that are characterised by a particular kind of intensity and that it is the intensity, or passion, of a religious person's belief that makes that belief religious. People sometimes report that an individual's beliefs about their favourite football team are like a religion because of the intense feelings and views they hold about their team.

A shrine to Elvis

A stall selling Liverpool FC Souvenirs

RELIGION	
Jewish	❑
Muslim	❑
Catholic	❑
Jedi Knight	✓

Jedi Knights wanted to be included in the census

A liturgical procession

Another view is that religious beliefs relate to an individual's most central life experiences. Paul Tillich, a Philosopher and Christian Theologian argued that religious beliefs are beliefs that concern an individual in a fundamental way, and he linked religious beliefs to their 'ultimate concerns'.

"Religion is the state of being grasped by an ultimate concern, a concern which qualifies all other concerns as preliminary and which itself contains the answer to the question of a meaning of our life." (Tillich 1976)

This definition of religious belief suggests that such beliefs usually relate to important life matters such as life and death, good and evil, human destiny and the origin of life, since these ideas can be classified as matters that are 'ultimate concerns' for human beings. The specific beliefs that relate to an individual's ultimate concerns will depend on their cultural background, their upbringing and their significant life experiences. With this definition of religious belief (belief as ultimate concern), there are further issues of how one can measure the extent to which a belief is an ultimate concern. This depends on the individual's own unique point of view and this cannot be easily measured.

Defining religious faith

Religious beliefs are seen as closely connected to ideas about religious faith. Faith is a technical term in some religious traditions, such as Christianity, and it refers to the way in which a religious person has a relationship of trust with their God or with the contents of their faith or teachings of their sacred books. The focus of religion is not people's intellectual beliefs (for example, 'I believe that gravity exists because of Newton's law of gravitation') but more about how they respond to life (for example, 'I believe in being kind to people, as it is part of my religious faith'). In this context, when people speak about their religious faith, the idea is that they are referring to aspects of religion that they are willing to live their lives by. Measuring faith can be harder than measuring belief since it can be difficult to know if a religious idea is something that a person really trusts and is willing to commit him or herself to. Research into religious faith is slightly different to research into some of the dimensions of religion referred to above in that such research would entail seeking to delve into people's deepest loyalty.

> **Activity**
>
> ### Researching faith
>
> 1 In groups, conduct a study within your class to find out about people's religion, faith and belief. You will need to operationalise each concept before you undertake your research.
> 2 Decide if you will use a quantitative or qualitative method of sociological research, or use mixed methods.
> 3 Identify any ethical concerns and make sure that your participants are protected from harm.
> 4 Present your findings to the class.
> 5 Write an evaluative paragraph explaining the strengths and weaknesses of your research.

Different types of religious institutions and movements

Sociologists use a number of key terms to describe different kinds of religious institutions. These terms, such as 'church' or 'denomination' (see below) can be seen as ideal types that do not perfectly describe actual religious institutions. The use of this typology is helpful for understanding religion but particular religious organisations may fit different terms, and there can be significant overlaps.

Churches and denominations

Sociologists such as Troeltsch (2009) have developed a number of terms to help them to describe or classify religious organisations. Within sociology, the term church refers to a type of large religious organisation that people might belong to because they are members of a particular society. For example, within the UK, some children might have been baptised in the Church of England and might be seen as belonging to that church long before they were old enough to freely choose to join. This practice relates to the idea that a church seeks to be universal, in other words, it is seen as being the organisation that all members of a society *should* belong to just because they are from that particular society. The Roman Catholic Church is another example which is prevalent within some European countries, such as Italy. These churches are large organisations and they are seen as closely linked to the societies within which they function. There can also be close links between the church and the state. An example of this link is that the Queen is both the Head of State within the UK and the Head of the Church of England. Traditionally, churches are seen as being conservative in terms of politics and social change and as supporting the existing social order. Churches will have strong organisational structures such as a hierarchy of religious professionals. In principle, a church will seek to have a monopoly of religious truth and will try to guard that truth from challenge. Churches will aim to appeal to all members of a society and people from all social classes might belong to a church. However, because of the link between the church and the social order, members of the upper classes might be prominent members of the church also.

A second useful term for classifying religious organisations is denomination. A denomination is, in some ways, similar to a church but there are differences. A denomination is seen as being a respectable religious organisation that fits into society and would accept its norms and values. It might be quite large in number of members but would not seek to be *the* organisation for everyone in that society. An example of a denomination within the UK might be the Methodist Church, which originally split off from the Church of England in the eighteenth century and appealed to a different kind of audience from the existing church structure.

A denomination works with awareness that there are other kinds of religious organisations around and it does not expect to be universal. It does not, for example claim that it is the sole possessor of religious truth. Within the USA, for example, there is no one established Christian church but there are many different denominations. A denomination is seen as appealing to members of different social classes and as less connected to the upper classes. In a similar way, a denomination is less connected to the state than a church. The use of these sociological terms can be quite complicated, since the same religious organisation might be classified as a church in one context and as a denomination in another context and both terms might seem to fit. So, the Church of England seems to be an example of a church within the UK and seems to be an example of a denomination within the USA (where it is called the Episcopalian Church).

Activity

What is a church?

1 Create an information leaflet explaining the key characteristics of a church.
2 Illustrate your leaflet with images that portray these characteristics.

The Archbishop of Canterbury

Activity

Denominations

1 Use the internet to find out about the origins of the Methodists in the UK.
2 Write a newspaper article explaining why they split off from the Church of England and include their key beliefs and values.
3 Write an evaluative paragraph assessing the usefulness of the terms 'church' and 'denomination' in showing the differences between these organisations.

Sects and Cults

Sociologists use the term sect to refer to a particular type of religious organisation that is very different to a church. Ernst Troeltsch (2009), who defined the difference between church and sect, suggested that sects are diametrically opposed to churches. A sect is seen as a type of small and intense religious organisation that does not accept the norms and values of society in a way that is seen as characteristic of churches. Rather than being integrated into the social order and as upholding the state, a sect is seen as deliberately disconnected from society (that is, opposed to the 'world'). Sect members would typically withdraw from contact with society in order to concentrate on their sect's beliefs and values. Contact with the wider society is seen as threatening to the existence of the sect. Sects claim a monopoly on religious truth and seek conformity to that truth from sect members. Unlike churches, sects might not have strong organisational structure with designated religious professionals such as priests, although there may be dominant charismatic religious figures who lead the group and exercise authority. An example of a sect, within seventeenth century Christianity, might be the Religious Society of Friends, or Quakers. This group separated itself from the Church of England and other groups, abolished the institution of priesthood and sought to adhere to a stricter code of ethics that set it apart from the wider society at the time (for example, the Quakers were opposed to all war or violence and refused to treat people differently because of their social position in society). The Quakers claimed that people could have a direct link to God within their meetings and used the truths gained to offer a criticism of the existing social order.

Sociologists have suggested that sects that manage to survive over time often seem to develop into denominations. For example, twenty-first century Quakers retain many of their distinctive beliefs, ideas and practices but function within British Christianity as a denomination (for example, they are members of a denominational organisation like 'Churches Together in Britain and Ireland'). On the other hand, some sects are groups that have broken away from denominations because they believe they have become compromised by society.

Activity

Sects

1 Use the internet to find out more about sects such as the Amish that have broken away from other religious organisations.
2 Make a diagram showing their development over time.

The term cult was introduced into sociology by the American sociologist Howard Becker (1950). Becker argued that this is a type of religious grouping that is not tightly organised like a sect and which is more of a loose association of individuals seeking spiritual enlightenment. Such groups might not have a formalised membership and participants might also be associated with other groups and organisations. Typically, a cult is seen as being associated with the teachings of a charismatic individual and it might be fairly short-lived. An example of a cult, in this sense, is 'Transcendental Meditation', which has an organisation devoted to propagating the teachings of Maharishi Mahesh Yogi (a religious teacher), and which seeks to teach the benefits of meditation for people in modern society experiencing stress and anxiety. The teachings of cults are seen as less challenging to contemporary norms and values. In traditional sociological terms, cults are different to sects in that they are less exclusive and less 'world-rejecting'.

Shoko Asahara, leader of the Aum Shinrikyo sect in Japan

In common sense understanding, however, the term cult has become interchangeable with the term sect and is often associated in the mind of the public with religious groupings that strictly adhere to the teachings of a specific individual and demand high levels of conformity and commitment from followers. This has led to many criticisms of cults within society. Cults are frequently described in the mass media as highly dangerous and are associated with moral panics. For example, the Branch Davidian Seventh-day Adventist religious group, which centred on the teachings of a charismatic individual named David Koresh in the late 1980s and was seen as diverging significantly from contemporary norms and values, was referred to as an example of a cult with highly negative connotations. This particular religious group was associated with the disastrous Waco siege in Texas in 1993, in which the FBI and other US law enforcement agencies tried to arrest Koresh and other followers for various crimes and which led to the deaths of 80 people including 22 children under the age of 17. There was considerable controversy in the USA about the causes of this event. Was the group to blame? Or was the FBI to blame? Media commentary tended to view the events as an example of what can happen when people become involved in cults.

The bad press associated with cults has meant that this specific sociological term has become less and less useful as its sociological definition is at odds with its wider use within society.

Some of the difficulties associated with the term cult have led sociologists to develop new terms to describe religious organisations and movements similar to cults and sects. New Religious Movements and New Age Movements (see below) are now part of sociological vocabulary.

New Religious Movements

The term New Religious Movement (NRM) was adopted within sociology as a way of distinguishing between different types of religious movements that develop either in their own right or as offshoots of existing organisations. A defining feature of an NRM is that the group is different from and separated from the dominant religious culture of the society within which it exists. This may mean that an NRM has completely different beliefs to the surrounding culture (and the dominant religion of the culture)

Activity

Cults

1 Use the internet to conduct research into newspaper stories about religious cults.
2 Analyse four stories and write a 200 word report explaining whether the typical description of the cult(s) conforms to the sociological definition or to the common sense view of the term.
3 Create a table to show the key characteristics of each of the following terms – churches, denominations, sects and cults.

Study

New Religious Movements, Roy Wallis (1984)

Roy Wallis has been applauded for creating a 'typology' which classifies NRMs in three different ways in order to explain and understand the differences between them.

World-rejecting

A 'world-rejecting' NRM advocates an attitude of rejection and criticism of the norms and values of the surrounding culture. An example of a world rejecting NRM might be the Unification Church, sometimes known as the Moonies.

World-accommodating

A world-accommodating NRM is often an offshoot from an established religious group. Wallis argues that world-accommodating NRMs are not interested in the surrounding culture and are focused on the spirituality of their members. These NRMs would distinguish between 'worldly' concerns and 'spiritual' matters and would focus on spiritual life. An example would be neo-Pentecostalism.

World-affirming

A world-affirming NRM, such as Transcendental Meditation (TM) is an NRM in which the norms and values of society are accepted and the beliefs and practices of the group help people to function within that society. For example, TM accepts that society creates stress and anxiety and uses mediation to help people to cope with stress and anxiety. It does not try to change society so that there is less cause for stress but rather focuses on self-actualisation and self-improvement.

1 Use textbooks and/or the internet to find out about one example of each of Wallis' types of NRMs.
2 Make a poster or write a short article illustrating the ways in which each can be seen as fulfilling Wallis' criteria.

or it may mean that the beliefs of the NRM share similarities with the wider religious culture but that the beliefs of the NRM are criticised by and rejected by the dominant religious culture. Jehovah's Witnesses are an example of a religious group that shares some of the same beliefs as Christian denominations (for example they believe in God and Jesus and read the Bible) but which is rejected by the larger Christian culture and has been classified as an NRM. The term 'New Religious Movement' has been used for older groupings such as the Church of Jesus Christ of Latter Day Saints, also known as the Mormons, which was created in 1830 and also of newer groupings such as the Falun Gong, which emerged in China in the 1990s.

New Age Movements

New Age Movement (NAM) is a sociological term, which refers to a broad movement that emerged in the 1970s and 1980s and which does not have the clear shape and structure that can be seen as characteristic of the other terms discussed above. While a church, a sect or denomination is seen as being a defined religious grouping with clear beliefs and an organisational structure, the New Age is a term which refers to an overall perspective on life and nature which can lead to various practices that people engage in on a voluntary basis and to a loose association with other people who share the same views and ideas.

New Age practices might include clairvoyance, trying to contact aliens, various types of meditation, trying to access spirit guides, belief in magic and a pursuit of healing and personal change. The concern for healing might lead to the practice of yoga, aromatherapy and/or reflexology. New Age practices are related to ideas around nature and ecology. New Age ideas centre on the personal subjective experience of the individual and there is a questioning of the role of tradition in relation to religion and spirituality. This is in spite of the fact that many New Age ideas and practices share links with older mystical traditions from established religions such as those of the 'East' including Hinduism, Buddhism and Taoism.

While some New Age movements can resemble NRMs organisationally, New Age ideas often spread in less structured ways. People might encounter New Age ideas through certain kinds of shops, seminars, public lectures and 'Mind, body and spirit' fairs which are held across the country. On the other hand, New Age ideas might be spread through music, film or TV programmes. New Age movements are often organised more through individual one-to-one meetings and small groups rather than weekly congregations, as in a church or

denomination. There are also large New Age gatherings associated with sacred sites such as Stonehenge.

It has been argued that the New Age can be seen as a response to the 'failure' of technologically driven societies to deliver a sense of meaning and purpose to their citizens. In this sense, the New Age can be thought of as a post-modern response to the 'failure' of modernism.

Mind, Body, Spirit Event

Saturday 6th May 2016
Wychwood Village Hall
10am – 4pm

A RELAXING EVENT WITH SOMETHING FOR EVERYONE!

Holistic therapies ~ One-to-One Readings
Workshops ~ Crystals ~ Refreshments

Mind, body, spirit event invitation

Study

The New Age, Heelas (1996)

Heelas studied the development of the New Age movement and concludes that it is an 'alternative counter-cultural movement' and a 'spirituality of our times'. According to Heelas, a key feature of the New Age is its challenge to the traditional views of mainstream society, 'the great refrain, running throughout the New Age, is that we malfunction because we have been indoctrinated – or, in the New Age sense of the term, been "brainwashed" – by mainstream society and culture. The mores of the established order – its materialism, competitiveness, together with the importance it attaches to playing roles – are held to disrupt what it is to be authentically human. To live in terms of such mores, inculcated by parents, the educational system and other institutions, is to remain the victim of unnatural, deterministic and misguided routines ...' (Heelas, 1996)

1 Read the above quote from Heelas and list the ways in which the New Age may be seen as a world rejecting movement?

2 From other information in this section, list the ways in which the New Age could also be seen as world-accommodating or world-affirming.

3 Write a speech either in favour or against the New Age, summarising the key arguments for the view you are taking.

Indeed, New Age Movements correspond fully to the postmodern cultural era in which religious people are encouraged to make use of the internet. New Age Movements can use the internet to acquire an awareness of different ideas and practices globally and pick and mix from these.

Religious Fundamentalism

So far we have discussed sociological terms such as church, denomination, sect or cult, which refer to types of organisational structure, which exist within religion. Religious fundamentalism can be defined as a religious movement or point of view rather than as a type of organisational structure. It has been argued that religious fundamentalism develops when liberal or modernist ideas are perceived as undermining people's religious faith and leading to secularisation. Within North American Christianity, the development of science, particularly the spread of Darwin's ideas about evolution and ways in which these ideas seemed to challenge the truth of the Bible, led to a movement back to the 'fundamentals' of the Christian faith. These include the literal infallible truth of the Bible, as well as other traditional Christian beliefs such as the Virgin Birth of Christ, and the belief in the bodily resurrection of Jesus. Such 'fundamentalist' teachings can exist within existing churches and denominations and can also lead to the formation of separate fundamentalist sects.

A defining feature of fundamentalism is close adherence to a sacred text such as the Bible or Qur'an. Another key aspect is an agenda to promote a wider following for fundamentalist ideas within society as a whole. This is linked to the frequent fundamentalist perception that society is decaying and that the world is heading towards some kind of disaster or 'end-time'. Fundamentalist ideas within different religious traditions can lead to political initiatives aimed at large scale social change to reverse this decline.

Religious fundamentalism can be a feature of religious traditions other than Christianity. For example, fundamentalist currents have been identified within Hinduism, Buddhism, Judaism and Islam. Almond et al (2003) point to politically significant fundamentalist movements in different countries – among Jews in Israel; Muslims in Pakistan and Chechnya; Hindus in India; Buddhists in Sri Lanka as well as Christians within the USA and elsewhere.

As well as religious fundamentalism being seen as a response to the threat of secularisation, it is also associated with social groups who feel marginalised in society. Bruce (2008) argues that the growth of fundamentalism often occurs amongst 'members of particular social strata that feel especially threatened, dispossessed or relatively deprived by modernization' (2008). This is seen as applicable within American society but also in a case like Palestine, where unemployed and disadvantaged young people find an appeal in the fundamentalist ideas of a social movement like Hamas.

Measuring religion, faith and belief

Sociologists continue to debate the complexities involved in measuring religion, faith and belief. Different measures contain advantages and disadvantages. We will examine measures of religious belief, 'religiosity', 'belief without belonging' and 'vicarious religion'.

Religious Belief

Sociologists have sought to measure religious belief using survey data. For example, the Equality and Human Rights Commission, which included data on belief in God over a number of years (Perfect 2011)

● 1991 – 45.8 per cent reported belief in God.
● 2008 – 36.7 per cent reported belief in God.

An advantage of such survey data is that it can provide useful evidence of patterns and trends in religion in society. For example, such data is sometimes used as an indication of decline in religious belief and there are debates between religious people and humanists as to the meaning of the statistics.

Perfect also reported on a 2010 survey of belief among people in European countries that there is 'some sort of spirit or life force' and found that in the UK 33 per cent share that belief. These statistics draw on similar surveys over a long period of time that include different types of religious belief. For example, the British Religion in Numbers (BRIN) website, which is a useful resource for statistics on belief, includes survey data on a bewildering variety of beliefs ranging from 'Belief in the Afterlife' and 'Belief in Angels', to 'Belief in Black Magic' and 'Belief in the Devil'. BRIN also reports on 'Belief that Dreams can predict the future' and 'Belief in ESP (extra sensory perception)' as well as 'Belief in Fate' and 'Belief in Flying Saucers'. Such beliefs may be very important for certain individuals but many would not be seen by religious people as indicative of religious belief. It is arguable that a disadvantage of conducting a survey, in which individuals are asked if they believe in specific beings or types of belief, does not go to the heart of what religious belief is in the context of religious participation. This is because religious believers may report that they share a particular belief because of their membership of a particular religious community such as a church. There is, of course, survey data on membership of religious organisations and these statistics can be compared with data on religious belief.

Day (2007) points out that some surveys of individual religious membership reflect a number of different types of religious participation –

- Adherents – Some people who belong to churches may be classified as religious 'adherents' (who believe in God and heaven, for example). These account for about half of the Christians in her survey. But others participate for different reasons such as a wish to belong to the church community rather than because of personal belief. Day outlines three other types of Christians who are not true 'adherents':
  - Natal Christians who describe themselves as Christians because they were baptised as babies or born into a Christian family.
  - Ethnic Christians who think they are Christians because that is a part of being British.
  - Aspirational Christians who view Christianity as a sign of goodness and respectability.

Day's research adds to the complexity of using survey data to decide on religious belief. There are obvious advantages to sociological research into religious belief since this data provides basic information as to what individuals report about their beliefs. This data can be presented both qualitatively and quantitatively. Disadvantages include the types of questions on belief that are asked in surveys (do they get to the heart of what people truly believe?) and whether they reflect belief or just membership of a community. This raises questions about the validity of the research. It may also indicate a problem of operationalisation because the meaning of the concepts involved may be interpreted differently.

Religiosity

We examined Smart's seven-dimension model for understanding religion earlier and noted that religious belief is just one dimension within that model and that different religious traditions place different levels of emphasis on belief relative to other dimensions such as ethics or spirituality. This illustrates the difficulty of measuring religion or religiousness. For example, it would not be sufficient to measure religion by measuring only religious belief if the particular religious adherent being studied belonged to a type of religious organisation that placed less emphasis on belief and more emphasis on ritual or experience. A useful concept within the sociology of religion that helps to address this problem is the concept of religiosity. This is a broader concept that is intended to capture some of the different aspects of what is typically involved in being a religious person. Religiosity can be seen as involving three elements.

- Cognition, including beliefs about what is known. Religious doctrine would be included here.
- Affect, including what a person feels about their faith. Spirituality is included here.
- Practices, including aspects of religious behaviour and participation in religious organisations and activities.

It is argued that an individual's religiosity can be measured better if all three of these aspects are taken into account. For example, Cornwall et al (1998) developed a model of religiosity to measure religious commitments among Mormons within the USA. They concluded that their 'analysis clearly supports the contention that religiosity is best viewed as multidimensional'. This means that a person might accept the truthfulness of a religious text, such as the

Bible or the Qur'an (belief) but never attend religious ceremonies or even belong to an organised religion (practice) showing that there are different ways for individuals to express religiosity. Another example of the multidimensional complexity of religiosity might be a person who attends devotional services within a particular religious tradition (practice) in order to experience oneness with God (spirituality) but have no orthodox religious beliefs. Cornwall et al's findings, that religiosity is multidimensional, was achieved by developing a questionnaire that asked people about all of the different aspects of their religious lives and sought to consider if different elements correlated with each other.

Examining religiosity yields some useful data on the links between religiosity and other aspects of people's experience. For example, religiosity on a global scale is associated with poverty in different nations (the USA is an exception to this trend). A Gallup poll entitled 'Religiosity Highest in World's Poorest Nations' (Gallup, 2010) found that rates of religiosity remain exceptionally high on a global scale where rates of poverty are high. 'One theory is that religion plays a more functional role in the world's poorest countries, helping many residents cope with a daily struggle to provide for themselves and their families. A previous Gallup analysis supports this idea, revealing that the relationship between religiosity and emotional wellbeing is stronger among poor countries than among those in the developed world'.

Measures of religiosity would seem to have advantages in that they provide a clearer picture of what religion actually means for people who participate in it. It is also more complicated to measure than straightforward survey questions on what people believe. A disadvantage of measuring religiosity would seem to be the difficulty of being able to pin down what people's participation in religion actually means to them. Cornwall et al's research

(1998) suggests that an individual's participation can take many different forms and the mix of 'cognition', 'affect' and 'practice' can be diverse.

Belief without belonging

Davie introduced the concept of belief without belonging in her 1994 book on Religion in Britain. She notes surprise at the popularity of the idea (Davie, 2015) and quotes Voas and Crockett to define what belief without belonging means; 'belief in the supernatural is high and reasonably robust while religious practice is substantially lower and has declined more quickly'. Davie suggests that belief without belonging is a dimension of modern religiosity and that creating a distinction between measures of 'believing' and measures of 'belonging' (as in participation in the activities of a religious organisation such as a church) will assist in the task of researching into and understanding the modern religious scene. Davie points to the low levels of active church participation among young people and working-class communities, alongside higher levels of belief in religious ideas and themes. She also notes exceptions to this, including higher instances of religious participation among specific working-class communities such as young working class males from Liverpool following on from the Hillsborough disaster in 1989. However, Rational Choice theorists (who point to the significance of individual choice in religion) argue that religious institutions thrive in a context where they have to compete for the allegiance of people whose religious needs are not being met. They argue that belief without belonging only exists when the prevailing religious culture does not have a number of competing groups (for example, a situation where there is a 'church' rather than 'denominations' or 'sects' in competition with each other). So, therefore, choice is limited and leads to belief without belonging because the choice of which religious group to belong to is narrow.

Study

Believing in belonging amongst young people, Day (2009)

'As a product of a certain historical era – and one raised in a church-attending family – it was initially difficult for me to explain ...'anomalies' I was to meet in my research – atheists who believe in ghosts, agnostics who despise religion and yet say they are Christian; apparently 'rational' humanists who believe in life after death and Christians who prefer talking to

their dead relatives than God or Jesus in prayer. Much of that did not correspond to what I had understood 'Christian' or 'religious' to be.' (Day, 2009)

Activity

1 Discuss Day's quote and write a paragraph explaining what you think she means by it.
2 Which theory/theories best support Day's findings about anomalies in young people's views?
3 How would you explain these anomalies?

An advantage of Davie's concept of belief without belonging is that it offers an explanation about the persistence of religious belief in the face of declining participation in religious attendance. A further disadvantage, which her critics have identified, is that it can be difficult to measure belief accurately to prove her thesis that there are high levels of belief alongside declining 'belonging'.

Vicarious religion

The Pope at a broadcast in 2014

Davie (2015) more recently argues that vicarious religion is an identifiable phenomenon within the British and European religious environment. In 'vicarious religion', people do not identify religious beliefs that they hold but identify religious persons, places and ceremonies that remain important to them. The term 'vicarious' means doing something on behalf of someone else and the idea of vicarious religion is that there is a small group of individuals who perform certain religious services on behalf of a larger majority of people. Davie notes that 'religion can operate vicariously in a wide variety of ways';

- Church leaders performing rituals on behalf of others, such as at times of birth or death, among people who would never normally attend church services themselves.
- Church leaders believing on behalf of others, and being willing to speak up about those beliefs in the media.
- Church leaders embodying moral codes on behalf of others, and being criticised if they do not stick to them.
- Churches offering a space for consideration of unresolved issues in society – such as moral issues surrounding birth and death or issues of sexuality.

- Churches as functioning as the focus for 'national grief' when major tragic events occur, such as the death of Princess Diana in August 1997.

Davie's notion of vicarious religion is used primarily to describe phenomena within Britain and Europe. Vicarious religion is also, arguably a feature of religious communities in different parts of the world and in different cultures and traditions. In Buddhist culture, there is a division between monastic communities and Buddhist adherents living nearby who do not themselves practice their faith in the same way as the monks within the monastery. Buddhist monks are understood to be performing a function on behalf of the 'ordinary' Buddhists living nearby. The ordinary Buddhists are supposed to support the monks in the monastery materially, by providing food.

A disadvantage of the concepts of vicarious religion and of belief without belonging is that it can be difficult to measure the extent of these phenomena. This is because they are difficult to pin down precisely. Bruce and Voas (2010) point out that vicarious religion can be taken as evidence of people in a secular society liking religious institutions because they perform useful secular functions. They point out that church services for the death of Princess Diana '... offered a convenient venue and trained personnel, but no one would have much cared if the person officiating at Diana's funeral was a lord rather than a bishop – what mattered was the pomp and circumstance'. Bruce and Voas' view is that vicarious religion can plausibly be seen as an example of secularisation rather than as an example of continued religious belonging on the part of the majority of people. However, their interpretation is not based on empirical research but is a theoretical point similar to that used by Davie as evidence of vicarious religion.

> **Activity**
>
> **Measuring religion, faith and belief**
> 1 Make a table that summarises the advantages/ disadvantages involved in measuring religion, faith and belief.
> 2 In your own words, explain the concepts of religious belief, religiosity, belief without belonging and vicarious religion.
> 3 Create your own resource such as a grid or poster and apply relevant sociological theories to the concepts above, for example postmodernism, Marxism and functionalism.

Check your understanding

Briefly define the following terms and give an example of each.

1 Dimensions of Religion
2 Religious Belief
3 Religious Faith
4 Church
5 Denomination
6 Cult
7 Sect
8 New Religious Movement
9 New Age Movement
10 Religious Fundamentalism
11 Believing without belonging
12 Vicarious Religion

Section summary

Make a copy of the following passage and fill in the gaps using the words given below

Sociologists study religion using the three concepts of _____, _____ and _____. Religion can be understood as having 7 _____ which capture the complexity of what religion means to people. According to Tillich, belief depends on the perspective of the religion being studied but can also be seen as a response to a person's _____ _____. Religious faith includes those features of religion that people put their _____ in.

There are a number of key terms used when studying religious _____. A _____ is a large religious body that claims to represent the truth for the whole of a society. This is different to _____ that are smaller and are linked to different social _____. A ____ is a small and intense religious group which may seek to enforce beliefs that are different to the rest of society. On the other hand, sociologists see a ____ as a group that inspires the individual to seek _____ growth.

___ _____ movements can be seen as _____ affirming, world-_____ and world accommodating. These three types of group are useful in classifying different movements. Another type of religious movement is the New ___ which is a type of loose-knit religious grouping that encourages individual spiritual change and _____.

Religious _____ entails believing in sacred ____ such as the Bible and may be concerned about the teachings of _____ including Darwin's theory of _____.

When measuring religious _____ sociologists use survey data that can produce _____ that show that patterns of belief change over time. There are advantages in seeking to measure the concept of _____ since this can include cognition, _____ and practice. High levels of religiosity are associated with _____ in many parts of the world but not the ____.

_____ has developed the concepts of belief without _____ and _____ religion to explain many of the statistics on religion in the contemporary UK. She contends that some people rely on religious _____ to perform religious _____ on their behalf. There are advantages and disadvantages with the use of these concepts and it is recognised that measuring religion, belief and faith needs to acknowledge the _____ involved.

rituals, belonging, USA, religiosity, belief, Age, New, spiritual, sect, classes, church, ultimate concerns, faith, leaders, poverty, statistics, fundamentalism, science, complexities, growth, Religious, world, cult, dimensions, religion, Davie, vicarious, affect, evolution, rejecting, denominations, organisations, trust, texts, beliefs

4.2 What is the role of religion, belief and faith?

Theoretical views of the role of religion, belief and faith for the individual and for society

Getting you thinking

Discuss and write brief answers to the following questions.
- What do you think the role of religion is for the individual?
- What role does religion perform for society?
- What do you think the main sociological theories, such as Marxism and Functionalism, would say about the role of religion for the individual and for society?

Functionalism

Functionalism offers a distinctive perspective on the role of religion, belief and faith for the individual and for society. Functionalist thinkers see religion as having a key, positive role in meeting society's needs.

Emile Durkheim (1858–1917) (Durkheim, 2008) argued that religion had a role in building social solidarity. He based his work on a study of religion in early societies such as aboriginal groups in Australia. Durkheim drew lessons from their experience to develop an understanding of religion more generally. His conclusion was that religion teaches a distinction between the sacred and the profane (the non-sacred). As a result, some objects and people were seen as having special meaning and others were seen as more commonplace and ordinary. Durkheim suggested that all societies work with this distinction and that particular objects come to hold a sacred symbolic significance for people.

Drawing on his research into aboriginal societies, Durkheim wrote about the significance of the totem as a religious and social symbol. Each aboriginal clan had their own totem, which was usually an animal or plant depicted in wood or stone, which they worshipped through rituals. A totem was 'the outward and visible form of ... the totemic principle of god' (Durkheim, 2008). However, Durkheim believed that the god being worshipped within religious rituals also represented society itself and the norms and values of the god were the norms and values of the society.

In other words, people were worshipping their society when they worshipped their god and the values of the god were the values necessary for the functioning of society. This relates to Durkheim's concept of the collective conscience which refers to the 'totality of beliefs and sentiments common to average citizens of the same society' (Durkheim, 1984) which society needs if it is to function well. A reason for the link that was made between the totem/god and the social order was that gods or totems were seen as being connected to the spirits of the dead ancestors of the clan itself. According to Durkheim, religion was the most central and significant institution in society and it had an enormous significance in terms of binding society together like a 'social glue'.

Critics have argued that Durkheim's view is based on a questionable sample of aboriginal societies. Dawson (2011) contends that one cannot generalise from the religion of early societies to the truth about what religion always is. It is also argued that religious values do not always accurately represent society's norms and values and that there can be a clash between society's values and the values that religion seeks to express and promote. Defenders of the functionalist view point to the continuing significance of religious values, beliefs and rituals for the functioning of societies across the world today.

Branislaw Malinowski (1884 – 1942) (1954) supports a functionalist view of the role of religion and based his theories on anthropological fieldwork among Trobriand Islanders who live on islands off the coast of New Guinea. Malinowski's ideas parallel those of Durkheim in his view of all religion as being based on the beliefs and practices of early societies. Malinowski seems to assume that the first form that a religion takes is likely to be the purest and most accurate form. He observed that religion had a function in regard to society and its values and that this function occurred in the context of religious rituals. However, rather than seeing such rituals as representing society itself in the form of a god or totem, Malinowski observed that rituals seemed to help society with difficult and stressful life events such as birth, puberty, marriage and death. These life events were seen as occasions when people's sense of their existence and their attachments to each other were threatened. In a basic sense, a religious ritual, such as a funeral, would serve various social functions at once; the bereaved person would be comforted by the beliefs around immortality expressed in the ritual and social relationships would be strengthened by the experience of joining together to support the family and friends of the person who had died.

Malinowski also examined rituals associated with difficult life events concerned with the work of fishing among the Trobriand islanders. When fishing was deemed to be especially dangerous, for example, outside the relative safety of the local lagoon, there would be rituals that were intended to offer protection from the risks involved. He observed that all rituals within this cultural context functioned to meet society's needs in times of stress and anxiety over difficult life events and, therefore, strengthened the society.

Criticisms of Malinowski's ideas are similar to the points that were raised with regard to Durkheim. Malinowski seems to make generalisations from the experience of a specific religious culture and this raises questions about the usefulness of such generalisations to very different kinds of societies. On the other hand, it is argued that religion does continue to function as a form of support in difficult life events and religious rituals do occur in many different parts of the world at significant life events such as birth and death.

Talcott Parsons (1902 – 1979) (1965) put forward a functionalist account of the role of religion in society. He contended that the social norms that guide people's behaviour are integrated into systems of values by religious teachings. An example might be the role of Christian moral guidelines, such as the Ten Commandments, and the ways in which these guidelines can have an effect on individual conduct and also on legal systems and family codes. In addition to the role of religion in teaching social norms, Parsons also follows Malinowski's view of the significance of religious rituals for people when responding to

challenging and difficult life events such as the death of a loved one and to unfairness and contradictions in the social order.

A criticism of Parsons' view is that religion often seems to have a divisive and non-integrative role in social life. It is argued that religious traditions can lead to conflict rather than bringing harmony and order.

The functionalist view more generally seems to relate to social contexts in which there is one religious order and one religious ethical code and it can be argued that it seems ill-suited to contexts where there is religious diversity and disagreement.

Another criticism of the functionalist perspective comes from proponents of liberation theology, discussed below. They argue that in societies where movements for social change and social equality were popular, such as Latin American countries, these were met with opposition from the Roman Catholic hierarchy. Therefore, the stance of the religious authorities in these countries seemed to create social division and conflict rather than social integration.

Activity

Religion and conflict

1 Using the internet and your own knowledge, make a table and list examples of where religion may be seen as causing conflict in society or between societies.

2 Add another column to your list with alternative explanations that you can think of for the conflict. You may wish to draw on theories that you already know and consider how they would explain the conflict, for example how would a feminist thinker respond?

Marxism

Marxism offers a view of the role of religion, belief and faith for the individual and for society which emphasises religion as a conservative force that is resistant to social change.

Marx (1818–1883) argued that society changes as a result of conflicts between social classes and he saw the different social institutions, including religious organisations, as part of the struggle between social classes. Marx grew up in a Christian society in nineteenth century Germany and was influenced by, among others, Ludwig Feuerbach (1804–1872), a well-known philosopher who argued that religious ideas are created by human beings and are not the product of a god. Feuerbach (2008) believed that key Christian ideas are invented by human beings and then projected onto God. Furthermore, the religious ideas that people engage with are alienating as they are experienced as being imposed upon them by God. Influenced by these ideas, Marx observed that, in practice, religious teachings are enforced by churches and that these teachings actually function to keep people in a state of oppression. They do this in various ways:

- Some religions, such as Christianity, teach people that there is an afterlife in which they will receive a reward for adhering to religious teachings in this life. This can mean that working-class people are not encouraged to seek to change their lives now but to wait for a change in the life to come after death.

- Religions may teach that God creates the social order and that people should accept their position in society without complaint. Marx was an historical thinker who analysed the social order in earlier societies such as those in mediaeval Europe and

he explored the ways in which religion taught that Kings and Queens were seen as exercising authority on behalf of God. He saw a similar pattern of religious teachings in the Christianity of his own era, in that religion was used to justify the power of the state.

While Marx saw religion as being an instrument of ruling class control, he also suggested that it offers emotional comfort for working-class people. However, he saw this comfort as illusory and acted like an intoxicant or drug. A famous quotation from Marx illustrates this view:

'Religion is the sigh of the oppressed creature, the heart of a heartless world, and the soul of soulless conditions. It is the opium of the people' (Marx, 1844)

Marx argues that religion expresses the suffering of the working class but that it does so in a way that discourages action for social change. Marxist theory describes society as comprised of a base and a superstructure. The base consists of those parts of society that have a strong and dominant economic effect. This includes institutions such as industrial corporations or banks. This economic base controls other elements of civil society (known as the superstructure) that may appear significant but have less real power. The superstructure includes political institutions such as parliament and religious institutions such as churches. In Marxist thinking, the power of religion is an ideological power, not a real economic power and it works by influencing people to accept their position in society and discourages efforts to bring about change. In this sense, religion is a form of 'false consciousness' that obscures the real picture of what is happening to people in their lives. Marxist thinkers view religion as being supported by the ruling class in order to keep the working class in a passive and dependent condition. Therefore, from this perspective, it is in the interests of the ruling class to encourage religiosity amongst the working class as a means of transmitting religious ideology that promotes 'false class-consciousness'. According to the Marxist view ruling-class people might not typically be religious in their personal lives but that they support religion in society in order to keep the working class under control. Marxists would argue that this is one of the reasons why daily acts of worship are a part of compulsory state education in some societies.

The making of the English working class, E. P. Thompson (1969)

E.P. Thompson, a Marxist historian, wrote a history of the growth of the working class in England from 1789 to 1832. His work was based on extensive historical research into the factors that led working people to define themselves as a class. Thompson analysed the Methodist Church, a prominent denomination that appealed to the working class during this period. He argued that it might have been expected that working class people would have become highly aware of the ways in which their lives were being controlled by the new industrial bourgeoisie of the time. Thompson believed, however, that the Methodist Church's small group meetings (called 'class meetings') and other aspects of church membership had the effect of making many working people conform to the discipline of working obediently in large industrial organisations which actually oppressed them. In this sense, he presented a Marxist view of the role of religion; that it serves the interest of the ruling class. However, other historians have argued that Thompson overstated his point and they suggest that many politically-aware working-class people had found that Methodist Church membership had assisted their ability to reflect on their life and to stand up for their rights.

1 Using an internet search engine such as Google, investigate the views of Methodism on social change.
2 Write a 250 word article explaining the views of famous Methodist thinker John Wesley on social change and also include information about current Methodist views on the matter.
3 Assess these views and write a paragraph using Methodism to support or challenge Marxist views on the role of religion.

According to Marxist thinkers, evidence of religion acting as a conservative force can be found within history and in the contemporary world. During the English Civil War in the 1640s, a key argument on the Royalist side (those who fought for King Charles I) was that the King ruled by 'Divine Right' and that citizens should never fight against him because they would be fighting against God.

Others argue against the Marxist view. They point out that there are often countervailing forces in times of social change. For example, during the English Civil War, groups such as the 'Levellers' and 'Diggers', argued for the rights of working people from a religious perspective.

Within the contemporary world, sociologists, such as Bruce (1988), have contended that Christianity is often aligned with the power structures of society. This can be seen in the links that are made in the USA between religion and the 'right-wing' politics of the Republican Party. Republican presidents such as Ronald Reagan and George W. Bush were viewed as depending on the votes of religious citizens and the vocal support of religious leaders for their power. Others argue that all US political figures including Democrats like Presidents Barak Obama, Bill Clinton and Jimmy Carter tend to appeal to religious ideas and to seek religious support.

There is a similar picture in other European countries and in other parts of the world where different religious traditions, such as Islam in Saudi Arabia or Hinduism in India, can be seen as working alongside the 'powers-that-be' and not necessarily in the interests of ordinary people. The Hindu caste system, for example, can be seen as reinforcing social division and inequality.

In evaluation, Friedrich Engels (1820–1895), a close associate of Karl Marx, argued for a view of early Christianity that mirrors some Neo-Marxist ideas about religion as a force for social change (see page 183). Engels (1895) pointed out that there were some striking similarities between early Christian groups and the working class movement that Engels and Marx were associated with in the nineteenth century. Both groups were movements of the working class and both looked to the future for a change in their fortunes. Engels believed that because early Christianity was a movement of the oppressed in society (the society of the Roman Empire), it could come to inspire a similar sense of opposition against the powers-that-be in later societies. When discussing the view of religion as promoting social change, it is also useful to consider evidence of religious thinkers working in Latin American countries, who adopted Marxist ideas to develop what is termed 'liberation theology' (see pages 183–4).

Overall, Marxist ideas provide a useful focus for the general debate in sociology as to whether religion is positive or negative and whether religion is a conservative force or a force for change.

Neo-Marxism

Neo-Marxism modifies traditional Marxist ideas about the role of different institutions in society. While Marxists argue that the ruling class controls all of society's institutions, including religious organisations, Neo-Marxists contend that such institutions are often not controlled *directly* by the ruling class but that influence is exercised *indirectly* by those who work for the institutions. It is argued that the people who work for banks, within the media or in churches don't necessarily see themselves as servants of the powerful but do what they honestly think is a good job. However, the effects of their work accords with the views of the ruling class partly because of their class background and socialisation into capitalist norms and values and also because of the expectations and culture within their organisations.

Another consequence of this view, however, is that religion (and other cultural institutions like the media) can be seen as having relative autonomy or some independence from the ideology of the ruling class. In other words, the experience of religious individuals may lead them to choose to fight against the power of the ruling class even when the institution they belong to, such as a Church or denomination, is a conservative force. In this sense, relative autonomy can enable religion to become an institution of empowerment for the proletariat. Within the USA, the role of religion in the 1960s civil rights movement is seen as an example of the relative autonomy of religion. Both Christianity, in the person of Martin Luther King, and Islam, in the person of Malcolm X had a role in inspiring people to work against the Vietnam War and against racism and economic injustice. It is arguable that religion within US society is both a conservative and radical force.

These ideas can be related to the concept of liberation theology which is often associated with neo-Marxist ideas.

Liberation Theology

Liberation theology is an approach to religious belief and practice that seeks to contribute to the struggle of oppressed people against economic forces and state repression. This form of religious teaching tries to connect to working-class people via 'base communities' in which individuals support each other and seek to counter the power of the ruling class. It is argued that, in that context, religion has functioned as a force for social change. Although, it can be

Study

Liberation Theology, Maduro and Romero (1982)

Otto Maduro (1945–2013) offered a Neo-Marxist perspective on religion. Brought up in Venezuela in a working-class family, Maduro studied the sociology of religion and specialised in Marxist ideas. He argued that Marx had offered an overly simplistic understanding of religion. Maduro thought that there was good evidence for the conservative role of Christianity within Latin America, including Venezuela itself, but he suggested that religion could work against the power of the ruling class and he provided evidence from Liberation Theology of religion's ability to be on the side of the poor.

Figure 4.13 Oscar Romero (1917–1980)

Oscar Romero provides an example of Maduro's ideas in action. He was a Roman Catholic priest and Bishop who, in 1977, became Archbishop of San Salvador in El Salvador, a small country in Latin America. Romero was a conservative Roman Catholic who supported traditional ideas. El Salvador was a country that was controlled by a few wealthy families and the army. Much of the population was poor and there was widespread political violence and repression. Many people believed that the Roman Catholic Church supported the ruling class in El Salvadorian society and some priests argued that the Church should side with the poor against the rich. Romero was seen as a conservative figure and a disappointment to those who were looking for change. However, after he became Archbishop, he began to speak out publically against the ruling class in El Salvador and called for support from elsewhere, for example, he appealed to the US president, Jimmy Carter, to stop sending weapons to the El Salvadorian army. Romero's role was a surprise to many people and he was nominated for the Nobel Peace Prize. On 24th March 1980, unnamed individuals assassinated Romero allegedly following orders from members of the El Salvadorian army.

Oscar Romero is seen as a good example of the relative autonomy of people within religion to serve the ruling class *and* to fight against the ruling class. He had been a conservative priest and had changed his mind and was seen as a champion of the poor.

1 Using an internet search engine, find out about Liberation Theology and 'base communities'.
2 Write a leaflet explaining about 'base communities' and the ways in which they represent a religious force for social change. Illustrate your leaflet with examples.
3 Write a paragraph about the concept of the relative autonomy of religion and include examples such as Oscar Romero.

argued that liberation theology has not always had long lasting effects on the societies within which it operates.

In evaluation, Neo-Marxism offers a more complex picture than traditional Marxist ideas about religion. Neo-Marxists consider that religion, like other cultural institutions within a class-based society *tends* to support the power of the ruling class but that it need not necessarily do so.

Weberianism

Max Weber (1864–1920) was a sociologist who argued that religion can be a force for social change as well as a conservative force. He presented a view of the individual as an agent who can be motivated by many factors including his/her ideas and beliefs. Marx had argued that people are motivated primarily by the economic realities of their lives – by their work and by the power of the wealthy in society. Marx can, therefore, be seen as a materialist who discounted the importance of ideals and ideas. Weber, on the other hand, is seen as advocating a social action theory in which people are motivated by meanings and motives, including religious ideas.

Weber's main work is contained in a book originally written in 1904 entitled The Protestant Ethic and the Spirit of Capitalism (Weber, 1958). This work gives a careful analysis of the factors that led to the development of the capitalist economic system in western societies. Marx had argued that capitalism developed due to conflicts between social classes, a conflict that was primarily to do with economic matters such as who owns what and who works for whom. Weber argued that capitalism developed in western societies partly as a result of religious ideas at the time. He pointed out that other countries did not develop capitalism even though the conditions seemed right (he was referring to India, which had similar economic conditions to England). What made the difference in the UK and some other European countries was what Weber called the 'protestant work ethic'. This phrase refers to a particular motivation to work hard experienced by some religious people who had been influenced by a seminal protestant religious thinker named John Calvin (1509–1564). Calvin argued that people get to go to heaven because they have been chosen by God – they belong to the 'elect' – but they can only know that God has chosen them if they show the evidence in their lives and if God blesses them with success. This situation is seen as creating a feeling of loneliness in people and a 'salvation anxiety' that motivated them to work hard to demonstrate to themselves and others that they belonged to 'the elect' and would be one of 'the saved'. Weber argued that this attitude was different to the motivation experienced by other sorts of religious teachings. This 'protestant work ethic' became linked with what is known as the 'spirit of capitalism' – an idea about pushing hard to make money for its own sake. Making money acquired a religious motivation as well as a business motivation. People were seen by Weber as being motivated in their work in a way that was similar to the devotion that they showed within their churches or monasteries or other religious institutions. Weber suggested that religion is a force for social change in the sense that capitalism would not have developed if the protestant work ethic hadn't been there. In addition to the religious ideas, Weber also believed that the technology needed to be right (such as the development of spinning machines) and that prevailing economic conditions needed to be in place too but he said that ideas and beliefs were major factors.

Weber (1963) also analysed other strands of religion as well as Calvinism. He pointed out that religions can be either ascetic (actively pursuing goodness or godliness in life) or mystical (passive and accepting). They could also be engaged in the world and the life of the world 'inner-worldly', or 'other-worldly', and detached from the world. This led him to identify four ideal types of religion:

1 Other-worldly mysticism (for example, Buddhism)
2 Inner-worldly mysticism (for example, Taoism in China and elsewhere)
3 Other-worldly asceticism (for example, Roman Catholic Monks)
4 Inner-worldly asceticism (for example, Calvinism)

According to Weber, these different forms of religious life would lead to different effects within society.

In evaluation, evidence for Weber's theorising is found in the detailed arguments that he advances within his work but it can be difficult to produce conclusive arguments for and against his ideas. For example, it has been suggested that capitalism did not develop very quickly or efficiently in some countries such as Scotland which had strong Calvinist influences within its population. This means that Weber may have been wrong since capitalism should have been stronger in that country due to the influence of Calvinism there. However, Gordon Marshall (Marshall,

1982), a modern Weberian scholar, points out that this argument betrays a misunderstanding of Weber's thought; Weber thought that Calvinism was an important factor in the development of capitalism but other factors could be important too and Scotland did not have enough skilled labour and did not have enough capital for investment to enable capitalism to develop quickly. Therefore, according to Marshall, Weber's view is not disproved.

An argument against Weber was advanced by Kautsky (1953), a Marxist scholar. He suggested that the capitalist economy came before the 'protestant work ethic' developed and that capitalism was actually a major factor that created Calvinist Protestantism. Kautsky suggests that it simply served the purpose of capitalism to have a system of ideas that supported their economic doctrines, so, instead of Calvinism coming first and contributing to the development of capitalism, it is capitalism that came first and contributed to the development of Calvinism. In contrast to this, Marshall argued that the earlier forms of capitalism that Kautsky refers to were not the successful forms of capitalism that came later and that Calvinism was necessary for this to develop. This type of argument can only be resolved if people agree on their definition of capitalism and on what counts as valid evidence.

Another argument against Weber is that Calvinists were successful capitalists for reasons other than their religion. It is argued that they were heavily involved in business because they were legally barred from other kinds of work (Calvinists were sometimes persecuted within European societies) and that their success wasn't because of their religion but because they didn't have any alternative source of income. Weberian scholars argue that other religious minorities (who also weren't allowed to do other kinds of work) did not develop capitalism in the same way as the Calvinists did. They think that Weber's ideas are more plausible.

Other sociologists argue that Weber ignored the effects of economic factors and class conflict in the emergence of capitalism. However, Weberian scholars point out that Weber's viewpoint was more complex and nuanced than that. They suggest that social change is caused by many factors, one of which is ideas and beliefs, which may include religious ones. A strength of Weber's ideas is that they are more sophisticated and multi-faceted.

Feminism

In a way that is in some respects similar to Marxism, feminist sociologists consider that religion usually serves the interests of a particular social group – in this case, men – rather than society as a whole. One feminist view typically put forward by radical feminists is that patriarchy (control by men) is a strong influence in society and that religions are usually patriarchal organisations. Evidence for this view is found in patterns of organisation within religions where leadership roles are often given to men rather than women in spite of the numerical superiority of women in some religious traditions such as Christianity. Examples include the role of priest or bishop within traditional Christianity, the role of imam in Islam and the role of rabbi in some strands of Judaism. In contrast, women are often seen as having a responsibility for religious nurture within the home and family. For example, Jewish women are seen as exercising a leadership role with respect to worship within the family home such as taking responsibility for the weekly Friday meal for Shabbat (or Sabbath).

Some feminists argue that the patriarchal dominance of men in positions of leadership within religions is the symptom of a deeper patriarchal bias in the central beliefs of religions. Many religious traditions describe God as male; God may be referred to as 'he' and may be addressed as 'Father' or 'Lord'. Rather than being a fact about God, this use of language is seen by some feminists as preventing women from achieving equality within those religions.

In addition to beliefs about God, feminists point to the prevalence of men as key figures within religions. Most religious traditions have male founders or prophets:

- Buddhism began with Siddhartha Gautama (the Buddha) who was male.
- Christianity was founded by Jesus.
- Hinduism originates with a long and complex tradition that includes worship of male and female deities. Major deities such as Krishna are male.
- Judaism has the roles of Abraham, Isaac, Jacob, and the teachings of Moses and the prophets.
- Muhammad (Pbuh) is the prophet of Islam.
- Sikhism has ten gurus beginning with Guru Nanak and all were male.

Feminists argue that religious symbolism such as ideas about God/gods or the gender of key religious figures and the preponderance of men in leadership roles within religion can have an effect on women's psychology. They suggest that it can be difficult for a woman to feel that she is a complete human being if the main language used within her religion does not affirm her gender in an explicit way.

Feminists believe that the features of religions described above suggest that religion has a conservative role in society. They argue that the continuing use of gender-specific symbolism as well as continuing patterns of patriarchal dominance within the organisation of religions can prevent the wider social change that is needed to bring about gender equality.

In addition to the above factors, feminists also point to patterns of overt violence and control of women within religion. El Saadawi (1980) refers to the practice of female circumcision within Islamic societies as an example of this. She contends that this practice is not true to Islam but is the result of a misinterpretation of the teachings of the Qur'an.

In evaluation, liberal feminists believe that reform of patriarchal religious organisations is possible. They argue that there is evidence of religious traditions changing to reflect gender equality within society. For example, the Church of England introduced women priests in 1992 and, by 2004, one in five priests in the Church of England were women. Subsequently, women were ordained as bishops within that Church. These changes reflect years of debate about whether women priests and bishops accord with their key beliefs. One argument deployed by proponents of women's ordination is that while Jesus chose 12 male disciples to be his leaders within the early church, he also had a surprisingly open and accepting attitude towards women in a way that was unusual for Jewish men at the time.

The Religious Society of Friends (or Quakers), which is a Christian denomination, has a strong tradition of equality between men and women since their inception in the seventeenth century. Most Quakers do not have the institution of priests or ministers and all

Study

The Goddess Movement, Carol Christ (1997)

Carol Christ is a feminist thinker who rejects images of God as male and ideas about religion that are patriarchal. She challenges male religious thinkers who see God as separate to human beings and separate to the earth. Instead, she proposes a feminist spirituality that promotes interconnectedness with nature. She writes about images of 'the Goddess' in human history and different religious cultures and suggests that people can experience a non-patriarchal view of religion when they discover the Goddess. Drawing from areas such as history, art, literature, and philosophy, Christ argues for the revolutionary effects of worshipping the Goddess which she sees as encouraging women to think about how they see themselves in relation to nature and each other. Christ is director of the Ariadne Institute and as part of her work there, she conducts pilgrimages to sacred sites in Greece containing artifacts of matriarchal religion. The quote below encapsulates her views about the role religion should have.

'Nurture life. Walk in love and beauty. Trust the knowledge that comes through the body. Speak the truth about conflict, pain, and suffering. Take only what you need. Think about the consequences of your actions for seven generations. Approach the taking of life with great restraint. Practice great generosity. Repair the web.' (Carol Christ)

1 Analyse the quote from Carol Christ above and write a sentence summarising what you think her view is on what the role of religion should be for the individual and society.

2 Using the internet, find out more about the Ariadne Institute and construct a presentation of your findings, include some visual images with your assessment of her views.

---

members of that group can speak up in the meeting for worship. Therefore, it can be argued that there has always been equality between women and men in some religious organisations.

Similarly within Sikhism, which originated in the Punjab region of northern India in the sixteenth century, there has been a strong tradition of equality between women and men during their history, although most religious leaders within Sikhism tend to be men.

Phenomenology

Phenomenology is a tradition within sociology that examines the ways in which individuals and groups give meaning to their everyday experience. Phenomenological sociologists, such as Alfred Schutz (1967), avoid study of the social structures (such as class or ethnicity) that other sociologists see as shaping human life and concentrate, instead, on the individual person's subjective understanding of the meaning of their experience. Phenomenology, therefore, shares much in common with interactionism within sociology. Edmund Husserl (1962), a key figure in the development of phenomenology suggested that understanding another person's experience requires one to temporarily put one's presuppositions to one side and just concentrate on their point of view. So, a sociologist might be an atheist or humanist but ought to put their ideas to one side in order to look at the world from the point of view of the religious person. Phenomenologists do not seek to classify social phenomena such as institutions or structures but try to look at experience through the eyes of the individual.

Paradoxically, phenomenology of religion has often been involved in developing ways of classifying religious phenomena that would be true to the thinking of religious believers. For example, Smart's seven-dimension model for understanding religions, referred to earlier (see page 167), is an example of a phenomenological approach to religion. These dimensions are seen by Smart as aids to help understand religious people's view of their faith. However, it can be argued that this attempt to classify religious phenomena cannot be true to phenomenology since phenomenology always pays attention to the view of the religious individual rather than to the ideas or categories of the scholar.

Phenomenology is a strong influence in the practice of ethnography, in which religions may be studied through researchers spending periods of times among members of religious communities to get a sense of the meanings that people give to their experience.

The phenomenological influence lies in the attempts to understand the 'world' of the religious individual rather than seeking to work out an understanding of religion based on a theory, such as Marxism or Weberianism.

Arguments for phenomenological views of religion centre on the idea that people's religious ideas are unique to them and the only way to understand religion is to 'see' it through the 'eyes of the believer'. Therefore, phenomenology favours qualitative rather than quantitative approaches to research into religion. Interpretivists would argue that this means that such research is high in validity and enables a much deeper understanding to be achieved.

Arguments against phenomenological approaches to religion, therefore, might be offered by those sociologists who favour a more quantitative or 'objective' approach to studying human individuals and their religious ideas.

Study

The Rumour of Angels (1969) and The Heretical Imperative (1979), Berger

Peter Berger is a sociologist who examined how religions exist in society. He drew on Schutz's work and also that of Weber and has been highly influential in the Sociology of Religion. Berger argues that modern society is characterised by an alienation from the sense of meaning that was evident in earlier societies that had a strong integrated religious culture. This has come about as a result of the rise of capitalism and he argues that this development was based on the Protestant reformation of the sixteenth century. He believes that individuals within modern society lack a definite religious meaning and are forced to choose their beliefs in a way that is different to previous centuries when an individual was part of a religion because of their culture and nation. This process of choice is what Berger termed the 'heretical imperative'. In earlier cultures, choosing one's beliefs was forbidden since the truth was known within one's own faith and culture and if you chose a belief, that would mean that you were disagreeing with everyone else's ideas. In the modern world, people are forced to choose and so they are all 'heretics'.

Berger argues that there are signs and 'whispers' of religious meaning in certain everyday experiences. For example:

- When a parent comforts a crying child who is scared of the dark, s/he might say that 'everything is alright'. This statement by a parent implies that the universe is trustworthy (s/he does not say 'everything *might* be alright but disasters might happen'). This is taken as evidence of religious belief in an everyday action by a loving parent.
- When people experience an 'absolute evil', such as the Nazi holocaust and the perpetrators seem to get away with it (and nothing is done to right the wrong), people sometimes decide that there *must* be a supernatural realm where things will be put right. Berger takes this as evidence of a religious belief that people develop from everyday life rather than from a religious tradition.
- When people are engaging in play or have a joyful experience, time can seem to stand still. This is an ordinary experience but is like an experience of eternity.
- When people laugh at their own limitations – they use humour – they can get the sense that human power is limited, that people are small parts of a great, huge world. This experience can create a religious feeling about life.
- Finitude. People ask questions about the limits of life – why am I here? Why must I die? Who am I?

These experiences are termed 'rumours of angels', as though angels have visited people and brought truths in their ordinary lives that point to 'heaven'.

1 Write a definition for Berger's concepts of the 'heretical imperative' and 'rumours of angels'.
2 Write an evaluative paragraph explaining what you see as the strengths and weaknesses of Berger's views.

Postmodernism

Postmodernism is a theory about how society has changed in the last 50 years. Advocates of postmodernism suggest that global society has moved from 'modernism' to 'postmodernism' and that there are large differences between the modern and the postmodern worlds. They argue that the change can be seen in a range of areas of social life such as art, architecture, music, film, TV programmes, politics, family life, customs, clothing and also religion. This change is a cultural change or cultural shift that has happened and there are a number of explanations for it.

Postmodern thinkers argue that the mass media is a large influence in the development of postmodernism since the media have helped to create a global awareness that is different to all previous periods of history. The use of the internet and the availability of devices such as tablet computers and smart phones that facilitate easy access to contemporary events and ideas mean that individuals are presented with a bewildering variety of choices as to what they might wish to buy, where they might wish to travel or live, what hair style or fashion they might wish to choose and what they ought to believe and value. Because of this huge range of choice, these thinkers suggest that the postmodern era is a time when people find it harder to believe in large theories about life, the universe and everything. In addition, postmodernists argue that there has been a shift from collectivism towards individualism which has resulted in no fixed ideologies and a more cynical outlook that is distrustful of big ideas that claim to know 'the truth'. Postmodernists refer to such theories as grand narratives. A religion would be seen as a 'grand narrative' about how the world came into existence and what will happen to the world in the end. It might also have clear ideas about how people should live their lives and what human destiny should be. What many grand narratives have in common is an idea about purpose. All events may be seen as fitting into a plan or purpose. In contrast, postmodern thinkers argue that people now have to choose what they wish to believe in because the grand narratives have lost their power.

Postmodernism has a distinctive view of religion. Rather than buying into the grand narratives of a religion, a postmodern view would be that religions offer people choices and individuals are sometimes seen as shopping around among religions choosing the bits that they like and discarding the rest. This has led to the use of the term 'spiritual shopper' to describe a postmodern type of religious person. Spiritual shopping would consist in picking and mixing bits and pieces from different religions and not worrying too much if they don't seem to fit together in the way they once did. This view of religion is contrasted with the older view of religion as offering authority to people and guiding people's lives. Now, individuals are seen as the authority on what they wish for and what is 'right' for them.

In some cities, religious buildings that have too few people attending acts of worship might be 'offered to' people from another faith tradition. An example is the occasion in 1983, when an Anglican Bishop in the south of England agreed to 'hand over a redundant Southampton church to a Sikh congregation'. This would have scandalised people in previous centuries (and some people are scandalised now) but a postmodern view would be that this type of scenario reflects the shift to a situation in which people can choose how they wish to worship and where. Some large organisations, such as a University, might have a multi-faith centre rather than distinct religious buildings. Such a centre would allow different styles of worship and meditation in the same place. The design of such a building might be circular rather than linear, reflecting the idea that there is no one 'road' or journey that people must follow in life.

In evaluation, some theorists argue that the global world created by the internet and the media is shallow and lacking in meaning. Religion as spiritual shopping can also be seen in this way. A postmodern response might be that in the time of the death of the grand narratives, people have no choice but to make use of the fragments of the older religions that still make some sense to them and combine them together in a personally satisfying way. One idea is that life is no longer a matter of destiny and more a matter of a project that you create for yourself.

In some respects, the phenomenon of believing without belonging, referred to earlier, can be taken as an example of a postmodern approach to religion, since an individual might choose to believe some parts of a religion but not to actually belong to that community.

Postmodernism and religion

Activity (continued)

ENGLAND

1 What postmodern ideas do the images above suggest?
2 Make a poster identifying and explaining key postmodern concepts such as 'pick and mix' related to religion. Illustrate each with a visual image.
3 Devise your own religion and present it to your class/group. You should be prepared to explain why you made the choices you did in creating your religion.
4 Make a table listing what you see as the strengths and weaknesses of the postmodern view of religion.

Theoretical views of the relationship between religion and social change

Functionalist views see religion as positive in society and they support a conservative view of religion. Durkheim, Malinowski and Parsons, among others, argued that religion functions to preserve and maintain social bonds, teaching and reinforcing social values and helping to maintain society's equilibrium in regard to difficult life events. Religion is seen as the 'glue' that binds society together. In this account, social change is an experience that drives society apart and religion is seen as a force that works to bind it together.

Marxism views religion as an inherently conservative element within society. Religious institutions are seen as having a negative role as they support the ruling class and religious beliefs teach people to accept their position in society and not to fight for social change. If an individual such as Oscar Romero or Martin Luther King does speak up for the poor, then they are exceptions and the institution that they belong to is seen as remaining unchanged in spite of their actions.

Neo-Marxism offers a more complex view that sees religion as a conservative force in society that has the potential to contribute to social change. This is because religious institutions are seen as relatively autonomous. In other words, people may be conservative in their beliefs and practices but they can adopt a different viewpoint and can then become part of a movement for social change. As a result, neo-Marxists see religion as both negative in terms of supporting the ruling class but also having the potential to make a positive contribution to society through supporting oppressed groups.

Weberian ideas about the role of religion in promoting social change contrast with Marxist ideas. Weber highlighted the role of religion as a force for social change. The social change that he was referring to was the emergence of capitalism and he pointed to the significance of certain specific religious ideas in the growth of capitalism. In a similar way, other religious ideas can be connected to different effects within society. For example, Islam provides examples of social change prompted by movements such as Boko Haram in Nigeria and ISIS in Iraq and Syria.

Check your understanding

Briefly define the following terms and give an example of each.

1 Social solidarity
2 Liberation theology
3 Collective conscience
4 Religion as the opium of the people
5 Religion as a conservative force
6 Relative autonomy
7 Protestant work ethic
8 The Goddess Movement
9 Phenomenology
10 Spiritual shopping

Section summary

Make a copy of the following passage and fill in the gaps using the words given below.

There are a number of sociological _____ that address the issue of what _____, belief and _____ mean for individuals and _____.

_____ suggest that religions create _____ and reinforce _____ and values. _____ based his work on a study of aboriginal religious _____ and he described the significance of the _____ as a way of symbolising society's norms and _____. Malinowski studied the culture of the Trobriand _____. He argued that religious _____ help societies to cope with _____ life events as well as creating stability. _____ saw religion as offering moral _____ and helping society to cope with tragic life _____. Some sociologists think that functionalism neglects evidence of religious _____ and the ways in which this contributes to social instability.

_____ is a social theory that views religion as a _____ force in society. Marx argued that religion is like _____ in that it dulls the senses and does not support people to fight against _____. Religious _____ are controlled by the _____ class and religious teachings are a form of false _____.

_____ disagrees with Marxist ideas in that they think that religion is relatively _____. Otto _____ provides examples of religious teachings such as those of _____ Theology that seem to prove that religion can promote social _____ and fight against _____.

_____ thought that religion contributes to social change. He described the development of _____ and suggested that the protestant ____ _____ is a key factor in creating the conditions for capitalism to grow. He saw _____ as a religious teaching that suggests that people can prove that they have been chosen by God by working hard and making _____.

_____ argues that religions are _____ organisations in which men occupy _____ roles and many famous religious teachers were men. Some feminists suggest that because God is pictured as ____ in some religious traditions, women can never have _____ within religion. Others suggested that there can be a view of religion in which male images of ___ are balanced by evidence of religious teachings about the _____.

_____ is a tradition within sociology that emphasises the unique perspective of the individual person rather than social structures such as class or ethnicity. This sociological viewpoint is evident in the practice of _____ fieldwork in which a sociologist might seek to understand a religion from its own point of view.

_____ argues that global society has changed and that people no longer believe in _____ _____ about life because there is so much choice available. They suggest that individuals are _____ _____ who pick and choose which religious practices suit them.

work, culture, conservative, male, Maduro, Liberation, leadership, Islands, institutions, theories, stressful, religion, Postmodernists, Phenomenology, patriarchal, Parsons, opium, norms, Neo-Marxism, narratives, stability, spiritual, society, shoppers, ruling, Weber, values, totem, ethnographic, ethic, equality, Durkheim, rituals, money, Marxism, inequality, Feminism, faith, events, consciousness, conflict, change, Capitalism, Calvinism, autonomous, injustice, guidance, grand, Goddesses, God, Functionalists

4.3 What are the patterns and trends of religion, belief and faith?

Getting you thinking –

1 Discuss the religions in these images and others that you know about and write a list of the norms and values that they hold about particular social groups based on social class, gender, ethnicity and age, for example what gender roles are expected? How are young people expected to behave?
2 Do you think that religion appeals to some social groups more than others? Write a paragraph explaining your thoughts.

When considering the patterns and trends of religion, belief and faith it is important to bear in mind that the picture is complex and it is necessary to take a multi-dimensional approach that recognises the interplay between different social characteristics. For example, when looking at social class and religion, the experience will be affected by age, gender and ethnicity so middle-aged working-class women from an ethnic minority background may well have a different experience to that of young working-class men from the majority ethnic group. This interplay is also true for patterns and trends of religion, belief and faith related to age, gender and ethnicity. These factors and the relationship between them are taken into consideration by the government's Office for National Statistics which produces a range of data including the Census conducted every 10 years (see page 194).

Another aspect to consider when studying patterns and trends of religion, belief and faith is the appeal of different types of religion to different social groups, for example, women participate in New Age religions more than men – this is discussed in further detail below.

The second section of this chapter also makes a useful contribution to understanding the patterns and trends of religion, belief and faith, particularly in the theoretical views provided by Marxism on social class and feminism on gender.

The 2011 Census 'Full story – What does the Census tell us about religion in 2011?', ONS May 2013

The ONS published the following key points about religion from their 2011 Census data.

- In 2011, Christianity had the oldest age profile of the main religious groups.
- The number of Christians has fallen and this was largely for people aged under 60.
- The number of people with no religion has increased across all age groups, particularly for those aged 20 to 24 and 40 to 44.
- In England and Wales, over nine in ten Christians (93 per cent) were white and nine in ten (89 per cent) were born in the UK, though the numbers have fallen since 2001.
- Nearly four in ten Muslims (38 per cent) reported their ethnicity as Pakistani, a 371,000 increase (from 658,000 to over a million) since 2001. Nearly half of all Muslims were born in the UK.

- The majority of people with no religion were white (93 per cent) and born in the UK (93 per cent) and these groups have increased since 2001.
- People with no religion had the highest proportion of people who were economically active, Christians and Muslims the lowest. Jewish people had the highest level of employment and Muslim people the highest level of unemployment.
- The main reason for Christians being economically inactive was retirement, for Muslims economic inactivity was mainly because they were students, or because they were looking after the home or family.

Source: ONS (2013)

1 Make an infographic to portray the data above. If you're not sure what an infographic is, try searching 'infographic' on Google images.
2 What do these key points from the 2011 Census tell us about religion in the UK in relation to social class, gender, ethnicity and age? Write a newspaper report outlining your analysis.

Social class

When thinking about the patterns and trends of religion, belief and faith in relation to social class, it is important to be aware that there is a long standing link between social class and religious participation. Historically, the higher classes were seen as the more religious and attended church more regularly than any other social class. Those in the lower classes who aspired to be like them would also attend church but, overall, traditionally the working class were regarded

as being the least religious social class. Evidence later in the section seems to challenge this view.

It is difficult to find specific numerical data about levels of religiosity by social class and it appears to be an understudied area in this respect. The 2011 Census, for example, analyses religion by categories of gender, ethnicity and age but not specifically social class.

Research consistently suggests that the greatest active religious involvement occurs amongst the middle classes. In terms of Christianity in the UK, organisations like the Church of England are associated with the middle and upper classes. The Anglican Church has been described as the 'Conservative Party at prayer' because its members are more likely to vote Conservative. Roman Catholicism, on the other hand, is regarded as primarily a working-class religion.

Membership of NRMs and NAMs

Patterns and trends of religion, belief and faith in relation to social class can be seen in participation in religious sects. Weber in writings first published in 1922 (1968) discussed the relationship between religion and marginalised groups. He described how sects arise in groups that are on the margins of society

Study

Churchgoing in the UK, Ashworth and Farthing (2007)

Research by Ashworth and Farthing (2007) confirms the view that church attendance is a more middle-class activity. They found that adults in professional, senior and middle management occupations have above average regular church attendance (22 per cent and 21 per cent respectively), as well above average proportions of fringe or occasional attendance.

Adults from skilled, semi-skilled and unskilled manual occupations have the lowest proportion of regular churchgoers (12 per cent) and the highest proportion who don't attend church and never intend to (37 per cent and 40 per cent respectively). Adults who are entirely dependent on the state long-term, through sickness, unemployment or old age etc., have the highest proportion who are not currently attending church and yet open to attending in future (8 per cent). Unemployed job seekers are less likely to have regular church attendance (7 per cent vs. 15 per cent national average) or to be fringe/occasional attendees (6 per cent vs. 10 per cent). Almost half (48 per cent) of unemployed people have never been to church and are unlikely to do so compared with a national average of a third (32 per cent).

1 Using data from Ashworth and Farthing's research make a chart or diagram showing their findings.
2 Write a list of as many reasons as you can think of for the differences in church attendance between different social classes.

and feel disprivileged. Weber argued that they offer their membership a 'theodicy of disprivilege' which gives them a religious explanation and justification for their suffering and disadvantage. This presents their disadvantaged position as a test of their faith while offering the promise of rewards in the future for keeping the faith.

This view is supported by Stark and Bainbridge (1987) who argue that world-rejecting sects offer 'compensators' to the deprived who cannot achieve the economic and material rewards seen as desirable. According to Stark and Bainbridge (1987), 'When humans cannot quickly and easily obtain strongly desired rewards they persist in their efforts and may often accept explanations that provide only compensators. These are intangible substitutes for the desired reward, having the character of I.O.U.s, the value of which must be taken on faith'. They also discuss how the wealthier in society are more likely to be drawn to world-accepting religious organisations that allow them to maintain their status and success. However, Stark and Bainbridge also identify high levels of religious participation among the middle and upper classes as being due to relative deprivation rather than as a means to preserve their privileged position. Although the higher classes are affluent, they perceive themselves to be spiritually deprived and seek fulfilment through religious involvement. The rise in cults and sects over the late twentieth and early twenty-first century has in part been explained by the feeling of relative deprivation experienced by the middle classes who join them in their search for meaning and a sense of community that is felt to be missing in the individualisation of contemporary society.

Bruce (1995) offers another view when he discusses New Age Movements. He argues that they appeal to the most affluent in society as they offer the promise of self-development and cohere with the individualism of modern society. He said that the New Age appealed particularly to 'university-educated middle classes working in the 'expressive professions' – social workers, counsellors, writers, and others whose education and work causes them to have an articulate interest in human potential' (Bruce, 1995).

However, when it comes to belief rather than practice, a study by Theos (2009) found that lifelong theists (people who identify as having always believed in God) come disproportionately from the lower class, whereas lifelong atheists (who identify as having never believed in God) are disproportionately from the middle class.

The intersection of social class, age, ethnicity and religion

Generally, more recent sociological research recognises the intersection between social class and other elements of stratification such as age and ethnicity i.e. the impact of the interplay between different social characteristics. The Religion and Society Research Programme, a collaborative venture between the government-funded Arts and Humanities Research Council (AHRC) and Economic and Social Research Council (ESRC), explores the inter-relationships between religion and society. They studied the experiences of young people growing up in areas of deprivation between 2009 and 2011. A team of researchers led by Elizabeth Olson went into areas of deprivation in Glasgow and Manchester, and conducted over 100 interviews with young people, neighbourhood elders, community service providers and faith leaders. Teams of young people in both cities were trained in video production and photography, leading to the production of two films and a travelling photography exhibition. The aim of the research was to understand how the characteristics of the places the young people lived, shaped and informed youth religiosity.

Read the extract from the research report below:

'... whilst community faith-based organisations are inspired to provide services for young people, the faith groups do not necessarily develop religious relationships with them. Young people perceived local churches as middle-class spaces for people who live 'better lives', which contrasted with their own experiences of growing up in areas of urban deprivation. Many young people didn't feel 'good enough' to engage with religious organisations in their communities. In contrast, secular youth clubs were not seen as welcoming places for discussing some of the issues central to young people's curiosities and concerns about life and death.

Some young participants did embrace aspects of 'traditional' religion in nontraditional ways. Many described deeply cultivated religious identities, evidenced by prayer, meditation, or practices that

focused on traditional and new sacred spaces. For some first or second generation migrants to the UK, the perceived secularism of their peers was viewed as emblematic of broader social problems. But for others, religious identity was not taken for granted and the British religious landscape provided new opportunities for spiritual exploration.

Belief in ghosts and spirits, ongoing bonds with lost family and friends, and the power of blessings and rituals, as well as atheism, were prevalent, once the researchers found an appropriate way to talk and listen to these young people about such subjects. Many had had early encounters with death and illness, often of a family member or close friend, and lived in insecure circumstances. Some reported feeling unable to cross certain streets or access certain areas, such as the park in their neighbourhood, due to gang boundaries and risk of violence. Their options for accessing religious and spiritual resources, or finding a space where belief could be discussed without ridicule, were restricted.

Two of the participants involved in making the films continued to study film and photography and one said, 'The adults [involved in making the film] let us express what we felt about religion and spirituality. They kept the paperwork to a minimum and didn't take over. We learnt by talking to ourselves and others, brainstorming ideas and taking pictures.' (Olson 2013)

1 Identify six key points from the study.
2 Write a newspaper article summarising the report including a reference to the way the data was gathered.
3 Using the study, write a paragraph explaining the link between religion, age and social class.
4 Discuss ways in which the religious experience of the young people in the study may differ from young people from higher social classes.
5 Write an evaluative paragraph explaining the intersection of social class with other social characteristics such as age and ethnicity.
6 Evaluate the methods the researchers used to gather data and add this to your evaluative paragraph.

Karl Marx, religion and social class

Read the quote from Marx below.

'Religious distress is at the same time the expression of real distress and the protest against real distress. Religion is the sigh of the oppressed creature, the heart of a heartless world, just as it is the spirit of a spiritless situation. It is the opium of the people. The abolition of religion as the illusory happiness of the people is required for their real happiness. The demand to give up the illusion about its condition is the demand to give up a condition which needs illusions.'

Marx, Critique of Hegel's Philosophy of Right

1 Write a paragraph or a list of bullet points in your own words explaining what you think he meant about the relationship between religion and social class.
2 Using your ideas, write an article or draw a cartoon strip showing Marx's view on the relationship between religion and social class.

Further evidence of the interplay of social class with other social characteristics can be seen in opinion poll data published in the run up to the 2015 UK General Election. A striking finding was that Muslims were more than twice as likely as the population as a whole to support the Labour Party, which was seen to be partly a function of their relatively deprived socio-economic status and, therefore, of class-based voting. (BRIN, 2015).

In terms of the views of the main sociological theories, as mentioned in the earlier section on the role of religion for the individual and society, Marxism and neo-Marxism are the key perspectives to discuss religion and social class. Marx saw religion as giving some comfort to the oppressed class but also as a transmitter of ruling class ideology to maintain the power of the bourgeoisie. However, neo-Marxists believe that religion can support the interests of those who are marginalised and deprived in society. They point to the way that liberation theology has been an important factor in raising the consciousness of impoverished communities and acting as an agent of social change to challenge inequality. Even earlier Marxist thinkers such as Engels, writing in the nineteenth century, also observed that the millenarian movements of Victorian society had sided with the poor (2001).

Main theories and their views on social class and religion

1 Using information from the above section on social class and previous sections on the role of religion for the individual and for society, make a grid like the one below showing how the main theoretical perspectives might respond to patterns and trends relating to social class and religion, belief and faith. Some examples are included to help you get started.

Theoretical view	View on social class and religion, belief and faith.
Functionalism	Religion is a unifying force that has the potential to bring different groups together …
Marxism	
neo-Marxism	
Weberianism	
feminism	A contemporary Marxist feminist might argue that gender is an important social division and will impact on the relationship between religion and social class e.g. working class women will have a different experience of religion to higher class women. A radical feminist might argue that gender is a more important social inequality when discussing religion.
phenomenology	
postmodernism	Social class is no longer an important social division. People are spiritual shoppers who can pick and mix their identity and beliefs.

2 Using the information in your table, write a paragraph explaining and evaluating the significance of social class and religiosity.

Gender

Evidence on patterns and trends of religion, belief and faith in relation to gender consistently shows that women score higher on measures of religiosity than men (1997). For example, research into church attendance by Ashworth and Farthing (2007) found that 19 per cent of women said they attended church regularly compared to 11 per cent of men.

In terms of patterns and trends of religious belief, Hunt (2005) cites a wide variety of indices through which women show higher rates of belief than men. The list goes beyond involvement with mainstream Christianity and new religions and shows that women are more likely than men to believe in 'the devil, heaven, hell, creationism, in ghosts, communication with the dead, ESP and astrology, and are more likely to report paranormal experiences.'

Sociologists have also identified a trend for women to be attracted to particular types of religions such as those associated with New Age spirituality.

Bruce and Trzebiatowska (2012) in their book, 'Why are Women more Religious than Men?', acknowledge and explore the spiritual gender gap in relation to the New Age which they divide into two strands; those associated with health and well-being and those concerned with spiritual enlightenment. They conclude that the appeal of the former for women and lack of appeal for men may be explained by the traditional ideas of masculinity and femininity that shape men and women's attitudes. Bruce and Trzebiatowska also contend that the parts of the New Age that are concerned with the spiritual tend to attract women because of the gendered nature of the activities that are constructed and also the lack of alternatives available to women.

Recent research on belief published by Voas for the UCL Institute of Education (2015), has shown a huge difference in the proportion of men and women who say they believe in God and life after death. The study involving more than 9,000 British people in their forties found that, 'Gender differences in religious belief are very substantial – 54 per cent of men, but only 34 per cent of women, are atheists or agnostics. The gap is even larger for belief in life after death – 60 per cent of women but only 35 per cent of men. Among believers, women are much more likely to be definite than men, and among non-believers, men are much more likely to be definite than women. Thus even controlling for belief in God, the gender gap in views about life after death are considerable.'

Sullins (2006) examined evidence across a range of societies and his findings show a complex picture of religion, belief and faith. He questions the universality of the gender gap in religiousness because there are notable exceptions, for example, among Jews and Muslims across the globe, men are significantly more religious than women. However, although he concludes that it appears that the gender gap in religiousness does not apply to the religions of the Middle East, he found reliable gender differences, where women are more religious than men, in samples taken from over sixty-five different countries and from seven different religions and sects. Sullins (2006) draws a distinction between 'affective religiousness' (personal piety) and 'active religiousness'

The Kendal Project and Gender, Heelas and Woodhead (2000–2002)

Between October 2000 and June 2002, Heelas and Woodhead studied the spiritual beliefs of the population of the town of Kendal in the UK with the aim of investigating 'patterns of the sacred in contemporary society', and they identified some interesting trends (some of which are also discussed as part of the section on secularisation later in this chapter). The study (known as the Kendal Project) examined regular attendance at a variety of different types of Christian churches and compared it to the popularity of other more informal forms of spirituality, including Eastern philosophies and holistic health approaches (which they together termed the 'holistic milieu') including yoga, transcendental meditation, aromatherapy, reflexology and tai chi etc, which sociologists would classify as part of the New Age.

They found that while participation in traditional forms of religion was declining, involvement in alternative spirituality was on the increase. Heelas and Woodhead also found that these forms of spirituality were particularly attractive to women with the majority of participants in New Age spiritualities being females aged between 45–60. They note that '80 per cent of those active in the holistic milieu in Kendal and environs are female; 78 per cent of groups are led or facilitated by women; 80 per cent of the one-to-one practitioners are women' (2005)

1 Use the internet to compile a list of at least 10 forms of New Age spirituality.
2 Discuss them and make a list of sociological reasons why women might find them attractive, for example, alternative spiritualities may offer a non-sexist environment.

(participation in organised religion) and argues that 'gender differences are much larger for the former than the latter in a wide variety of cultures'. In terms of accounting for such differences, Sullins argues (2006) that 'together social factors explain most and in some contexts all of the gender differences in religiousness'. This is in contrast to some explanations that cite psychological differences as the reason for the religious gender gap.

These kinds of findings have led sociologists to believe that there is a pattern suggesting a religious gender gap in which women are more religious than men and that such gender differences exist across different religions and countries.

Explanations for the patterns and trends of religion, belief and faith in relation to gender

Sociologists have proposed a number of explanations for the patterns and trends of gender differences in both personal belief and participation in religious organisations.

1 **Structural location** – the different labour market and family roles occupied by men and women in the social structure means that men take their values from their commitment to their work and also have less opportunity for religious involvement.

The nature of women's domestic and nurturing role in child-rearing in the family encourages greater religious behaviour. However, De Vaus and McAllister (1987) tested structural location theory and concluded that 'the child-rearing role and differing attitudes towards work do not account for the greater religiousness of women. By contrast, the lower rate of female work force participation is an important explanatory factor'. Deprivation theory and the concept of relative deprivation has also been used to explain how women's subordinate role in the structure of society both in the workplace and in the domestic sphere leads them to seek comfort through a belief system that offers them solace and redemption. In this sense, religion acts as a compensator for women's exploitation. When examining participation in religious organisations such as new religious movements, research has shown that women are more likely to join sects than men. Early research by Glock and Stark (1965) used deprivation theory and the concept of compensators to explain such gender differences. They argue that people are attracted to religion because they feel deprived in some way and that religion offers compensation for various forms of deprivation including social, organismic and ethical deprivation. Glock and Stark believe that women are more likely to experience these forms of deprivation and that this explains their higher level of sect membership. Women are more likely to be socially deprived as they have less status and fewer opportunities than men and sects tend to attract impoverished groups. Organismic deprivation relates to physical and mental health problems and women are more likely to suffer from ill health so they seek healing through religion. Women are also more likely to suffer ethical deprivation, which relates to losing faith in the values of society. Women are more likely than men to be morally conservative and see the world as in moral decline, so are drawn to world-rejecting sects who hold this view. Glock and Stark's work on deprivation theory has been elaborated upon by a number of theorists over the years and the concept of religion as offering compensation remains as a credible explanation for gender differences in religious affiliation. Marxist-feminists would argue that, in this regard, religion acts as a form of false consciousness for women and prevents them from taking action against their oppressed position in capitalist society. However, some researchers have argued that there are more positive reasons for women's religiosity rather than a sense of deprivation.

2 **Differential socialisation** – this view contends that males and females are socialised into different norms, values and roles with males being encouraged to develop aggression and competitiveness and females learning behaviour related to nurturing. It is argued that women are more religious because they are socialised to be more passive, obedient and caring and these are characteristics valued by religion. Sullins (2006) contends that social factors play an important role in the origins of gender differences and religiosity. From his research, he found that aspects of socialisation, parental religious involvement and the child's own religious involvement at age 11 or 12, and the degree to which friends are involved in religion, account for a significant portion of the variability in religiosity. These findings, in turn, suggest that gender differences in religiosity may exist in part, due to the influence of important agents of socialisation, such as parents or peers (Stark, 2002).

3 **Risk behaviour** – the concept of 'risk preferences' has been used to explain the greater religiousness of women in many different parts of the world. This refers to the tendency of an individual or group to choose a risky or less risky option. Women are often considered to be more risk averse than men and so take fewer risks. In terms of religious belief, it has been argued that women are less willing to take the risk that there isn't a god than men and that this explains women's higher levels of religiosity. According to research by Miller and Hoffmann (1995) this accounted for 40 per cent of gender differences in religiosity. Risk preferences is an explanation that has been used by both sociologists and psychologists to explain women's greater religiosity and it is part of a debate about whether risk behaviour is formed as a result of nature or nurture. Indeed, Stark (cited in Hunt 2005) has added that physiological differences between men and women may help to explain the irreligiousness of males.

> ## Activity
>
> ### Gender difference and religiosity
> 1 Discuss the three reasons for gender differences in religiosity given above and identify at least one evaluation point for each of the reasons.
> 2 What other sociological explanations can you think of for the patterns and trends in gender and religiosity? Make a list of your ideas.

In evaluation, Davie and Walter (cited in Hunt 2005) have reviewed the explanations that have been put forward and identify a number of contradictions, for example, they argue that deprivation theory goes against the experience of some deprived groups and white working-class men who have low rates of religiosity. Davie and Walter acknowledge the complexity involved in understanding gender differences in religious behaviour and conclude that 'a review of the reasons for women's greater religiosity leaves more questions than it provides answers.' (cited in Hunt 2005, p87)

Women, religion and power

When seeking to understand demographic differences in religiosity, some sociologists have been interested in examining the role of power, for example, Marxists have commented on the ways that religion reinforces inequalities in relation to social class and economic power. Woodhead (2004), in a paper entitled 'Gender Differences in Religious Practice and Significance', argues that power is an important concept when it comes to understanding religion as a social institution, 'religion(s) can and do play active roles in: reinforcing and legitimating dominant power interests; generating resistance to dominant power; resourcing groups with little social power; resourcing reconfigurations of power.' She created a typology to examine different forms of religion in relation to gender and power and she identified four main 'types'.

- Consolidating – religion which accepts, reinforces and places power with the dominant gender order in society, for example fundamentalist religious groups within Christianity, Judaism and Islam which defend 'traditional' gender roles, family values involving male leadership and female domesticity and the traditional nuclear family.

- Tactical – religion which accepts prevailing patterns of gender power distribution, but within which women participate in fulfilling ways e.g. through forming women-only groups within the structure where they can shape the agenda and can almost be seen as practicing their own parallel religion and as a result used by women 'to tip the balance of power more in their favour than would otherwise be the case'. This may be found in some mainstream Christian churches.

- Questing – religion which works within the existing gender order and aims to use sacred power to transform the situation of those involved and move towards a position of greater personal or group advantage. This covers a broad range of New Age religions from groups involved in paganism to self-spirituality such as yoga and reiki.

- Counter-cultural – religion which actively opposes the existing gender order and seeks to change it and create alternatives where there is female empowerment e.g. the Goddess feminist movement. According to Woodhead, 'counter-cultural forms of religion seek to consolidate gains for women (achieved since the 1950s) and minimise the losses by bringing about permanent change which will dissolve essentialist ideas about male–female hierarchical difference, and replace them with a social order in which power is no longer unequally distributed along gender lines.'

Activity

Woodhead's forms of religion

1. Use the internet to find out more about the forms of religion referred to above.
2. Using your findings and the information above, complete a case study of one example of each form of religion mentioned above and write up your findings in a 250 word report.
3. In groups, discuss and note down the ways that Woodhead's typology is useful in helping to understand the relationship between gender and religiosity e.g. you may wish to consider the appeal of the different types she identifies.

Study

Women in religion, Jean Holm (2001)

In the introduction to the book *Women in Religion* (2001), Jean Holm seeks to explain the subordinate role of women in religion. Firstly, she takes an historical approach and argues that the position of women in religion was higher at an earlier period in history. Holm points to notable examples from early founders or leading figures of major world religions to support this view:

- 'The Buddha acceded to the request of his disciple, Ananda, and allowed the creation of a nuns' as well as a monks' order, and so provided women for the first time with an alternative to domesticity.'
- 'Jesus included women among his followers, and is recorded as having welcomed contact with women who were regarded as 'beyond the pale' in the society of his day, while Paul, who has suffered from the reputation of being a misogynist, declared that there was 'neither male nor female; for you are all one in Christ Jesus'.'
- 'Muhammad greatly enhanced the status of women in Arabia, ensuring that they were entitled to a share of inheritance, taking steps to provide for widows who were left destitute, and banning infanticide (which usually affected girl babies), and he is even recorded as having appointed a woman to lead the prayers in a household of men and women.'
- 'Guru Nanak proclaimed the equality of men and women, and both he and the Gurus who succeeded him allowed women to take full part in all the activities of Sikh worship and practice.' (2001)

Holm also contends that there is a contradiction between the classical teachings of religions about the equality of men and women and the reality of women's lives. She believes that this contradiction is the result of the way that men have interpreted and transmitted sacred texts, created religious institutions and controlled worship. She believes that this has resulted in women's experiences and achievements being largely neglected. She sees the unequal position of women in religion as a reflection of a wider social context in which men are generally seen as superior to women.

However, Holm is often regarded as holding a liberal feminist viewpoint as she sees some evidence that change is happening and that there are signs of hope that reforms will bring greater gender equality to religion. She believes, for example, that research is now being undertaken and published that uncovers the part that women have played in religious activities over time. She also sees evidence of women speaking up about the inequalities they experience in religion. Holm argues that the spread of the influence of women's movements across the globe, including in

Asia and the Middle East, has and will bring about improvements in women's position. She believes that, to be successful, these movements need to take on their own distinctive characteristics that reflect the cultures they exist in.

Holm concludes that, despite wide ranging debate amongst women's movements about the role of religion, including those that take an anti-religion stance, religion has the potential to be both oppressor and to play a part in liberation.

1 Summarise Holm's views in a short article of approximately 250 words outlining the key arguments she makes.
2 Holm's writing was first published in 1994. From your own knowledge and using an internet search engine, make a list of changes that have happened since then, both in religion and more widely, that might give Holm further hope that gender inequalities in religion are improving. Include examples from different societies.
3 Write an evaluative paragraph giving your assessment of Holm's views.

Gender and secularisation

Gendering Secularisation Theory, Woodhead (2007)

Woodhead is an influential writer in the sociology of religion and she has also contributed to the secularisation debate which is discussed more generally later in this chapter. Woodhead examined how social changes like feminisation of the labour market have affected women's attitudes to religion. Her research has contributed to an understanding of the role of gender in secularisation.

Woodhead (2005) found that changes in female roles are having an impact on their religious commitment. She identifies three groups of women –

Home-centred women – whose priority is home and family, and they tend to be Christian as it affirms their priorities.

Jugglers – combine home and work, likely to be found in alternative spirituality as it does most for this category, of women who are affirming their commitments to family and also endorsing female empowerment.

Activity (continued)

Work-centred women – who are likely to abandon the church as it doesn't fit with their busy work schedules.

1 Discuss and then write a detailed paragraph for each category explaining the effect of domestic and/or workplace roles on women's religiosity.

2 Make a poster or other visual image to illustrate the three groups of women identified by Woodhead and include a brief description of each to capture the details of your discussion.

Brierley (2006) also contributes to the debate on gender and secularisation. Drawing on data from the fourth English Church Census which took place in 2005, he found that women are now leaving the church at a faster rate than men, increasing the percentage of men in the church from 42 per cent to 43 per cent. Twice as many women as men had stopped regular church attendance between 1998 and 2005. One-third of the women stopping were aged 30 to 44. Brierley contends that there is evidence to suggest that this change could be due to the strains of juggling home, family and work and that many women take jobs on Sundays because of the availability of childcare provided by their partner.

It can be seen from the discussion so far, that the relationship between gender and religion, belief and faith is complex and is affected by wider social changes such as changes in the labour market. Another social change that has had an important impact is the increasingly multi-cultural and multi-faith nature of British society. This means that a multi-dimension approach is needed to understand the patterns and trends of religion, belief and faith in relation to gender.

Perfect (2011) produced a briefing paper for the Equality and Human Rights Commission in which he examined findings from The Citizen Survey in England and Wales. The survey had asked those who stated that they had a religion whether they considered they were actively practising it or not. The findings show considerable gender variations across different religions.

Perfect reported that, 'The survey found that a higher proportion of female (38 per cent) than male (25 per cent) Christians stated that they actively practised their religion in 2008–09; Hindu women (78 per cent) were also more likely to state this than Hindu men (65 per cent), but there were no significant gender differences for Muslims, Sikhs or Buddhists' (2011). This research confirms that the nature of religiosity and gender in contemporary Britain is not clear-cut and that for some religions there appears to be little in the way of a gender gap at all.

While much of the research suggests that religion tends to reinforce traditional gender inequalities, there is also evidence that proposes that religion can have a positive impact on women and even be a force for promoting gender equality. For example, Leila Badawi (1994) contends that Islam has positive features specifically for women. She points out that Islamic women are able to keep their own family name when they marry and that most converts to Islam are women. Watson (1994) adds that wearing the veil can be important for women as an expression of personal identity. Furthermore, the Goddess Movement, discussed in the previous section, shows that religion can be female-focused and empowering for women.

Activity

Does religion benefit women?
Construct a debate addressing the proposal that women are more religious than men because of the benefits it brings to them, listing evidence for and against this view.

Respondents actively practising their religion, England and Wales, 2008–09 (per cent)							
	Christian	Muslim	Hindu	Sikh	Buddhist	Other	All
Men	25	79	65	66	64	46	31
Women	38	82	78	66	69	56	42

Source: Ferguson and Hussey (2010)

Ethnicity

Sociologists have identified distinctive patterns of religiosity among members of minority ethnic communities. Contrary to patterns of secularisation within British society and in other European countries, there are clear indications that some minority ethnic groups retain strong affiliation with religious beliefs and practices. Evidence for this is found in the quantitative data obtainable from the National Census, other statistical data from the Office for National Statistics (ONS) and data collected by the Home Office Citizenship Survey.

For the first time, the 2001 census asked people to identify their religious affiliation on the main census form (previously this question had been located on a separate sheet) and this data yielded information about the religious allegiance of people from minority ethnic backgrounds. For example, apart from individuals with a Chinese background, statistics for people reporting that they had no religion were lower among members of minority ethnic groups than for the white British people. 1.36 per cent of Asian or Asian British people reported that they had no religion, as compared to 18.48 per cent of white British people. In a similar way, 7.66 per cent of black or black British people reported that they had 'no religion'. In addition, minority ethnic groups reported that their religion corresponded to their country of birth or origin. For example, an Asian individual from India would be likely to answer Hindu, Muslim or Sikh on the census form and a white Irish person would be likely to answer Roman Catholic. This phenomenon of minority ethnic groups' religiosity corresponding to their country of origin and the low figures for 'no religion' has continued into the 2011 census in which statistical changes in the ten year period reflected patterns of migration. For example, the largest proportion of foreign born residents were Christian (3.6 million) and the highest proportion of Christians – over 1.8 million (53 per cent) – arrived in the period 2001 to 2011, which included 464,000 people from Poland following Poland's accession into the European Union. Also over a third of Buddhists arrived between 2007 and 2011. This compared to 14 per cent before 1981. This latter development corresponded to patterns of migration from countries such as Thailand, Sri Lanka and China (ONS, 2011). Similarly, in 2011, around 1 in 7 (14 per cent) of the foreign born population said that they had no religion which compared to 27 per cent of people born in the UK.

However, statistical data collected via questionnaires such as the National Census in 2011 has identifiable limitations. The creators of the census question on religion acknowledge that the question does not address the issue of the extent to which people practice their religion (Final Recommended Questions for the 2011 Census – Religion 2009). Of significance for discussion of patterns and trends in relation to ethnicity is the extent to which the greater religiosity of members of minority ethnic groups represents a real contrast to the pattern of decline in established religions identified by some sociologists. This requires exploration of the meaning of the statistics in people's lived experience.

Modood et al (1997) published research that seemed to show that the religion of minority

---

Activity

2011 Census data on religion by ethnicity
The 2011 Census produced the following data.

- England and Wales had become more ethnically diverse with more people identifying with minority ethnic groups. Despite the white ethnic group decreasing in size, it was still the majority ethnic group that people identified with (86 per cent).
- Over nine out of ten Christians in England and Wales were white (93 per cent) accounting for 30.8 million people. Within this group white British was the largest group (28.7 million people, 86 per cent). Over 1.6 million people (5 per cent) identified with 'other white'.
- Muslims were more ethnically diverse. Two-thirds of Muslims (68 per cent) were from an Asian background, including Pakistani (38 per cent) and Bangladeshi (15 per cent). The proportion of Muslims reporting as black/African/Caribbean/black British (10 per cent) was similar to those reporting as 'Other' ethnic group (11 per cent).
- 93 per cent of people (13.1 million) with no religion were from a white background.
- The majority of Hindus and Sikhs were from an Asian ethnic background (96 per cent and 87 per cent respectively). As with Muslims, Buddhists were also ethnically diverse.

Source: ONS (2013)

1 Write a 250 word newspaper article reporting on the findings above answering the question, 'What does the Census data tell us about religion and ethnicity in Britain in 2011?'

ethnic groups can be a source of explicit and active commitment. For example, their research asked participants to consider the question 'How important is religion to how you live your life?' This revealed that many members of minority ethnic groups rated their religion highly in terms of how they live their lives. Modood et al noted:

'Nevertheless, while only 5 per cent of whites aged 16–34 said that religion was very important to how they led their lives, nearly a fifth of Caribbeans, more than a third of Indians and African Asians, and two thirds of Pakistanis and Bangladeshis in that age group held that view. Non-white Anglicans are three times more likely than white Anglicans to attend church weekly, and well over half of the members of black-led churches do so. Black-led churches are a rare growth point in contemporary Christianity. The presence of ethnic minorities is changing the character of religion in Britain.'

Although Modood et al's study was published in 1997, a more recent ONS report from 2011, described similar findings:

'The proportion of those who had identified a religion and also said that they actively practised it varied according to the religion. Only 32 per cent of those who reported themselves as Christians actively practised their religion. In contrast, 80 per cent of Muslims actively practised their religion, the highest proportion of those with a religion who actively practiced. Two-thirds or more of Hindus, Sikhs and Buddhists actively practised their religion (70 per cent, 66 per cent and 66 per cent respectively). Among people in the 'other religion' category, 51 per cent said that they were actively practising.'

One example of this trend is the growth of Pentecostal churches within the UK. Sociologists have studied Pentecostal churches in an effort to understand the characteristics of these institutions and to explain their appeal for members of minority ethnic groups. Ken Pryce, in his acclaimed 1979 study of African Caribbeans in Bristol found that Pentecostal churches have a variety of functions for black people within their specific situation which may help to explain their appeal.

It is useful to consider the characteristics of Pentecostal churches. Pentecostal churches share many of the same beliefs as other mainstream Christian churches but with distinctive emphases –

- Pentecostal churches are frequently fundamentalist
- Religious teachings are presented in an accessible way
- Religious worship is lively and emotionally engaging in a way that contrasts sharply with traditional styles of worship within, for example, the Church of England (although there are some Church of England services which share characteristics of Pentecostal services).
- There is an emphasis on religious experience rather than just on religious teaching.
- Pentecostals emphasise the possibility of healing of the body and of psychological healing.
- There can be a sense of hope based on a literal reading of biblical narratives. Biblical narratives describe God as an active agent leading people to freedom from oppression (for example, the story of Moses). A literal reading of this narrative can mean that minority ethnic groups can come to believe that God will similarly liberate them from the problems they experience including discrimination and economic disadvantage.

Roger Beckford in 'Dread and Pentecostal' (2000) describes ways in which black Pentecostal churches can draw on the experience of minority ethnic groups from the Caribbean to construct a type of black liberation theology (for more on Liberation Theology see page 183). This suggests that Pentecostalism can serve a function for this particular minority ethnic group that meets needs associated with their own experience of migration and assimilation into a different culture.

The English Church Census (Brierley, 2006) showed that, from 1998 to 2005, church attendance among minority ethnic groups increased by 23 per cent. Brierley argues that this is partly a result of immigration but also because of the intense community involvement in black churches.

Activity

Changing patterns and trends in religious participation

Read the newspaper article below.

Survey shows Pentecostals outnumber Methodists at church services in England

Research has found that Pentecostals now outnumber Methodists at church services in England. For the first time ever, attendance figures for Methodism, a century-old branch of Christianity, sits behind the Church of England and the Roman Catholic Church. The English Church Census, conducted by the independent charity Christian Research, and funded in part by the Economic and Social Research Council shows that Sunday attendance at Methodist churches has fallen from 289,400 in 2005 to about 278,700 in 2006. The number of people attending Pentecostal churches on an average Sunday has risen to more than 288,000.

According to Dr David Voas, a senior researcher at the School of Social Sciences at Manchester University, 'Methodism is dying in Britain. By contrast, immigration from Africa and elsewhere has led to growth in Pentecostal churches, where the worship style is more flamboyant...Black churchgoers in inner London, where they outnumber white attendees, are an important source of growth in the context of the national decline in church attendance...So it is significant that 40 per cent of Pentecostals, but only four per cent of Methodists, are black... It seems inevitable that the Methodist Church will be reabsorbed into the Church of England. The Pentecostals have appeared out of nowhere in the last couple of decades, but it remains to be seen whether they can make significant inroads into the white population.'

Attendance at Methodist churches has declined by a quarter between 1998 and 2005 resulting in the closure of 264 churches. In comparison, Pentecostal church attendance has increased by a third and new churches have opened. In 2005, the Church of England saw its biggest congregations since the Millennium for Christmas Eve and Christmas Day services with 2.8 million worshippers in attendance.

Commenting on the survey data, the Rev Jonathan Kerry, the co-ordinating Secretary for Worship and Learning for the Methodist Church in Great Britain, said, 'It's always good news to hear of growth amongst Christians, regardless of denomination – we are not in competition...Methodism was born out of revival movements in the 18th century. However, like many historic denominations, the Methodist Church now struggles to respond to new movements of God's spirit without feeling that it is betraying the past.'

Adapted from Petre, J. (2006)

1 Write a paragraph to explain the key trends.
2 Add a further paragraph explaining in your own words what this article is telling us about ethnicity and religion in the UK.

Investigating Religion, John Bird (1999)

John Bird, in his book Investigating Religion (1999) explains the relative strength of minority ethnic religiosity in the following ways:

- Many minority ethnic groups originate in societies with high levels of religiosity.
- Religion can act as a basis for social solidarity. For example, a religious community can be a point of contact, a source of marriage partners, a place where individuals access social welfare etc.
- Religious commitment can be associated with maintaining other aspects of an individual's ethnic identity including language and customs etc.
- There can strong family pressure to maintain commitment to religion.

- Religion can help members of minority ethnic groups to cope with oppression. For example, Bird drew on the work of Pryce (1979) to argue that Pentecostalism can function to assist adjustment to a society in which black people suffer from discrimination and social injustice.

Bird argues, therefore, that the religion of minority ethnic groups has a social and cultural significance that is separate from the specifically religious commitment that the religion requires.

1 Using the internet, investigate some of the points above to find contemporary examples and/or evidence to support the point e.g. for the third bullet point Sikh children learning to speak Punjabi at their local Gurdwara.
2 Write up your findings in a leaflet explaining the appeal of religion to different minority ethnic groups.

Sociologists have offered a range of explanations for key patterns and trends of religiosity among members of minority ethnic groups. The work of John Bird offers a number of ideas.

In a similar vein, Roy Wallis and Steve Bruce, leading proponents of secularisation, argue that religion has a continuing social role within a secularising society when a group or community has need for their religious tradition to support them in some way. In that case, 'religion finds or retains work to do other than relating individuals to the supernatural' (1992). They argue that the religion of minority ethnic groups continues to function as.

- Cultural defence – in which the religion helps a minority ethnic community to protect its sense of identity in an 'alien' culture.
- Cultural transition – in which the religion helps the minority ethnic group to cope with the process of migration. In such times, mosques and churches etc. can become sites for networking and integration.

However, Wallis and Bruce argue that the vigour of minority ethnic religion is a temporary phenomenon as such groups will integrate into the secularising societies of the UK and Western Europe.

Evidence for Wallis and Bruce's view can be found in the statistical data for differences between the religion of older and younger members of minority ethnic groups. Modood et al pointed out in their research that younger members of minority ethnic groups are, on average, less likely to return a positive answer to the researcher's question as to the importance of their religion for how they live their lives.

Other theorists have pointed to the different responses that minority ethnic groups can make to the challenge of adapting to the cultural environment of the UK or other European countries. For example, George Chryssides (1994) describes three different types of response:

- **Apostasy** – where religious beliefs are given up in the context of an alien cultural environment.
- **Accommodation** – where religious beliefs are adapted to the new cultural environment.
- **Renewed vigour** – where a religion is reasserted as a response to what might be perceived as a threat to its existence.

Ethnicity and the importance of religion

	White	Caribbean	Indian	African Asian	Pakistani	Bangladeshi	Chinese	All ethnic minorities
All	13	34	47	43	73	76	11	46
16–34	5	18	35	37	67	67	7	35
35-49	13	43	56	40	81	92	8	52
50+	20	57	59	64	83	81	31	62
Weighted count	2857	779	637	400	437	145	194	2592
Unweighted count	2857	587	627	373	595	298	109	2589

Modood et al 1997, page 308

As with other social characteristics, an understanding of the patterns and trends of religion, belief and faith is best achieved by considering the impact of other factors such as age.

The table below shows responses by age and ethnicity to the statement 'Religion is very important to how I live my life'

1 Analyse the information in this table and write a 200 word report explaining the significance of age on the importance of religion for minority ethnic group members.

Wallis and Bruce's view would predict that, in the end, minority ethnic groups will accommodate themselves to the cultural environment of the host community and will secularise over time. However, Chryssides suggests that, in general, minority ethnic religions have tended to respond with accommodation and renewed vigour to the task of settling into UK society.

One example of 'renewed vigour' is Islam, which has an appeal to members of some minority ethnic groups. Minority ethnic groups that follow Islam are primarily drawn from countries within which Islam is the predominant faith tradition such as Pakistan or Bangladesh. Islam is also relatively strong among individuals and communities from an African Caribbean background, alongside Christianity. There are various explanations for the appeal of Islam:

- Islam is often presented as a fundamentalist faith, which shares the characteristics of other successful fundamentalist movements, such as Christian Fundamentalism.

- Islam among minority ethnic groups within the UK can be seen as a response to the revival of Islam within the global context. Gilles Kepel, in his book, 'The Revenge of God' (1994) argues that there is a resurgence of Islam, alongside Christianity and Judaism, and that the Islamic faith of minority ethnic groups is a response to that resurgence.

- Islam can be seen as a point of opposition and critique for older and younger members of minority ethnic groups concerned that the policies and practices of UK and western governments, including the USA, provoke conflict and oppression within a global context.

- The institutions of Islam, the mosque, the role of the Imam, ethical teachings and social relationships, function as a source of community and identity within UK and European societies.

Ethnicity and RE in schools

As the UK has become a more diverse country, in terms of ethnicity, language and religion, successive governments have used a variety of strategies to promote cohesion. Religious Education (RE) is mandatory in state-funded schools and has been seen as a way of fostering tolerance and understanding. Theorists have examined and evaluated the way that RE and multi-faith approaches are presented in schools and the impact of this on the attitudes of young people. Some critics have argued that the content of RE in the UK is questionable and have advocated that it is re-shaped to take account of the lived experience of multi-faith Britain.

Activity

Young people's attitudes towards religious diversity, Robert Jackson.

Recent research, outlined below, has investigated young people's attitudes towards religious diversity across the UK and the impact that RE has upon these attitudes. Its findings show the significance of the wider, especially local, context with which RE in a school interacts.

A summary of the research was published on the 'Religion and Society' website:

'The research was conducted between 2009 and 2012 by a multidisciplinary team at Warwick Religions and Education Research Unit led by Professor Robert Jackson. It was funded by the Religion and Society Programme. As part of the project, a national survey was completed by nearly 12,000 students aged between 13 and 15 in schools across the UK. As another part of the project, team members visited a sample of secondary schools in rural, urban and suburban areas of England, Northern Ireland, Scotland, and Wales – and London as an exceptional case – to hold discussion groups with young people. Through these discussions, the young people involved had input into the focus of the survey. Analysis of the large amount of data generated is ongoing, but findings are emerging.

Much depends on whether religions form minorities or majorities in the school and wider community. In some schools, students who belonged to a religious minority felt that teaching about minority faiths provided fuel for teasing and bullying in their school. In other areas, such as inner-city Birmingham, religion was seen as a normal part of everyday life even if students were not themselves religious. This can be compared with rural Sussex, where religion was seen as something strange by pupils who normally had very little direct experience of active faith. In contexts like this, religious students said they avoided discussing their faith in order to fit in. In contrast, in Protestant schools in Northern Ireland and on a Scottish island, being seen to be actively Christian brought respect. In some Northern Irish and Scottish schools researchers also found strong awareness of the areas' histories of sectarianism.

In one school the researchers encountered ethnic, linguistic and religious self-segregation, along with divisions of space at school, e.g. in the playground. Such divisions reflect residential divisions in the local area. In another school much more antipathy was reported by white, British young people towards recently arrived Polish pupils because of the linguistic divide, rather than with schoolmates from the long-standing local Pakistani-origin Muslim community. Thus local patterns of residency, migration and religious practice have an impact upon young people's attitudes to others.

According to the survey young Hindus and Muslims generally feel accepted in the UK. Being religious is positively related to wellbeing for young people, though religious students can be at risk of bullying due to their religious identity, and religious dress remains a contentious issue. Interacting directly with other young people from different backgrounds affects students' attitudes and understanding. The media also influence perceptions about religion and religious people, as does RE. Generally, those who do not belong to a religious group are less interested in learning about religions, but RE does help students to understand people from different religions.

In evaluating patterns and trends of religion, belief and faith, it is important to be aware of the differences experienced across different ethnicities and also to look at the interplay with other social characteristics such as age. The picture is complex and there is significant evidence to suggest that ethnicity is strongly related to religiosity. There is speculation, however, about the impact that secularisation may have on the future impact of ethnicity and there is considerable disagreement amongst sociologists about this matter.

Age

Evidence from a range of sources suggests that, as with previous social characteristics, patterns and trends of religion, belief and faith related to age cannot be easily captured in a simple statement and that the interplay with other social characteristics must be taken into account to achieve an accurate understanding. Overall, research seems to suggest that young people, taken as a whole, are less interested in religion than other age groups and that those over 65 are the most interested.

The 2011 Census provides the following data on age and religion:

● Christians had the oldest age profile of all the main religious groups. Muslims had the youngest age profile, followed by people with no religion.
● In 2011, Christianity had the oldest age profile of the main religious groups.
● Despite falling numbers, Christians formed the largest religious group in England and Wales in 2011. The fall in the number of Christians between 2001 and 2011 was largely in people aged under 60.
● The number of people with 'no religion' has increased across all age groups, particularly for those aged 20 to 24 and 40 to 44.
● Muslims were the second biggest religious group and have grown in the last decade. There were increases across all age groups in both men and women.

BRIN (June, 2015) also provide useful information on patterns and trends of religious affiliation related to age. They analysed and compared data taken from the 1983 and 2013 BSA (British Social Attitudes) surveys. The main focus was the proportions identifying as Anglican with comparisons made with other religious affiliation – Anglican, Catholic, other Christian, other religion, and no religion. They noted clear differences based on age, 'in 1983 – 16 per cent of those aged 18–24 identified as Anglican compared to 32 per cent of those in the next oldest age group (25–34). The proportion that identified as Anglican amounted to a majority of those aged 65 and over, two-fifths of those aged 35–44, and nearly half of those aged 45–64 years of age.' Whereas, from data taken from the BSA 2013 survey, they found that 'it is apparent that the proportions identifying as Anglican have fallen across all socio-demographic groups. The marked age differential is still present. While just 3 per cent and 4 per cent of those in the 18–24 and 25–34 age groups, respectively, identify as Anglican, this steadily increases to more than a third of those aged 65–74 (36 per cent) and 75 and over (35 per cent).' (BRIN, June, 2015)

2011 Census data shows that four in ten people with no religion were aged under-25 and four in five are under 50, with the biggest increases seen amongst the 20–24 age group and those aged 40–44. In comparison, the 2011 Census found that 88 per cent of Muslims are under 50 and nearly half of Muslims are under 25. Although this pattern is not new, as Muslims also showed the youngest age profile in 2001, by 2011, the number aged under-25 had increased by 505,000.

A YouGov poll of 18–24 year olds conducted in 2013 found that the place of religion in young people's lives was 'smaller than ever' (YouGov 2013).

Activity

Data on age and religion

1 Write a short report to summarise what the statistical data on age and religion outlined on this page and the pages above is telling us.

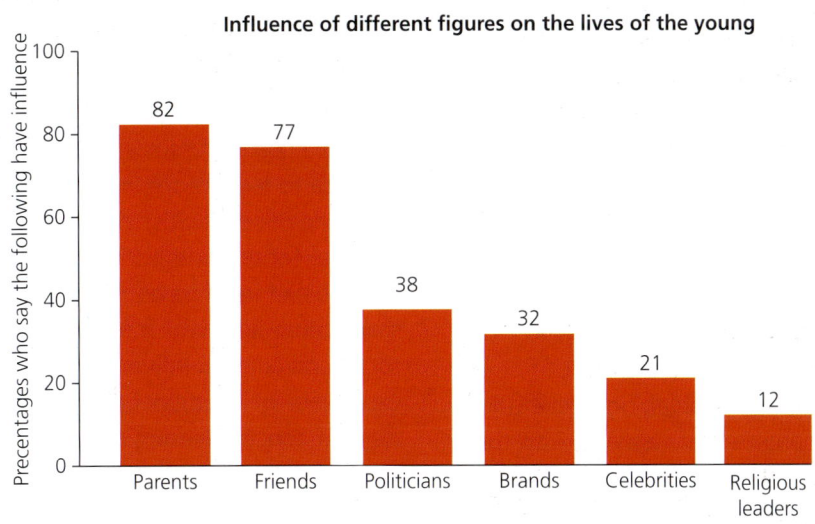

Explanations for the patterns and trends of religion, belief and faith in relation to age

There are a range of reasons put forward to explain the lack of interest in religion reported by a large proportion of young people. Some sociologists have contended that other influences have become more significant. For example, Marxist theorist, Miliband (1969) believed that the media had replaced religion to become the new opium of the people and it can be argued, therefore, that because young people interact with the media more than other age groups, it may have a more significant impact as an agent of socialisation.

Voas and Crockett (2006) analysed evidence from major British social surveys in an attempt to explain the trend of continuous decline of religion throughout the twentieth century. They contend that this decline is overwhelmingly generational in nature and has not been offset by any positive effects of an ageing population. This is because they believe that evidence shows that British people do not get more religious as they get older. They argue that this intergenerational decline is the product of transmission from parents to children as each generation is less likely to socialise their children into religious beliefs than the previous generation. Voas and Crockett note that there is a view that the decline may be tempered by immigration of people who are more religious than the existing population and higher fertility rates among the religiously active population. However, they argue that while evidence shows that the non-white minority ethnic immigrant population is significantly more religious than the white population, the rates of intergenerational decline (between immigrant parents and British-born children) are almost as high as for the white population.

Voas and Crockett's views are challenged by research undertaken by Mirza et al (2007) who contend that British-born Muslims are more committed to Islam than their older, first generation relatives. Their report argues that 'research into the attitudes of Muslims in Britain showed that there is a growing religiosity amongst the younger generation of Muslims. They feel that they have less in common with non-Muslims than their parents and they show a stronger preference for Islamic schools and sharia law. Religiosity amongst younger Muslims is not about following their parents' cultural traditions, but rather, their interest in religion is more politicised. There is a greater stress on asserting one's identity in the public space, for example, by wearing the hijab.'

Woodhead (2007) agrees that young Muslim women regard wearing the hijab as an important part of their religious identity but also as a creative expression of commitment to British national identity. She refers to the concept of 'Muslim chic' which she describes as a 'careful and often lavish attention to style mixed with a very deliberate nod to faith'.

Roof's study of changes to American religious life offers a view that may be applied to an understanding of trends and patterns in religion, belief and faith related to age. Roof (2001) notes that 'in large chain bookstores the "religion" section is gone and in its place is an expanding number of topics including angels, Sufism, journey, recovery, meditation, magic, inspiration, Judaica, astrology, gurus, Bible, prophesy, evangelicalism, Mary, Buddhism, Catholicism, and esoterica.' He believes that such changes, apparent since the 1980s and credited to the post-war baby boomer generation and their quest for meaning, reflect a shift away from traditional religion to more diverse expressions. He believes the 'quest culture' of the baby boomers has created a spiritual marketplace of new spiritual beliefs and practices. Roof's work suggests that religious life is being reshaped and this change may explain the decline in traditional religious participation among the young.

Lynch (2010) discusses the changing nature of belief and young people. He reported on a workshop that brought together 21 participants from Britain, Sweden, Finland, Poland, Russia, and the United States of America to explore the meanings of belief in relation to young people across different religious, secular and national contexts. In his report he proposes that ideas about belief need to be re-imagined into something much more fluid which responds to historical, social and cultural influences and fits with the lived experience of young people. Lynch refers to 'alternative ways of conceptualising belief' that are under development. He also recognises that 'the concept of 'belief' remains meaningful to many young people, and is used by them to refer to their identities, affiliations, opinions and convictions'.

Study

Youth on Religion (YOR), Madge et al (2014)

The Youth On Religion (YOR) study conducted in 2011 and published in 2014 used a mixed-methods approach to investigate the identities of religious and non-religious young people in the UK. The data was gathered from schools and colleges in three British multi-faith locations. There were 10,500 responses by 13 to 18 year-olds to an online survey and qualitative data was collected from 157 people aged 17–18 who participated in focus groups and paired interviews. The principal research objectives were to find out about:

1 Young people's religious identity and its meaning, the importance of religion in their lives and how they express their religiosity.

2 The factors that influenced the negotiation of religious identity including: age, gender, socio-economic status, family, friends, geographical location, school, media, religious leaders and world events. The study also looked at issues of agency and choice, and tensions and changes over time.

3 The effect of religion on young people's everyday life including; sense of purpose, morality, what they wear and eat and expectations of dating and marriage.

4 The role of religion on society and in their local and national communities.

While the YOR study acknowledge that young people's religious journeys are personal and individual, they found that most young people said that their religious identity began with the influence of the family as they absorbed the beliefs and practices of their upbringing. As they moved into adolescence and early adulthood they developed their own approach to their religious identity and there were various influences on this process. They felt personal agency and choice were important in the decisions they made about their religiosity. However, the study also found that the decisions that the young people made about their religious journey was influenced by a range of agencies of socialisation including peers, media, school and religious leaders. The young people also reported life events to be an important influence on believing, with 'bad' things making belief less strong and 'good' things making belief stronger.

The researchers developed a typology of religiosity to help them distinguish between participants in the interviews and this typology was confirmed by patterns of responses to the survey. The typology identified four categories of religiosity amongst the participants in the study:

- 'Strict Adherents (devout and largely following the teachings and traditions of their faith position)'
- 'Flexible Adherents (also devout but more influenced by the Western context of their lives)'
- 'Pragmatists (usually religious to a degree, but more exploratory than Adherents in their outlook)'
- 'Bystanders (for whom religion impinges little on their lives)'.

1 Make notes on the key points of the study.

2 Discuss how the agents of socialisation mentioned might influence religiosity.

3 In groups, plan and present your own research proposal to study religious identity in your area. Include your aims, methods and some sample questions you would use to find out about young people and the factors that shape their religious identity (which may be based on faith or no-faith).

4 You could also conduct a survey to find out if the typology used in the YOR study is useful in categorising religiosity in your school or college.

Research also shows that young people are drawn to some religions more than others and that they find some appeal in world rejecting religious movements. Aldridge (2013) notes that such movements have tended to attract better-off young white people who are able to 'drop out' and who have good prospect of being able to re-enter society after time away. One notable example of a world rejecting movement is the Moonies. This group was the subject of an acclaimed study by Eileen Barker called The Making of a Moonie (1984). She found that those young people who had become Moonies were well-educated and came from highly respectable families where traditional values were held to be important. Some converts saw such movements as a refuge from society and some were attracted by the ideals. Barker concluded that there were a number of factors that explained why some young people became converts to such groups including their disposition before they joined, the broader social context, the positive appeal of the movement such as its ideals, and the actual process of indoctrination that was used. Other researchers have used Deprivation Theory (referred to earlier in the chapter – see page 199) to explain the appeal of world rejecting movements.

Religion and ageing

In terms of explaining the greater religiosity of older people, a number of explanations have been put forward. A report produced by NORC on various international surveys covering 42 countries, 'Belief About God Across Time and Countries' (NORC, 2012) found that belief is highest among older adults. According to the report, 43 per cent of those aged 68 and older are certain that God exists, compared with 23 per cent of those aged 27 and younger. One explanation is that there is a cohort effect whereby young people who are more likely to doubt the existence of God hold onto their disbelief as they age, meaning that societies as a whole are tending to become more secular. However, the NORC study suggests that people change their beliefs over time and one proposition from the report is that as people age they become more religious because of their increasing awareness of mortality.

Davie and Vincent (1998) explored the interconnections between religion and old age. They acknowledge that the relationship is complex but they contend that in Western societies there is still an association of religious rituals with key moments in the life course such as birth, adolescence, marriage and, importantly, death. They believe that, to a certain extent, religion continues to play a part in shaping the transitions between one stage of life and the next. There is a view that people become more conservative as they age and, as religion is often associated with more traditional ideas, as people age they may become more religious. Davie and Vincent also consider the possibility that older people may be more religious because of cohort effect – those growing up in a more secular world have different beliefs from those who grew up in a more religious environment.

There is some evidence to suggest that religion has beneficial effects for people as they get older. For example, Coleman (2011) found that, in the case of the experience of bereavement in later life, religion had a positive effect in the following ways.

- Benevolent religious cognitions – religion provides a positive perspective on loss and gives the reassurance of meaning to the deceased
- Biblical assurances – people are able to draw upon various passages (such as gospels, psalm) to reinforce acceptance
- Religious ritual – prayer and church services regulate emotions and create a sense of closeness to the deceased
- Spiritual capital – church itself provides opportunities for activities, contacts and taking on new roles

Religion, belief and faith in a global context

Change in the significance of religion in societies

As you will have seen from the activity above, so far we have looked at patterns and trends of religion, belief and faith relating to social class, gender, ethnicity and age pertaining to UK and elsewhere across the globe. Immediately below, we will look more generally at global patterns of change in the significance of religion in societies. In section 4, further below, we will focus more on patterns of change in the UK.

The US Centre for Global Christianity's 'Christianity in its Global Context, 1970–2020' report (2013) identified a number of changes in the significance of religion in societies. They draw on the findings of the 'World Religions Database' (WRD) which, in turn, drew on 'best estimates at multiple dates for the period 1900 to 2050 ... using sources ... such as censuses and surveys' (WRD; Leiden/Boston – Brill, 2008). The 2013 report compared statistics for religious affiliation from 1970 to 2010:

- 'In 1970, nearly 82 per cent of the world's population was religious. By 2010 this had grown to around 88 per cent, with a projected increase to almost 90 per cent by 2020'. It suggests that religious 'adherence is growing largely due to the continuing resurgence of religion in China'.
- 'In 1970 Christianity and Islam represented 48.8 per cent of the global population; by 2020 they will likely represent 57.2 per cent'.
- 'The global North is becoming more religiously diverse, with more countries becoming home to a greater number of the world's religions'.
- Religious diversity is decreasing in many areas of the global South with many countries experiencing growth of mainly one religion, typically either Christianity or Islam.

(Centre for the Study of Global Christianity, 2013, page 6).

Since the WRD is based on estimates from censuses and surveys from different parts of the world in contexts where it is difficult to be certain about validity and reliability, one must be cautious about the specific figures provided but the general patterns described are of interest when considering religious change in a global context.

The WRD picture of change can be compared with figures produced by the market research company WIN/Gallup International, which questioned 63,898 people (around 1,000 in each country) at the end of 2014. WIN/Gallup produced some comparative figures that are useful for examining the current global picture. A press release published in April 2015 about the data contained the following points –

'New research this Easter shows that worldwide six out of ten (63 per cent) citizens say they are religious, while one in five (22 per cent) say they are not and one in ten (11 per cent) consider themselves convinced atheists. In Africa and the Middle East more than 8 out of 10 people (86 per cent and 82 per cent respectively) portray themselves as religious while 7 out of 10 say so in Eastern Europe and America (71 per cent and 66 per cent respectively) and 6 out of 10 (62 per cent) in Asia, say they are.' (WIN/Gallup, 2015).

Jean-Marc Leger, president of Win/Gallup International Association, reported the finding that globally an average of two-thirds of people still consider themselves to be religious. He said that –

'Religion continues to dominate our everyday lives and we see that the total number of people who consider themselves to be religious is actually relatively high. Furthermore, with the trend of an increasingly religious youth globally, we can assume that the number of people who consider themselves religious will only continue to increase.' (WIN/Gallup, 2015)

The global picture that these research findings describe appears to reflect the resurgence of different religions in various parts of the world and also seems to reflect the significance of the growth of religious fundamentalism deriving from different religious traditions including Christianity, Islam, Judaism, Buddhism and Hinduism.

Jose Casanova (1994 and 2003) considers that globally many issues show an increase in religious influence and power. For example, the collapse of communism, the growth of Republican politics in the USA (and the effects of US policies globally), the development of politics and policies in Northern Ireland etc., all appear to show the effects of religions on social and political life. Casanova describes the ongoing widespread influence of religions on social and political life as the 'deprivatisation' of religion. He also suggests that the effects of religion cross national boundaries particularly in relation to Islam and Christianity.

1 Examine the following religions map and list of statistics.

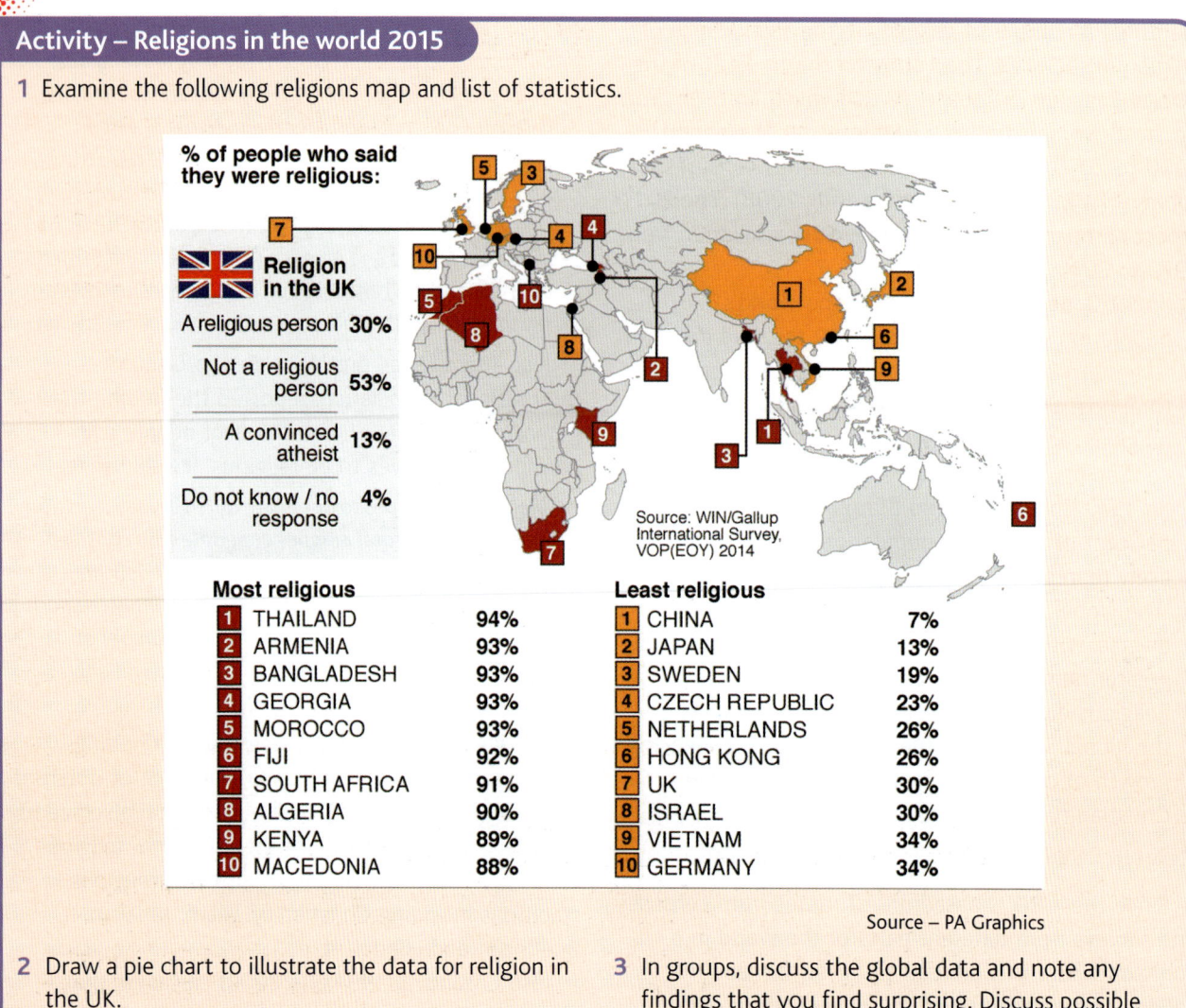

% of people who said they were religious:

Religion in the UK

A religious person	30%
Not a religious person	53%
A convinced atheist	13%
Do not know / no response	4%

Source: WIN/Gallup International Survey, VOP(EOY) 2014

Most religious	
1 THAILAND	94%
2 ARMENIA	93%
3 BANGLADESH	93%
4 GEORGIA	93%
5 MOROCCO	93%
6 FIJI	92%
7 SOUTH AFRICA	91%
8 ALGERIA	90%
9 KENYA	89%
10 MACEDONIA	88%

Least religious	
1 CHINA	7%
2 JAPAN	13%
3 SWEDEN	19%
4 CZECH REPUBLIC	23%
5 NETHERLANDS	26%
6 HONG KONG	26%
7 UK	30%
8 ISRAEL	30%
9 VIETNAM	34%
10 GERMANY	34%

Source – PA Graphics

2 Draw a pie chart to illustrate the data for religion in the UK.

3 In groups, discuss the global data and note any findings that you find surprising. Discuss possible explanations for such findings and share your ideas with the class.

Differences in the significance of religion between societies

In the above section, we have examined evidence of changes in the significance of religion in societies and discovered some key differences between societies. In addition to the differences noted above, the points below are also significant.

In some societies, such as those of western Europe, there is evidence of a decline in the power and influence of traditional religions such as Christianity, and a decline in active participation in religious institutions. However, alongside the evidence of decline, there is evidence of what appears to be continuing belief in religious ideas alongside low levels of participation in religious institutions. The phenomenon of 'belief without belonging' (Davie, 2015) appears to exist in different societies. Davie developed her model 'belief without belonging' within the UK context but there is also, for example, evidence that in Canada 75 per cent of people do not attend church but 80 per cent of people hold religious beliefs (Bibby, 2009).

In addition, in societies where religious traditions appear to be in decline, there is evidence of a resurgence of religion as spirituality. In contrast to the phenomenon of 'deprivatisation' of religion referred to above, there is evidence of a change to privatised religious forms including the spirituality of the New Age and postmodern types of 'spiritual shopping' in some societies. The Kendal project referred to earlier (see page 199) pointed to the huge number of 'spiritual' activities outside of the mainstream churches that individuals and groups were engaging in.

There appears to be a large difference between societies in which religions retain a large, and perhaps, growing influence on social and political life and societies in which the direction of change is towards religion as significant within the private sphere of spirituality and personal development. We will examine these changes in greater detail and with a focus on developments within the UK in the next section on secularisation.

Activity

Global religious trends

1 Do you think that the data on global trends suggests that religion is declining or increasing?
2 Make a mind-map to illustrate the changes and differences relating to religion, belief and faith in a global context.

Check your understanding

Briefly define the following terms and give an example of each:

1 theodicy of disprivilege
2 deprivation theory
3 theists
4 the intersection of social class, age, ethnicity and religion
5 the New Age
6 holistic milieu
7 risk preferences
8 cultural defence
9 cultural transition
10 apostasy
11 cohort effect
12 deprivatisation

Section summary

Make a copy of the following passage and fill in the gaps using the words given below.

When examining patterns and trends in religiosity, _____ and faith, sociologists look at the four particular social characteristics – social class, gender, ethnicity and _____ and the _____ between them. The ONS is a key source of _____ data which helps to establish patterns and trends and enables _____ to be made between different social categories such as age and gender. When studying the relationship between social class and religious participation, sociologists believe that the _____ classes are more religious. However, Weber argued than there is a _____ of disprivilege which offers a religious explanation and justification for the suffering and disadvantage of marginalised groups in society which would include the _____ class. Research suggests that women are more religious than men and are attracted to some religions in particular such as New Age _____. Heelas and Woodhead in the _____ project studied such alternative informal spiritualities, known together as the holistic _____. The _____ movement also attracts women and is seen as _____. However, _____ view is that more traditional forms of religion can be _____ to women because of the way they are interpreted and implemented by men. When studying ethnicity and religiosity, _____ research shows that religion is important in the way some people from minority ethnic groups live their lives. Other theorists believe that religion plays an important function in providing both _____ defence and transition. Religion can be seen as an important source of identity for some minority ethnic young people, for example, _____ argues than wearing the hijab can help young Muslim women assert their religious identity in public. Age in general is also an important factor in religiosity with evidence showing a pattern of _____ people being _____ religious than older people. _____ examined religious identity in young people in a study called _____ on Religion and found that this was influenced by a number of factors including _____, media, school and religious leaders. The young people in the study also reported personal _____ to be important in their decisions about religion. Coleman found that religion can be important for _____ people as it gives them benefits such as spiritual _____. It is important to understand patterns of religion, belief and _____ in a _____ context. Research shows that some countries, like _____ have changed their behaviour towards religion with fewer people attending church but _____ of people saying they hold religious beliefs. Sociologists predict that over the next few years countries like _____ will become more religious and that by 2020 _____ of the world's population will be religious.

Section summary (continued)

Modood's, less, agency, global, young, 80 per cent, milieu, capital, faith, Canada, empowering, Mirza, theodicy, Kendal, comparisons, Madge, spirituality, cultural, intersection, peers, China, higher, 90 per cent, quantitative, belief, age, Holm's, working, goddess, oppressive, older, Youth

4.4. Is secularisation occurring?

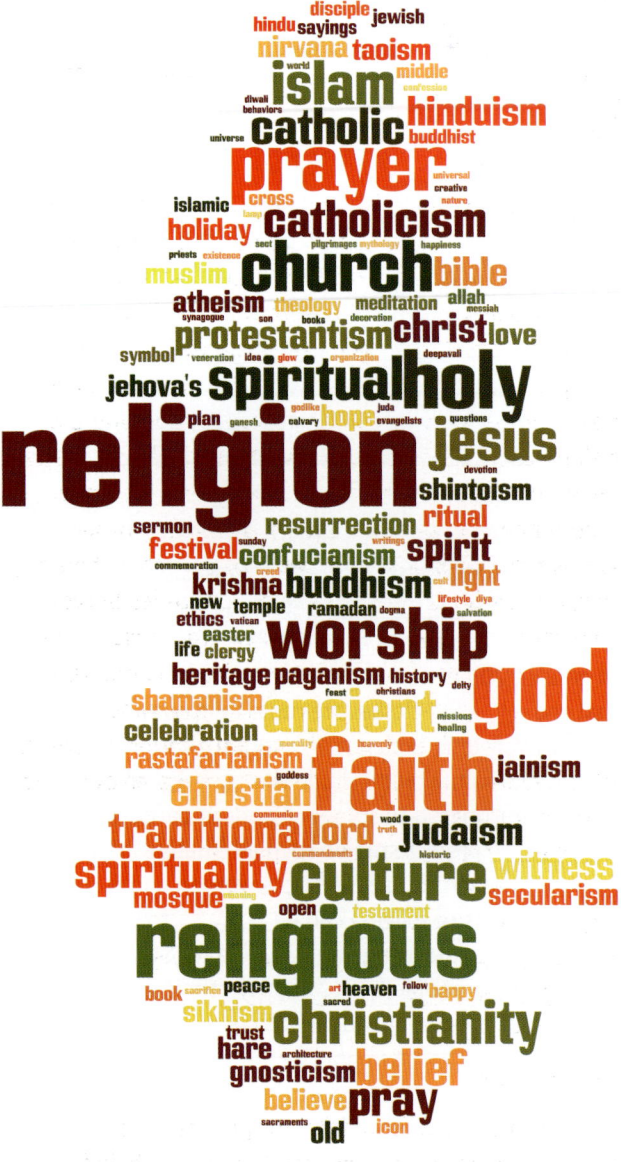

Secularisation is the process by which society becomes less religious. Many sociologists believe that religion is still an important institution that carries society's values, helps to create stability and offers individuals and communities a sense of meaning and purpose. However, other sociologists provide evidence that as society changes over time, religion is becoming less important. They point to statistics for religious belief and religious practice that show that religion is in decline. They argue that the power and influence of religion in society is waning.

Those who argue against secularisation contend that the evidence is less definite and that the global picture of religious belief, practice and influence is very different to the situation in Europe and the UK. We will examine the debates on secularisation in relation to measurements of religious belief, religious practice and the power and influence of religion in society. We will then consider the main debates between those who argue for secularisation and those who argue against it. We will also look at religion and social policy.

Debates on secularisation in relation to religious belief

One approach to the discussion of secularisation is to examine evidence within the context of religious belief. Religious belief is a distinct aspect of religion that some religious traditions emphasise and others do not. Many religious individuals believe in God but some religious traditions do not contain a belief in God (such as Theravada Buddhism) and the God that people believe in is very differently understood in different religions. This diversity of view means that examining evidence for secularisation in relation to religious belief is complicated by the wide variety of beliefs that religious people hold in society.

There may also be diversity within a religion. For example, Christianity is a prominent world religion which is numerically strong in the UK and throughout the world. For some Christian traditions, such as the Roman Catholic Church, there are many detailed beliefs that all adherents are encouraged to hold and which may be influential in their lives. For other Christian groups, such as the Religious Society of Friends (or Quakers), there is little emphasis on formal

Activity

Is religion still important to society?

1 Using some of the words in the image above and the knowledge you have gained from this chapter so far, make a list of all the evidence that indicates that religion is still important in society – you can include statistics, concepts, studies and theories.

2 Make a further list that suggests that religion is becoming less important.

statements of belief and different members may hold very different ideas. The picture is similar in other religious traditions; beliefs may be an important aspect of a religion for some individuals and groups and less important for others. Statements of religious belief may be used in the context of religious worship. For example, within traditional Church of England services, participants would be asked to recite one or other of the 'creeds', which are ancient statements of belief. It is not certain, however, that the recitation of such summaries of religious belief within the context of worship means that church members actually attach importance to such belief in a way that is different from other traditions where there is no recitation of creeds.

In addition, there are beliefs that can be held to be central to a religious tradition and other beliefs that are less central. For example, there is a tradition within Sikhism that men have uncut hair and use a turban or dastaar to hold the hair in place. There are also beliefs within Sikhism about God and about how God's will is revealed to human beings through the teachings of the ten gurus, including the Guru Granth Sahib or Holy Book. Some Sikh men eschew the wearing of turbans and may cut their hair and beards but retain their belief in God and in the teachings of the gurus. This raises the issue of how one could rightly measure decline in religious beliefs within that tradition, in that one would need to decide which beliefs were the central ones that indicated that secularisation had or had not occurred (Matthen 2013).

In a similar way, members of the Roman Catholic Church are taught specific beliefs about sexual practices and the use of contraception. There is evidence that many members do not stick to these beliefs (that is, they use contraception) but do adhere to other beliefs such as belief in God and Jesus and in regular attendance at Sunday mass.

These variations within the patterns of belief among religious people mean that discussion of secularisation is complicated by the way in which beliefs are followed by the members. With these caveats in mind, it is useful to consider the evidence for decline in religious belief that proponents of secularisation put forward. They argue that it is important to look at the extent to which people adhere to the beliefs that are taught by the religious tradition that is prominent within a given society, for example, the matter of belief in God.

The British Social Attitudes Survey reports a decline in belief in God within the UK;

Belief in God, Great Britain, 1991, 1998 and 2008 (per cent)			
	1991	1998	2008
Believe and always have	45.8	47.6	36.7
Believe, didn't before	5.9	4.2	5.1
Not believe, did before	12.1	11.6	15.2
Not believe, never have	11.6	13.2	19.9
Can't choose	22.7	21.7	21.7
Not answered	1.8	1.7	1.5
Total (per cent)	100.0	100.0	100.0
Base	1,222	815	1,975

Source: Perfect, D. (2011)

These statistics would seem to indicate that British people believe in God as a core religious idea (in UK culture) to a lesser extent. Those who answered that they believe in God and always have declined over a 17-year period from 45.8 per cent to 36.7 per cent. There is a small but significant increase in those reporting that they do not believe in God and never have and those who do not believe in God and did before. Logically, of course, people might have rejected belief in God as defined by a religion but that now hold a new and different religious belief, in other words this could be a religious change rather than a religious decline. The British Social Attitudes Survey also considers evidence for society's response to less clear and specific beliefs. They produced comparative data about people's response to the following question; 'Which of these statements comes closest to your beliefs?' and offered the statements below (with percentage answers for the UK):

- Believe there is a God – 37 per cent
- Believe there is some sort of spirit or life force – 33 per cent
- Do not believe there is any sort of spirit, God or life force – 25 per cent
- Don't know – 5 per cent

(Perfect 2011, page 14)

These figures offer a different picture to the straightforward idea of decline in religious belief. A shift in belief in God from 45.8 per cent to 36.7 per cent is a significant change between 1991 and 2008 but the additional figure of 33 per cent for people believing that 'there is some sort of spirit or life force' suggests that there may be a large element of religious change – change to a different sort of religious belief – rather than a pattern of secularisation or decline.

Religion in Britain – A Persistent Paradox, Grace Davie (2015)

Grace Davie has written about the phenomenon of religion in the UK more widely and has produced evidence to support some interesting concepts; 'belief without belonging' and 'vicarious religion' (see pages 175 and 177). Davie has updated her earlier seminal text on Religion in Britain Since 1945 (1994) and has written about factors that influence religion within the UK.

- **Britain's cultural heritage**
  This refers to the assumption within UK society that the country's Christian background remains an ongoing point of reference. The UK's inherited link with Christianity and, in particular, the role of the Church of England and other relatively established denominations including the Methodist Church, the Presbyterian and Congregational Churches (now the United Reformed Church) and the Quakers have a role in shaping UK culture.
- **The inherited model of religion**
  This refers to an awareness that the churches often have a place at particular moments in people's lives such as within certain ceremonies and also for occasions when tragic events have occurred.
- **A shift from 'obligation' to 'consumption'**
  This reflects a change of emphasis among actively religious people within the UK where religion appears more as a choice – where people operate as 'consumers' of religion – rather than as an obligation or duty.
- **New arrivals – the religion of immigrant communities**
  This factor points to the changes that the religions of immigrant communities have made, numerically and in terms of national debates about religion, such as those concerning faith schools and debates about the law on blasphemy.
- **Secular reactions to religion**
  This includes reference to prominent secular voices within society, such as Richard Dawkins, and their reaction to religion.
- **Britain's secularity as an exceptional case – different to global patterns**
  This refers to the notion that the pattern of religious activity in the UK and in Western Europe is different to the global pattern.

1 Discuss and make notes on each of Davie's points and write down an example for each.
2 Discuss the ways in which these influences show a paradox, as indicated in the title of Davie's book. Write an evaluative paragraph to explain your thoughts on this.
3 Write a 200 word report showing how Davie's ideas contribute to the secularisation debate.

With this in mind, it is worthwhile considering the work of Paul Heelas on the New Age and what he terms the 'holistic milieu'. Heelas (1996) quotes a 1993 Gallup poll that suggested that 72 per cent of people see a sacred presence in nature. These figures indicate that changes in religious belief may points to a change to a different kind of 'privatised religiosity' rather than evidence of religious decline.

We have previously examined the phenomenon of 'believing without belonging' (see page 175) and this phenomenon also indicates that assessing secularisation in terms of religious belief is difficult, since the beliefs that people hold may not be associated with a specific religious institution but may be important for the individual.

Sociologists who favour the idea that secularisation is occurring (such as Bruce, 2011), suggest that the belief of 'privatised religion' or the 'holistic milieu' is not the same kind of religious belief at all, in that religious belief as classically defined is a strong influence on people's lives and is closely linked to religious practice and to the cultural impact of religion. In this view, the shift from 'belief in God' to 'belief in a spirit or life force' is evidence of secularisation as it shows that the influence of religion has declined.

As referred to above, Davie identified the notion of the UK and Europe as exceptional cases (2015). She was referring to the wide divergence between statistics for religious believing in the UK and Europe and for the rest of the world. Davie does not suggest that 'believing without belonging' is a global phenomenon but a UK one and she argues that the picture is very different elsewhere. Norris and Inglehart (2011) have developed the idea that religious resurgence and decline can be correlated with the level of 'existential security' (the feeling that survival is secure enough) experienced by people within a society. The authors argue that when people feel secure about their survival and wellbeing (they have a sense of 'existential security'), then religion

The Sea of Faith, Don Cupitt (1984)

Don Cupitt is a Church of England priest who worked for many years as a senior chaplain and lecturer at the University of Cambridge. He has written numerous books on religion. In 1984, he published a book, the Sea of Faith (SCM, 1984), which was based on a TV series that he presented, of the same name. The book examines the process of secularisation and suggests that religious people, including members of the Church of England, may wish to belong to the Church and practice their religion without believing in God or in any supernatural beliefs. A group of fellow religious individuals, including other Anglican priests, formed the Sea of Faith network to spread this idea and to support Christians and others who do not believe in God as an actual existing being.

The Sea of Faith raises a question as to whether secularisation is a process of decline where people no longer believe or whether secularisation is a process of change where people can now have different beliefs about science and the natural world and still be religious.

1 Watch some excerpts from the Sea of Faith episodes on Youtube, particularly the first one and make notes on the key ideas.
2 In what ways do the ideas correspond to some sociological theories of the role of religion in society? Make a poster or mind-map showing the links. (You may wish to start with some functionalist views).
3 Hold a debate on whether it is possible for religion to be a human creation.

may decline but when people feel less secure about their survival and wellbeing, they are inclined towards religion. Norris and Inglehart argue that the growth in religious belief in poor countries is greater than the decline in 'richer' countries. They note; 'we believe that the importance of religiosity persists most strongly among poorer nations, facing personal survival-threatening risks.'. They observe; 'The world as a whole now has more people with traditional religious views than ever before – and they constitute a growing proportion of the world's population'. Norris and Inglehart draw on the World Values Surveys from 1981 to 2001 as well as other evidence (such as Gallup polls) to establish the global trends as well as to provide support for their existential security thesis. The picture for religious belief is taken to be different in the UK as well as other wealthier nations and the global trend towards religious adherence and belief is seen to be contrary to the decline in religious belief in the UK and western Europe.

Debates on secularisation in relation to religious practice

At the beginning of this chapter (page 167), we examined the 'dimensions of religion' (Smart, 1998) and noted that religious belief is one aspect of religion which is emphasised in some religious traditions and not others. 'Religious practice' is a general term which refers to all of the activities that religious individuals might engage in.

Religious practices may include:

- Attendance at places of worship.
- Participation in worship and related activities in the home.
- Personal devotion, such as praying, meditating or reading sacred literature, such as holy books.
- Religious journeys to sacred places (also known as 'pilgrimages').
- Attending religious occasions which mark significant life events, such as ceremonies for birth, coming of age, marriage and death (also known as 'rites of passage').
- Becoming members of a religious institution, which may include attending ceremonies to initiate an individual into membership of a religious organisation.

Data about religious practices can be a useful source of information as to the extent of religious decline or resurgence. In the UK, much of the data gathered focuses on the Christian tradition. Census data from the mid-nineteenth century to the present can be used to gauge the extent of changes in attendance for religious worship over time. In 1851, the Census recorded that 40 per cent of the population attended church. This figure had declined to 35 per cent in 1900 and to 20 per cent in 1950. Data from Church Census figures chronicled a similar decline. Brierley (2006) noted that 12 per cent of people attended Sunday services in 1979 and that this had declined to 6.3 per cent on a given Sunday in 2005. These figures seem to point to a massive decline in religious practice in that attendance at church services on a Sunday is an important indicator of religious practice within the religious tradition which has historically been seen as the most important within the UK. It may also be that the figures reflect a change in religious practice rather than a decline. Many churches have religious events during the week as well as at the weekend. It can be argued, therefore, that if one adds mid-week services to the Sunday figures, they will provide a more accurate picture of what is happening. The Church of England suggested in 2010 that mid-week services added 20 per cent to the weekly attendance figures. However, overall, church attendance figures do seem to provide evidence of decline in mainstream Christianity.

The picture of decline that derives from national census and church census data can be complicated by different effects among Christian denominations and among different religious groups. For example, statistics for religious participation among some Christian groups can be much larger than the figures for mainstream churches such as the Church of England, the Methodist Church and the United Reformed Church. So-called 'Free Churches' such as Baptist churches have demonstrated some increases in attendance figures and Pentecostal churches, as well as Eastern Orthodox churches have shown increases in attendance figures. This suggests that some religious organisations are not part of religious decline in the same way as others. Some sociologists have sought to aggregate the figures somewhat. For example, some religious denominations have succeeded in opening new churches (Brierley, 2006) but there is evidence that a larger number of churches closed than new ones were opened, so combining those figures shows a net decline. So, although there is a general pattern of decline, this conceals evidence of growth among some religious groups.

Less overt and official types of religiosity such as individual devotions, for example, prayer or meditation in the home, are harder to calculate than attendance figures. Qualitative research into patterns of 'religious nurture' (how children acquire religiosity) suggest that much religious instruction and learning occurs within the family and is undertaken by women in the home (Jackson et al, 1989). This type of religious activity is hard to quantify but may be important in an enduring sense.

Some sociological research examines statistics for attendance at key religious ceremonies such as Christian baptisms and other rites of passage. Figures from 'British Religion in Numbers' demonstrate evidence of decline in Christian ceremonies that mirrors the attendance figures:

- Baptisms have declined by 70 per cent since the 1920s.
- Church marriages have declined by 20 per cent since 1900.
- Confirmation ceremonies have fallen by 25 per cent in a 7 year period to 2009.
- Religious funerals dropped 21 per cent in a 7 year period to 2009.

These figures of decline (with exceptions) can be contrasted with the global picture and with the situation within the United States of America where many people continue to attend church and profess Christian belief. A striking contrast in regard to this is the way in which many US presidents declare publically their adherence to Christian belief but a British Prime Minister might well down play his/her religious commitment. A famous example of this is Tony Blair, Prime Minister from 1997 to 2007, who was a Christian but whose spokesperson declared, in answer to a question about the Prime Minister's beliefs, 'We don't do God' (Brown, 2003). More substantially, the global picture of Christian religious practice suggests that the UK is something of an exception. The 'Christianity in its Global Context, 1970–2020' report (2013) stated that; 'Christianity is expected to grow as a proportion of Africa's population, from 143 million in 1970 (38.7 per cent of the continent's population), to 630 million by 2020 (49.3 per cent). In Asia, Christianity is growing more than twice as fast as the general population, mostly through conversions, though it is still a minority religion there (only 8.2 per cent in 2010)'. This wider picture for Christianity reflects the growth of Pentecostal churches within these countries as well as others. A concern with some of the statistics for religious adherence in different countries is that demonstrably reliable statistics are frequently not available and sociologists are comparing 'valid' and 'reliable' data with estimates. Nevertheless most sociologists accept that the picture for religious practice globally is very different to the pattern of overall decline in the UK.

We have seen in the previous section on ethnicity, that decline in attendance within some traditional religious groups can be contrasted with growth in membership and participation in religious groups where migrant groups supplement the membership from UK born members. This includes 'black' Pentecostal groups and Islam as well as Roman Catholic migrants from EU countries such as Poland. There is also evidence of growth in religious practice among members of New Religious Movements (NRMs) as well as older sects such as the Mormons or Jehovah's Witnesses. Supporters of secularisation point out that the growth in smaller NRMs do not typically compensate for decline in larger religious institutions. More substantially, a mixed methods study like the Kendal Project (Woodhead and Heelas, 2002) suggests that many people are participating in NRMs and

activities that could be classified as part of the New Age Movement (or the 'holistic milieu') in ways that are hard to quantify accurately. Part of the change here is a shift from overt religious commitment where people are asked to declare their loyalty through religious membership and attendance towards a more subjective 'privatised' style of spirituality. This may reflect change rather than decline.

Activity

Secularisation in relation to religious practice

1 Make a mind-map summarising the evidence for and against secularisation in relation to religious practice. Add in evidence from the earlier section on patterns and trends in religion, belief and practice in relation to ethnicity to show the impact of Britain as a multi-faith society. You could also include evidence relating to gender and age. Add in any other relevant points that you can think of, for example is the digital world having an impact on religious practice?
2 Discuss the arguments and identify strengths and weaknesses for both sides. Add these points of evaluation to your mind-map.
3 Do you agree that religious practice is changing rather than declining? Write a paragraph supporting or refuting this view.

Debates on secularisation in relation to power and influence of religion in society

Sociological theories of religion, from the time of Durkheim (1858–1917), have examined religious traditions from the perspective of their role in society as a whole. The secularisation debate can be examined from the point of view of the individual and it can also be considered in terms of the impact on society, e.g. how much power and influence does religion have in society?

Jose Casanova (2003) has suggested that there is a division between two key meanings of the term secularisation. He argues that secularisation can refer to:
- 'the secularisation of societal structures or the diminution of the significance of religion'
- 'secularisation in the narrower sense of the decline in religious beliefs and practices among individuals'

223

Hitherto, we have examined the second 'narrower' meaning. Casanova argues that the first meaning is more significant from a sociological perspective, since sociologists are interested in the significance of religion in society – how much power and influence religion has and whether its power has waned or increased.

On this account, the key issue with respect to debates about secularisation is not whether religious individuals have certain beliefs or practice in a particular way but whether a religious institution is involved in social life and can exercise power and influence within it. Within the UK, a model for this might be the changing fortunes of the Church of England. The Church of England has a link to the state via the role of the monarch as head of the church as well as head of state. Religious figures from the Church of England are members of the House of Lords and all parts of England are linked to Church of England 'parishes' with priests or vicars in charge. Church of England services would have traditionally been used to celebrate births, marriages and deaths and these key events would have been shaped by the influence of the Christian religion.

One part of the argument for secularisation is that people are increasingly celebrating births and marriage and commemorating deaths without using the Church of England. For example, statistics for births, marriages and deaths, as referred to above, indicate that large percentages of these ceremonies occur in secular environments, such as a marriage in a registry office, and increasing numbers of people form relationships and create a home together without a specific commitment ceremony to mark the occasion.

Within the political sphere, secularisation may be seen in the lack of obvious power and influence that religious leaders seem to possess when political decisions are made. Some sociologists, such as Martin (1969), draw a contrast between the current situation in the UK and the situation in earlier times when Christian churches appeared to possess considerable power and political leaders such as monarchs strived to gain control over religious institutions because of their power and wealth. An example of this is the case of King Henry VIII who broke with the Catholic Church in Rome and formed the Church of England so that he would have more direct control over the finances and religious decisions, such as granting himself the power to divorce. This political dynamic continued over the next 100 years or so and was a major factor in the English Civil War in the mid-1600s. This situation can

be contrasted with the UK today where the opinions of religious leaders are not typically decisive or even seen as relevant in political debates.

In a similar way, it is arguable that the beliefs and opinions of different religious believers are not especially influential in public debates or in the formation of public policies. In some countries, such as the USA, the policies of political parties or leaders will explicitly seek to gain the views and garner the support of groups of religious people. In that way, those religious people will exercise power and influence in society. In Great Britain, it is arguable that most religious teachings are not heeded in the public sphere. Examples might include Roman Catholic and other religious institutions' opposition to abortion which appears to have had little effect on public policy. One might also point to religious criticism of the practice of usury – the lending of money for interest – which is a key foundation for the capitalist social order and which exists in spite of centuries of religious opposition. A similar case can be made in regard to religious criticism of policies on war such as are expressed in Quaker pacifist ideas.

On the other hand, it has been argued that religion still plays a prominent role in some aspects of social life in the UK. In state schools in England and Wales, daily acts of collective worship that are 'wholly or mainly of a broadly Christian character' (Education Reform Act 1988) are still mandatory and Religious Education is a legal requirement. In theory, at least, this means that the intention of the state is that many children growing up in Britain will be exposed to Christian religious ideas.

As previously discussed, the global picture is very different. Some commentators have argued that, internationally, many policies and events are influenced by religious teachings and ideas. Some sociologists have argued that modern international affairs cannot be comprehended without an understanding of religion and that religions are a growing force (Kepel, 1994). For example, it can be argued that significant global events such as the fall of the Berlin Wall and political conflicts in the Middle East cannot be understood without reference to religious factors.

Religious influence and power within UK society seems to be in decline and that situation contrasts with the situation globally and, particularly, in the USA. Debates about secularisation require attention to this as well as to data on religious belief and practice.

Religion and influence on society

1 Using the internet, find out about the kind of non-religious ways that people in the UK observe births, marriages and deaths and note down three examples for each. You may wish to add some images in illustration.
2 Consider what these examples tell us about secularisation in the UK and add your thoughts to your notes.
3 Write notes to evaluate the argument that religion is still significant because of its mandatory role in schools.

Theoretical views on secularisation

Pro-secularisation theorists

We have examined the secularisation debate via the three areas of religious belief, religious practice and the power and impact of religion on society. We will now consider some of the arguments of those sociologists who are convinced by the evidence for secularisation.

Many of the founding figures of sociology wrote about religion and expressed opinions about the future of religion. Marx, for example, believed that religion, including the Christianity of his day, was based on illusory ideas that encouraged working-class people to accept their position in society. Marx thought that religion would disappear as society changed for the better and class divisions were erased within the communist society of the future. Marx, therefore, predicted that secularisation would occur.

Weber on rationalisation and disenchantment

Weber also thought that as society changed, religion would no longer have the key place that it had once occupied. This judgment came in spite of the fact that Weber saw religion as a major factor in the development of capitalist society. He believed that as society developed, it would be governed more by rational thinking and 'efficient' bureaucracy and less by the values and standards of religion. As part of rationalisation, Weber believed that a process of disenchantment would occur whereby people would lose faith in magic and supernatural ways of understanding and affecting the world. Rational ways of thinking would make it increasingly difficult for people to consider using such interventions to have an impact on the world and so secularisation would occur.

Although coming from a very different perspective about society generally, early functionalist thinker Durkheim shared Weber's view that religion would be replaced more scientific ways of understanding the world. Later sociologists have developed the ideas of Marx, Weber and Durkheim and produced detailed theories on secularisation.

Wilson based his view on the evidence of religious decline in belief, practice and social influence. He stressed the consequences of the process of societalisation in modern societies and on this basis he formulated his thesis that secularisation is linked to the decline of community. Wilson stated provocatively that 'when the local community dies, religion declines with it' (1982).

Wilson pointed out that the economy, the polity, law, education, art and the family function independently of religious values, norms and practices. Searching for an explanation for this, he cited changes in society due to processes of rationalisation and societalisation. He also pointed out that the processes of industrialisation, urbanisation, rationalisation and bureaucratisation have undermined religious institutions.

Wilson's certainty that the empirical evidence clearly demonstrated that religious institutions had lost their social significance did not mean he thought religion had ceased to play an important role. He argued that religion had become privatised. In the private sphere religion often continues and 'It offers another world to explore as an escape from the rigours of technological order and the ennui that is the incidental by-product of an increasingly programmed world' (Wilson, 1985).

Secularisation, Steve Bruce (2011)

Bruce has produced a complex theory about secularisation that draws together different elements –

He argues that secularisation is caused by the following factors.

- **Structural differentiation**
  As society develops and changes, different institutions separate and are less interconnected. This means that churches or other religious bodies have less of a role as a unifying force that binds everyone together as in medieval times. One example of this is the separation between the church and the state and the way that political decisions can be taken without consulting religious leaders.
- **Social differentiation**
  As society develops, different social groups are less physically connected to each other, they live in different physical environments, and people's view of society is less unified. Religion, such as Christianity in the UK, had described society as being bound together under God with mutual obligations and relationships. When social differentiation occurs, it is less possible for people to have that viewpoint – it becomes less believable to think of everyone as connected in that way.
- **Individualism**
  This is seen as a characteristic of modern societies in which people are less connected to organisations and institutions and see themselves as individuals who make their own way in life.
- **Societalisation**
  This term refers to the change that occurs when society becomes larger and people are less connected to each in small communities like village, towns or communities. When society is large scale and work environments are large and impersonal (like a factory), people may feel less connected to their community and this undermines religions which were traditionally organised in small groups (local parish churches where everyone knows everyone else).

- **Schisms**
  Many religions have split over the years and there is typically no church for a whole society but a number of different denominations and sects.
- **Pluralism**
  This is the result of the diversity of different religious groups in society. People do not see one religious truth but a whole number of different truths and different groups. One effect of pluralism is that religious commitment becomes a matter of private choice rather than being a matter of something that people have to believe, hence the use of the term 'privatisation' of religion.
- **Technology**
  Bruce thinks that technology has an effect on religion. When people can solve problems using technology, they are less likely to believe that they need a God to provide solutions. The development of technology is something that occurs as society develops and changes.

Overall, Bruce thinks that these changes in society create a situation in which people find it hard to believe in a religion as an absolute truth. They may choose to have religious beliefs but these will exist in a privatised way and will be less significant for society. Society will be secular and religion will be a personal choice with little social significance.

Bruce accepts the evidence for religious decline in regard to belief and practice. For example, he points to the increase in people who report in surveys that they do not believe. He considers that evidence for privatised religion such as Davie on 'belief without belonging' (1994) or Heelas on the 'holistic milieu' (1996) is also evidence of secularisation in that he sees privatised religion as part of religious decline also.

1 Using Bruce's ideas, write a 250 word newspaper article putting forward his case in support of secularisation.
2 Follow this up by drafting some online comments responding to the article with criticisms of the views it contains.

Pro-secularisation theorists such as Bruce (2011) and Wilson (1996) argue that secularisation is an irreversible change in society. This judgment is based on the idea that individuals do not simply lose their faith. Bruce contends that people's beliefs change because of large scale social changes that affect the whole of society. Pro-secularisation sociologists suggest that everything in the UK's social environment has become disconnected from religion in a way that is different to previous times.

They consider that secularisation is likely to occur more widely as all societies experience the same kinds of changes that have occurred in the UK and in Europe. So, secularisation is likely to occur globally even if it has not done so yet.

A problem for the secularisation thesis is the phenomenon of religion in the USA. The USA retains consistently higher statistics for religious belief, religious practice and it also shows evidence for the power and influence of religion in society. For example, within the USA, there was evidence in 2003 that 40 per cent of people attended church regularly, a figure that was approximately the same as the figures for 1939. This is contrary to the decline in church attendance within the UK and in some European countries. On a wider scale, there is evidence that US religion is very influential in the development of US politics and has been a significant factor in the policy choices of various US presidents. This runs alongside the view that US society appears to possess many of the characteristics identified by Bruce in the Study box above. For example, structural and social differentiation are evident in US society as is individualism and societalisation. In addition, US religious denominations are characterised by the schisms that Bruce identifies as key factors in the development of religious pluralism in which religion is more a matter of choice rather than an absolute truth which all must accept.

The US example is a strong test for proponents of the secularisation thesis. However, Bruce, for example, argues that there is evidence of the changes in American religion that he describes elsewhere. He suggests that the development of religion in the USA mirrors the shift to a 'weaker', more privatised style of religiosity that lacks the unifying power of traditional religions. However, this does not seem to take account of the power politics of what is termed the 'New Christian Right' in America. The New Christian Right is a term used mainly in the US to describe right-wing political groups that are characterised by their strong support of socially conservative policies. Christian conservatives principally seek to apply their understanding of the teachings of Christianity to politics and public policy by proclaiming the value of those teachings or by seeking to use those teachings to influence law and public policy. Therefore, the evidence is unclear as to whether US society is secularising or not. Bruce argues that the development of secularisation can be uneven but that the US will, in the end, follow the UK and Europe. It is important to note that pro-secularisation sociologists do not necessarily think that religion will disappear. They argue, rather that it will be less socially significant and influential. Hence, the idea that high figures for church attendance do not necessarily disprove secularisation. It is also pointed out, for example, by Hadaway et al

(1993), that the reported figures for church attendance may be somewhat exaggerated by US citizens' wish to appear more religiously active than they actually are. Their research showed that some people state that they have attended Sunday worship but have not done so – the researchers went so far as to count the number of cars outside the church on a Sunday morning! – and they hypothesised that church attendance is socially approved of in US society and so people exaggerated when asked to respond in a survey.

Pro-secularisation sociologists such as Bruce also argue that the religiosity that was identified by Heelas and Woodhead in the Kendal Project (see page 199) was an example of the weaker kind of religion which is actually evidence for secularisation rather than against it. Bruce points out that many of the activities that people engaged in in the Kendal study, such as Tai Chi or yoga, could be described simply as recreation or as pseudoscience rather than being genuinely spiritual.

The pro-secularisation arguments advanced by Bruce, amongst others, is a consistent and powerful attempt to explain the evidence of religious decline within the UK and western Europe. In addition, the arguments and evidence are used to justify a prediction that secularisation will affect all parts of the world in time, although many people will remain religious as a personal choice.

Theoretical views on secularisation

Anti-secularisation theorists, including postmodern views

We have seen that proponents of secularisation do not contend that religion will decline completely and disappear from human culture. Rather, they argue that religion will occupy a less socially significant, privatised place within society. In a similar vein, sociologists who argue against secularisation do not simply dismiss the evidence for religious decline but suggest that a more complicated picture of decline and resurgence is evident within the global religious scene. We will examine the views of a number of sociologists who argue against secularisation as promoted by Bruce and others. However, these researchers typically do not simply deny the evidence for religious decline but offer a more nuanced approach.

Peter Brierley is a researcher who examines evidence for religious decline and resurgence. He worked for many years for a Christian research organisation and his interest in this area of research is informed by his own faith. Brierley presents evidence for the growth of religious groups within the UK as well as in a global context, with particular emphasis on Christian churches. A part of Brierley's research concerns evidence for church membership and church attendance provided by church census information as well as by national census data and other relevant surveys. Brierley's key finding is that many indices of decline, from a Christian perspective, are not as drastic as they can seem at first sight. He argues that the rate of decline in church membership and participation has slowed significantly in the last 15 years or so and this provided the title for his 2006 book 'Pulling out of the Nosedive'. For example, Brierley notes a slower overall decline in church attendance between 1998 and 2005 compared to the period 1989 to 1998. Brierley distinguishes carefully between churches which seem to be declining, such as the Church of England, and churches whose growth in the UK mirrors their patterns of growth elsewhere, including Pentecostal churches, Eastern Orthodox churches and the 'Fresh Expression' churches (churches that take a distinctive form to meet local needs, for example, a surfers' church in Cornwall or, a youth church in a skate park). Brierley notes that these churches share a missionary and expansionist zeal that means that they actively seek growth and new members. The implication is that secularisation is occurring where churches do not actively seek growth. The sociological significance of Brierley's research lies in the patient collection of data that supports the view that secularisation is not an inevitable development but one that reflects the situation where religious bodies do not actively seek new members.

Activity

Fresh Expression churches

1 Using the internet, find out more about Fresh Expression churches.
2 Write a leaflet with images and text to inform people about these new types of churches.
3 Assess the view that Fresh Expression churches represent evidence against secularisation.

what are... fresh expressions of church?

they are forms of church that:

listen to people and enter their culture

serve those outside the reach of the existing church ✗

make discipleship a priority

✝ intentionally form church

fresh expressions ✚ freshexpressions.org.uk

We have made frequent reference to the work of Grace Davie. Her 1994 book on 'Religion in Britain since 1945' introduced the concept of 'believing without belonging' (see page 175) as a way of accounting for the fact that many people seemed to report a continuing engagement with religious belief alongside an unwillingness to actively participate in religious institutions. Her later concept of 'vicarious religion' (see page 177) pointed to the significance of continued engagement with institutional religion from the standpoint of 'vicariously' allowing religious leaders to speak on behalf of people and to articulate ethical standpoints . Davie does not deny evidence for religious decline where it exists but argues for an appropriate complexity in engaging with the evidence. Her main contention remains that decline in orthodox religious practice does not mean straightforward decline in religious believing and that the patterns of decline in the UK and Europe are different from and not to be confused with the broader picture in the USA and in other countries. In that sense, the UK and Europe are exceptions to the more general picture of growth and resurgence of religious faith in other parts of the world.

Woodhead and Heelas (see page 199) argue against a straightforward secularisation thesis in their research on religious life in the town of Kendal in Cumbria. They report that a huge variety of religious activities were occurring within a five mile radius of Kendal in a given period of time. Alongside traditional religious activity within churches, there were 23 yoga groups, 7 tai chi groups, 7 dancing groups, 4 earth-based spirituality groups, 4 interfaith groups, 4 therapy groups, 4 women's groups, 3 Buddhist groups as well as Baha'i and Sai baba groups. Woodhead and Heelas argue that all of these groups were concerned with spiritual growth. A particular concern for the researchers was to test their belief that society is undergoing religious change rather than religious decline. Heelas had discussed his ideas about religious change in his 1996 book on the 'New Age Movement'. Part of the significance of the Kendal Project was to provide evidence for the author's view that a shift was occurring from religion to spirituality and that secularisation in relation to traditional religious groups such as Christian Churches could occur alongside growth of alternative spiritualties such as those of the New Age.

> ### Activity
>
> **The Kendal Project**
> 1 Consult the website for the Kendal Project and find out about the history of the project and the methods used.
> 2 Identify the findings of the research.
> 3 From your knowledge and understanding of research methods, evaluate the research.
> 4 Write up the information you have discovered in a 500 word report or seminar presentation.

Jose Casanova (2005) brings an evaluative tone to the debate and proposes a way forward for the discussion. He analyses the ways in which sociologists from the USA study American religions and he suggests that their stance is very different to British and European sociologists. Sociologists from the USA tend to believe that European sociologists are misguided in asserting that secularisation is happening and is an irreversible process. He proposes that both stances lack balance and that a pooling of ideas will enable sociology to understand the emergent pattern of religion in the global context. Casanova argues that globally, religion is neither declining nor growing but that there are variations within different countries as well as between countries. He argues that religions remain powerful and influential in different places but also that patterns of decline in some societies such as the UK are significant.

A key part of the critique of secularisation arises from postmodern thinking on religion. We have discussed postmodernist ideas about religion on page 189. They propose a way of approaching religion that is different to modern and pre-modern styles of religious thinking and practice. If pre-modern thinking is connected to religion and modern thinking is critical of religion because the modern view is committed to science and rationality, postmodern thinking sees religion as a possible choice for people as they seek to come to terms with the global consumer culture of the twenty-first century. In a way that partially parallels the thinking of the Kendal researchers, postmodern thinkers such as Lyon (2000) suggest that religion offers the possibility of choice in terms of lifestyle and narrative to confused individuals within postmodern culture. By this account, religion is not disappearing or declining as society changes. Religion will still have a continuing role but only in the context of choice and only from a standpoint that goes beyond the metanarratives of traditional religious thinking that offer claims to the truth.

Anti-secularisation thinking within sociology, including postmodern ideas, does not provide proof that secularisation is wrong. Much of the evidence for secularisation is accepted but further evidence is provided for the view that religion also remains strong globally as well as in the UK, depending on how it is measured.

> **Activity**
>
> ### The secularisation debate
> Prepare for a secularisation debate by gathering as much evidence as you can for both sides of the debate. When you have assembled the evidence in note-form or a mind-map, evaluate it and come to your own assessment of whether secularisation is occurring or not.

Religion and social policy

In terms of examples of religion and social policy in the UK, we have referred earlier to the mandatory nature of worship and religious education in schools in England and Wales. We have also looked at the relationship between the Church of England and the state.

The UK government has, since 2010, enshrined in UK law the human rights that are typically protected in international guidelines such as the United Nations' Universal Declaration of Human Rights and others. UK law guarantees a citizen's rights in regard to their religion and different aspects of their religion. It provides legal protection against discrimination on the grounds of religion. The provisions of the law are summarised below:

- The law guarantees the right to freedom of thought, conscience, religion or belief.
- People cannot be compelled to disclose or adopt religious or other beliefs. There may be limited ways in which the expression of religion can be curtailed – see below.
- An employer may not discriminate against an employee because of his/her religion or beliefs.
- Religion or belief means any religion, religious belief or similar philosophical belief (such as Humanism).
- People may not be discriminated against because of her/his religion or belief or perceived belief or because of being associated with a particular religion or belief.

- Direct discrimination may be allowed in specific work situations such as employing a person to work for a religious organisation and requiring them to be someone who believes in that particular religion.
- Indirect discrimination is not lawful. This is where a person is discriminated against because of an aspect of their religion that is disliked by others (such as wearing religious clothing). There may be situations in work where it is lawful to discriminate on these matters (if wearing particular religious clothing can be shown to be unsuitable in a specific work context, for example) but in general indirect discrimination on the grounds of religion or belief is unlawful.
- Harassment and victimisation, including bullying on the basis of religion or belief is unlawful. This includes situations in which a person complains (such as at work) and is victimised for complaining. This can include being victimised because of an association with a religion or belief. For example, some people from an Asian background were subjected to harassment and victimisation because of a reaction against the events of 9/11.
- Giving information to an employer about ones' religion or belief is advised but not required in law.
- Employers are not required to provide time off for religious observance or special facilities for prayer, for example, but they are advised to do so where possible.
- Organisations and employers should consider if their policies and practices indirectly discriminate against people on the basis of their religion or belief.
- Holidays for religious observance should be requested from employers and employers are not required to accede but would be advised to do so if possible. The requirements of a business take some priority.
- Work dress codes should not discriminate on the basis of religion and should assist people to wear religious clothing as appropriate. A health and safety risk would override a religious requirement in a work context.
- Work situations should not discriminate on the basis of religion or belief when it comes to food, unless the needs of the business override the religious requirement.
- Religion and belief may lead to an individual disagreeing with a person's sexual orientation. They may not discriminate against others on the basis of these religious views or beliefs since people are protected in law on the basis of their sexual orientation.

(Equality Act 2010)

The above points summarise current provision for human rights as they pertain to religion and belief. Such legally binding rights can, of course, change according to current political thinking and the policies of the government of the day. According to the government, the ethical and political thinking that is enshrined in current UK law should guide the ways in which the UK government responds to human rights violations in other countries.

Social policy regarding religion is not without its critics. Field (2010) argues that government responses to the rights of Muslims in the UK has prioritised 'counter-terrorism' and 'community cohesion', when considering the perceived alienation of many Muslim people within UK society rather than the effects of UK foreign policy.

The Sociology of Religion has been an important area of research since the origins of sociology as a discipline. It continues to shed light on the changing nature of religion, belief and faith in the UK and across the globe. Sociologists have sought to both define and measure religion, belief and faith and have produced useful categories for understanding different kinds of religious organisations. Different theoretical frameworks within sociology have developed distinctive perspectives on religion that continue to inform contemporary thinking. Sociologists have also examined religion and religious phenomena in relation to different social groups. It is probably within the debates about secularisation that there has been most disagreement among sociologists and this continues to be a lively area of discussion.

Check your understanding

1 Privatised religiosity
2 Rationalisation
3 Disenchantment
4 Structural differentiation
5 Social differentiation
6 Societalisation
7 Pluralism
8 New Christian Right

Section summary

Make a copy of the following passage and fill in the gaps using the words given below

Secularisation is the process by which society becomes _____ religious. The secularisation _____ encompasses both sides of the view and, as yet, there has been no conclusive resolution that has proved whether religion is in decline or not. Sociologists have attempted to gather evidence of secularisation in relation to measurements such as religious _____, religious practice and the power and _____ of religion in society. Data suggests that belief in God has declined but that a broader belief in some sort of spirit or ____ _____ has emerged. _____ data also shows evidence of decline in some institutions but increase in others. Pro-secularisation theorists argue that religion has lost its ____ in society and that _____ ideas no longer shape society. However, anti-secularisation theorists believe that religion has _____ rather than declined. The findings of the _____ Project are cited as evidence that there has been a shift from religion to _____. _____ agree that religion has changed and is no longer a _____ but instead it offers people _____ as part of their _____. When looking at the _____ context, the picture is very different with evidence of religion growing in some countries _____ than others with an overall trend towards religious _____. The USA retains consistently _____ statistics for religious belief, religious _____ and it also shows evidence for the power and influence of religion in society. Overall, the question of whether secularisation is occurring or not is a _____ one with evidence for both sides of the debate. A key issue is how secularisation is _____ and measured.

attendance, spirituality, practice, postmodernists, more, complex, metanarrative, religious, higher, choice, defined, Kendal, adherence, life force, global, power, belief, changed, less, debate, influence, lifestyle

Practice questions

1 In what ways does age influence religiosity? [10]

2 To what extent is data on religious practice useful in measuring patterns and trends in religion? [20]

3 Outline and evaluate the view that secularisation is occurring. [40]

Glossary

academic education education in general subjects rather than towards a specific career or job related skills, for example English Literature, Maths, History and Sociology are all academic subjects.

academic-vocational divide the idea that the education system has traditionally been divided between academic and vocational education with academic studies generally having a higher status (see academic and vocational education).

academies schools which are free from control by local authorities but still follow the national curriculum and are funded by central government. Academies were originally intended to transform failing secondary schools but under the coalition government all primary and secondary schools could request moving to academy status.

alienation this is a concept used by Marx to describe the sense of powerlessness, lack of control and disconnectedness felt by the proletariat created by exploitation at work and capitalism.

anomie a concept used by Durkheim to describe a state of normlessness, in which the social bonds which hold a society or community together have broken down, leading to a lack of social order. The more individual aspect of this concept was developed by Merton, describing how an individual may experience anomie when society's goals and values seem unachievable, creating a 'strain' and potentially leading to deviance.

anti-school subculture a group of pupils in a school who share a common set of attitudes and values involving resistance to school rules and discipline and rejection of the value of academic success (see also pro-school subculture).

bulimic society young uses this concept to describe the way in which contemporary society is apparently inclusive, with its focus on consumption of material possessions as a route to happiness available to all, but is also exclusive, excluding the poorest and most deprived in society who are unable to access these things.

canteen culture this concept refers to the attitudes and values exhibited by the police in their off-duty socialising. Canteen culture within the police force is argued to include a normalisation of racist attitudes.

city technology colleges a type of secondary school directly funded by central government rather than local authorities specialising in technology based subjects. commodification of education the process by which education comes to be seen as a product to be bought and sold rather than as a public service available as a right to everyone (see also marketisation).

cohort effect the effects of shared life experiences of a group being studied such as being born around the same time, exposed to the same events in society and influenced by the same demographic trends. Sharing such similar experiences makes the group quite unique to study.

collective conscience a concept associated with functionalism and in particular Emile Durkheim. It refers to the universally shared beliefs, ideas and moral attitudes which function as a uniting force within society and help to bring social integration, social solidarity and social order.

colonisation where a more powerful country seeks to dominate a less powerful country.

comprehensive schools secondary schools which are not selective but accept pupils of all abilities and aptitudes.

conformist subculture term used by Hargreaves to describe the pro-school subculture (see also delinquescent subculture and pro-school subculture).

converter academies academy schools which were set up after 2005 by the coalition government. They are schools which have voluntarily converted to academy status rather than being obliged to convert because of being classified as an underperforming school.

core subjects the subjects regarded as the most important by the devisers of the national curriculum; English, maths and science. Standard Assessment Tests and key stages 1, 2 and 3 were based on these subjects.

correspondence principle term used by Bowles and Gintis to describe how the organisation of schooling is similar to the organisation of workplaces so that pupils are socialised to accept the discipline of work

counter-school culture term used by Willis to describe the culture of pupils who oppose the values and rules of the school.

crisis of masculinity a situation where young males have become increasingly uncertain about masculine identity and male roles due to the decline of traditional male jobs in heavy industry, male unemployment and more women becoming wage earners in families.

CSEW The Crime Survey for England and Wales, which was previously called the British Crime Survey (BCS). This is an official and large-scale victim survey, carried out annually on behalf of the Government.

cultural capital term used by Bourdieu to describe knowledge, attitudes and values possessed by members of the higher social classes which enable them to be more successful in the education system (see also habitus, economic capital and social capital).

cultural defence refers to the idea that as various groups recognise that their cultural practices may be threatened by homogenising forces, they protect and reinforce their own cultures to make sure that they remain distinct.

cultural deprivation a lack of the norms, values and attitudes required to ensure success in education.

cultural factors factors explaining success or failure in education relating to cultural background e.g. attitudes towards education and use of language.

cultural homogenisation a process whereby as globalisation occurs, a world culture emerges which means that local cultural practices are less significant.

cultural reproduction the process whereby children of the dominant class tend to end of the same class position as their parents because they possess cultural capital which enables them to be more successful in education and work.

cyborg an entity which is part human part machine.

debt aversion fear of building up large debts as a result of taking out loans to go to university. Some sociologists have suggested this may deter working-class students from going on to higher education.

delinquescent subculture term used by Hargreaves to describe the anti-school subculture (see also conformist subculture and anti-school subculture).

deschooling the process of removing responsibility for education from qualified teachers and formal schools advocated by Ivan Illich.

deviant career using this concept of 'career', Becker described the process by which the deviant label is accepted, and how this affects the choices subsequently available to and made by the individual. For example, he or she may be rejected by some social groups and denied access to opportunities, and may then join with others who are similarly labelled, as part of a deviant subculture.

digital all forms of information that can be reduced to binary code, which can then lead to the proliferation (growth) of small and large-scale phenomena.

digital divide refers to growing disparity between those who have access to the internet and digital forms of communication and those who do not. Those who do not are even more likely to experience exclusion, marginalisation and a lack of social capital as a result, further reinforcing inequality.

digital revolution refers to the huge shift in communication over the past two decades in terms of the ways in which information is stored and shared.

disintegrative and reintegrative shaming Braithwaite suggests that disintegrative shaming involves labelling the criminal or deviant themselves, suggesting they are a bad person, whereas reintegrative shaming involves labelling the deviant or criminal act as bad, rather than the person, preventing a master status from forming. The former is arguably more likely to lead to reoffending.

division of labour the way work is divided up among members of a social group.

double deviance this term refers to the negative perception of female offenders, especially those involved in violent offences and/ or offences against children. They are seen as being deviant against their femininity as well as against society's laws.

Ebacc Abbreviation for the English Baccalaureate, a performance measure for any student who achieves grade C or above at GCSE in English, mathematics, history or geography, two sciences and a language.

economic capital wealth in the form of money or material possessions (see also cultural capital and social capital).

edgework a concept used by Lyng to describe exploring the edges that exist along cultural boundaries and undertaking activities which push and test those boundaries.

Education Action Zones (EAZs) a scheme set up the Labour government in 1998 to target extra funding in order to raise educational attainment in certain deprived inner city areas.

Education Maintenance Allowances (EMAs) launched in 2004, EMAs offered a weekly cash allowance to young people aged 16–19 from lowincome families who remained in education.

education market a term used to describe the situation resulting from educational policies which encourage schools to compete like private businesses, for example the introduction of performance league tables, parental choice and funding according to student numbers.

education poverty children who attend school for less than four years can be defined as in education poverty.

educational triage a process whereby teachers and schools divide pupils into three categories, those who will definitely succeed, those who will definitely not succeed and those who may succeed and then concentrate more attention and resources on the third group than the other two.

elaborated code of speech term used by Bernstein to describe a complex form of speech where details are spelt out and meanings are more explicit, used in situations where the context is not familiar to the listener for example in education (see also restricted code of speech).

equal opportunities policy policies formulated by schools and other educational institutions promoting equal treatment for all students typically focusing on equality in terms of gender, ethnicity and disabilities.

equality of opportunity the principle that everyone in society should be given the same chances in education or employment.

essentialised a view of women is a view in which women are seen as sharing similar qualities and characteristics. This view has been criticised for assuming women are the same and share the same characteristics when this is not the case.

ethnocentric curriculum the organisation of knowledge and teaching so that it reflects the culture of the dominant ethnic group and marginalises the cultures of less influential ethnic groups.

ethnographic research focusing on small scale case studies, typically using a mixture of qualitative methods.

Excellence in Cities (EIC) a scheme launched by the Labour government in 1999 which replaced Education Action Zones and gave extra funds to education authorities in inner city areas to boost attainment for students from low income backgrounds.

faith schools schools which focus on the ethos of a specific religion, the most common type are Church of England Schools. Such schools can be state funded or independent.

false consciousness a concept in Marxist theory which refers to situations in which the working class adopt the perspective of the ruling class in society because they are not able to see that they are exploited and oppressed, and do not, therefore, struggle against their oppression. Social institutions such as the media, education and religion are said to promote ruling class ideology that encourages this false view.

feminisation of education the process by which it is suggested that education has become associated with feminine qualities.

focal concerns a term used by Miller to describe the values of working-class boys, which include smartness and toughness.

formal curriculum the way learning is organised in schools through timetabled subjects (see also hidden curriculum).

formal-learning-type skills the kind of skills encouraged by formal education. For example, based on reading and writing.

formula funding a system of funding schools based on a formula whereby schools receive additional funding for every extra pupil enrolled.

foundation subjects subjects which are part of the national curriculum but which are not core subjects, for example history, PE or modern languages.

free schools a new type of school which are set up by parents, charities or faith groups but which are funded by central government. Free schools have greater freedom to design their own curriculum and run their own affairs than most state schools.

gender apartheid economic and social sexual discrimination against individuals because of their gender or sex. It is a system enforced by using either physical or legal practices to relegate individuals to subordinate positions.

gender parity index (GPI) a measure of the ratio of girls to boys enrolled at different levels of education.

gender socialisation the process by which males and females learn attitudes and behaviour regarded as appropriate to their gender roles.

General National Vocational Qualifications (GNVQs) A form of vocational qualification relating to general occupational areas, rather than any specific job, e.g. business studies or health and social care. There were two levels of GNVQ, namely the Intermediate level (equivalent to four General Certificates of Secondary Education) and Advanced level (equivalent to two Advanced-level General Certificates of Education).

global organised crime this term describes criminal activities pursued by organised groups which cross national borders, such as the trafficking of drugs, people and arms.

global village refers to the idea that physical distance is much less of an issue in communication between people, which gives people the ability to create and maintain much stronger social relationships.

globalisation the compression of time and distance which results in increasing interdependence of societies across the globe resulting in an increasingly global culture, economics and politics

glocalisation the process by which the global and the local become intertwined (a combination of the words 'globalisation' and 'localisation'), used to describe products and services that are both developed and sold to global customers but designed so that they suit the needs of local markets as well, and the way in which local conditions impact on global phenomena.

grammar schools secondary schools which select children on the basis of academic ability using the 11+ exam (see also tripartite system).

grant maintained schools schools which were permitted to opt out of the control of local education authorities and manage their own finances by the Conservative government from 1988 onwards.

green crime this terms usually refers to criminal activity which affects the environment, such as the dumping of toxic waste and the poaching and trafficking of endangered species. additionally, it may be used to refer to legal activities which are seen as harmful to the environment such as deforestation.

habitus a set of cultural expectations which guide individuals in making choices in life and in what is regarded as normal reasonable behaviour. According to Bourdieu it is the habitus of the higher social classes which gives them greater cultural capital (see cultural capital).

hidden curriculum attitudes and behaviour which are taught through the school's organisation and teachers' attitudes rather than through the formal timetabled subjects (see also formal curriculum).

holistic milieu the activities of a group or one-toone that are not part of traditional religion and are run by mind-body-spirit practitioners, such as yoga. They are associated with New Age spirituality and typically happen within their own individual contexts rather than through organised schools or businesses and reflect a desire for self-spirituality and personal experience.

homogenisation whereby culture becomes increasingly similar all over the world, and differences between societies become less noticeable.

hyper-femininity an exaggerated form of femininity associated with concern about hair, makeup, clothing and body shape.

hypermasculinity this refers to an exaggerated form of stereotypical masculine behaviour, emphasising traits such as aggressiveness and toughness.

ideological and repressive state apparatus These terms are used by neo-Marxist Althusser to describe the two ways in which social control is carried out. The RSA is the system of formal control which has an obvious controlling function using force, and includes the police and armed forces. ISAs, such as religion and education, control us more informally, but just as powerfully, using ideology.

ideological state apparatus term used by Althusser to describe agencies such as the education system and mass media which serve to transmit the dominant ideology and help justify the power of the ruling class.

independent schools schools which are not controlled or funded by the state. individualisation term used by Beck to describe the process whereby individuals start to give greater priority to their own needs over norms and duties prescribed by traditional roles in society.

institutional racism this refers to racism within the social processes and practices of an institution. It has been widely applied to the police, in the wake of the McPherson Report on the flawed police investigation into the murder of the black teenager Stephen Lawrence.

interactionism a sociological perspective properly known as symbolic interactionism which focuses on the small-scale interaction between individuals in everyday social situations.

interdependent the way in which people, companies and social groups are becoming increasingly reliant on each other in a variety of different ways.

interpretirism an approach to sociology which advocates using method which allow sociologists to understand the meanings and interpretations of those they study, typically using qualitative methods.

Islamophobia this term refers to prejudice against, hatred towards, or fear of the religion of Islam or Muslims. It is argued that Islamophobia has grown since 9/11 and has been amplified by the media, but may also affect the way the police and courts react to all Asians.

key stages stages in the national curriculum – key stage 1: years 1–3; key stage 2: years 4–6; key stage 3: years 7–9; key stage 4: years 10–11.

labelling a process identified by interactionists by which individuals are categorised or typed usually according to stereotypical characteristics, for example individuals may be labelled as 'criminals' by police officers or as disruptive students; by teachers.

lad culture a form of cultural identity found among young males associated with macho masculinity and a disdain for academic achievement.

ladettes girls and young women who adopt traditionally masculine or laddish styles of behaviour, for example assertiveness, overt sexuality and heavy drinking (see also lad culture).

league tables a system of ranking schools by performance in standard assessment tests and public examinations such as GCSEs and A Levels (see also national curriculum).

learning webs a system advocated by Ivan Ilich whereby people learned from others who had already mastered a skill or form of knowledge rather than qualified teachers. Learners would be introduced to potential teachers via a learning web (see deschooling).

level of illiteracy a measure of the proportion of the population who cannot read and write.

liberation theology a movement in Christian theology, developed mainly by Latin American Roman Catholics, which attempts to address the problems of unjust economic, political, or social conditions.

local education authorities (LEAS) Bodies under the control of local councils with a responsibility for providing education in each local government area.

marginalisation this is a process of social exclusion being pushed to the edges of society. Some social groups are more likely to feel economically, socially and politically marginalised in contemporary society. Left realists link this concept to criminality and deviance, alongside relative deprivation and the formation of subcultures.

market forces see marketisation

market in education see marketisation

marketisation the process whereby educational institutions has been increasingly subjected to competition and encouraged to behave more like private businesses (see also New Right).

master status this concept is most associated with the interactionist Becker, and describes how a (deviant) label can become the controlling and defining interpretation of an individual, through which all the actions that a person performs or has previously performed will be evaluated.

material deprivation a lack of money and the things that money can buy, for example a balanced diet, good housing or materials to help with a child's education such as a computer, books or private tuition.

media convergence the way that a whole range of different kinds of information can be combined and delivered in one format. For example, videos, text and images can all be stored and accessed on one website.

meritocracy a system where the most important and well-rewarded positions in society are allocated according to merit or ability.

metanarrative a term used in postmodernism which, put simply, is a 'big story' that claims to know the truth and to be able to explain everything that happens in society. In sociology, the main theories such as functionalism and Marxism would be described by postmodernists as metanarratives.

military-style policing this refers to the tough, 'conflict' policing favoured as a form of social control and deterrence by some right-wing criminologists. Military-style policing tactics may include more use of weapons such as tasers, plastic bullets, watercannons or guns, and the use of horses and riot gear.

mixed ability teaching organisation of teaching and learning in groups of mixed ability rather than setting or streaming.

moral panic an over-reaction by society to a small problem which is blown out of proportion by the media.

multicultural education an approach to education which emphasises the equal validity and status of all cultures.

multiple victimisation this refers to the idea that particular types of people, such as those in poverty, are more likely to be victims of several different types of crime as a result of their circumstances and vulnerability.

muted group a group such as some women who have no way in which they can communicate with others due to their oppressed and controlled position in society.

myth of underachievement term used by Heidi Mirza to suggest that black girls actually perform well in education and the idea they underachieve is based on negative stereotypes.

nanny state term used by New Right thinkers to describe the idea that the state has taken on too much responsibility for the welfare of individuals.

national curriculum a curriculum all schools were ordered to adopt by the 1988 Education Reform Act. It laid down what was to be learned within compulsory subjects at each of four key stages and established standard assessment tests to measure progress at the end of each stage.

National Vocational Qualifications (NVQs) a framework for vocational qualifications introduced in the 1980s aiming to eventually offer comparable qualifications for all occupational areas at a variety of levels.

neoliberalism a political ideology which advocates that the state should intervene in society and the economy as little as possible and leave the running of society to market forces (see also New Right).

networked global society refers to the idea that in the post-industrial society, the focus is on information as a result of new forms of communication.

new deal a scheme introduced by Labour in 1998 which offered 18–24 year olds who had been out of work for six months support and training to assist them in returning to work.

New Labour a label often applied to the Labour government of Tony Blair (1997–2007) reflecting Blair's rejection of many old Labour Party policies (such as nationalisation of key industries and comprehensive education) and his drive to create a new modernised Labour Party.

New Right a political movement which particularly influenced Conservative government policies from 1979 onwards. It emphasised individualism and self-reliance and the replacement of state planning and control by free markets and competition (see also neoliberalism).

new vocationalism a series of policies introduced by governments from the late 1970s which attempted to strengthen vocational education and training (see vocational education).

official statistics statistics collected by government agencies such as the Department for Education.

Ofsted (Office for Standards in Education) The government body which inspects and reports on the quality of schools, colleges and local authority children's services.

open enrolment a system of allocation to school places whereby parents can in theory apply to any school within their area rather than being confined to the catchment area of a single school.

opium of the people a concept associated with Karl Marx which contends that religion is used by the ruling class to transmit its ideology and has the effect of an opiate which stupefies or dulls the senses and so stops the working class from taking action against their oppression.

over- and under-policing Left realists consider that certain offences and communities are policed too heavily, i.e. 'over-policed', causing a breakdown in community relations with the police and breeding mistrust, whereas other crimes, such as white-collar crime and domestic violence, are 'under-policed' and should be taken much more seriously.

particularistic values values which give priority to personal relationships (see also universalistic values).

police recorded crime statistics officially published statistics which include all the crime recorded by the police in a given period. They are separately recorded for England and Wales, for Scotland and for Northern Ireland.

positivist an approach to sociological research which advocates using similar methods to natural sciences, for example analysis of quantitative data.

post-war consensus a term describing the situation after the Second World War where both main political parties agreed to a substantial range of issues, for example educational policies.

primary and secondary deviance these concepts are used by interactionist Lemert to describe the difference between deviant behaviour which everyone partakes in (primary deviance) and that which is consciously engaged in as an expression of a deviant self-concept (secondary deviance).

privatised religiosity a shift in religious practice and belief that marks a change from public expressions such as church attendance to more individual, private forms.

pro-school subculture a group of pupils in a school who share a common set of attitudes and values involving conformity to school rules and discipline and pursuit of the value of academic success (see also anti-school subculture).

public degradation ceremonies rituals in which deviant individuals are publically shamed or ridiculed. functionalists suggest that such ceremonies are important in reaffirming the norms and values of the majority.

pupil premium a scheme launched by the coalition government in 2011 which gave additional funding to schools for every free school meal child enrolled.

pupil subcultures see pro-school subcultures and anti-school subcultures

racialised expectations expectations of teachers towards pupils based on their ethnic or racial background.

rationalisation a concept associated with Weber which refers to a situation in society where actions are based on rational calculation and efficiency rather than moral, religious or supernatural thinking.

relative autonomy a term used by some neo-Marxists to describe the idea that schools and other institutions, such as the church, are not completely shaped by the needs of employers and the economy but have a degree of independence or autonomy and play their own independent role in maintaining capitalist society.

relative deprivation this concept refers to feelings of deprivation and discontentment which people may experience when they compare themselves and what they have to others in their society. Expectations are not met, which can lead to feelings of frustration and resentment. Left realists link this concept to criminality and deviance, alongside marginalisation and the formation of subcultures.

religion is a feature of almost all human cultures. It can be seen as consisting of a number of different dimensions and may include ideas and beliefs about the origin of the universe and of human destiny.

religions belief refers to the beliefs held by a religious person that concern matters central to their religious beliefs. Religious beliefs often concern significant life events and may be held with particular intensity or devotion.

religiosity refers to the various aspects of religious activity, commitment and belief.

religious faith describes the relationship of trust that a religious person might have with their god, or special book, or with key religious leaders.

religious fundamentalism religious groups who literally interpret a religious text and express the desire to return to a more traditional way of life.

repeat victimisation this refers to the idea that some victims of crime will experience repeat instances of the same crime over a prolonged period, such as victims of abuse or domestic violence.

resistance term used by some neo-Marxists to describe how members of the working class fight back against their subordinate position in the capitalist system.

resistance within accommodation term used by Martin Mac an Ghaill to describe a strategy used by some black students whereby they do not openly resist the authority of teachers but still prefer to organise their own learning as they see fit.

restorative justice This approach to dealing with offenders focuses on addressing the consequences of their actions, and often involves them meeting with the victim to explore the impact of their crime. It would be a policy favoured by left-wing approaches to crime.

restricted code of speech term used by Bernstein to describe a simple shorthand form of speech used where explanation and detail is not necessary, for example in situations of social familiarity (see also elaborated code of speech).

retributive punishment retribution can be viewed as the opposite to rehabilitation and restorative justice techniques, and emphasises the severity of punishment to deter offenders and ensure they are fully punished for their actions. The ultimate retributive punishment would be the death penalty, but also much longer prison sentences and harsher conditions within prisons are favoured by some right-wing criminologists.

reverse colonisation where the colonised (or those who have been colonised in the past) reassert their culture and authority.

risk society term used by Beck to describe contemporary societies which are characterised by greater uncertainty and awareness of risk.

ritualists term used by Tony Sewell to describe a group of students who were outwardly fairly conformist but who had little real commitment to success in education.

role allocation the process of determining (for example by school exams) which individuals are suitable for which positions in society (for example occupations).

secondary modern schools a form of secondary school developed as part of the tripartite system in the 1940s (see tripartite system) offering general education for children who were defined as of average or below average ability by the 11+ exam. Most secondary modern schools converted to comprehensive schools in the 1960s and 1970s (see comprehensive schools).

secondary stage of socialisation the process of learning norms and values which builds on the learning of primary socialisation in families and preparing young people to move into the adult world.

secularisation the decline in religion where religious attendance, practices and beliefs have become less significant in society and the power and influence of religion within society is in decline.

self-concept term used by interactionists to describe the way a person sees themselves often based on how they are defined or labelled by others (see also labelling).

self-report study social research which questions a sample of respondents about crimes or deviant acts in which they have been involved as perpetrators, in a given period.

setting a system of placing pupils in teaching groups according to ability where pupils may be in different sets or abilitygroups for different subjects (see also streaming).

sexism negative or unfounded beliefs and attitudes about people based on their sex or gender.

sexualised hyper-feminine identity a term used by Archer et al to describe an identity adopted by some working class girls involving achieving status through sexual attractiveness and personal appearance than academic success.

shop-floor culture a term used by Paul Willis to describe the culture of male manual workers which he suggests is the basis for the counter-school culture of some working class boys.

situational and environmental crime prevention these terms are sometimes used interchangeably. Situational crime prevention includes specific measures which make particular crimes harder to commit and/ or capture more likely, such as 'target hardening' e.g. security devices to make cars harder to steal. Environmental crime prevention usually refers to wider measures relating to the public environment which can make any deviant behaviour less likely, such as street lighting and the planning of housing estates and shopping centres, creating more 'defensible space'.

social capital a Marxist idea that refers to useful social contacts and networks which can be used to increase a person's economic capital or to gain an advantage in a competitive education system (see also cultural capital and economic capital).

social control the formal and informal ways in which people are persuaded to obey rules and conform. Formal social control is overtly carried out, for example by the government and the Criminal Justice System. Informal social control is less obviously exerted by agencies such as the education system, the family and religion.

social democratic theory an approach to social policy and education which emphasised the role of the state in encouraging social justice and equality of opportunity by providing basic services such as education, health care and social security free and as a right for all.

social exclusion the process by which some members of society are denied or excluded from opportunities available to others, for example progression to higher education or access to well-paid secure employment .

social inequalities refer to the differences in life chances, social capital and power between different groups, which appear to be reflected and reinforced through digital forms of communication.

social media new forms of shared information which involve different types of communication, based on new forms of technology.

social networking sites the latest development in digital media, which enable people to create relationships of all types online, offering immediate contact globally.

social order general conformity to a society or community's shared norms and values, so that society is peaceful and predictable. Sociologists do not always agree about how and why social order is achieved, and in whose interests it works.

social reproduction the process by which new generations of workers are prepared to take their place in capitalist society, typically in a similar social class position to their parents.

social solidarity a functionalist concept that relates to the sense of unity and connectedness that individuals feel towards their society based on shared values and beliefs. Social solidarity is important in establishing social integration and social order.

social variation model an approach which rejects the idea that working class children are culturally deprived or inferior and suggests that the simply have a different culture which is a variation from the dominant upper, middle class culture.

societalisation is associated with the process of secularisation. It refers to the growth of society that happens through modernisation and leads to fragmentation and loss of community. People become disconnected from each other and only interact with society as a whole rather than at local level and this undermines religion which is traditionally organised through local groups.

special schools schools which cater specifically for pupils with special needs (SEN) for whom education in mainstream schools is considered unsuitable. These may include pupils with physical disabilities, such as blindness. or severe learning difficulties.

specialist schools a type of secondary school which emphasises a subject specialism in their curriculum, for example technology, business or arts. They may select up to 10 per cent of their pupils by aptitude in this subject area. Most have now converted to become academies.

spectacular subcultures his term describes the highly visible and often confrontational youth subcultures, particularly found in the 1960s and 70s such as mods and punks, which were seen by neo-Marxists as a form of resistance against social class inequality and Capitalism.

sponsored academies type of academy whereby a school deemed to be failing is sponsored by another school or chain of schools responsible for supporting the new academy and ensuring its success in place of the local education authority.

standard assessment tests (SATs) tests which originally took place at the end of each key stage of the national curriculum in order to measure the level of pupils' progress. SATs now only take place at the end of key stage 2 and at the end of key stage 4 (in the form of GCSEs).

status frustration a term, used by Albert Cohen, to describe how some young people are unable to achieve status in society by conventional means (for example success in education) so may turn toward anti-school or even criminal behaviour as an alternative means of achieving status.

streaming a system of placing pupils in teaching groups according to ability where pupils are in the same stream or ability group for every subject (see also setting).

subterranean values this concept, used by Matza, describes the 'deviant' values that we all have, such as risk-taking, danger, aggression and greed. These are not peculiar to criminals, but the majority of people may control their expression of these values or express them in more socially acceptable ways.

Sure Start a scheme set up the Labour government in 1998 with the aim of giving children the best possible start in life through improvement of childcare, early education, health and family support.

technical schools a form of secondary school specialising in technical education which was part of the tripartite system from the 1940s onwards. Few technical schools were built meaning that in most areas it was in reality a bipartite system (see tripartite system).

techniques of neutralisation Matza argues that these are ways in which individuals justify deviant behaviour to themselves and others, despite knowing that it is wrong. They may include a 'denial of responsibility' (blaming others) and a 'denial of harm' (claiming that no-one suffered).

the chivalry thesis/ factor this term suggests that a 'chivalrous' or paternalistic attitude exists within the male-dominated criminal justice system towards women, which can lead to female offenders receiving more lenient treatment.

the dark figure a term referring to crime which has taken place in a given period but which does not appear in the official statistics, because it has not been recognised, reported or recorded.

the square of crime this is a concept developed by left realists to demonstrate the importance of understanding any crime from various angles/ perspectives, including the view of the offender and the formal agencies of control, but also the societal reaction and the victim's perspective.

theodicy of disprivilege the religious explanation and justification for social inequality and deprivation that proposes that there will be rewards in heaven as compensation for poverty on earth.

Third Way an idea proposed by Tony Blair that New Labour should pursue policies which were neither socialist nor capitalist but which represented a Third Way between these two extremes.

totem an object or animal, usually from the natural world, that is adopted as an emblem by a particular group or society as it is believed to hold spiritual significance.

Transnational Corporations (TNCs) large companies who conduct their business in various parts of the world, buying and selling simultaneously around the globe.

tripartite system the selective system of secondary education operating in most parts of England and Wales from the 1940s to the 1970s. Children were selected for one of three types of schools by the 11+ exam (see grammar schools, technical schools and secondary modern schools). From 1965 onwards the tripartite system was gradually replaced by comprehensive schools.

typed the categorisation of students by teachers into types based on their behaviour or characteristics.

universalistic values values which apply equally to all members of society (see also particularistic values).

value added a measure of how far pupils progress between the end of one stage in education and the end of the next.

victim survey social research which questions a sample of respondents about crimes of which they have been victims, in a given period.

virtual community online groups of people who share interests and build relationships without necessarily being physically near to one another.

Vocational A Levels a new name for Advanced General National Vocational Qualifications.

vocational education education which focuses on developing skills which are directly relevant to the world of work (see also new vocationalism).

Vocational GCSEs a new name for Intermediate General National Vocational Qualifications.

wastage of ability the idea that many working-class children's talents and abilities are not recognised or fully used by the education system.

white-collar crime this term is often used to refer to crime committed by professionals in the course of their employment. However, it is also sometimes used to include the criminal behaviour of entire companies or industries.

women's movement a feminist movement which reached its height in the 1970s. It aimed to fight for equality between men and women in all areas of social life.

Youth Training Scheme a scheme set up in 1983 by the Conservative government to provide one year of training with employers for unemployed 16 and 17 year olds with the aim of reducing youth unemployment.

zero tolerance This term is associated with right realists such as Wilson, and refers to a crime reduction strategy by which small misdemeanours and incivilities are cracked down on and punished, with the aim of creating a culture where the rules are respected and everyone adheres to them, preventing more serious crimes from being considered.

References

Abbas, T. (2004), 'After 9/11: British South Muslims, Islamophobia, multiculturalism and the state', *American Journal of Islamic Social, Sciences*, 21(3): 26-8

Adams, R. (2013), 'Working-class students shun top universities, says study' *The Guardian*, 13 November

Adler, F., (1975), *Sisters in Crime: The Rise of the New Female Criminal*, New York: McGraw-Hill Agnew, R. (2006), *Pressured into crime*, Los Angeles: Roxbury

Aldridge, A. (2013), *Religion in the Contemporary World – A Sociological Introduction*, Cambridge – Polity Press

Almond, G., Scott Appleby, R., & Sivan, E., (2003), *Strong Religion – The Rise of Fundamentalisms Around the World*, Chicago – University of Chicago Press

Althusser, L. (1970), 'Ideology and Ideological State Apparatuses', in Althusser, L. (1977), *Lenin and Philosophy and other Essays*, London: New Left Books

Althusser, L. (1972), 'Ideology and ideological state apparatus – Notes towards an investigation' in Cosin, B.R. (ed.), *Education, Structure and Society*, Harmondsworth – Penguin

Anderson, E. (1990), *Streetwise*, Chicago: University of Chicago Press

Archer, L. and Francis, B. (2007), *Understanding Minority Ethnic Achievement – Race, Gender, Class and 'Success'*. London – Routledge

Archer, L. Halsall, A. and Hollingworth, S. (2007), 'Class, gender, (hetero)sexuality and schooling – paradoxes within working-class girls' engagement with education and post-16 aspirations', *British Journal of the Sociology of Education* 28 –2, pp. 165–180

Ark. [www.arkschools.org, accessed September 2015]

Arnett, G. (2014), 'A-level results 2014: the full breakdown', *The Guardian*, 14 August 2014

Arnott, M. (1999), *Closing the Gender Gap – Postwar Education and Social Change*, Cambridge – Polity Press

Ashworth, J., & Farthing, I. (2007), 'Churchgoing in the UK', Middlesex – Tearfund

Badawi, L. (1994), 'Islam', in Holm, J., *Women in Religion*, (pp. 84–112), London, Pinter

Bagdikian, B. (2004), The New Media Monopoly, Boston: Beacon Press

Baird, A. (2012), 'Negotiating pathways to manhood: rejecting gangs and violence in Medellín's Periphery', *Journal of Conflictology,* 3 (1) p. 30–41

Ball, S. (2008), *The Education Debate*, Bristol – Policy Press

Ball, S. (2013), 'Free schools – our education system has been dismembered in pursuit of choice' *The Guardian*, 23 October

Barker, E. (1984), *The Making of a Moonie*, Oxford – Blackwell

Bartlett, S. and Burton, D. (2012), *Introduction to Education Studies*, London – Sage

Beck, U. (1992), *Risk Society – Towards a New Modernity*, London – Sage

Becker, H. (1966), *Outsiders: Studies in the Sociology of Deviance*, New York: The Free Press

Becker, H. P. (1950), *Through Values to Social interpretation – Essays on Social Contexts, Actions, Types and Prospects*, California – Duke University Press

Becker, H. P. (1950), *Through Values to Social Interpretation*, Durham, N.C. – Duke University Press

Berger, P. (1969), *A Rumour of Angels – Modern Society and the Rediscovery of the Supernatural*, Garden City – Doubleday Anchor

Berger, P. (1979), *The Heretical Imperative – Contemporary Possibilities of Religious Affirmation*, New York – Harper Collins

Bernstein, B. (1961), 'Social class and linguistic development – a theory of social learning' in Halsey, A.H., Floud, J. and Anderson, C.A. (eds.), *Education, Economy and* Society, New York – The Free Press

Bernstein, B. (1970), 'A socio-linguistic approach to social learning' in Worsley, P. (ed.), *Modern Sociology – Introductory Readings* (Harmondsworth – Penguin)

Bernstein, B. (1971), 'Education cannot compensate for society' in Cosin, B.R. et al (eds.), *School and Society* (London – Routledge and Kegan Paul)

Bernstein, B. (1972), 'Language and social context' in Giglioli, P. (ed.), *Language and Social Context*, Harmondsworth – Penguin

Bernstein, B. (1973), *Class, Codes and Control*, London – Paladin

Berry, R. (2011), 'Older people and the internet: towards a system map of digital exclusion', London: The International Longevity Centre

Bibby, R. (2009), 'Canada's data-less debate about religion – The precarious role of research in identifying implicit and explicit religion', Alberta – Presented at the Annual Meeting of the Canadian Society for the Study of Religion Vancouver – June 2008

Bingham, J. (2014), 'Churches are best social melting pots in modern Britain', *The* Telegraph, London – Continuum

Bjorklund, D. (1998), *Interpreting the Self: Two Hundred Years of American Autobiography, Chicago*: The University of Chicago Press.

Bjornberg, U. & Dahlgren, L. (2003), *Policy – The case of Sweden*, York – University of York

Blanden, J. and Gregg, P. (2004), 'Family income and educational attainment – a review of approaches and evidence for Britain', *Oxford Review of Economic Policy*, 20 (2). pp. 245 – 263

Boellstorff, T. (2008), *Coming of Age in Second Life: An Anthropologist Explores the Virtually Human,* Princeton: Princeton Press

Bonger, W. (1916), *Criminality and Economic Conditions*, Boston: Little, Brown & company

Bourdieu, P. (1971), 'Intellectual field and creative project' and 'Systems of education and systems of thought' in Young, M. (ed.), *Knowledge and Control*, London – Collier-Macmillan

Bourdieu, P. (1974), 'The school as a conservative force – scholastic and cultural inequalities' in Eggleston, J. (ed.), *Contemporary Research in the Sociology of Education*, London – Methuen

Bourdieu, P. (1984), *Distinction – A Social Critique of the Judgement of Taste*, London – Routledge and Kegan Paul

Bourgois, P. (1995), *In Search of Respect*, Cambridge: CUP

Bowles, S. and Gintis, H. (1976), *Schooling in Capitalist America*, London – Routledge and Kegan Paul

Bowling, B. and Phillips, C. (2006), 'Young black people and the criminal justice system', Submission to the House of Commons Home Affairs Committee Inquiry October 2006

Bowling, B., Parmar, A. and Phillips, C. (2003), 'Policing ethnic minority communities' in Newburn, T. (ed.), *Handbook of Policing*, Devon: Willan Publishing

Box, S. (1983), *Power, Crime and Mystification*, London: Tavistock Publications

Boyle, R. (2005), Press the red button now: television and technology,' *Sociology Review*, Nov

Boyle, R. (2007), The 'now' media generation, *Sociology Review*, September

Braithwaite, J. (1989), *Crime, Shame and Reintegration*, Cambridge: Cambridge University Press

Braithwaite, J. (2004), 'Restorative justice and deprofessionalization', in *The Good Society* 13 (1), 28–31

Brierley, P. (2006), *Pulling Out of the Nosedive. A Contemporary Picture of Churchgoing – What the 2005 English Church Census Reveals*, Tonbridge – Christian Research

BRIN. (2015, March), 'Religious voting intentions', [www.brin.ac.uk]

British Council (2014), *Can higher education solve Africa's job crisis? Understanding graduate employability in Sub-Saharan Africa*, [British Council website]

Bruce, S. (1995), *Religion in Modern Britain*, Oxford – Oxford University Press

Bruce, S. (2008), *Fundamentalism*. Cambridge – Polity Press

Bruce, S. (2011), *Secularisation – In Defence of an Unfashionable Theory*, Oxford – OUP

Bruce, S., & Trzebiatowska, M. (2012), *Why are Women more Religious than Men?,* Oxford – Oxford University Press

Bruce, S. and Voas, D. (2010), 'Vicarious religion – an examination and critique'. *Journal of Contemporary Religion*, 25(2), 243-259

Burns, J. and Bracey, P. (2001), 'Boy's underachievement – Issues, challenges and possible ways forward', *Westminster Studies in Education,* 24, pp 155–66

Callender, C. and Jackson, J. (2005), 'Does the fear of debt deter students from higher education?' *Journal of Social Policy*, 34 (4). pp. 509–540.

Campbell, A. (1981), *Girl Delinquents*, Oxford: Blackwell

Capra, F., (1982), *The Turning Point – Science, Society and the Rising Culture*, New York – Bantam Books

Carlen, P. (1983), *Women's Imprisonment*, London: Routledge and Kegan Paul

Carlen, P. (1987), 'Out of care into custody' in Carlen, P. and Worrall, A. (eds.), *Gender, Crime and Justice*, Milton Keynes: Open University Press, pp. 126 – 160. 1987

Carrabine, E., Iganski, P., Lee, M., K. Plummer, K. and South, N. (2004), *Criminology: A Sociological Introduction*, London: Routledge

Casanova, J. (2003), 'Beyond European and American exceptionalism – towards a global perspective, in Davie, G., Heelas, P., & Woodhead, L., *Predicting Religion – Christian, Secular and Alternative Futures* (pp. 17–29), Aldershot – Ashgate

Castells, M. (2000), *End of Millenium* (2nd edn.) Oxford: Blackwell

Castells, M. (2000a), Materials for an exploratory theory of the network society. *British Journal of Sociology*, 51(1) (January/March 2000), p. 5–24

Castells, M. (2000b), *The Rise Of The Network Society*, (2nd ed.). U.S.: Blackwell Publishing

Cavadino, M. and Dignan, J. (2001), *The Penal System: An Introduction*, 3rd edn., London: Sage

Center for the Study of Global Christianity, (2013, June), 'Christianity in its global vontext, 1970–2020 – Society, Religion, and Mission', Massechussets – Gordon-Conwell Theological Seminary

Centre for Social Justice, (2013), 'The Centre for Social Justice Slavery Report, UK, 2013', [http://www.centreforsocialjustice.org.uk]

Chambliss, W. (1973), 'The saints and the roughnecks', in *Society*, 11, 1, 24–31, Nov-Dec 73

Chambliss, W. (1975), 'Toward a political economy of crime', in *Theory and Society*, 1975, 2 (1): 149–170

Chan, J. (1997), *Changing Police Culture: Policing in a Multicultural Society*. Melbourne: Cambridge University Press.

Charlesworth, S. (1999), *A Phenomenology of Working-class Experience*, Cambridge: Cambridge University Press

Chesney-Lind (1989), 'Girls, crime and woman's place: towards a feminist model of female delinquency', *Crime and Delinquency*, 35 (1), 5–29

Chesney-Lind, M. (1997), *The Female Offender: Girls, Women and Crime*, University of Michigan: Sage

Chowdry, H., Crawford, C. and Goodman, A. (2010), *Outcomes in the secondary school years – evidence from the Longitudinal Study of Young People in England*, York – Joseph Rowntree Foundation

Christ, C. (1997), *Rebirth of the Goddess: Finding meaning in feminist spirituality*, Abingdon - Routledge

Cicourel, A. (1969), *The Social Organisation of Juvenile Justice*, New York: Wiley

Clarke, R.V.G., (1980), 'Situational crime prevention: theory and practice', in *British Journal of Criminology*, 20 (2): 136–47

Clements, B. (2015, June 3), 'Socio-demographic groups and religious affiliation in Britain', [www.brin.ac.uk]

Cloward, R. and Ohlin, L., (1961), *Delinquency and Opportunity*, Glencoe: The Free Press

Cochrane, A., and Pain, K. (2000), 'A globalising society' in Held, D. (ed.), *A Globalising World: Culture, Economics, Culture*, London: Routledge

Cochrane, K., (2013), 'The fourth wave of feminism: meet the rebel women', *The Guardian*, 10 December 2013

Coffey, A. (2001), *Education and Social Change*, Buckingham – Open University Press

Cohen, A., (1955), *Delinquent Boys: the Culture of the Gang*, New York: The Free Press

Cohen, N., (2011), 'Define gender gap? Look up Wikipedia's contributor list', *The New York Times*, 30 January 2011

Cohen, P., (1972), 'Sub-cultural conflict and working class community', in *Working Papers in Cultural Studies*. No.2. Birmingham: University of Birmingham

Cohen, R, and Kennedy, P. (2000), *Global Sociology*, London: MacMillan

Cohen, S., (1985), *Visions of Social Control*, Cambridge: Polity Press

Collins, R., (2005), *The Sociology of Philosophies: A Global Theory of Intellectual Change*, Harvard University Press

Colman, A.M. and Gorman, L.P. (1982), 'Conservatism, dogmatism, and authoritarianism in British Police Officers', *Sociology*, 1982, vol. 16, pp. 1–11.

Colman, P. G., (2011), *Belief and Ageing – Spiritual Pathways in Later Life*, Bristol – Policy Press

Connor, H. Tyers, C. Modood, T. Hillage, J. (2004), *Why the Difference? A closer look at higher education minority ethnic students and graduates*, Research Report RR552, London – Department for Education and Skills

Cooper, M., (2013), 'Why are so many women 'seen but not heard' on social media?', *The Telegraph*, 29 October 2-13

Cornford, J. and Robins, K. (1999)'New media' in J Stokes and A Reading (eds.) *The Media in Britain: Current debates and developments*, London: Macmillan

Cornwall, M. Albrecht, S. L. Cunnigham, P. H. and Picther, B. L. (1998), 'The dimensions of religiosity – a conceptual model with an empirical test', in J. T. Duke, *Latter-day Saint Social Life – Social Research on the LDS Church and its Members*, (pp. 203–230), Prov, Utah – Brigham Young University

Croall, H. (1993), 'White collar crime: scams, cons and rip offs' in *Sociology Review*, November 1993

Croall, H. (2001a), *Understanding White Collar Crime*. Buckingham: Open University Press.

Cropwood Round-Table Conference, December 1980, Issue 13 of the Cropwood Conference Series.

Cupitt, D. (1984), *The Sea of Faith*, London – BBC Books

Dahlgreen, W. (2013, June 24), 'British youth reject religion', [yougov.co.uk]

Davidson, K. and Alexis, J. (2012), *Education – A pathway to success for black children – a guide to overcoming barriers to educational excellence*, London – KAD Publishing

Davie, G. (1994), *Religion in Britain since 1945 – Believing without belonging*, Oxford – Balckwell

Davie, G. (2015), *Religion in Britain – A Persistent Paradox*, Chichester – WILEY Blackwell

Davie, G. and Vincent, J. (1998), 'Religion and old age', in *Ageing and Society*. 18 (1), p. 101-110

Davie, G. and Walter, T. (1998), 'The religiosity of women in the modern West. *The British Journal of Sociology*, 49 (4), p. 640–660

Davis, K. (1961), 'Prostitution, in Merton', in Merton, R.K. and Nisbet, R.A., (eds.) *Contemporary Social Problems*, New York: Harcourt Brace Jovanovich

Davis, K. and Moore, W.E. (1945), 'Some principles of social stratification', *American Sociological Review,* 10

Davis, M. (1994), 'Beyond Blade Runner: Urban Control – the ecology of fear', Open Magazine Pamphlet Series, New York: The New Press

Dawson, A. (2011), *Sociology of Religion*, London – SCM Press

Day, A. (2007), 'Believing in belonging – religion returns to sociology', Mainsteam. Network

Day, A. (2009), 'Believing in belonging – an ethnography of young people's constructions of belief', [www.esrc.ac.uk]

De Vaus, and McAllister. (1987), 'Gender Differences in Religion – A test of the structural location theory'. *American Sociological Review*, 52, p. 472–481

Denscombe, M. (2001), 'Critical incidents and the perception of health risks: the experiences of young people in relation to their use of alcohol and tobacco', *Health, Risk and Society*, 3 (3), 293–306.

Department for Children, Schools and Families (2009), *Deprivation and Education*, London – DfCSF

Department for Children, Schools and Families (2009a), *Breaking the link between disadvantage and low attainment – Everyone's business*, London – DfCSF

Department for Education (2010), *The Impact of Sure Start Local Programmes on Five Year Olds and their Families*, London – DfE

Department for Education (2011), *Youth Cohort Study & Longitudinal Study of Young People in England – The Activities and Experiences of 19 year olds – England 2010,*

Department for Education (2013), *Level 2 and 3 attainment by young people in England measured using matched Administrative Data: Attainment by Age 19 in 2012*, London – DfE

Department for Education (2014), *GCSE and Equivalent Attainment by Pupil Characteristics in England, 2012/13*, London – DfE

Dobash, R.P. and Dobash, R. E. (1979), *Violence Against Wives*, New York: The Free Press

Dunne, M. and Gazeley, L. (2008), 'Teachers, social class and underachievement', *British Journal of the Sociology of Education* 29 –5 pp.451–463

Durkheim, E. (1958), *The Rules of Sociological Method*, translated by Sarah A. Solovay and John H. Mueller, Glencoe: The Free Press

Durkheim, E. (1961), *Moral Education*, Glencoe – Free Press

Durkheim, E. (1984), *The Division of Labour in Society*, New York – The Free Press

Durkheim, E. (2008), *The Elementary Forms of the Religious Life*, Oxford – Oxford University Press

Dustmann, C. Machin, S. and Schönberg, U. (2008), *Educational Achievement and Ethnicity in Compulsory Schooling*, London – Centre for Research and Analysis of Migration

Elliot, A. (2001), *Concepts of the Self*, Malden: Blackwell Publishers Inc.

Erikson, K (1966), *Wayward Puritans: A Study in the Sociology of Deviance*, New York: John Wiley and Sons

Evans, G. (2007), *Educational Failure and Working Class White Children in Britain*, Basingstoke – Palgrave Macmillan

Fairweather, N. and Rogerson, S. (2003), 'The Problems of Global Cultural Homogenisation', *Info, Comm & Ethics in Society*, 1, 7–12

Faludi, S (1999), *Stiffed: The Betrayal of American Man*, London: Chatto & Windus

Farrington and Morris (1983), 'Sex, sentencing and reconviction', *British Journal of Criminology*, 23: 229–248

Farrington, D. (1989), 'The origins of crime: the Cambridge study of delinquent development', Home Office Research and Planning Unit, Research Bulletin, no. 27, London, HMSO

Farrington, D. (2001), 'What has been learned from self-reports about criminal careers and the causes of offending?', Home Office online report

Farrington, D. P. (1990), 'Age, period, cohort and offending' in Gottfredson, D.M and Clarke, R.V. (eds.) *Policy and Theory in Criminal Justice*, Aldershot: Avebury

Farrington, D. P. (2000a), 'Adolescent Violence: Findings and Implications from the Cambridge Study' in Boswell, G., (ed.), *Violent Children and Adolescents: Asking the Question Why* (pp. 19–35). London: Whurr

Farrington, D. P. Gallagher, B., Morley, L., St.Ledger, R. and West, D. J. (1990), 'Minimizing attrition in longitudinal research: methods of tracing and securing cooperation in a 24-year follow-up study' in Magnusson, D, and Bergman, L., (eds.) *Data Quality in Longitudinal Research*. Cambridge: Cambridge University Press.

Farrington, D. P. Knapp, W. S., Erickson, B. E. & Knight, B. J. (1980), 'Words and Deeds in the Study of Stealing'. *Journal of Adolescence*, 3, 35–49.

Farrington, D.P (1986), 'Age and Crime' in Tonry, M. and Morris, N. (eds.) *Crime and justice: An Annual Review of Research*, Vol. 7, pp189–250

Feinstein, L. (2003), 'Inequality in the early cognitive development of children in the 1970s cohort', *Economica*, 70, 277

Ferguson, C., & Hussey, D. (2010), '2008–09 Citizenship Survey – race, religion and equalities topic report', London – Communities and Local Government

Ferrell, J. (1999), 'Cultural Criminology', *Annual Review of Sociology*, 1999, 25: 395–418

Feuerbach, L. (2008), *The Essence of Christianity*, New York – Dover Publications

Field, C. (2010), 'Muslim opinions and opinions of Muslims – British experiences', [www.brin.ac.uk]

Field, C. (2015, August), 'Religion and Social Capital'. Retrieved from British Religion in Numbers, [www.brin.ac.uk]

Filmer, D. (2007), *Education inequalities around the world*. [Commonwealth Education Partnerships]

Finn, D. (1987), *Training without Job*, London – Macmillan

FitzGerald, M. and Sibbitt, R. (1997), 'Ethnic monitoring in police forces: a beginning', Home Office Research Study 173. London: Home Office.

Foster, P., Gomm, R. and Hammersley, M. (1996), *Constructing Educational Inequality*, London – Falmer Press

Foucalt, M. (1977), *Dispiline and Punish: the Birth of the Prison*, translated by Alan sheridan, London: Allen Lane, Penguin

Francis, B. (2000), *Boys, Girls and Achievement – Addressing the Classroom* Issues. London – Routledge/Falmer

Francis, B. (2005), *The Impact of Gender Constructions on Pupils' Learning and Educational Choices –*

Francis, B. and Skelton, C. (2005), *Reassessing Gender and Achievement*, London – Routledge/Falmer

Francis, B. Hutchings, M. and De Vries, R. (2014), *Chain Effects – The impact of academy chains on low income* students, London – Sutton Trust

Francis, L. (1997), 'The psychology of gender differences in religion', *Religion*, 27(1), p. 81–96

Franko Aas, K. (2007), *Globalization and Crime*, London: Sage

Friedrichs, D. (1996), *Trusted Criminals: White-collar Criminals in Contemporary Society*, Belmont: Wadsworth

Fuller, M. (1984), 'Black girls in a London comprehensive school' in Hammersley, M. and Woods, P. (eds.) *Life in School, the Sociology of Pupil Culture*, Milton Keynes – Open University Press

Gaine, C. and George, R. (1999), *Gender, 'Race' and Class in Schooling – a New Introduction*, London – Falmer Press

Gallie, D. (1994), 'Are the unemployed an underclass? Some evidence from the ocial Change and Economic Life Initiative', in *Sociology* 28(3)

Gallup, & Crabtree, S. (2010, August 31), 'Religiosity Highest in World's Poorest Nations', [www.gallup.com]

Garside, J., (2014), 'Ofcom: Six year olds understand digital technology better than adults', *The Guardian*, 7th August 2014, [accessed 1st September 2015]

Gastrow, P. (2013), 'How big is the threat? Scope and patterns of organized crime', Keynote address from 'Being Tough is not Enough: Curbing Transnational Organised Crime', International Expert Conference 28 February – 1 March 2013, Friedrich-Ebert-Stiftung, Berlin

Gewirtz, S. Ball, S.J. and Bowe, R. *Markets, Choice and Equity in Education*, Buckingham – Open University Press

Giddens, A. (1990), *The Consequences of Modernity*, Cambridge: Polity

Giddens, A. Duneier, M. and Appelbaum ,R, (2005), *Introduction to Sociology*, New York: W.W Norton and Company

Gillborn, D. (1990), *Race, Ethnicity and Education – Teaching and Learning in Multi-Ethnic Schools*, London – Unwin-Hyman/Routledge

Gillborn, D. (2008), *Racism and Education – Coincidence or Conspiracy?*, London – Routledge

Gillborn, D. (2011), 'There's no black in the baccalaureate' *The Guardian*, 12 June 2011

Gillborn, D. and Youdell, D. (2000), *Rationing Education – Policy, Practice, Reform and Equity*, Buckingham – Open University Press

Gillborn, D. and Youdell, D. (2001), 'The new IQism – intelligence, "ability" and the rationing of education' in Demaine, J. (ed.), *Sociology of Education Today*, Basingstoke – Palgrave

Gilroy, P. (1982), 'The myth of Black vriminality' in *The Socialist Register*, London: Merlin Press

Gilroy, P. (1982a), 'Police and thieves' in Centre for Contemporary Cultural Studies, *The Empire Strikes Back – Race and Racism in '70s Britain*, London: Hutchinson

Gilroy, P. (1982b), 'Steppin' out of Babylon – race, class and autonomy' in Centre for Contemporary Cultural Studies, *The Empire Strikes Back – Race and Racism in '70s Britain*, London: Hutchinson

Glock, C. Y., & Stark, R. (1965), *Religion and Society in Tension*, Chicago – Rand McNally

Glynn, M. (2014), *Black Men, Invisibility, and Desistance from Crime: Towards a Critical Race Theory*, Abingdon: Routledge

Goldstraw-White, J. (2010), 'It's not like I'm a real criminal' in *Sociology Review*, November 2010

Gordon, D. (1973), 'Capitalism, class and crime in America' in *Crime and Delinquency* 19(2) London: Sage

Granovetter, M. (1973), The strength of weak ties, *American Journal of Sociology,* 78,p.1360–1380.

Gunter, A. (2008), 'Growing up bad: Black youth, `road' culture and badness in an East London neighbourhood' in *Crime, Media, Culture*, December 2008 4: 349–366

Gwakh, B., (2011), 'The Taliban's internet strategy', [http://www.rferl.org] September 9 2011

Hadaway, C. K., Marler, P. L., & Chaves, M. (1993), 'What the polls don't show – a closer look at chucrh attendance', *American Sociological Review*, 58 (6), p. 741–752

Hall, S. and Jefferson, T. (eds.), *Resistance Through Rituals*, London: Routledge

Hall, S., Critcher, C., Jefferson, T., Clarke, J. and Roberts, B. (1978), *Policing the Crisis: Mugging, the State, and Law and Order*, London: MacMillan

Hall. S. (1999), 'From Scarman to Stephen Lawrence' in *History Workshop Journal*, 48 (1999), 187–97

Halsey, A.H., Floud, J. and Anderson, C.A. (1961), *Education, Economy and Society*, New York – The Free Press

Halsey, A.H., Heath, A. and Ridge, A.M. (1980), *Origins and Destinations – Family, Class and Education in Modern Britain*, Oxford – Clarendon

Hanmer, J. and Saunders, S. (1984), 'Well-founded fear: a community study of violence to women', London: Hutchinson

Hannan, J. (2001), *Improving Boys' Performance*, Dunstable – Folens

Hargreaves, D. (1967), *Social Relations in a Secondary School*, London – Routledge and Kegan Paul

Hargreaves, D., Hester, S. and Mellor, F. (1975), *Deviance in Classrooms*, London – Routledge and Kegan Paul

Hart, W. E. (2011), 'Mind, Self and Facebook', [www.academia.edu], accessed 28 September 2015

Hartley-Parkinson, R. (2015), 'How religious are you? UK among least religious countries in the world', *metro.co.uk* 13 April 2015

Hasan, M. (2012), 'Ten things they don't tell you about academies', *New Statesman* 22 March

Hedderburn, C. and Gunby, C. (2013), 'Diverting Women from custody: the importance of understanding sentencers' perspectives', *Probation Journal*, Vol. 60. No.4, pp. 32–45

Heelas, P. (1996), *The New Age Movement – Religion, Culture and Society in the Age of Postmodernity*, Oxford – Blackwell

Heelas, P., & Woodhead, L. (2005), *The Spiritual Revolution*, Oxford – Blackwell

Heidensohn, F. (1986), 'Models of justice: Portia or Persephone? Some thoughts on equality, fairness and gender in the field of criminal justice', *International Journal of the Sociology of Law*, 1986, 14(3): 298–298

Heidensohn, F. (1996), *Women and Crime* (2nd ed.), Basingstoke: MacMillan

Hirschi, T. (1969), Causes of delinquency, Berkeley: University of California Press

Hobbs, D. and Dunnighan, C. (1998), 'Glocal organized crime: context and pretext' in Ruggiero, V. et al (eds.) *The New European Criminology: Crime and Social Order*, London: Routledge

Holdaway, S. (1996), *The Racialisation of British Policing*, Basingstoke: Macmillan.

Holland, D., Liadze, I., Rienzo, C. and Wilkinson, D. (2013), *BIS Research Paper No. 110, The relationship between graduates and economic growth across countries*, London – Department for Business Innovation and Skills

Hollingworth, S. (2014), 'Race, class and teenage subcultures' 26 March, [http –//www.racecard.org.uk]

Home Affairs Select Committee (2007), 'Young black people and the criminal justice system', House of Commons

Hood, R. (1992), *Race and Sentencing: A Study in the Crown Court*, Oxford: Clarendon Press

Horst, H. and Miller, D. (2012), *Digital Anthropology*, London: Bloomsbury

Hough, J.M. and Mayhew, P. (1985), 'Taking account of crime: Key findings from the second British Crime Survey', HMSO

House of Lords Constitutional Committee, (2009), 'Surveillance: the citizen and the State', The Stationary Office

Howard, R. (2011), *Digital Jesus: The Making of a New Christian Fundamentalist Community on the Internet*, New York: NYU Press

Hudson, B.A. (1997), 'Social Control', in Maguire, M. Morgan, R. and Reiner, R. (eds.) *The Oxford Handbook of Criminology* (2nd ed.), Oxford: Clarendon Press

Hughes, D. (1999), 'Pimps and predators on the internet, globalizing the sexual exploitation of women and children', Rhode Island: University of Rhode Island

Hunt, S. (2001), *Christian Millenarianism*, Bloomington – Indiana University Press

Hunt, S. (2005), *Religion and Everyday Life*, Abingdon, Oxon – Routledge

Husserl, E. (1962), Phenomenology and the Foundations of the Sciences, Hingham, MA – Kluwer Boston Inc

Illich, I. (1973), *Deschooling Society*, Harmondsworth – Penguin

IPSOS Mori, 'Big data', [https://ipsos-mori.com/researchareas/digitalresearch/bigdata.aspx [accessed on 1st September 2015]

Ireson, J., Hallam, S. and Hurley, C. (2001), 'Ability grouping in secondary school – effects at key stage 4', London – Institute of Education, University of London

Jackson, C. (2006), *Lads and Ladettes in School – Gender and a Fear of Failure*, Buckingham – Open University Press

Jackson, C. (2006), *Lads and Ladettes in School: Gender and the Fear of Failure*, Maidenhead: Open University Press

Jackson, R. (1989), 'Religious education – from ethnographic research to curriculum development', in Campbell, J. & Little, V., *Humanities in the Primary School*, Lewes – Falmer

Jackson, R. (2012), 'Young people's attitudes towards religious diversity'. [www.religionandsociety.or.uk]

Jackson, R. *et al* (2012), 'Place makes a big difference to young people's attitudes to religious diversity in the UK', [www. religionandsociety.or.uk]

James, J. & Thornton, W. (1980), 'Women's liberation and the female delinquent' in *Journal of Research in Crime and Delinquency*, 17(2), 230–244

Jones, T., Maclean, B. and Young, J. (1986), *The Islington Crime Survey*, Aldershot: Gower

Katz, J. (1988), *Seductions of Crime*, New York: Basic Books

Katz, J. and Jackson-Jacobs, C. (2004), 'The criminologists' gang' in C. Sumner, C. (ed.), *Blackwell Companion to Criminology*. London: Blackwell. Pp.91–124

Kautsky, K. (1953), *Foundations of Christianity*, New York – Russell and Russell

Kingdon, G. and Cassen, R. (2007), *Understanding Low Achievement in English Schools,* Case Paper 118, London – Centre for Analysis of Social Exclusion

Kinsey, R. (1984), 'The Merseyside Crime Survey: First Report', Liverpool: Merseyside County Council

Kirkpatrick, D. (2010), *The Facebook Effect: The Real Inside Story of Mark Zuckerberg and the World's Fastest Growing Company*, Virgin

Klein, D. (1973), 'The etymology of female crime: a review of the literature', in *Issues in Criminology* 1973, 8: 3–30

Labov, W. (1973), 'The logic of nonstandard English' in Keddie, N. (ed) *Tinker, Tailor… The Myth of Cultural Deprivation*, Harmondsworth – Penguin

Laney, D. (2001), '3D Data Management: Controlling Data Volume, Velocity, and Variety', Stamford: META Group

Lawson, T, Heaton, T. and Brown, A. (2010), *Education and Training*, Basingstoke – Palgrave Macmillan

Lea, J. and Young, J. (1982), 'Race and Crime' in *Marxism Today*, August, p. 38–39

Lea, J. and Young, J. (1993), *What is to be done about Law and Order?* London: Pluto Press

Lees, S. (1989), 'Learning to Love; Sexual Reputation, Morality, and the Social Control of Girls' in Cain, M. (ed.), *Growing Up Good: Policing the Behaviour of Girls in Europe*, London: Sage Publications

Lemert, E. (1951), 'Primary and secondary deviance'. *Social Pathology*, New York: McGraw-Hill

Li, N., and Kirkup, G. (2007), 'Gender and Cultural difference in internet use: a study of China and the UK', *Computers and Education* 48(2), Feb London Victoria, (2015), 'LV= Cost of a child: from cradle to college', [http://www.lv.com/upload/IFARebrand- 2009/pdf/2015/jan/coac-report-final.pdf [accessed on 1st September 2015].

Lombroso, C. and Ferrero, W. (1898), *The Female Offender*, New York: D. Appleton & Company

London – DfE Department for Education (2012), *GCSE and Equivalent Attainment by Pupil Characteristics in England, 2010/11*, London – DfE

Lynch, G., & Day, A. (2010, July 22), 'Young people and the cultural performance of belief', [www.religionandsociety.org.uk]

Lyng, S. (2005), *Edgework: the Sociology of Risk-Taking*, New York: Routledge

Mac an Ghaill, M. (1992), *Young, Gifted and Black – Student-Teacher Relations in the Schooling of Black Youth*, Milton Keynes – Open University Press

Mac an Ghaill, M. (1994), *The Making of Men – Masculinities, Sexualities and Schooling*, Milton Keynes – Open University Press

Madge, N., Hemming, P. J., & Stenson, K. (2014), *Youth On Religion – The Development, Negotiation and Impact of Faith and Non-Faith Identity*, Sussex – Routledge

Malinowski, B. (1954), *Magic, Science and Religion and other Essays*, New York – Anchor Books

MarketingProfs, (2012), 'Age not gender drives most social media use' [www.marketingprofs.com, accessed on 5th August 2015]

Marshall, G. (1982), *In Search of the Spirit of Capitalism – An Essay on Max Weber's Protestant Ethic Thesis*, Aldershot, Hampshire – Gregg Revivals

Marshall, T.F. (1998), 'Restorative justice: an overview' in Newburn, T. (ed.) (2009), *Key Readings in Criminology*, Cullompton: Willan Publishing

Marx, K. (1844), 'Introduction to a Contribution to the Critique of Hegel's Philosophy of Right', [www.marxists.org]

Marx, K. (1844, February 10), 'A Contribution to the Critique of Hegel's Philosophy of Right – Introduction', [www.marxists.org]

Matthen, M. (2013), 'The Sikh turban is NOT a religious symbol'. [New APPS – Art, Politics, Philosophy, Science]

Matthews, R. and Young, J. (1992), 'Reflections on realism', in Young, J. and Matthews, R. (eds.) *Rethinking Criminology: The Realist debate*, London: Sage

Mayer, A. E. (2000). A Benign Apartheid – How Gender Apartheid has been Rationalized, *UCLA Journal of International Law and Foreign Affairs*, p. 237

McVie, S. (2004), 'Patterns of deviance underlying the age-crime curve: the long-term evidence', *British Society of Criminology*, Vol. 7. Selected papers from the 2004 British Criminology Conference, Portsmouth July 2004

Mertens, S. and D'Haenens, L., (2010), 'The digital divide among young people in Brussels: Social and cultural influences on ownership and use of digital technologies', *Communications: The European Journal of Communication*, 35(2), p. 187–207

Merton, R.K. (1938), 'Social structure and anomie', in *American Sociological Review* 3, p. 672–682

Messerschmidt, J. (1993), *Masculinities and Crime*, Lanham, Maryland, Rowman and Littlefield

Miliband, R. (1969), *The State in Capitalist Society*, London – Weidenfeld and Nicholson

Miller, A., & Hoffman, J. (1995), 'Risk and religion – an explanation of gender differences in religiosity', *Journal for the Scientific Study of Religion*. 34 (1), p. 63–75

Miller, D. (2011), *Tales from Facebook*, Cambridge: Polity

Miller, W. (1958), 'Lower class culture as a generating milieu of gang delinquency', Journal *of Social Issues*, 14.

Ministry of Justice (2012), 'Statistics on race and the criminal justice system, published under Section 95 of the Criminal Justice Act 1991

Ministry of Justice, (2014), 'Women and the Criminal Justice System 2013', The Stationary Office

Miranda, J. P. (2004), *Marx and the Bible – A Critique of the Philosophy of Oppression*, Oregon – Wipf & Stock

Mirza, H. (1992), *Young, Female and Black*, London – Routledge

Mirza, M., Senthilkumaran, A., & Ja'far, Z. (2007, January 29), 'Living apart together – Britsih Muslims and the paradox of multiculturalism', [Policy Exchange]

Modood, T. (2004), 'Capitals, ethnic identity and educational qualifications', *Cultural Trends*, vol 13, no 2, pp 247–50

Modood, T., Nazroo, J., Smith, P., Virdee, S., & Beishon, S. (1997), 'Ethnic minorities in Britain – diversity and disadvantage', [PSI Policy Studies Institute]

Mosher, D.L. (1991). 'Macho men, machismo, and sexuality', *Annual Review of Sex Research*, 2, 199–247

Mumsnet, (2012), 'Rape and Sexual Assault Survey (21 Feb – 6 March 2012)' [www.mumsnet.com]

Murray, C. (1984), *Losing Ground*, New York: Basic Books

Murray, C. (1990), *The Emerging Underclass*, London: IEA

Murray, C. (2005), 'The advantages of social apartheid', The Sunday Times, 3 April

Murray, C. and Herrnstein, R. (1994), *The Bell Curve*, New York: The Free Press

National Literacy Trust (2012), *Boys' Reading Commission – The report of the All-Party Parliamentary Literacy Group Commission*

Nightingale, C. (1993), *On the Edge*, New York: Basic Books

Norris, P., & Inglehart, R. (2011), *Sacred and Secular – Religion and Politics Worldwide*, Cambridge – CUP

North, A. (2012), 'Successes and challenges in Afghan girls' education' BBC News Asia, 11 October

Ofcom website available online www.ofcom.org.uk (February 17th 2012), [accessed on 1st September 2015]

Office for National Statistics. (2013, April), 'Full story – What does the Census tell us about religion in 2011?', [ons.gov.uk]

Olson. (2013), 'Loss, creativity, and social class', [religionandsociety.org.uk]

Painter, K. and Farrington, D. (1999), 'Street lighting and crime: diffusion of benefits in the Stoke-on-Trent Project', *Crime Prevention Studies*, 10, p. 77–122

Palfreyman, D. (2002), 'Book Reviews – Does Education Matter? Myths about Education and Economic Growth by Alison Wolf' *Policy and Practice in Higher Education*, 6(4)

Palmer, S. (2013), 'Black perspectives on race, crime and justice' in Phillips, C. and Webster, C. (eds.) *New Directions in Race, Ethnicity and Crime*, Oxford: Routledge

Parsons, T. (1961), 'The school as a social system' in Halsey, A.H., Floud, J. and Anderson, C.A. (eds.) *Education, Economy and Society*, New York – The Free Press

Parsons, T. (1965), 'Religious perspectives in Sociology and Social Psychology', in Lessa, W. A., & Vogt, E. Z., *Reader in Comparative Religion – an Anthropological Approach*, 2nd edition, New York – Harper & Row

Parsons, T. and Bales, F.B. (1955), *Family, Socialisation and Interaction Process*, New York: The Free Press

Perfect, D. (2011), 'Briefing Paper 1 – Religion or Belief', Equality and Human Rights Commission

Phillips, C. and Bowling, B. (2002), 'Racism, crime and justice', *Longman Criminology Series*, Longman: Harlow

Pitts, J.(2008), *Reluctant Gangsters: The Changing Face of Youth Crime: The Changing Shape of Youth Crime*, Willan Publishing

Platt, L. (2007), *Poverty and Ethnicity in the UK*, Bristol – Policy Press

Plummer, K. (1979), 'Misunderstanding labelling perspectives', in Downes, D. and Rock, P. (eds.) *Deviant Interpretations*, Oxford: Martin Robertson

Plummer, K. (1996), 'Symbolic interactionism and forms of homosexuality' in *Queer Theory/ Sociology*, Siedman, S. (ed.), Blackwell

Pollak, O. (1950), *The Criminality of Women*, Philadelphia: University of Pennsylvania Press

Potter, G. (2010), 'What is green criminology?' in *Sociology Review*, November 2010

Presdee, M. (2002), *Cultural Criminology and the Carnival of Crime*, London: Routledge

Procek, E. (1980), 'Psychiatry and the social control of women', in *Women and Crime: Papers presented to the*

Public Administration Committee (2014), 'Caught red-handed: why we can't count on police recorded crime statistics', House of Commons

Reay, D. (1998), *Class Work – Mothers' Involvement in their Children's Primary Schooling*, London – UCL Press

Reay, D., David, M.E. and Ball, S. (2005), *Degrees of Choice – Class, Race and Gender and Higher Education*, Stoke-on-Trent – Trentham Books

Richardson, H., (2011), ' African Caribbean boys "would rather hustle than learn"', BBC News, 21 October

Richardson, J. T. E. (2010), 'Widening participation without widening attainment – The case of ethnic minority students', *Psychology Teaching Review*, British Psychological Society

Rikowski, G. (2002), 'Globalisation and education – a paper prepared for the House of Lords Select committee on Economic Affairs, Inquiry into the Global Economy

Rikowski, G. (2005), 'In the dentist's chair – a response to Richard Hatcher's critique of *Habituation of the Nation* – Part One', , www.flowideas.co.uk]

Robertson, R. (1995), 'Glocalization: time, space and homogeneity – heterogeneity?' in Featherstone, M., Lash, S. and Robertson, R. (eds.) *Global Modernities*, London: Sage

Roof, W. C. (2001), *Spiritual Marketplace*, Princeton – Princeton University Press

Rose, K., (2012), 'UK social media statistics', [www.socialmediatoday.com], January 6th 2014

Rosenthal, R. and Jacobson, L. (1968), *Pygmalion in the Classroom* (New York – Holt, Rinehart and Winston)

Russo, A. (2006), The Feminist Majority Foundation's campaign to stop gender apartheid – The Intersection of feminism and imperialism in the United States,

International Feminist Journal of Politics, 8, (4) (December) – 557–580

Sabbagh, D. (2010), 'Murdoch media to control over a fifth of UK news consumption', *The Guardian*, 30 December

Sabberg, D., (2010), 'Murdock to control 22 percent of the media', *The Guardian* [online] 30th December 2010 [accessed 1st September2015]

Schutz, A. (1967), *The Phenomenology of the Social World*, Evanston, Il – Northwestern University Press

Scraton, P. (1985), *The State of the Police: Is Law and Order out of Control?* London: Pluto Press Ltd.

Sellgren, S. (2010), 'Rise in ethnic minority students at UK universities' BBC News website, 3 February

Selvarajah, S. (2014), 'Violin, clarinet, football and choir – the costs and benefits of extra-curricular activities', [Sutton Trust website, accessed 4 September 2015]

Sewell, T. (1997), *Black Masculinities and Schooling*, Stoke-on-Trent – Trentham Books

Shapland, J et al (2008), 'Restorative Justice: Does Restorative Justice affect reconviction. The fourth report from the evaluation of three schemes', Ministry of Justice Research Series 10/08. London: Ministry of Justice

Sharpe, S. (1976, 1994 2nd ed) *Just Like a Girl*, Harmondsworth – Penguin

Shaw, C. R. (1966), *The Jack-Roller: A Delinquent Boy's Own Story*, London: University of Chicago Press

Shaw, L, & Gant, L. (2002), 'In defence of the internet: the relationship between internet communication and depression, loneliness, self-esteem, and perceived social support', *Cyberpsychology and Behaviour*, 5 (2), 2002

Simon, J. (1988), 'The Ideological Effects of Actuarial Practices', *Law and Society Review*, 22 (4), 772–800

Sippitt, A. (2014), 'Measuring social mobility – How does the UK perform?', [https –//fullfact.org]

Skelton, C., Francis, B., Carrington, B., Hutchings, M. Read, B. and Hall, I. (2006), *Investigsating Gender as a Factor in Primary Pupil-Teacher Relations and Perceptions*, London – ESRC

Smart, C. (1976), *Women, Crime and Criminology*, London: Routledge and Kegan-Paul

Smart, N. (1998), *Dimensions of the Sacred – An Anatomy of the World's Beliefs*. Berkeley, CA – University of California Press

Smart, N. (1998), *The World's Religions*, Cambridge – CUP

Smith, D. J. & Gray J. (1985), 'Police and people in London: The PSI report', Aldershot: Gower

Smith, T. and Noble, M. (1995), *Educational Divides – Poverty and Schooling in the 1990s*, London – CPAG

Social Exclusion Unit (2002), 'The SEU Report', Ministry of Justice

Soothill, K., Ackerley, E. and Francis, B. (2004), 'Profiles of Crime Recruitment' in *British Journal of Criminology*, No. 44, 401–418

Speed, M. and Burrows, J. (2006), 'Sentencing in cases of theft from shops', Sentencing advisory panel, Research report 3

Spender, D. (1983), *Invisible Women – The Schooling Scandal*, London – Women's Press

Stanko, B. (2000), 'The day to count: a snapshot of the impact of domestic violence in the UK', Criminal Justice 1: 2

Stark, R. (2002), 'Physiology and Faith – Addressing the 'Universal' Gender Difference in Religious Commitment', *Journal for the Scientific Study of Religion*, 41 (3), 495–507

Stark, R., & Bainbridge, W. (1987), *A Theory of Religion*. New York – P. Lang

Steer, L., Rabbani, F. and Parker, A. (2014), 'Primary Education Finance for Equity and Quality – An Analysis of Past Success and Future Options in Bangladesh', [Brookings Institution website]

Strand, S. (2008), *Minority Ethnic Pupils in the Longitudinal Study of Young People in England – Extension Report on Performance in Public Examinations at Age 16*, London – Department for Children, Schools and Families

Sullins, D. P., (2006), 'Gender and Religion – Deconstructing Universality, Constructing Complexity', *American Journal of Sociology*, 838–80

Sullivan, A. (2001), 'Cultural capital and educational attainment' *Sociology*, 35 (4), November.

Survival International, 'The Uncontacted Indians of Brazil', [www.survivalinternational.org, accessed 1st September 2015]

Sutherland, E. and Cressey, D. (1955), 'Differential Association', in *Principles of Criminology* (5th ed.) Chicago: J.P. Lippincott and co.

Sutherland, E. H. (1949), *White Collar Crime*, New York: Dryden

Theos, (2013), 'The spirit of things unseen – belief in post-religious Britain', [Theos]

Theos. (2009), 'Class and religion in the UK', Retrieved April 2015, from demas.wordpress.com

Thomas, W. (1907), *Sex and Society*, Boston: Littlebrown and Company

Thomas, W. (1923), *The Unadjusted Girl*, New York: Harper and Rowe

Tillich, P. (1976), *The Future of Religions*, New York – Greenwood Press

Tombs, S. (1999), 'Health and safety crimes: (in)visibility and the problems of ''Knowing'', in P. Davies, P. Francis and V. Jupp (eds.), *Invisible Crimes: Their Victims and their Regulation*, London: Macmillan.

Troeltsch, E. (2009), *The Social Teaching of the Christian Churches*, Louisville – Westminster John Knox Press

Troeltsch, E. (2009), *The Social Teaching of the Christian Churches*, Westminster – John Knox Press

Turkle, S. (2013), *Life on the screen: Identity in the age of the Internet*, New York: Simon & Schuster

UK Government. (1988), *Education Reform Act*.

UK Government. (2010), *Equality Act 2010*.

UNESCO (2012), *World Atlas of Gender Equality in Education* (Paris – UNESCO)

UNESCO (2013), *EFA Global Monitoring Report* (Paris – UNESCO)

United Nations (2014), *The Millennium Development Goals Report 2014*, New York – UN

United Nations Interregional Crime and Justice Research Institute, International Conference on Environmental Crime, 29–30 October 2012

United Nations Office on Drugs and Crime (2004), United Nations convention against transnational organized crime and the protocols thereto, United Nations, New York

Vargas, J., (2012), 'How an Egyptian revolution began on Facebook', *The New York Times*, 17 Feburary 2012

Vincent, C., Rollock, N., Ball, S. and Gilborn, D. (2013), 'Raising Middle-class Black children – parenting priorities, actions and strategies', *Sociology*, 47 (3). p. 427–442

Vincett, G., Sharma, S., & Aune, K. (2013), *Women and Religion in the West – Challenging Secularization*, Aldershot – Ashgate

Voas, D. (2015, January 1), 'The mysteries of religion and the lifecourse', Retrieved from Centre for Longitudinal Studies

Voas, D., & Crockett, A. (2006), 'Generations of decline – religious change in 20th century Britain',. *Journal for the Scientific Study of Religion*, 45 (4), pp. 567-584

VSO (2011), *Gender Equality and Education*, London – Voluntary Service Overseas

Waddington, P.A.J., Stenson, K. and Don, D. (2004), 'In proportion: race and police stop and search', in *British Journal of Criminology*, 2004, 44(6): 889–914

Walford, G. (2005), 'Introduction – education and the Labour Government' *Oxford Review of Education,* 31 (1), p. 3–9

Walklate, S. (2006), *Imagining the Victim of Crime*, London: McGraw-Hill International

Wallis, R. (1984), *The Elementary Forms of the New Religious Life*, London – Routledge & Kegan Paul

Watson, H. (1994), 'Women and the veil – personal responses to global process,', in Ahmed, A. S., & Donnan, H., *Islam, Globalization and Postmodernity*, London – Routledge

Weber, M. (1968), *Economy and Society*, New York – Bedminster Press

Weekes-Bernard, D. (2007), *School Choice and Ethnic Segregation – Educational Decision-making among Black and Minority Ethnic Parents*, London – Runnymede Trust

West, D. J. & Farrington, D. P. (1977), *The Delinquent Way of Life*, London: Heinemann.

William, D. and Bartholomew, H. (2004), 'It's not which school but which set you're in that matters – the influence on ability-grouping practices on student progress in mathematics'. *British Educational Research Journal*, 30 (2), 279–294.

Williams, K., Papadopoulou, V. and Booth, N. (2012), 'Prisoners' childhood and family backgrounds: Surveying Prisoner Crime Reduction (SPCR) longitudinal cohort study of prisoners', Ministry of Justice

Willis, P. (1977), *Learning to Labour*, Farnborough – Saxon House

Wilson, B. (1982), *Religion in Sociological Perspective*, Oxford – Oxford University Press

Wilson, B. (1985), 'Secularization – the inherited Model', in Hammond, P. E., *The Sacred in a Secular Age*, Berkeley – University of California Press

Wilson, B. (1996), 'Secularisation as an irreversible process', in Bruce,S., *Secularisation – In Defence of an Unfashionable Theory*, Cambridge – CUP

Wilson, J.Q. (1975), *Thinking About Crime*, New York: Basic Books

Wilson, J.Q. and Herrnstein, R. (1985), *Crime and Human Nature*, New York: Simon & Schuster

Wilson, J.Q. and Kelling, G.L. (1982), 'Broken Windows', *Atlantic Monthly*, March 1982

Winlow, S. (2001), Badfellas: *Crime, Tradition and New Masculinities*, Oxford: Berg

Wiseman, J. (1998), *Global Nation? Australia and the Politics of Globalisation*, Cambridge: Cambridge University Press.

Wolf, A. (2002), *Does Education Matter? Myths about Education and Economic Growth*, London – Penguin

Woodhead, L. (2004), 'Gender Differences in Religious Practice and Significance', in Beckford, J. A., and Demerath, N. J., *The Sage Handbook of the Sociology of Religion*, London – Sage

Woodhead, L. (2007), 'Gendering secularisation theory'. *Social Compass*, 55 (2), p. 187–193

Woodhead, L. (2007), 'Lifting the veil on religion and identity'. Retrieved from ESRC – www.esrc.ac.uk/_images/The%20Edge%2024_tcm8-8231.pdf

Woods, P. (1979), *The Divided School*, London – Routledge

World Inequality Database on Education, The., 'Percentage of children aged 3-6 years above primary school entrance age who have never been to school'. [www.education-inequalities. org/, accessed September 2015]

Young, J. (1971), *The Drugtakers*, London: Paladin

Young, J. (1986), 'The failure of criminology: the need for a radical realism', in Matthews, R. and Young J. (eds.), *Confronting Criminology*, London: Sage

Young, J. (1988), 'Risk of crime and fear of crime: a Realist critique of survey-based assumptions', in Maguire, M. and Pointing, J. (eds.), *Victims of crime: A new deal?*, Milton Keynes, Philadelphia: Open University Press

Young, J. (1992), 'Ten Points of Realism', in Young, J. and Matthews, R. (eds.), *Rethinking Criminology: The Realist Debate*, London: Sage

Young, J. (1999), *The Exclusive Society: Social Exclusion, Crime and Difference in Late Modernity*, London: Sage

Young, J. (2003), 'Merton with energy, Katz with structure: The sociology of vindictiveness and the criminology and transgression', in *Theoretical Criminology*, London: Sage

Young, T. (2012), 'Free schools – the research lab of state education?' *The Guardian*, 3 October

Younger, M. and Warrington, M. with Gray, J. Rudduck, J. McLellan, R. Bearne, E. Kershner, R. and Bricheno, P. (2005), *Raising Boys' Achievement,* DfES Research Report no 636, London – Department for Education and Science

Zhao, S. (2006), 'Do Internet users have more social ties? A call for differentiated analyses of internet use', *Journal of Computer-Mediated Communication*, 11(3), p. 844–862

Zimring, F. (2011), *The City that Became Safe: New York's Lessons for Urban Crime and its Control*, Oxford: Oxford University Press

Index